# Theoretical Criminology

# Theoretical Criminology

## Third Edition

by the late
George B. Vold
and
Thomas J. Bernard

New York   Oxford
Oxford University Press
1986

Oxford University Press

Oxford   New York   Toronto
Delhi   Bombay   Calcutta   Madras   Karachi
Kuala Lampur   Singapore   Hong Kong   Tokyo
Nairobi   Dar es Salaam   Cape Town
Melbourne   Auckland

and associated companies in
Beirut   Berlin   Ibadan   Mexico City   Nicosia

This revision was prepared under the editorial direction of Edward Sagarin.

Published by Oxford University Press, Inc., 200 Madison Avenue
New York, New York 10016

Library of Congress Cataloging in Publication Data
Vold, George B. (George Bryan), 1896–1967.
   Theoretical criminology.
   Includes index.
   1. Criminal anthropology.   2. Crime and criminals.
3. Deviant behavior.   4. Social conflict.   I. Bernard,
Thomas J.   II. Title.
HV6035.V6   1986   364.2   85-11558
ISBN 0-19-503616-6

Printing (last digit): 9 8 7 6 5 4 3 2 1
Printed in the United States of America

# Foreword to the Third Edition

In 1958 an event of extraordinary importance in the field of criminology occurred: the publication of a work by George B. Vold, carrying the simple title *Theoretical Criminology*. It was the crowning achievement of a man of distinction, and it did not take long before it gained recognition and acceptance as the leading book in the field concentrating more or less exclusively on the theoretical aspects of the study of crime. It was primarily for this contribution that the American Society of Criminology honored Vold by bestowing on him in 1966 the prestigious Edwin Sutherland Award. A year later Vold died, but his book remained and his reputation survived, soon to become known to an entire generation of criminologists who were children when his major publication first appeared.

George Bryan Vold, son of Norwegian immigrants, was born in South Dakota in 1896, and if indeed, as would seem apparent, his middle name was given for the American politician and orator, there was nothing to indicate in his later career that he would follow in the footsteps of the man for whom he was named. From early manhood, his was a distinguished intellectual career. He received his master's degree in sociology from the University of Chicago in 1924, when that school came close to dominating the discipline, and then went on to broaden his education by doing his doctoral work at the University of Minnesota, receiving his Ph.D. in 1930. A few years later he became full professor at Minnesota, where he spent the remainder of his academic career. He studied the Massachusetts prison system, returned to Minnesota to serve on the state's Crime Commission, wrote important works on parole and police training, and capped his career with the publication of *Theoretical Criminology.*

That it was accepted from its inception as the foremost work in the field is obvious (although traditional textbooks, not concentrating on theory, were better known to more students). It is interesting today to look at the assets of that first edition, which is now (thanks to Tom Bernard) a museum piece. It contained extraordinary early chapters on the origins of criminology, the classical, neoclassical, and positivist schools, and then systematically and convincingly developed a social conflict vision of society that Vold found applicable to crime. His conflict approach was not essentially Marxist in that it was not the class conflict that enabled him to explain crime but the myriad of group belongings and group conflicts inherent in a society.

Although the book was extremely well received and was sold, read, studied, discussed, and debated for many years, two things became increasingly apparent. First, Vold had chosen to omit from his work many modern criminological theories and theorists whose importance he did not recognize or who, he may have felt, deserved no place in the pantheon of architects of criminological theory. Yet without such people the book was incomplete, even if one were to agree with Vold's apparently negative view of their contribution. Second, much had occurred in theoretical criminology since 1958— new theoretical formulations, the discovery of some evidence that the biological predilection theory could not be dismissed quite so cavalierly as many had long believed, and above all a considerable development of conflict theory, by Marxists, neo-Marxists, and anti-Marxists, without whose formulations one could not hope to grasp how a society enmeshed in its own internal conflicts would show evidence of such conflicts through the individual criminal acts of a minority of its residents.

Thus it was time for a revised edition of Vold's work, and for this task a brilliant young man, Thomas J. Bernard, was chosen. A second edition appeared in 1979, and I wrote then that the new material captured Vold's essence and that the old material was left intact, or updated at times, so that what Vold had written was preserved.

Now another edition appears, and, rightly, Thomas Bernard is Vold's collaborator, although the two never met. Bernard has built on Vold, reexamined what each of them had written, synthesized the material, introduced concepts that were only being born when he was doing his first revision, but, above all, I believe that he felt a little more freedom in dealing with the original work than he did the first time around. He was no longer circumscribed; the second edition had established his place as Vold's logical successor, and the third could be the work that the two of them might have written had they worked together today.

Had Vold lived to see the third edition of this book, he could not have chosen a better collaborator than Tom Bernard, and he would have been pleased, very pleased, with the end product.

*City University of New York and* Edward Sagarin
*John Jay College of Criminal Justice*

# Acknowledgments

In preparing this edition of *Theoretical Criminology*, I again have had the privilege and pleasure of working with Edward Sagarin. Ed possesses all of the attributes of a superb editor: an astonishingly broad base of knowledge, an unerring eye for detail, and a willingness to spend the time and effort necessary to analyze thoroughly and comment thoughtfully. This book has benefited greatly from Ed's wisdom and experience, and I have benefited as well. For that I wish to express to him my most sincere thanks. To the extent that there are errors or inadequacies here, they undoubtedly exist because I failed to take his advice on some point and insisted on going my own way.

Many thanks are also owed to present and former faculty members of the School of Criminal Justice at the State University of New York at Albany, where I spent three productive years as a doctoral student after preparing the second edition of this book. Much of what is new in the third edition reflects knowledge that my professors managed to beat into my skull only with considerable difficulty. It seems to me that more knowledge got through than they believed at the time. Thanks and appreciation are also due to my colleagues in the Administration of Justice program at The Pennsylvania State University. It is my good fortune to work in a wonderfully congenial atmosphere with a truly fine group of people for whom I have the highest respect. In various direct and indirect ways they have all contributed to the writing of this book.

I would particularly like to thank Myer Guzy for his help in preparing the chapter on Marxist criminology. In addition, I would like to thank Steven F. Messner, David O. Friedrichs, Robert Price, Arthur Patterson, W. Byron Groves, Gary Potter, J. Philip Jenkins, and D. T. M. Senarath for reading and commenting on various chapters. My spouse, Wendy J. Moran, deserves special thanks for the love and support she has given me (along with our second son, Brian) while I worked on this book. Finally, I would like to dedicate this book to my parents, Edward L. and Frances M. Bernard, in the hope that I can be as good a parent to my children as they are to me.

*State College, Pennsylvania*                                    T. J. B.
*May 1985*

# Contents

1. Theory and Criminology    3

Spiritual explanations—Natural explanations—Criminal behavior
as freely chosen—Criminal behavior as caused—The behavior
of criminal law—The explanation of crime as a function of the frame
of reference

2. Classical Criminology    18

Preclassical writers and ideas—Beccaria and the classical school—
The neoclassical school—Assessing Beccaria's theory—
Contemporary classicism: Deterrence and econometrics—
Implications and conclusions

3. The Positive School    36

Cesare Lombroso—Enrico Ferri—Raffaele Garofalo—
Contemporary positivism

4. Theories Related to Physical Characteristics    47

Forerunners of physical–type theories: Physiognomy and
phrenology—Criminal anthropology: Lombroso to Hooton—
Body type theories: Kretschmer to Cortés—Conclusion

5. Theories Related to Intelligence     67

Background ideas and concepts—Intelligence testing and crime—
Later studies: Delinquency, race, and IQ—
Implications and conclusions


6. Biological Factors and Criminal Behavior     84

Crime as a hereditary defect—The study of twins—The study
of adoptees—XYY chromosomal complement—Biochemical
imbalance—Central nervous system functioning—Learning
disabilities—Autonomic nervous system functioning—
Implications and conclusions


7. The Personality of the Offender     108

Historical background: Psychiatry as a springboard for
psychoanalytic theory—Sigmund Freud and psychoanalysis—
Psychoanalytic explanations of criminal behavior—
Research using personality tests—Psychopathy, sociopathy,
and the antisocial personality—The prediction of future
dangerousness—Implications and conclusions


8. Crime, Poverty, and Economic Inequality     130

Historical background: Guerry and Quetelet—Crime and
unemployment—Counting poor people—Interpreting
the studies—Poverty, economic inequality, and relative
deprivation—Implications and conclusions


9. Durkheim, Anomie, and Modernization     143

Emile Durkheim—Crime as normal in mechanical societies—
Anomie as a pathological state in organic societies—
Assessing Durkheim's theory of crime—Conclusion


10. The Ecology of Crime     160

The theory of human ecology—Research in the "delinquency
areas" of Chicago—Later criticisms and replications—
Policy implications—Conclusions

11.  Strain Theories

Robert K. Merton and Anomie in American Society—Strain as
the explanation of gang delinquency—Assessing strain theories—
Policy Implications—Conclusion


12.  Criminal Behavior as Normal Learned Behavior      205

Basic psychological assumptions—Tarde's laws of imitation—
Sutherland's differential association theory—Cultural and
subcultural theories—The learning process and criminality—
More recent theories of the normal learning process—
Assessing Sutherland's theory—Conclusion


13.  Social Control Theories      232

Early control theories: Reiss to Reckless—Matza's *Delinquency
and Drift*—Hirschi's *Causes of Delinquency*—Assessing control
theories—Implications and conclusions


14.  Deviance and Social Reaction      249

Reactive definitions of crime—Social reaction theories of criminal
behavior—Social reaction views of enforcing criminal laws—
Social reaction views of enacting criminal laws—
Implications and conclusions


15.  Conflict Criminology      269

Sellin's culture conflict theory—Vold's group conflict theory—
Quinney's theory of the social reality of crime—Turk's theory
of criminalization—Chambliss and Seidman's analysis of the criminal
justice system—A unified conflict theory of crime—Conflict
explanations of the behavior of criminal law—Conflict explanations
of criminal behavior—Policy implications—Conclusion


16.  Marxist Criminology      299

General overview of Marxist theory—Early Marxist views
of crime—Marxist views of criminal behavior—
Marxist views of the behavior of criminal law—Marxist views
of criminology—Conclusion

17. Criminology Theory and Specific Types of Crime    317

Victimless crimes—Organized crime—White-collar crime—
Conclusion


18. Theory, Research, and Policy    340

Theory as the basis for research—Criminology theory
and crime policy—Conclusion


19. Assessing Criminology Theories    358

Theories of criminal behavior—Theories of the behavior
of criminal law—Conclusion


Index    365

# Theoretical Criminology

# CHAPTER ONE

# Theory and Criminology

Criminology as a field of study has been well documented by a long line of excellent and distinguished textbooks, both European and American, going back many decades.[1] Most of these texts concentrate on presenting facts known about the subject of criminality. For example, they discuss such subjects as the extent and distribution of criminal behaviors in society; the characteristics of criminal law and procedure; the characteristics of criminals; and the history, structure, and functioning of the criminal justice system. The theoretical material presented in these texts is usually somewhat limited. Almost all texts review the major theories about the causes of criminal behavior, and some texts present other theoretical material such as

---

1. A few of the recent, readily available American textbooks in general criminology may be mentioned: Joseph F. Sheley, *America's "Crime Problem,"* Wadsworth, Belmont, Cal., 1985; Vernon Fox, *Introduction to Criminology*, 2nd ed., Prentice-Hall, Englewood Cliffs, N.J., 1985; D. Stanley Eitzen and Doug A. Timmer, *Criminology*, John Wiley, New York, 1984; Don C. Gibbons, *Society, Crime, and Criminal Behavior*, 4th ed., Prentice-Hall, Englewood Cliffs, N.J., 1984; Robert L. Bonn, *Criminology*, McGraw-Hill, New York, 1984; William B. Sanders, *Criminology*, Addison-Wesley, Reading, Mass., 1983; Martin R. Haskell and Lewis Yablonsky, *Criminology: Crime and Criminality*, 3rd ed., Houghton Mifflin, Boston, 1983; Charles W. Thomas and John R. Hepburn, *Crime, Criminal Law, and Criminology*, William C. Brown, Dubuque, Iowa, 1983; Larry J. Seigel, *Criminology*, West, St. Paul, 1983; Sue Titus Reid, *Crime and Criminology*, 3rd ed., Holt, Rinehart and Winston, New York, 1982; Harry E. Allen, Paul C. Friday, Julian B. Roebuck, and Edward Sagarin, *Crime and Punishment: An Introduction to Criminology*, The Free Press, New York, 1981; Sheila Balkan, Ronald J. Berger, and Janet Schmidt, *Crime and Deviance in America: A Critical Approach*, Wadsworth, Belmont, Cal., 1980; Richard Quinney, *Criminology*, 2nd ed., Little, Brown, Boston, 1979; Donald Glaser, *Crime in Our Changing Society*, Holt, Rinehart and Winston, New York, 1979; Edwin H. Sutherland and Donald R. Cressey, *Criminology*, 10th ed., Lippincott, Philadelphia, 1978; and Gresham M. Sykes, *Criminology*, Harcourt Brace Jovanovich, New York, 1978.

sociology of law, philosophy of punishment, or theories of correctional treatment.

As a text in theoretical criminology, this book does not concentrate on presenting the facts known about criminality, although at least some of those facts are presented in the various chapters. Rather, this book concentrates on the theories used to explain those facts. The theories themselves, then, rather than the facts about criminality, are the focus of this book.[2]

A theory is a part of explanation.[3] Basically, an explanation is a sensible relating of some particular phenomenon to the whole field of knowledge. The whole field of knowledge is the background of contemporary culture—the world of information, beliefs, and attitudes that make up the intellectual atmosphere of any people at any particular time or place. Thus, when modern people see a train move along the railroad tracks, they "explain" that phenomenon to themselves in terms of their knowledge of internal combustion engines. Primitive people also had explanations that enabled them to account for such phenomena, but they used primitive concepts such as the power of spirits or demons.

Scientific theories are one kind of explanation. In general, scientific theories make statements about the relationships between two classes of phenomena.[4] For example, some scientific theories in criminology make statements about the relationship between characteristics of criminal punishments (e.g., certainty and severity) and the volume of criminal behaviors in society. Other scientific theories make statements relating certain biological, psychological, and social characteristics of individuals to the likelihood that they will engage in criminal behaviors. Still other scientific theories make statements relating the characteristics of individuals to the likelihood that they will be defined and processed as criminals by the criminal justice system.

The key characteristic of a scientific theory is that it makes statements that can be disproved.[5] Explanations that cannot be disproved

2. Some recent criminology texts that focus on theoretical material include Gwynn Nettler, *Explaining Crime*, 3rd ed., McGraw-Hill, New York, 1984; Francis T. Cullen, *Rethinking Crime and Deviance Theory*, Rowman and Allanheld, Totowa, N.J., 1984; J. E. Hall-Williams, *Criminology and Criminal Justice*, Butterworths, London, 1982; William V. Pelfrey, *The Evolution of Criminology*, Anderson, Cincinnati, 1980; Don C. Gibbons, *The Criminological Enterprise: Theories and Perspectives*, Prentice-Hall, Englewood Cliffs, N.J., 1979; and Ian Taylor, Paul Walton, and Jock Young, *The New Criminology*, Harper and Row, New York, 1973.

3. Arthur L. Stinchcombe, *Constructing Social Theories*, Harcourt, Brace & World, New York, 1968, pp. 3–5.

4. Ibid., pp. 15–17.

5. Ibid., pp. 5–6.

are not scientific. The general process of attempting to disprove a scientific theory involves deriving specific empirical assertions from the theory and comparing those assertions to observations made in the real world; that is, the assertions of the theory are tested against the observed world of the facts. If the observations are inconsistent with the assertions of the theory, then the theory is falsified. If the observations are consistent with the assertions of the theory, then the theory becomes more credible, but it is not proved; there are always alternative theories that might also explain the same observations.

A theory can gain a great deal of credibility if all the reasonable alternative theories are shown to be inconsistent with the observed world of facts. At that point the theory might simply be accepted as true. However, it is always possible that some new facts will be discovered in the future that are inconsistent with the theory, so that a new theory will be required. For example, Newton's laws of physics were accepted as true for 200 years, but they were replaced by Einstein's theory of relativity at the beginning of this century due to the discovery of some new facts.[6]

All theories are consistent with the basic facts of the phenomenon they are trying to explain. For example, all the theories discussed in this book are consistent with the basic facts known about crime. No one is going to take a theory seriously if it makes assertions that are inconsistent with well-known and widely accepted facts. While each theory is consistent with the basic facts, each also implies that there will be many less important facts, ones that are not well known or widely accepted. It is on these relatively minor points that most testing of theories takes place. If the observed facts are inconsistent with these relatively minor points, then the theory itself may be said to be falsified.

These relatively minor points become especially important when there are several theories competing to explain the same set of facts.[7] Such points can then generate a great deal of theory and research by adherents of the competing theories. An example would be the behavior of identical twins each of whom was raised in a different environment.[8] Although very few cases of such twins exist, they have been the subject of a great deal of theory and research. The reason

6. Thomas S. Kuhn, *The Structure of Scientific Revolutions*, University of Chicago Press, Chicago, 1969.

7. Stinchcombe, op. cit., pp. 24–28.

8. See Susan L. Farber, *Identical Twins Raised Apart: A Reanalysis*, Basic Books, New York, 1981.

is that theories that propose a genetic model for human behavior logically imply that identical twins, because they possess identical genetic endowments, should behave similarly even if they are raised in different environments. In contrast, theories that propose environmental factors as the primary influences on behavior logically imply that people raised in different environments should behave differently, even if they have identical genetic endowments. Both genetic and environmental theories are consistent with the basic facts known about human behavior, and it is only on such fine points as the behavior of identical twins raised apart that the different implications of the theories can be tested.

Criminology has been blessed (or cursed, depending on one's point of view) with a very large number of theories. The extent to which these theories are supported by the facts is another question entirely. Fifty years ago Michael and Adler reviewed crime theories and concluded: "The assurance with which criminologists have advanced opinions regarding the causes of crime is in striking contrast to the worthlessness of the data upon which those opinions are based."[9] Michael and Adler's judgment was harsh even at the time, but the point needs to be kept in mind as the various theories are reviewed. Another point to keep in mind was raised recently by Gould, who commented: "Some topics are invested with enormous social importance but blessed with very little reliable information. When the ratio of data to social impact is so low, a history of scientific attitudes may be little more than an oblique record of social change."[10] It may be that the history of changing theories of crime reflects more about changing attitudes and values than it does about the changing state of scientific knowledge.[11]

In the broad scope of history, there are two basic types of theories of crime. One relies on spiritual, or other-world, explanations while the other relies on natural, or this-world, explanations. Both types of theories are ancient as well as modern, but only the natural theories can be called scientific since the spiritual explanations cannot be disproven.

## 1. SPIRITUAL EXPLANATIONS

Spiritual explanations of crime are part of a general view of life in which many events are believed to be the result of the influence of

9. Jerome Michael and Mortimer J. Adler, *Crime, Law and Social Science*, Patterson Smith, Montclair, N.J., 1971, p. 169.

10. Stephen Jay Gould, *The Mismeasure of Man*, Norton, New York, 1981, p. 22.

11. Cf. Ysabel Rennie, *The Search for Criminal Man*, Heath, Lexington, Mass., 1973.

otherworldly powers. For example, primitive people regarded natural disasters such as famines, floods, and plagues as punishments for wrongs they had done to the spiritual powers.[12] They responded by performing sacred rites and rituals in order to appease those powers. In the Middle Ages in Europe a spiritual view of the world was joined to the political and social organization of feudalism to produce the beginnings of the criminal justice system.[13] Originally, crime was a largely private affair in which the victim or the victim's family obtained revenge by inflicting a similar or greater harm on the offender or the offender's family. The problem was that private vengeance had a tendency to start blood feuds that could continue for many years until one or the other family was completely wiped out. The feudal lords therefore instituted methods by which God could indicate who was innocent and who was guilty. The first such method was trial by battle, in which the victim or a member of his or her family would fight the offender or a member of his or her family. God was said to give victory to the innocent party. The family of the loser then had no grounds for exacting vengeance on the family of the winner, and the blood feuds were ended.

The problem with trial by battle was that great warriors could commit as many crimes as they wanted, secure in the knowledge that God would always find them innocent. Thus, somewhat later in history, trial by ordeal was instituted. In this method the accused was subjected to difficult and painful tests, from which an innocent person (protected by God) would emerge unharmed while a guilty person would die a painful death. For example, a common method of determining whether a woman was a witch was to tie her up and throw her into the water.[14] If she floated she was considered innocent, but if she sank she was guilty. Other forms of ordeal included running the gauntlet and walking on fire. Trial by ordeal was condemned by the Pope in 1215 and was replaced by compurgation, in which the accused gathered together a group of 12 reputable people who would swear that he or she was innocent. Again, the idea was that no one would lie under oath for fear of being punished by God. Compurgation ultimately evolved into testimony under oath and trial by jury.

Spiritual explanations of crime appeared in the New World in the Puritan colony on Massachusetts Bay. During the first 60 years of its existence, this colony experienced three serious "crime waves" thought

12. Graeme Newman, *The Punishment Response*, Lippincott, Philadelphia, 1978, pp. 13–25.
13. Harry Elmer Barnes, *The Story of Punishment*, 2nd ed. revised, Patterson Smith, Montclair, N.J., 1972, pp. 7–10.
14. Newman, op. cit., p. 97.

to be caused by the Devil. The most serious of these "crime waves" occurred in 1792, when the community was thought to have been invaded by a large number of witches.[15] Our modern prison system originated in association with a spiritual explanation of crime. Around 1790 a group of Quakers in Philadelphia conceived the idea of isolating criminals in cells and giving them only the Bible to read and some manual labor to perform. The Quakers thought criminals would then reflect on their past wrongdoings and repent.[16] They used the term *penitentiary* to describe their invention, a place for *penitents* who were sorry for their sins. Today, some religious individuals and groups still attribute crime to the influence of the Devil. For example, Charles Colson, who was special counsel to President Richard M. Nixon and who served seven months in prison for his part in the Watergate affair, attributes crime to sinful human nature.[17] He argues that religious conversion is the only "cure" for crime and now spends much of his time bringing that Christian message to prisoners.

Spiritual explanations provide a way of understanding crime that is satisfactory to some people. The problem with these theories is that, because spiritual influences cannot be observed, they cannot be disproved. Thus these theories cannot be considered scientific, even if some thoughtful and intelligent people believe that they represent the best explanation of crime.

## 2. NATURAL EXPLANATIONS

Spiritual explanations make use of otherworldly powers to account for what happens; natural explanations make use of objects and events in the material world to explain the same things. Like the spiritual approach, the natural approach to explanation is ancient as well as modern. The early Phoenicians and Greeks developed naturalistic, this-world explanations far back in their history. For example, Hippocrates (460 B.C.) provided a physiological explanation of thinking by arguing that the brain is the organ of the mind. Democritus

15. Kai T. Erikson, *Wayward Puritans*, John Wiley, New York, 1966.

16. Harry Elmer Barnes and Negley K. Teeters, *New Horizons in Criminology*, Prentice-Hall, New York, 1945; Negley K. Teeters, *The Cradle of the Penitentiary: The Walnut Street Jail at Philadelphia, 1773–1835*, Temple University Press, Philadelphia, 1955.

17. Charles Colson, "Toward an Understanding of the Origins of Crime," in John Stott and Nick Miller, eds., *Crime and the Responsible Community*, Hodder and Stoughton, London, 1980. See also David R. Wilkerson, *The Cross and the Switchblade*, B. Geis, New York, 1963; Oral Roberts, *Twelve Greatest Miracles of My Ministry*, Pinoak, Tulsa, 1974, Ch. 9; Gerald Austin McHugh, *Christian Faith and Criminal Justice: Toward A Christian Response to Crime and Punishment*, Paulist Press, New York, 1978.

(420 B.C.) proposed the idea of an indestructible unit of matter called the atom as central to his explanation of the world around him. With Socrates, Plato, and Aristotle, the ideas of unity and continuity came to the fore, but the essential factors in all explanations remained physical and material.

By the first century B.C. Roman thought had become thoroughly infused with the naturalism of the Greek scholars. Roman law, for example, fused the demonology of the Hebraic tradition with the naturalism of the Greeks to provide a natural basis for penalties as well as for rights. The Hebrew doctrine of divine sanction for law and order merged with Greek naturalism and appeared in Roman law as a justification based on the "nature of things." Thus the rule of kings by divine right became a natural law looking to the nature of things for its principal justification. In the sixteenth and seventeenth centuries writers such as Hobbes, Spinoza, Descartes, and Leibniz studied human affairs as physicists study matter, impersonally and quantitatively. Modern social science continues this natural emphasis. The disagreements among social scientists are well known, but at least they have in common that they seek their explanations within the physical and material world.

In criminology, as in other social sciences, modern thought that calls itself scientific has abandoned the spiritual approach as a frame of reference. Within the natural approach, however, one can distinguish three essentially different and in some ways contradictory frames of reference, based on three essentially different ways of thinking about crime. The differences among these frames of reference are so fundamental that they involve different conceptions of the basic problem that the discipline of criminology attempts to solve,[18] as well as different definitions of the terms *crime* and *criminal*. Because of these fundamental differences, communication between criminologists who hold different frames of reference is often difficult. Critics may pass judgment on research efforts from the viewpoint of their own particular frame of reference rather than from the viewpoint of general methodological integrity and intellectual honesty.

These three frames of reference within the natural approach will be identified and briefly described in the paragraphs that follow. Two of the frames of reference focus on the behavior of criminals. The first argues that criminal behavior is freely chosen, while the second argues that it is caused by forces beyond the control of the individual. The third frame of reference views crime primarily as a function

18. The idea that a science is defined by the problem it attempts to solve is based on the conception of normal science as "puzzle-solving" in Kuhn, op. cit.

of the way the criminal law is written and enforced. Thus, it focuses on the behavior of criminal law rather than the behavior of criminals.

## 3. CRIMINAL BEHAVIOR AS FREELY CHOSEN

First, there is the view that intelligence and rationality are fundamental human characteristics and are the basis for explaining human behavior. In this view humans are said to be capable of understanding themselves and of acting to promote their own best interests. Societies are formed because people rationally decide to make them according to patterns that seem "good" to them—either monarchies or republics, totalitarian dictatorships or democracies. The key to progress is said to be intelligent behavior brought about by careful training and education. Each person is said to be master of his or her fate, possessed of free will rather than driven by spirits or devils.

This is the frame of reference of classical criminology, as well as of classical thinking in other fields such as philosophy, political science, and economics. Within this frame of reference crime and criminals are usually defined from a strictly legal point of view.[19] Crime may be defined as the commission of any act prohibited by criminal law, or the omission of any act required by it, and a criminal is defined as any person who commits a crime. Crime is seen as a product of the free choice of the individual, who first assesses the potential benefits of committing the crime against its potential costs. The rational response of society is to increase the costs and to decrease the benefits of crime to the point that individuals will not choose to commit crime. The problem that criminologists attempt to solve, then, is to design and test a system of punishment that would result in a minimal occurrence of crime. Thus this perspective is concerned with theory and research on the question of deterrence.

## 4. CRIMINAL BEHAVIOR AS CAUSED

Next is the view that behavior is determined by factors beyond the individual's control. This view implies that humans are not self-determining agents free to do as they wish and as their intelligence directs. Rather, it is more accurate to say that people can only be-

19. Clarence R. Jeffery, "The Structure of American Criminological Thinking," *Journal of Criminal Law, Criminology and Police Science* 46: 663–64 (Jan.–Feb. 1956).

have as they have already been determined to behave. Thinking and reasoning are actually processes of rationalization in which individuals justify their predetermined courses of action, rather than processes by which individuals freely and intelligently choose what they want to do. Humans have changed and developed through a slow process of evolution, and not because intelligence has led to increasingly rational choices.

This is the frame of reference of positivist criminology, as well as of positivist thinking in other fields such as psychology, sociology, and philosophy. These theories arose in criminology after classical theories had dominated the field for about 100 years and repeated manipulations of the punishment systems had failed to produce the expected reductions in crime. In a sense, these theories were offered as explanations of why classical theories had failed; if the criminal's behavior was determined by factors beyond his or her control, then punishment would have no effect.

Within this frame of reference, the problem that criminologists attempt to solve is the identification of the causes of criminal behavior. The original positivist criminologists looked to biological factors, but later criminologists shifted their focus to psychological and then to social factors in their attempts to find these causes. At the present time, some criminologists hold that criminal behavior can be explained by one type of factor, while other criminologists take a multiple-factor approach, holding that there are many factors that increase or decrease the likelihood of a person engaging in criminal behavior.[20]

For the past 100 years the search for the causes of criminal behavior has dominated criminology, and most modern theories fall within this framework. Consequently, most of the chapters in this book are concerned with various explanations of those causes. Even such recent developments as Marxist theories of criminology can be said to fall within this framework to the extent that they describe criminal behavior as being caused by the capitalist economic system.[21] In fact, this framework dominates criminology to such an extent that some criminologists hold that the search for the causes of criminal behavior is identical with criminology itself. Other criminologists, however, including the classical criminologists already mentioned, hold

20. Travis Hirschi and Michael Gottfredson, eds., *Understanding Crime: Current Theory and Research*, Sage, Beverly Hills, Cal., 1980, pp. 7–19.

21. Cf. David F. Greenberg, *Crime and Capitalism*, Mayfield, Palo Alto, Cal., 1981, especially pp. 17–18.

that criminologists should attempt to solve other types of problems. Explaining the causes of criminal behavior is not necessarily the only way to explain crime.

Criminologists who search for the causes of criminal behavior find it difficult to work within the framework of strictly legal definitions of crime, such as those used by the classical criminologists. That is because the law frequently distinguishes between legal and illegal actions on the basis of extremely fine points ("technicalities") that have no bearing on the idea of causation. The law also groups behaviors into legal categories when those behaviors are not similar to each other from the point of view of causation. Therefore, criminologists who search for the causes of crime tend to use various "natural" definitions of crime which focus on the "nature" of the behavior itself rather than on its legal definition. For example, Mannheim defends the view that criminology should study all antisocial behavior, whether it is legally a crime or not.[22] Sutherland regarded crime as behavior that is harmful to society and used this definition to pursue his studies on white-collar crime.[23] Sellin defined crime in terms of violations of group conduct norms,[24] and the Schwendingers defined it in terms of violations of basic human rights.[25] Cressey found it necessary to replace a variety of legal categories of financial crime with the concept of criminal violation of financial trust.[26] He claimed that this definition included all forms of criminal behavior that were similar from an economic and sociological point of view, but excluded other forms of criminal behavior. He was then able to proceed with a causal analysis of this behavior.

22. Hermann Mannheim, *Comparative Criminology*, Houghton Mifflin, Boston, 1965, pp. 14–15.

23. E. H. Sutherland, "White Collar Criminality," *American Sociological Review* 5 (1): 1–12 (Feb. 1940). Each edition of Sutherland's text contains the statement "Obviously, legal definitions should not confine the work of the criminologist; he should be completely free to push across the barriers of legal definitions whenever he sees noncriminal behavior which resembles criminal behavior." E. H. Sutherland and D. R. Cressey, *Criminology*, 9th ed., Lippincott, Philadelphia, 1974, p. 21. In the 10th edition (1978, p. 23), Cressey has qualified the statement by adding the following: "It is an error, however, to call such noncriminal behavior *crime*, no matter how repulsive it may be."

24. Thorsten Sellin, *Culture Conflict and Crime*, Social Science Research Council, New York, 1938.

25. Herman and Julia Schwendinger, "Defenders of Order or Guardians of Human Rights?" *Issues in Criminology* 5 (2): 123–57 (Summer 1970).

26. Donald R. Cressey, *Other People's Money*, The Free Press, Glencoe, Ill., 1953.

## 5. THE BEHAVIOR OF CRIMINAL LAW

Theories of the causes of criminal behavior have dominated criminology for over 100 years, but since about 1960 some criminologists have begun to address a very different question: why some individuals and behaviors are officially defined as criminal and others are not. The theories that these criminologists propose have been described in a variety of ways but will be called "theories of the behavior of criminal law" in this book because they focus on how the criminal law itself is written and enforced.[27]

The criminologists who hold this view focus on the processes by which humans create the social world in which they live. They argue that the phenomenon of crime is socially constructed when a society defines certain people and actions as criminal, and that any of a wide variety of people and actions may, at one time or another, be the subject of these definitions. These criminologists therefore study the processes by which particular sets of people and actions are defined as criminal at particular times and places.

The following example is presented to illustrate this frame of reference. Consider the most serious of all crimes, murder. A classical criminologist might attempt to measure the effects of different types of enforcement and punishment policies on the incidence of murder in a society. A positivist criminologist might study the biological, psychological, or social characteristics of murderers in order to determine what caused their behavior. A criminologist who studies the behavior of criminal law, in contrast, might study the types of killings defined as murder by the law, and attempt to determine why

---

27. This term is derived from Donald Black, *The Behavior of Law*, Academic Press, New York, 1976. Black's term is broader in that it includes all "governmental social control." The present term includes only the criminal law and excludes other forms of governmental social control since those other forms do not influence the distribution of official crime rates. In the second edition of the present book, theories of the behavior of criminal law were described as "critical criminology," following the lead of Gresham Sykes, "The Rise of Critical Criminology," *Journal of Criminal Law and Criminology* 65 (2): 206–13 (June 1974). However, it appears that the term *critical criminology* is more appropriately reserved for a branch of radical criminology. The term *new criminology* has also been used to describe these theories. See Gibbons, op. cit., pp. 167–71; Charles E. Reasons, "Social Thought and Social Structure, *Criminology* 13 (3): 332–65 (Nov. 1975); Robert F. Meier, "The New Criminology," *Journal of Criminal Law and Criminology* 67: 461–69 (Dec. 1976); Eugene Doleschal and Nora Klapmuts, "Toward a New Criminology," *Crime and Delinquency Literature* 5 (4): 607–26 (Dec. 1973). Both the terms *critical criminology* and *new criminology* may be misnomers (see Robert F. Bohm, "Radical Criminology: An Explication," *Criminology* 19 (4): 565–89 (Feb., 1982), but there is as yet no commonly accepted term to describe this emerging perspective. The term *theories of the behavior of criminal law* has been chosen to focus on the essential characteristics of this frame of reference while avoiding some of the problems with the other terms.

these killings are selected for definition as murders while other killings are not. They might also study the set of people defined as murderers by the police and courts and attempt to determine why this
particular group had been selected out of all the people whose behaviors resulted in the deaths of other people.

These criminologists might study systematic differences in the enforcement of laws that result in certain groups being disproportionately processed by the criminal justice system. They might argue,
for example, that wealthy and powerful groups are systematically
weeded out of the criminal justice system at successive decision points,
so that the end result of the system is that poor and powerless groups
are disproportionately convicted and imprisoned. Thus wealthy and
powerful people who kill may be less likely to be arrested, tried, or
convicted at all, or they may be convicted of a less serious offense
and given a more lenient sentence.

These criminologists may also examine differences in the types of
deaths that are defined as murders by the law. For example, *felony
murder* laws make an offender liable for first degree murder if a death
results from the commission of certain "dangerous" felonies such as
forcible rape, robbery, arson, or burglary. No premeditation or intent is required, as the intent to commit the lesser offense is trans-
ferred to the greater one.[28] Under this law, if a shopkeeper has a
heart attack and dies while being robbed, a person could be charged
with first degree murder if he or she was driving the getaway car,
did not go inside the store, and had no weapon. If convicted, such
an offender could then receive the death penalty.[29]

In contrast with the severity of this law are the extremely lenient
laws associated with serious injuries and deaths resulting from the
actions of corporate executives. Even the most outrageous examples
of deliberate decisions resulting in numerous injuries and deaths may
not be defined as crimes at all, or, if they are defined as crimes, the
penalties may be limited to a minimal and symbolic level.[30] Many
serious injuries and deaths associated with corporate decision making occur where there is the intent to commit a lesser offense (for
example, to violate health or safety laws), combined with the full
knowledge that the decision may result in serious injury and death

28. Hazel B. Kerper, *Introduction to the Criminal Justice System*, West, St. Paul, 1972, pp.
111–12.

29. A similar case in which the offender did receive the death penalty is *Woodson v. North
Carolina*, 96 S. Ct. 2978 (1976).

30. E.g., see Gerald M. Stern, *The Buffalo Creek Disaster*, Vintage, New York, 1976; Kai T.
Erikson, *Everything in its Path*, Simon and Schuster, New York, 1976.

to numbers of innocent people. If a law similar to the felony murder law were applied to corporate decision making, then many corporate executives might find themselves convicted of murder and sentenced to death.

Theories of the behavior of criminal law suggest that the volume of crime and the characteristics of criminals are determined primarily by how the law is written and enforced. Most people convicted of crimes are poor, but not because poverty causes crime. Rather, the actions typical of poor people are more likely to be legally defined as crimes, and the laws applying to such crimes are more likely to be strictly enforced. Burglary, larceny, armed robbery, and auto theft are all crimes typically committed by the poor, and the laws applying to these crimes are strictly defined and enforced. Fraud, embezzlement, corruption, and other kinds of white-collar crimes are typically committed by wealthier people. But the laws applying to these crimes are neither defined nor enforced as strictly, despite the fact that these crimes can cause many serious injuries and deaths and can result in large property losses. In general, both rich persons and poor persons can be vicious, brutal, greedy, and deceptive, but the poor person with these characteristics is more likely to be defined as a criminal than is the rich person. Thus differences in the crime rates between rich and poor persons may primarily reflect differences in the behavior of criminal law rather than differences in the behaviors of individuals.

Classical criminologists use "legal" definitions of crime, and criminologists who seek the causes of criminal behavior use "natural" definitions. The criminologists who propose theories of the behavior of criminal law use what might be called a "labeling" definition. The terms *crime* and *criminal* are defined as labels applied to certain people and events by the official law enactment and law enforcement agencies. The problem these criminologists attempt to solve, therefore, is analyzing the processes by which these labels are applied in order to explain the distribution of official crime rates among the various groups in society.

## 6. THE EXPLANATION OF CRIME AS A FUNCTION OF THE FRAME OF REFERENCE

It is fairly obvious from the preceding discussion that the explanation of crime depends on the frame of reference. Each approach usually regards itself as self-sufficient; none falls back on any of the others for confirmation or verification. The meaning of theories and supporting research is taken from within the general point of view; abandon the point of view, and its theories and research become useless and meaningless. Thus science with its naturalistic approach has abandoned the satisfying argument of spiritual explanations. To those who believe in spiritual influences, this does not invalidate their frame of reference; it only points out that scientists are in error and unable to recognize the true sources of crime when they encounter them. Such individuals do not need, and have no interest in, the natural explanations of behavior. They are satisfied that they already have a more adequate explanation.

Something very similar also may be true of those who reject spiritual explanations and accept natural explanations but have different frames of reference. The classical criminologist holds on to the view that crime can be judged in terms of deliberateness, intent, and understanding of right and wrong. These criminologists view the search for the causes of crime as a fundamentally wrongheaded endeavor that produces no beneficial results. In contrast, criminologists who search for the causes of criminal behavior reject both the spiritualism of some religious individuals and the free will of the classical criminologists. Within this frame of reference, however, some criminologists focus on social factors and hold that there is little or no role for biological and psychological factors in the causes of criminal behavior. Other criminologists may argue that biological or psychological factors explain substantial amounts of criminal behavior, and social factors enter into the picture through their interaction with the biological or psychological factors. Finally, criminologists who propose theories of the behavior of criminal law may regard both classical theories and theories that search for the causes of criminal behavior as fundamentally misinterpreting the phenomenon of crime. In their view, the volume of crime in society and the characteristics of criminals are both reflections of the operations of the criminal justice system, not the behavior of individuals.

In the chapters that follow, the implications of some of these general propositions will be examined in much greater detail. The chapters have been organized primarily for the sake of convenience and clarity; no necessary separateness or mutual exclusiveness should be inferred. Some theoretical positions are logically incompatible; others are notably interdependent. In general, the chapters are organized in the historical sequence in which the theories originated, so that the earliest theories are presented first. This is intended to provide the reader with a sense of how the field of criminology has evolved over time. Each chapter presents modern as well as historical materials; that is, each chapter brings the work of the early theorists up to date by presenting more recent theories and research that take the same general point of view. Thus, for example, classical theories are presented first since they originated before other types of criminology theories. The chapter then presents some of the contemporary work being done within the frame of reference of classical thought. The earliest theories of the causes of criminal behavior focused on the biological and psychological characteristics of the individual criminal, so that chapters covering these topics are presented next. Each of these chapters also presents modern work within this frame of reference.

The major theories in criminology are presented in Chapters 2 through 16. Chapter 17 applies criminological theories to some specific types of crime, with the intention of illustrating the different types of questions that are asked within the different criminological frames of reference. Finally, Chapter 18 discusses the interrelationships among theory, research, and crime policy, and Chapter 19 provides a conclusion that assesses the current state of criminology theories.

## RECOMMENDED READINGS

Clarence Ray Jeffery, "The Historical Development of Criminology," in Hermann Mannheim, ed., *Pioneers in Criminology*, Patterson Smith, Montclair, N.J., 1972. A history of the development of criminological ideas through 1970, including a discussion of the decline of positivism and the ideas that are taking its place.

Eugene Doleschal and Nora Klapmuts, "Toward a New Criminology," *Crime and Delinquency Literature* 5 (4): 607–26 (Dec. 1973). Analysis of the development of criminology in the classical, positivist, and interactionist schools.

Don C. Gibbons and Peter Garabedian, "Conservative, Liberal and Radical Criminology: Some Trends and Observations," in Charles E. Reasons, *The Criminologist: Crime and the Criminal*, Goodyear, Pacific Palisades, Ca., 1974. Another analysis of the three stages of criminological development.

Travis Hirschi and David Rudisill, "The Great American Search: Causes of Crime 1876–1976," *Annals of the American Association of Political and Social Sciences* 423: 14–22 (Jan. 1976). Developments in criminology over the last 100 years.

Raymond J. Michalowski, "Perspective and Paradigm: Structuring Criminological Thought," in Robert F. Meier, ed., *Theory in Criminology: Contemporary Views*, Sage, Beverly Hills, Cal., 1977, pp. 17–39. Outlines three basic perspectives—the consensus, pluralist, and conflict—and three scientific paradigms—the positivist, interactionist, and socialist—in the contemporary study of crime.

Frank P. Williams III, "The Sociology of Criminological Theory: Paradigm or Fad," in Gary F. Jensen, ed., *Sociology of Delinquency: Current Issues*, Sage, Beverly Hills, Cal., 1981, pp. 20–28. The different types of criminological theories are tied to different social values, and are not actually competing views of reality.

# CHAPTER TWO

# Classical Criminology

The literature of criminology often refers to the classical and the neoclassical schools of criminological thought. These terms or labels are used to designate some important ideas in the long history of trying to understand, and trying to do something about, crime. The classical school is usually associated with the name of the Italian scholar Cesare Bonesana, Marchese de Beccaria (1738–94). Its later modification, the so-called neoclassical school, is very similar as far as basic ideas and conceptions about the human nature are concerned. Both represent a sort of free-will, rationalistic hedonism that is part of a tradition going back many centuries.

## 1. PRECLASSICAL WRITERS AND IDEAS

The backgrounds of classical criminology involve the entire scope of preceding intellectual history, which had developed a theory of society and engendered a great deal of discussion about the relationship between the individual and the group. These themes or problems had been the concern of the writers of antiquity. The more immediate background for Beccaria included the scholasticism of St. Thomas Aquinas and theories of the social contract writers such as Hobbes, Locke, Voltaire, and Rousseau.

Beccaria wrote in a period when the theology of the Church Fathers and the doctrine of the divine right of kings were pitted against the intellectualism and rationalism of the social contract thinkers. People of that time were familiar with and accustomed to accept, as a matter of course, the general thought pattern and arrangements suggested in the following outline.

1. Humans had originally existed in a state of nature, grace, or innocence.

2. The emergence from this state involved the application of *reason* as *responsible* individuals:

   a. According to the Doctrine of the Fall (sin in the Garden of Eden), all people live in suffering and pain because the first human pair chose to disobey the divine injunction.

   b. Under social contract theories, individuals come together and contract to form a society; that is, presumably, they consider the pros and cons—what to gain and what to lose—and come to deliberative agreement to live together in a society, each giving up something to gain something else.

3. Human will was accepted as a psychological reality, a faculty or trait of the individual that regulates and controls behavior:

   a. In general, the will was free—that is, there were no limitations to the choices an individual could make.

   b. God and the Devil could influence will—and so apparently could nature, i.e., impulses or instincts—yet in specific action of the individual the will was free. Thus:

   i. Montesquieu found that society results from four impulses or desires: peace, hunger, sex, and social desires (sociability).

   ii. Rousseau made desire for companionship the basis for the formation of society.

   iii. Hobbes conceived of fear as an elemental drive causing humans to form societies and accept the necessary restraints. All these, apparently, affected the will, yet in individual action the choice was free.

   iv. Voltaire recognized that will may be strong or weak, thus influencing behavior, but still did not question the basic doctrine of will as the motive, or mainspring, of human behavior.

4. The idea was accepted that the principal instrument for control (affecting the will to behave) of behavior is fear—especially fear of pain.

5. Punishment (i.e., infliction of pain, humiliation, and disgrace) as a principal method of operating to create fear was necessary to influence the will and thus to control behavior.

6. Society had the right to punish the individual, and to transfer this right to the political state exclusively for execution. This follows logically with the state as the strongest practical authority.

7. Some code of criminal law, or, better, some system of punishments for forbidden acts, was accepted. With the growth and development of the na-

tional states, the limited controls of the feudal chiefs was replaced with centralization in the realm of the law, the courts, and the police.

These were the established ideas of the time. There was dissatisfaction and protest, but they were directed against procedure and personal abuse, not the basic frame of reference of the thought pattern of the time. Beccaria was such a protest writer who sought to restate the conditions under which acts should be called crimes, as well as to reformulate the appropriate punishments. He nowhere questioned the psychology of the day or the explanation for human behavior then current; he merely sought to reform the system of punishments.

## 2. BECCARIA AND THE CLASSICAL SCHOOL

Cesare Bonesana, Marchese de Beccaria, was an indifferent student who had some interest in mathematics.[1] After completing his formal education, he joined with Allessandro Verri, an official of the prison in Milan, and with his brother Pietro Verri, an economist, in a group of young men who met regularly to discuss literary and philosophical topics. Beccaria was given an assignment in March 1763 to write an essay on penology, a subject about which he knew nothing. With help from the Verri brothers, the essay was completed in January 1764, and was published under the title *Dei deliti e delle pene (On Crimes and Punishments)* in the small town of Livorno in July of that year, when Beccaria was 26 years old.

Beccaria's career, otherwise, was that of a university professor and government official whose ability in mathematics led to a number of original and brilliant applications of quantitative methods to the field of social and political study.[2] His general thought followed that of the French rationalists, and his economic thought was not far from that of his illustrious English contemporary, Adam Smith (1723–90), who has been called "the father of quantitative economics."[3]

Beccaria, in common with his contemporary intellectuals, pro-

---

1. An account of the life and work of Beccaria may be found in Elio D. Monachesi, "Pioneers in Criminology: Cesare Beccaria (1738–94)," *Journal of Criminal Law, Criminology and Police Science* 46 (4): 439–49 (Nov.–Dec. 1955), reprinted in Hermann Mannheim, *Pioneers in Criminology*, Patterson Smith, Montclair, N.J., 1972, pp. 36–50.

2. See *Encyclopedia of the Social Sciences*, vol. II, Macmillan, New York, 1930, pp. 488–89.

3. See Charles Gide and Charles Rist, *History of Economic Doctrine*, Heath, Boston, 1913; also *International Encyclopedia of the Social Sciences*, vol. II, Macmillan and The Free Press, New York, 1968, pp. 37–38.

tested against the many inconsistencies in government and in the management of public affairs. In keeping with this basic orientation, he proposed various reforms to make criminal justice practice more logical and rational. He objected to existing practices on many grounds, but especially to the capricious and purely personal justice the judges were dispensing and to the severe and barbaric punishments of the time. Judges did what the law could not well do, differentiate in terms of the circumstances and special considerations of a particular case. Thus judges exercised the power to add to the punishments prescribed by law penalties in keeping with their personal views of the special circumstances involved. This arbitrary and tyrannical practice of power, in which the judges took the part of one class in its struggle with the members of other classes in a society rapidly becoming mobile and fluid, was the substance against which much of the protest writing of the period was directed. It was, after all, only 20 years before the French Revolution, the climax of such protests, with the consequent overthrow of much of the smug complacency of the status quo.

In the light of the preceding discussion, it is interesting to look at Beccaria's ideas as expressed in his own words in relation to some of the basic principles of his system of justice.

1. On the contractual society and the need for punishments:[4]

Laws are the conditions under which independent and isolated men united to form a society. Weary of living in a continual state of war, and of enjoying a liberty rendered useless by the uncertainty of preserving it, they sacrificed a part so that they might enjoy the rest of it in peace and safety. The sum of all these portions of liberty sacrificed by each for his own good constitutes the sovereignty of a nation, and their legitimate depositary and administrator is the sovereign. But merely to have established this deposit was not enough; it had to be defended against private usurpations by individuals each of whom always tries not only to withdraw his own share but also to usurp for himself that of others. Some tangible motives had to be introduced, therefore, to prevent the despotic spirit, which is in every man, from plunging the laws of society into its original chaos. These tangible motives are the punishments established against infractors of the laws.

---

4. Cesare Beccaria, *On Crimes and Punishments,* translated by Henry Paolucci, Bobbs-Merrill, Indianapolis, 1963, pp. 11–12. This and the following quotations are reprinted with permission of the publisher, Bobbs-Merrill Educational Publishing, Inc., © 1963.

## 2. On the function of legislatures:[5]

Only the laws can decree punishments for crimes; authority for this can reside only with the legislator who represents the entire society united by a social contract. . . . But a punishment that exceeds the limit fixed by the laws is just punishment plus another punishment; a magistrate cannot, therefore, under any pretext of zeal or concern for the public good, augment the punishment established for a delinquent citizen.

## 3. On the function of judges:[6]

Judges in criminal cases cannot have the authority to interpret laws, and the reason, again, is that they are not legislators. . . . For every crime that comes before him, a judge is required to complete a perfect syllogism in which the major premise must be the general law; the minor, the action that conforms or does not conform to the law; and the conclusion, acquittal or punishment. If the judge were not constrained, or if he desired to frame even a single additional syllogism, the door would thereby be opened to uncertainty.

Nothing can be more dangerous than the popular axiom that it is necessary to consult the spirit of the laws. It is a dam that has given way to a torrent of opinions. . . . Each man has his own point of view, and, at each different time, a different one. Thus, the "spirit" of the law would be the product of a judge's good or bad logic, of his good or bad digestion; it would depend on the violence of his passions, on the weakness of the accused, on the judge's connections with him, and on all those minute factors that alter the appearances of an object in the fluctuating mind of man. . . . The disorder that arises from rigorous observance of the letter of a penal law is hardly comparable to the disorders that arise from interpretations.

## 4. On the seriousness of crimes:[7]

The true measure of crimes is . . . the *harm done to society.* . . . They were in error who believed that the true measure of crimes is to be found in the intention of the person who commits them. Intention depends on the impression objects actually make and on the present disposition of the mind; these vary in all men and in each man, according to the swift succession of ideas, of passions, and of circumstances. It would be necessary, therefore, to form not only a particular code for each citizen, but a new law for every crime. Sometimes, with the best intentions, men do the greatest

5. Ibid., pp. 13–14.
6. Ibid., pp. 14–15.
7. Ibid., pp. 64–65.

injury to society; at other times, intending the worst for it, they do the greatest good.

## 5. On proportionate punishments:[8]

It is to the common interest not only that crimes not be committed, but also that they be less frequent in proportion to the harm they cause society. Therefore, the obstacles that deter man from committing crime should be stronger in proportion as they are contrary to the public good, and as the inducements to commit them are stronger. There must, therefore, be a proper proportion between crimes and punishments.

## 6. On the severity of punishments:[9]

For punishment to attain its end, the evil which it inflicts has only to exceed the advantage derivable from the crime; in this excess of evil one should include the certainty of punishment and the loss of the good which the crime might have produced. All beyond this is superfluous and for that reason tyrannical. . . .

The severity of punishment of itself emboldens men to commit the very wrongs it is supposed to prevent; they are driven to commit additional crimes to avoid the punishment for a single one. The countries and times most notorious for severity of penalties have always been those in which the bloodiest and most inhumane of deeds were committed, for the same spirit of ferocity that guided the hand of the legislators also ruled that of the parricide and assassin.

## 7. On the promptness of punishments:[10]

The more promptly and the more closely punishment follows upon the commission of a crime, the more just and useful will it be. I say more just, because the criminal is thereby spared the useless and cruel torments of uncertainty . . . [and] because privation of liberty, being itself a punishment, should not precede the sentence except when necessity requires. . . . I have said that the promptness of punishment is more useful because when the length of time that passes between the punishment and the misdeed is less, so much the stronger and more lasting in the human mind is the association of these two ideas, *crime and punishment*.

8. Ibid., p. 62.
9. Ibid., pp. 43–44.
10. Ibid., pp. 55–56.

### 8. On the certainty of punishments:[11]

One of the greatest curbs on crime is not the cruelty of punishments, but their infallibility. . . . The certainty of a punishment, even if it be moderate, will always make a stronger impression than the fear of another which is more terrible but combined with the hope of impunity; even the least evils, when they are certain, always terrify men's minds. . . . Let the laws, therefore, be inexorable, and inexorable their executors in particular cases, but let the legislator be tender, indulgent, and humane.

### 9. On preventing crimes:[12]

It is better to prevent crimes than to punish them. That is the ultimate end of every good legislation. . . . Do you want to prevent crimes? See to it that the laws are clear and simple and that the entire force of a nation is united in their defense, and that no part of it is employed to destroy them. See to it that the laws favor not so much classes of men as men themselves. See to it that men fear the laws and fear nothing else. For fear of the laws is salutary, but fatal and fertile for crimes is one man's fear of another.

Beccaria also emphasized that the laws should be published so that the public may know what they are and support their intent and purpose; that torture and secret accusations should be abolished; that capital punishment should be abolished and replaced by imprisonment; that jails be made more humane institutions; that the law should not distinguish between wealthy and poor or between nobles and commoners; and that a person should be tried by a jury of his peers, and that when there were class differences between the offender and the victim, one-half of the jury should be from the class of the offender, and the other half from the class of the victim. Beccaria summarized his ideas in a brief conclusion to his book:[13]

In order for punishment not to be, in every instance, an act of violence of one or of many against a private citizen, it must be essentially public, prompt, necessary, the least possible in the given circumstances, proportionate to the crimes, dictated by the laws.

Beccaria's ideas were quite radical for his time, so he published his book anonymously and defended himself in the introduction against charges that he was an unbeliever or a revolutionary. In fact, the

11. Ibid., pp. 58–59.
12. Ibid., pp. 93–94.
13. Ibid., p. 99.

book was condemned by the Catholic church in 1766 for its rationalistic ideas.[14] But despite Beccaria's fears and some opposition, his little book was extremely well received by his contemporaries. The first French translation appeared in 1766, and Voltaire provided an elaborate commentary. The first English translation appeared in 1767 under the title *An Essay on Crimes and Punishments*. In the preface to that edition, the translator noted that the book had already gone through six editions in Italian and several in French, and commented that "perhaps no book, on any subject, was ever received with more avidity, more generally read, or more universally applauded."[15]

Following the French Revolution of 1789 Beccaria's principles were used as the basis for the famous French Code of 1791. Gillin discussed this effort in the following words:[16]

It attempted to apply Beccaria's principle of "equal punishment for the same crime." It adopted his suggestions that crimes should be arranged in a scale, that to each crime the law should affix a penalty, and that the legislators should make the law, while the judges should only apply it to the cases that came before them for trial. On the other hand, it failed to adopt methods whereby the injustice inherent in the application of "equal punishment for the same crime" should be prevented. While in that dictum Beccaria had in mind the abuse of arbitrary punishments by the judges and the favoritism shown the powerful by the courts, in actual practice in the French courts it was extended to accused persons who were unequal in another sense— the insane and the sane, the minor and the adult, the idiot and the person of normal intelligence. In this code there was an attempt not only to legislate on every crime, but to fix by statute the penalty for each degree of each kind. Nothing was left to the judgment of the court, except the question of guilt. There could be no abatement for extenuating circumstances, no added penalty for the heinousness of the way in which a particular crime was committed. The punishments were as absolutely fixed as they had been in the Salic Law more than a thousand years before, although they were not quite on the same basis.

It seems fair to characterize the classical school as administrative and legal criminology. Its great advantage was that it set up a procedure that was easy to administer. It made the judge only an instrument to apply the law, and the law undertook to prescribe an

14. Ibid., p. xi.

15. Ibid., p. x.

16. John L. Gillin, *Criminology and Penology*, 3rd ed., Appleton-Century-Crofts, New York, 1945, p. 229. Reprinted by permission of Helen N. Gillin.

exact penalty for every crime and every degree thereof. Puzzling questions about the reasons for or causes of behavior, the uncertainties of motive and intent, the unequal consequences of an arbitrary rule, these were all deliberately ignored for the sake of administrative uniformity. This was the classical conception of justice—an exact scale of punishments for equal acts without reference to the individual involved or the special circumstances in which the crime was committed.

As a practical matter, however, the Code of 1791 was impossible to enforce in everyday situations, and modifications were introduced. These modifications, all in the interest of greater ease of administration, are the essence of the so-called neoclassical school.

## 3. THE NEOCLASSICAL SCHOOL

The greatest practical difficulty in applying the Code of 1791 came from ignoring differences in the circumstances of particular situations. The Code treated everyone exactly alike, in accordance with Beccaria's argument that only the act, and not the intent, should be considered in determining the punishment. Thus first offenders were treated the same as repeaters, minors were treated the same as adults, insane the same as sane, and so on. No society, of course, will permit its children and other helpless incompetents to be treated in the same manner as its professional criminals. The French were no exception. Modifications in practice began, and soon there were revisions of the Code itself.

The Code of 1810[17] tipped the lid just a little in permitting some discretion on the part of the judges. In the Revised French Code of 1819 there is definite provision for the exercise of discretion on the part of the judges in view of certain objective circumstances, but still no room for consideration of subjective intent.

The set, impersonal features of even this revised *Code Napoléon* then became the point of attack for a new school of reformers whose cry was against the injustice of a rigorous code and for the need for individualization and for discriminating judgment to fit individual circumstances. These efforts at revision and refinement in application of the classical theory of free will and complete responsibility— considerations involving age, mental condition, and extenuating circumstances—constitute what is often called the neoclassical school.

17. In addition to the *Revolutionary Code* of 1791, other Napoleonic codes of the period often mentioned are *Code de procédure civile*, 1806; *Code de commerce*, 1807; *Code d'instruction criminelle*, 1808; the *Code pénal*, 1810; and the revised *Code pénal*, 1819.

Thus, the neoclassical school represented no particular break with the basic doctrine of human nature that made up the common tradition throughout Europe at the time. The doctrine continued to be that humans are creatures guided by reason, who have free will, and who therefore are responsible for their acts and can be controlled by fear of punishment. Hence the pain from punishment must exceed the pleasure obtained from the criminal act; then free will determines the desirability of noncriminal conduct. The neoclassical school therefore represented primarily the modifications necessary for the administration of the criminal law based on classical theory that resulted from practical experience.

### 4. ASSESSING BECCARIA'S THEORY

The neoclassical view is, with minor variations, "the major model of human behavior held to by agencies of social control in all advanced industrial societies (whether in the West or the East). . . ."[18] Its widespread acceptance in contemporary legal systems is probably a result of the fact that this view provides support for the most fundamental assumption on which those systems are based. Classical criminology provides a general justification for the use of punishment in the control of crime. Since punishment for that purpose has always been used in the legal system, it should not be surprising that this is the theory to which legal authorities adhere.

In addition, classical theory was attractive to legal authorities for a more general reason. It is based in social contract theory, which holds that all people have a stake in the continued existence of the authority structure, since without it society would degenerate into a "war of all against all." Since crime contributed to this degeneration, it was ultimately in the best interests of all people, even criminals, to obey the law. Social contract theorists saw crime as a fundamentally irrational act, committed by people who, because of their shortsighted greed and passion were incapable of recognizing their own long-term best interests.[19] The fact that crime was concentrated in the lower classes was taken to be a symptom of the fact that these classes were filled with irrational, dangerous people.[20]

18. Ian Taylor, Paul Walton, and Jock Young, *The New Criminology*, Harper & Row, New York, 1973, pp. 9–10.

19. Ibid., p. 3.

20. See, for example, the discussion of Locke's view of the irrationality of the lower classes in C. B. MacPherson, *The Political Theory of Possessive Individualism*, Oxford University Press, New York, 1962, pp. 232–38.

The ease with which the classical system of justice could be administered rested largely on this view. It supported the uniform enforcement of laws without questioning whether those laws were fair or just. Specifically, social contract theorists did not take into account the fact that some societies are unfair. For some groups, the costs of adhering to the social contract may be few and the benefits great; for other groups, the costs may be great and the benefits few. The latter group will probably have less allegiance to the social contract, a fact that may be expressed in the form of a higher crime rate.

That is a far different perspective than the view that high-crime groups are filled with irrational and dangerous people. Rather than relying solely on punishments, it would imply that an additional way to reduce crime is to make the costs and benefits of adhering to the social contract more uniform among the different groups in society. This option was not attractive to the social contract theorists, who were themselves members of the propertied class. Thus they addressed the problem in such a way as to justify the existence of inequalities. Hobbes, for example, argued that lower-class persons could adhere to the social contract if they were taught to believe that the status quo was inevitable.[21] Locke maintained that all persons were obligated to obey the laws of society, since all gave their "tacit consent" to the social contract. But he also argued that only persons with property were capable of making the laws, since only they were capable of the fully rational life and only they would defend the "natural right" of the unlimited accumulation of property.[22]

Beccaria's position on defending the status quo was somewhat confusing. He argued that it was natural for all to seek their own advantage, even at the expense of the common good, and that this was the source of crime. Thus he did not share the view of the social contract theorists that criminals were essentially irrational. He was fully aware that the laws (which he said "have always favored the few and outraged the many") could impose massive injustices on the poor.[23] He went even further by arguing that the laws themselves could create crime:[24]

To prohibit a multitude of indifferent acts is not to prevent crimes that might arise from them, but is rather to create new ones. . . . For one motive that drives men to commit real crime there are a thousand that drive them to

21. Ibid., p. 98.
22. Ibid., pp. 247–51.
23. Beccaria, op. cit., p. 43.
24. Ibid., p. 94.

commit those indifferent acts which are called crimes by bad laws. . . .
The majority of laws are nothing but privileges, that is, a tribute paid by
all to the convenience of some few.

Thus Beccaria was not solely concerned with the establishment of a
system of punishment. He recognized the problem of inequality in
society, and implied that it was wrong to punish lawbreakers when
the laws themselves were unjust. This aspect of Beccaria's writings
is sometimes ignored, so that classical criminology is identified with
the social contract position that crime is essentially irrational.[25]
    On the other hand, Beccaria wanted to "defend humanity without
becoming a martyr." This led him to take some unusual positions.
For example, Beccaria argued that the death penalty was ineffective
because a thief would reason as follows:[26]

What are these laws that I am supposed to respect, that place such a great
distance between me and the rich man? He refuses me the penny I ask of
him and, as an excuse, tells me to sweat at work that he knows nothing
about. Who made these laws? Rich and powerful men who have never
deigned to visit the squalid huts of the poor, who have never had to share
a crust of moldy bread amid the innocent cries of hungry children and the
tears of a wife. Let us break these bonds, fatal to the majority and only
useful to a few indolent tyrants; let us attack the injustice at its source. I
will return to my natural state of independence; I shall at least for a little
time live free and happy with the fruits of my courage and industry. The
day will perhaps come for my sorrow and repentance, but will be brief, and
for a single day of suffering I shall have many years of liberty and of pleasures.

The radical perspective of this passage is clear, as is the reason that
Beccaria feared the official reaction to his book. On the other hand,
the implication that Beccaria drew from this discussion was that the
death penalty should be replaced by extended imprisonment at hard
labor. His reasoning was that such a punishment was actually more
terrible than the death penalty, since the threat of "a great number
of years, or even a whole lifetime to be spent in servitude and pain,"
would make a much stronger impression on a potential offender than
the threat of execution.[27]
    Thus Beccaria seems to have implied that there are broader social

25. See, for example, Taylor, Walton, and Young, op. cit., pp. 1–10.
26. Beccaria, op. cit., p. 49.
27. Ibid., pp. 49–50.

causes behind the crime problem, but he did not make these arguments explicit. One of the effects of the neoclassical adaptation of Beccaria's theory was to prune carefully all of these radical elements from his work, leaving only the easily administered system of punishment as the response to crime.[28]

## 5. CONTEMPORARY CLASSICISM: DETERRENCE AND ECONOMETRICS

The classical school was the dominant perspective in criminology for approximately 100 years, until it was replaced by the positivist search for the causes of crime. After another 100 years substantial interest returned to the classical perspective in criminology, beginning in the late 1960s. This revival of interest was associated with a dramatic shift away from the positivist-oriented indeterminate sentencing structures and back to the determinate sentences similar to the French Code of 1791.[29]

Two principal branches of contemporary classicism can be identified. The whole question of deterrence has been the subject of voluminous literature in criminology in recent years.[30] Here an attempt has been made to develop the classical perspective in the light of modern knowledge of the human behavioral sciences, as well as through empirical studies of the effects of certainty and severity of punishment on crime rates. While deterrence theory and research has been dominated by criminologists and sociologists, the other branch of contemporary classicism has been dominated by economists. The field of economics holds a view of man that is quite similar to that of the classicists. For example, economic theory holds that a person analyzes the costs and benefits when he decides to buy a hamburger instead of a T-bone steak, or a Volkswagen instead of a Cadillac. The costs and benefits include not merely monetary factors, but factors such as taste, comfort, prestige, and convenience.

28. For a radical interpretation of Beccaria's theory, see Lynn McDonald, *The Sociology of Law and Order*, Faber and Faber, London, 1976, pp. 40–42. McDonald argues that Beccaria's is a "complete and recognizable conflict theory."

29. See the entire issue of *Corrections Magazine* 3 (3) (Sept. 1977).

30. For a review of theoretical issues, see Franklin E. Zimring and Gordon J. Hawkins, *Deterrence*, University of Chicago Press, Chicago, 1973; Johannes Andenaes, *Punishment and Deterrence*, University of Michigan Press, Ann Arbor, Mich., 1974; and Jack P. Gibbs, *Crime, Punishment, and Deterrence*, Elsevier, New York, 1975. Gibbs's book reviews the empirical studies, as does Alfred Blumstein et al., *Deterrence and Incapacitation*, National Academy of Sciences, Washington, D.C., 1978. For a briefer but very thorough presentation of both theory and empirical studies, see E. A. Fattah, "Deterrence: A Review of the Literature," *Canadian Journal of Criminology* 19 (2): 1–119 (Apr. 1977).

Econometric techniques[31] have been developed to analyze these factors in terms of the resulting economic choice. Beginning with an article by Gary S. Becker in 1968,[32] many economists have approached crime as a similar economic choice. They have therefore applied their techniques to the analysis of criminal behavior, as well as to the choices of the criminal justice system.

The economic perspective views the decision to commit a crime as essentially similar to any other decision—that is, it is made on the basis of an analysis of the costs and benefits of the action. Because crime is seen as a free choice of the individual, the theories of crime which discuss cultural or biological "causes" are seen as unnecessary.[33] For example, Sullivan describes the choice of a career as a thief as follows:[34]

The individual calculates (1) all his practical opportunities of earning legitimate income, (2) the amounts of income offered by these opportunities, (3) the amounts of income offered by various illegal methods, (4) the probability of being arrested if he acts illegally, and (5) the probable punishment should he be caught. After making these calculations, he chooses the act or occupation with the highest discounted return. To arrive at a discounted return he must include among his cost calculations the future costs of going to prison if he is apprehended. It is in this sense that the criminal is understood to be a normal, rational, calculating individual.

The benefits of a criminal action may include not only increases in monetary wealth, but also increases in psychological satisfaction as well as the possibility of achieving these increases with very little effort. The expected cost of the crime is normally computed as the total cost associated with the punishment of the crime times the probability that the punishment will be imposed. For example, if the crime is usually punished with a fine of $1,000, and the probability of the punishment being imposed is 1/10, then the expected cost of the crime is $100. If the person can gain more than $100 in the crime, then it would be in his interest to commit it.[35] Often the

31. This term refers to the use of mathematical techniques to test and apply economic theories. See Richard F. Sullivan, "The Economics of Crime: An Introduction to the Literature," *Crime and Delinquency* 19 (2): 138–49 (Apr. 1973).

32. Gary S. Becker, "Crime and Punishment: An Economic Approach," *Journal of Political Economy* 76 (2): 169–217 (Mar.–Apr. 1968).

33. Becker, op. cit., p. 14; Sullivan, op. cit., p. 139.

34. Sullivan, op. cit., p. 141.

35. George J. Stigler, "The Optimum Enforcement of Laws," *Journal of Political Economy* 78: 526–36 (May–June 1970).

costs and benefits cannot be computed in monetary terms, such as when the costs include time in prison or the social disapproval of arrest and conviction, or when benefits include the satisfaction of revenge or of outwitting the authorities. However, the individual must still compare these costs and benefits in order to decide whether the action is "worth it" to him or her.

This calculation does not presume that the criminal has a crystal ball to foresee future events. Many people make mistakes in calculating their future payoffs, and when they do, they end up in dead-end jobs or in bankruptcy. When criminals make similar mistakes, they may end up spending the better part of their lives in prison. As Sullivan says, "The basic economic assumption does not maintain that people do not make mistakes but rather that they do their best given their reading of present and future possibilities and given their resources."[36]

Economic theories can also be used to explain the policies of various criminal justice agencies. The economic view maintains that if society were willing to pay the social costs, virtually all crime could be eliminated.[37] These social costs would include a tremendous increase in budgets of criminal justice agencies, as well as the willingness to convict large numbers of innocent people.[38] By maintaining the crime rate that we have, our society is saying in effect that the cost of reducing crime to a lower level is more than we are willing to pay. If crime were reduced to a lower level, it would result in a net social loss, since the costs would be greater than the benefits we would receive. Therefore, according to economic theory, the present level of crime represents an "optimality condition," the point at which the total social loss for the society is minimized.[39]

## 6. IMPLICATIONS AND CONCLUSIONS

The classical and neoclassical schools represent an abandoning of the supernatural as an explanation of criminal behavior. Instead of viewing humans as puppets of the supernatural, the early classical criminologists argued that humans act on the basis of reason and intelligence and therefore are responsible for their own actions. To that

---

36. Sullivan, op. cit., p. 142.

37. Becker, op. cit., pp. 18–19.

38. John R. Harris, "On the Economics of Law and Order," *Journal of Political Economy* 78: 165–74 (Jan.–Feb. 1970). See also Stigler, op. cit., p. 80.

39. Becker, op. cit., pp. 18–24; Stigler, op. cit.; Sullivan, op. cit., p. 143.

extent classical criminology marks the beginnings of the natural approach to criminal behavior.

The classical school also marks the beginnings of the rationalistic,
bureaucratic approach to criminal procedure. As such, the classical
school was responsible for a wide-ranging reformation and restructuring of the criminal justice system. But after 100 years of such reforms there was considerable dissatisfaction with the ability of classical ideas to achieve reductions in criminal behavior. This ultimately
resulted in a break with the classical system of thinking, beginning
with the positive school of Lombroso and his pupils. That school extended to criminology some of the ideas about human behavior that
were beginning to dominate biology, medicine, psychiatry, psychology, and sociology at that time. In part, this school proposed an explanation of the failure of classicism to reduce crime: if crime is caused
by forces beyond the control of the individual, then punishing the
criminal will not be effective. Instead of punishing criminals, positivist criminologists argued that it is necessary to address the causes
of criminal behavior whether they be biological, psychological, or
social.

The recent revival of interest in classical criminology seems to reflect, at least in part, dissatisfaction with the effectiveness of positivist-
oriented policies for the control of criminal behavior, just as the
original switch to positivism reflected a dissatisfaction with the effectiveness of classically oriented policies.[40] Whether punishing criminals will be more successful today than it was 100 years ago remains
to be seen. Several recent reviews of the empirical research on the
question of deterrence have all concluded that at the present time it
is not possible to say whether or to what extent punishments actually deter crime.[41]

The appeal of classicism rests on its promise of crime control
through manipulations of the criminal justice enforcement and punishment systems. As such, it is more attractive than the later theories that argue that crime can be reduced only by changing more
fundamental social arrangements, such as redistributing legitimate

40. For example, James Q. Wilson, *Thinking About Crime*, 2nd ed., Basic Books, New York,
1984; Ernest van den Haag, *Punishing Criminals*, Basic Books, New York, 1975.

41. See, for example, Gibbs, op. cit., p. 217; Daniel Nagin, "General Deterrence: A Review
of the Empirical Evidence," in Alfred Blumstein, Jacqueline Cohen, and Daniel Nagin, eds.,
*Deterrence and Incapacitation: Estimating the Effects of Criminal Sanctions on Crime Rates*,
National Academy of Sciences, Washington, D.C., 1978, p. 136; Charles R. Tittle, *Sanctions
and Social Deviance*, Praeger, New York, 1980, p. 24; Linda S. Anderson, "The Deterrent
Effect of Criminal Sanctions: Reviewing the Evidence," in Paul J. Brantingham and Jack M.
Kress, eds., *Structure, Law, and Power*, Sage, Beverly Hills, Cal., 1979, pp. 120–34.

opportunities or changing the capitalist economic system. Ultimately classicism must be judged on the basis of its ability to produce the results it promises.

## RECOMMENDED READINGS

Cesare Beccaria, *On Crimes and Punishments*, translated by Henry Paolucci, Bobbs-Merrill, Indianapolis, 1963. A small book, easily read, which continues to hold a great deal of force.

Jeremy Bentham, "An Introduction to the Principles of Morals and Legislation," in *The Works of Jeremy Bentham*, ed. by John Bowring, Russell & Russell, New York, 1962. Bentham's basic ideas on crime and punishment.

Hermann Mannheim, ed., *Pioneers in Criminology*, Patterson Smith, Montclair, N.J., 1972. Contains brief accounts of the lives and works of Cesare Beccaria (by Elio Monachesi, pp. 36–50), Jeremy Bentham (by Gilbert Geis, pp. 51–68), and criminal law reformer Edward Livingstone (by Joseph Mouledoux, pp. 69–83.)

Coleman Phillipson, *Three Criminal Law Reformers: Beccaria, Bentham and Romilly*, Dutton, New York, 1923; reprinted by Patterson Smith, Montclair, N.J., 1970. A more detailed account, focusing on the application of classical theory to the problems of reform.

Marcello Maestro, *Cesare Beccaria and the Origins of Penal Reform*, Temple University Press, Philadelphia, 1973. The first full biography of Becarria in English, with an excellent bibliography and a foreword by Norval Morris.

Michel Foucault, *Discipline and Punish: The Birth of the Prison*, Pantheon, New York, 1977. Beccaria's ideas are placed in the context of the "great transformations" from rural, feudal, agricultural societies to urban, capitalist, industrial societies. These ideas gained acceptance because they met the needs of emerging power groups and because they justified a vast expansion of state power over the lives of ordinary citizens.

Philip Jenkins, "Varieties of Enlightenment Criminology: Beccaria, Godwin, de Sade," *British Journal of Criminology* 24 (2): 112–30 (Apr. 1984). Beccaria's book gained widespread acceptance because it suggested an administrative solution to the problem of crime that could be implemented without changing basic social structures. Thus it diverted attention from more radical theories that were developing at the time.

Charles A. Murray and Louis A. Cox, Jr., *Beyond Probation*, Sage, Beverly Hills, Cal., 1979. On the basis of an experimental program in Chicago, the authors conclude that imprisonment reduces delinquency more than does community treatment.

Alfred Blumstein, Jacqueline Cohen, and Daniel Nagin, eds., *Deterrence and Incapacitation: Estimating the Effects of Criminal Sanctions on Crime Rates*, National Academy of Sciences, Washington, D.C., 1978. A close scientific look at available evidence on deterrence and incapacitation.

Andrew von Hirsch, *Doing Justice: The Choice of Punishments*, Hill & Wang, New York, 1976. A modern attempt to construct a uniform punishment system in the face of widespread sentencing disparity, similar to the efforts of Beccaria and Bentham.

The Twentieth Century Fund Task Force on Criminal Sentencing, *Fair and Certain Punishment*, Background Paper by Alan M. Dershowitz, McGraw-Hill, New York, 1976. Another modern attempt to address the same problems Beccaria and Bentham did.

Peter Schmidt and Ann D. Witte, *An Economic Analysis of Crime and Justice*, Academic Press, New York, 1984. Includes a critical review of econometric models of criminal behavior and the test of a new model.

Daniel Glaser, *Crime in Our Changing Society*, Holt, Rinehart and Winston, New York, 1978, pp. 83–99. Assessment of the costs and benefits of crime, and whether crime "pays."

Peter Letkemann, *Crime as Work*, Prentice-Hall, Englewood Cliffs, N.J., 1973. Crimes against property are a precarious means of earning a living.

CHAPTER THREE

# The Positive School

The century between Beccaria and Lombroso marks a shift in thinking that is of such magnitude that it can well be described as an intellectual revolution. During this century, the logic and basic methodology of objective science became well established. Interpretations
of scientific investigations began to provide a new intellectual approach, a new system of explanation of all phenomena, including the
accumulated heritage of history, custom, and religion. Answers to
ancient questions about human nature began to be given in the terms
of objective science rather than religion or philosophy. Darwin's book,
*On the Origin of Species* (1859), brought about the final break with
the thought of the past. In that book Darwin presented evidence that
humans were the same general kind of creatures as the rest of the
animals, except that they were more highly evolved or developed.
The ancestors of modern people were less highly evolved and were
part of a continuous chain linking humans to the earliest and simplest forms of animal life.

This was the intellectual atmosphere of educated people in Europe and America in the second half of the nineteenth century. Animal experimentation was becoming an accepted way of learning about
humans in physiology, medicine, psychology, and psychiatry. Humans were beginning to appear to scientists merely as one type of
creature, with no special links to divinity. Even more important, humans were beginning to be understood as creatures whose conduct
was influenced, if not determined, by biological and cultural ante-
cedents rather than as self-determining beings who were free to do
what they wanted. Lombroso was a part of, even a creature of, this

intellectual world. He made use of it in his thinking about crime just as Beccaria had made use of his particular world 100 years before.

## 1. CESARE LOMBROSO

Born in Venice of a Jewish family, Cesare Lombroso (1835–1909) was educated in medicine and became a specialist in psychiatry. His principal career was academic as a professor of legal medicine at the University of Turin. His name came into prominence with the publication of his book, *L'uomo delinquente (The Criminal Man)*, in 1876. In that book Lombroso proposed that criminals were biological throwbacks to an earlier evolutionary stage, people more primitive and less highly evolved than their noncriminal counterparts. Lombroso used the term *atavistic* to describe such people. The idea that some individuals might be reversions to an earlier evolutionary stage was originally suggested by Darwin, who had written: "With mankind some of the worst dispositions which occasionally without any assignable cause make their appearance in families, may perhaps be reversions to a savage state, from which we are not removed by many generations."[1]

Lombroso's theories will be presented in more detail in Chapter 4, but as a founder of the positive school of criminology he is something of an anomaly. It has been Lombroso's fate to be known principally for the earliest formulation of his theory of criminality—his theory of the atavistic criminal. The real basis of the positive school, however, is the search for the causes of criminal behavior. That search is based on the conception of multiple factor causation, where some of the factors may be biological, others psychological, and still others social.

No doubt stimulated by his distinguished pupils, Ferri and Garofalo, Lombroso did much by way of documenting the effects of many of these factors. As his thinking changed over the years, he looked more and more to environmental rather than biological factors. This change and growth in his thinking was evidenced by the increases in the number of pages in successive editions of *L'uomo delinquente*. In its first edition in 1876, Lombroso required 252 pages to explain his theory of evolutionary atavism as the cause of crime. Twenty years later, in the fifth edition of his book, he needed over 1900 pages to include all the items that appeared to be related to crime causation. Those included such things as climate, rainfall, the price of grain,

---

1. Charles Darwin, *Descent of Man*, John Murray, London, 1871, p. 137.

sex and marriage customs, criminal laws, banking practices, national tariff policies, the structure of government, church organization, and the state of religious belief. Lombroso's last book, *Crime, Its Causes and Remedies*, was a summary of his life work specially prepared for American readers. Published in 1911, two years after Lombroso's death, it includes discussions of many factors related to crime causation, of which by far the largest number are environmental rather than biological.

Lombroso's later, more mature thought therefore included many factors other than the physical or anthropological. He maintained that there are three major classes of criminals: (1) *born criminals*, to be understood as atavistic reversions to a lower or more primitive evolutionary form of development, and thought to constitute about one-third of the total number of offenders; (2) *insane criminals*, i.e., idiots, imbeciles, paranoiacs, sufferers from melancholia, and those afflicted with general paralysis, dementia, alcoholism, epilepsy, or hysteria (strange bedfellows, to be sure); and (3) *criminaloids*, a large general class without special physical characteristics, not afflicted with recognizable mental disorders, but whose mental and emotional makeup are such that under certain circumstances they indulge in vicious and criminal behavior (a concept perhaps not very different from the category of psychopathic personality of later psychiatric and psychological theories). Lombroso conceded that well over one-half of all criminals were not born criminals in the sense that he used the term, nor were they insane or epileptic, but their defects were more subtle and involved; these he called criminaloids.

By the time of Lombroso's death in 1909 it was evident that his theories were too simple and naïve. Anthropology had more and more abandoned the conception of uniform, linear evolution with humans as the end product (and the nineteenth-century Englishman as nature's perfect handiwork), and then the notion of the criminal as a physically atavistic type became quite meaningless. Psychiatry and psychology were already marshaling evidence to show that the relationship between crime and epilepsy, or between crime and insanity, was much more complex and involved than Lombroso assumed.

Present-day positivism in criminology has developed its own system of ideas in which little remains of Lombroso per se. Other writers[2] had anticipated his views and constructed somewhat similar formu-

---

2. See Havelock Ellis, *The Criminal*, 2nd ed., Scribner, New York, 1900, for a discussion of Lombroso's predecessors. Ellis mentions more than 20 authors who had previously explored in part the probable relation between physical character, mental traits, and criminal behavior. Several editions of this book have been reprinted.

lations long before he came on the scene. Because of these earlier authors, several modern criminologists maintain that Lombroso should not be considered the founder of positive criminology. Lindesmith and Levin[3] point to the analysis of criminal statistics carried out by A. M. Guerry (1802–66) and Adolphe Quetelet (1796–1874).[4] Quetelet focused on the observation that the French national crime statistics, which had been compiled since 1825, were remarkably constant from one year to the next. He argued that this regularity was caused by various natural factors, such as age, sex, and climatic conditions. Guerry attempted to account for different crime rates in different localities, as well as changes in the crime rates of a single locality, by analyzing differences in general social conditions and in legislation. Both these men studied crime from the perspective of analyzing its causes, but both focused on social rather than biological conditions. Savitz, Turner, and Dickman point to the research on phrenology carried out by Franz Joseph Gall (1758–1828), claiming that it was clearly scientific and bears some resemblance to modern research on the relationship between violence and the anatomy of the brain.[5]

These criminologists speculate on why Lombroso's work received so much more attention than did that of other early criminologists. Lindesmith and Levin state:[6]

It may be that the theory of the born criminal offered a convenient rationalization of the failure of preventive effort and an escape from the implications of the dangerous doctrine that crime is an essential product of our social organization. It may well be that a public, which had been nagged for centuries by reformers, welcomed the opportunity to slough off its responsibilities for this vexing problem.

Radzinowicz made a similar comment:[7]

It served the interests and relieved the conscience of those at the top to look upon the dangerous classes as an independent category, detached from

3. Alfred A. Lindesmith and Yale Levin, "The Lombrosian Myth in Criminology," *American Journal of Sociology* 42: 653–71 (1937). See also Sawyer F. Sylvester, "Adolphe Quetelet: At the Beginning," *Federal Probation* 46 (4): 14–19 (1982), for a comparable argument.

4. Quetelet and Guerry will be discussed at more length in Chapter 8 of this book.

5. Leonard Savitz, Stanley H. Turner, and Toby Dickman, "The Origin of Scientific Criminology; Franz Joseph Gall as the First Criminologist," in Robert F. Meier, ed., *Theory in Criminology*, Sage, Beverly Hills, Cal., 1977, pp. 41–56. Gall's work is further discussed in Chapter 4 of this book.

6. Lindesmith and Levin, op. cit., p. 670.

7. Leon Radzinowicz, *Ideology and Crime*, Columbia University Press, New York, 1966, pp. 38–39.

the prevailing social conditions. They were portrayed as a race apart, morally depraved and vicious, living by violating the fundamental law of orderly society, which was that a man should maintain himself by honest, steady work.

Savitz maintained that Lombroso's theories met with such great success because they coincided with the rise of Social Darwinism, which justified racism and inequality on the basis of evolutionary principles.[8]

In spite of these criticisms, Lombroso's name is one that will long be remembered as important in the development of criminological thought. As Sellin has well said:[9] "Any scholar who succeeds in driving hundreds of fellow students to search for the truth, and whose ideas after half a century possess vitality, merits an honorable place in the history of thought."

### 2. ENRICO FERRI

The most widely known of Lombroso's pupils was probably Enrico Ferri (1856–1928). Born in the Italian province of Mantua, Ferri attended the University of Bolgna where he became interested in statistics, especially as applied to the study of crime. He continued his studies in Paris, where he made a recognized contribution to the analysis of French crime for the period 1826–78. In this analysis he made comparisons between French statistics and those available for Italy.

Ferri's first major publication was *The Theory of Imputability and the Denial of Free Will*, published in 1878 when he was 21 years old. It was an attack on the concept of free will and foreshadowed much of the general view of human behavior that was to characterize his life work. After his year of study in France Ferri returned to the University of Turin, where he became a pupil of Lombroso. The two men complemented one another's thinking to a considerable extent. Ferri was a young socialist who, although interested in Lombroso's ideas of basic biological causation of crime, nevertheless consistently placed more emphasis on the interrelatedness of social, economic, and political factors in a situation always made up of many factors.

8. Leonard D. Savitz, Introduction in Gina Lombroso-Ferrero, *Lombroso's Criminal Man*, Patterson Smith, Montclair, N.J., 1972, pp. v–xx.

9. Thorsten Sellin, "The Lombrosian Myth in Criminology," *American Journal of Sociology* 42: 896–97 (1937). This is a critical comment on the article by Lindesmith and Levin cited in footnote 3.

Lombroso gave Ferri a more mature and balanced conception of objective or "positive" methodology.

By 1884, at the age of 27, Ferri had developed his ideas in two major publications. His famous fourfold classification of criminals as insane, born, occasional, and criminal by passion first appeared in *The Homicide;* his expanded thought on the whole problem of crime was developed in his *Criminal Sociology.* His original thesis was that crime is caused by a great number of factors classified as (1) physical (race, climate, geographic location, seasonal effects, temperature, etc.), (2) anthropological (age, sex, organic and psychological conditions, etc.), and (3) social (density of population, customs, religion, organization of government, economic and industrial conditions, etc.). In his more fully developed thought he discussed a large number of *équivalents des peines* (substitutes for punishment), or, more accurately, preventive measures. Among these he mentioned free trade, abolition of monopolies, inexpensive workmen's dwellings, public savings banks, better street lighting, birth control, freedom of marriage and divorce, state control of the manufacture of weapons, provision for marriage of the clergy, establishment of foundling homes, provision for public recreation, and so on, through a long list of social betterment measures. His preventive measures were in line with the political theory to which he subscribed—that the state is the principal instrument through which better conditions are to be attained.

Active in politics, Ferri was soon elected a deputy to the Italian Parliament by the Socialist party. In 1890 he changed universities, going to the University of Pisa as professor of criminal law, and thus, paradoxically, taking over the position held for so long by a great Italian leader of the classical school, Francesco Carrara (1805–88). The height of Carrara's career had been his effort to secure the adoption of a consistent, classically oriented penal code for the newly unified Italy, the Penal Code of 1889. So great was the prestige of Carrara, and so deeply ingrained were the views of the classical school, that Ferri found himself unable to influence Italian legal thinking.

Ferri continued his political activity as a socialist, and was soon (1893) dismissed from his university position. He founded the Socialist paper *Avanti* in 1896 and did not return to academic life until 1904, when he was made professor of criminal law at the Royal University in Rome. After World War I Ferri was asked to chair a commission to prepare a new penal code for Italy. The result, usually called the Ferri Project or Ferri Draft, was a document in keeping

with Ferri's positivistic theories and socialistic orientation.[10] It denied moral responsibility, rejected the concepts of punishment and
retribution, and emphasized the need for professionalism among all
those who dealt with criminals. Ferri had great hopes for this document, but they were not fulfilled. In 1922, the year after Ferri
completed his draft, Mussolini took power in Italy. Despite Ferri's
efforts, his draft was rejected by the Italian Chamber of Deputies.
Ferri resigned from the Socialist party in 1924, and later wrote favorably about the efforts of the Fascist government to deal with crime.

Sellin summarized Ferri's attitude towards Fascism as follows: "As
for Fascism, he saw something of value in it, so far as criminal justice was concerned, because it represented to him a systematic reaf-
firmation of the authority of the state against the excesses of individualism, which he had always criticized."[11] Sellin's statement highlights
one of the problems of positivistic theory, namely, the ease with which
it fits into totalitarian patterns of government. It is centered on the
core idea of the superior knowledge and wisdom of the scientific expert who, on the basis of scientific knowledge, decides what kind of
human beings commit crimes, and prescribes treatment without
concern for public opinion and without consent from the person so
diagnosed (i.e., the criminal). There is an obvious similarity between the control of power in society advocated in positivism and
the political reality of centralized control of the life of the citizen by
a government bureaucracy indifferent to public opinion. This is further exemplified in the life and work of Garofalo.

3. RAFFAELE GAROFALO

Raffaele Garofalo (1852–1934) is considered the third great Italian
positivist. Born in Naples of a family of Spanish origin, though of the
Italian nobility, young Garofalo turned to a university education in
law and a career in government. At a relatively early age he became
a magistrate in the Italian courts and held a number of important
positions in various parts of Italy, in which he achieved considerable
distinction. He held the position of professor of criminal law at the
University of Naples and was later named a Senator of the Kingdom.
In 1903 he was appointed by the minister of justice to revise the

10. Thorsten Sellin, "Enrico Ferri," in Hermann Mannheim, ed., *Pioneers in Criminology*,
Patterson Smith, Montclair, N.J., 1973, pp. 375–76.

11. Ibid., p. 377. See also Philip Jankins, "The Radicals and the Rehabilitative Ideal, 1890–
1930," *Criminology* 20 (3–4): 347–72 (Nov. 1982), for a discussion of the ease with which early
socialists accepted a Fascist orientation.

code of criminal procedure, but this project had to be abandoned because of the political difficulties of the Italian government.

An active, prolific writer, Garofalo produced a succession of books and monographs on the subject of crime and criminals from 1880 on. The titles of his books—*Criminal Attempt by Insufficient Means, Indemnification of Persons Injured by Crime, The Socialist Superstition, International Solidarity in the Repression of Crime*—give some clue to the range of his interests and scholarship. He is best known, however, for his major work, *Criminology*, first issued as a monograph in 1880 and then expanded and published in regular book form in 1885. It has been reprinted and revised a number of times and translated into French, Spanish, and Portuguese. An English translation was published in the United States in 1914.[12]

Like Lombroso and Ferri, Garofalo was a self-conscious positivist, rejecting the doctrine of free will and supporting the position that crime can be understood only where it is studied by scientific methods. Since science deals with universals, he attempted to formulate a sociological definition of crime that would be such a scientific universal, one that would "designate those acts which no civilized society can refuse to recognize as criminal and repress by means of punishment."[13] Such acts would constitute *natural crime;* that is, they would be offenses violating the two basic altruistic sentiments common to all peoples in all ages, namely, the sentiments of *probity* and *pity.* His "natural" definition of crime, as formulated by Gillin, is as follows:[14]

Crime is an immoral and harmful act that is regarded as criminal by public opinion because it is an "injury to so much of the moral sense as is represented by one or the other of the elementary altruistic sentiments of probity and pity. Moreover, the injury must wound these sentiments not in their superior and finer degrees, but in the average measure in which they are possessed by a community—a measure which is indispensable for the adaptation of the individual to society."

Quaint as the terminology is, it still clearly indicates a psychological orientation rather than the physical-type orientation of Lombroso, whose approach had become known as "criminal anthropol-

12. Raffaele Garofalo, *Criminology*, Little, Brown, Boston, 1914. (The bibliographical notes are from the translator's preface, p. xiii.)

13. Garofalo, op. cit., p. 33.

14. Quoted from John Lewis Gillin, *Criminology and Penology*, 3rd ed., Appleton-Century-Crofts, New York, 1945. This in turn is an adaptation and quotation from Garofalo, op. cit., pp. 33–34. Reprinted by permission of Helen N. Gillin.

ogy." Garofalo identified with neither Lombroso nor Ferri, though
he examined many of their ideas and offered numerous criticisms.[15]
He conceded that his own work could be included in the school of
criminal anthropology only on condition that "it be granted that of
this science criminal psychology is the most important chapter."[16]

Having had a distinguished career as a magistrate, Garofalo was
naturally concerned with reforms in criminal procedure and in the
practical problem of what to do with the criminal. In a chapter[17] entitled "The Law of Adaptation" he outlines in detail a theory of punishment based on the simple Darwinian principle of adaptation with
elimination of those unable to adapt. Society, like any natural body,
must similarly eliminate those who show by criminal behavior that
they are not adapted to civilized life. Three means of elimination are
suggested: (1) *death* for those whose acts grow out of a "permanent
psychologic anomaly which renders the subject forever incapable of
social life"; (2) *partial elimination,* including long-time or life imprisonment and transportation for those "fit only for the life of nomadic
hordes or primitive tribes," as well as the relatively mild isolation of
agricultural colonies for young and more hopeful offenders; (3) *enforced reparation* for those lacking in altruistic sentiments who have
committed their crimes under exceptional circumstances not likely
to occur again.

Garofalo argued that his theory of punishment met the three basic
conditions necessary to make it an effective instrument of public policy, namely, (1) it satisfied the deep-seated public demand for punishment of the offender simply because he committed a crime; (2)
its general principle of elimination was sufficiently intimidating to
contribute to deterrence; and (3) the social selection resulting from
its operation offered hope for the future by slow eradication of the
criminals and of their progeny. In support of this last point he referred to the low crime rates in contemporary England and ascribed
them to the effect of earlier harsh capital penalties, which had killed
off most of the English criminal stock—hence, there was now no
progeny of similar moral degeneracy to bedevil English society. He
also noted the large proportion of failure when the reform of criminals had been attempted, notably in certain institutions in France
and at the Elmira Reformatory in New York.[18]

In the light of these ideas about the nature of the criminal and the

15. Cf. Garofalo, op. cit., pp. 132–34, for criticisms of Ferri's classification of crime.
16. Ibid., author's preface, p. xxx.
17. Ibid., Part II, Ch. IX, pp. 370–408.
18. Ibid., p. 401.

course of action necessary for his ultimate control, it is not surprising to find that Garofalo managed to adapt to the Mussolini regime in Italy.

## 4. CONTEMPORARY POSITIVISM

The essential point of the positive school in criminology is the application of the scientific method to the study of the biological, psychological, and social characteristics of the criminal in the attempt to determine the causes of criminal behaviors. As such, positive criminology is based on several assumptions. First, by searching for the *causes* of criminal behavior, positive criminology assumes that human behavior is determined, at least to a certain extent, by forces that are beyond the control of the individual. Second, by searching for the causes of *criminal behavior,* as opposed to other human behaviors, positive criminology assumes that the causes of criminal behavior differ, at least to a certain extent, from the causes of noncriminal behaviors. Because of this assumption, the search for the causes of criminal behavior often takes the form of a search for differences between criminals and noncriminals. Some theorists propose that the differences are biological or psychological or social, whereas others emphasize a multiple-factor approach, which combines elements of each. But the differences are then used to explain why one person becomes a criminal while another does not.

Most contemporary scientific criminology is positivist in method and in basic formulations. In the chapters that follow, the major theories of crime causation within this frame of reference will be examined. If it seems that the evidence often turns out to be negative (or at least inconclusive) under careful examination, it must not be concluded that such results defeat the interests of a developing scientific criminology. It is just because the formulations of positivism are specific, and thus susceptible to investigation, that so many of these theories have been disproven.

The failure of criminologists to establish the causes of criminal behavior reflects the fact that there is as yet no adequate theory of human behavior, either criminal or noncriminal. But there are reasons beyond mere historic interest for studying older theories of crime, even those that have been discredited. Such theories normally have been based in intuitive notions about crime and criminals, many of which retain their popular appeal even at the present time. It is only by studying these theories and the methods by which they have been tested that popular preconceptions about crime that do not stand up can be discarded and contemporary issues and questions raised. What will be attempted in the following chapters, then, is a clarification of what is known and what is not known, with discussions as to what may reasonably be concluded from present information.

RECOMMENDED READINGS

Cesare Lombroso, *Crime: Its Causes and Remedies*, 1912; reprinted by Patterson Smith, Montclair, N.J., 1968. Lombroso's final work, emphasizing both biological and environmental factors in the causation of crime.

Gina Lombroso-Ferrero, *Lombroso's Criminal Man*, 1911; reprinted by Patterson Smith, Montclair, N.J., 1972. A concise presentation of the work of Lombroso, written by his daughter for American readers. Also of interest are the original Introduction by Lombroso, and the new Introduction to the Reprint Edition by Leonard D. Savitz.

Enrico Ferri, *Criminal Sociology*, Little, Brown, Boston, 1917; reprinted by Agathon, New York. Ferri's basic work in criminology.

Raffaele Garofalo, *Criminology*, 1914; reprinted by Patterson Smith, Montclair, N.J., 1968. Garofalo's basic work.

Hermann Mannheim, ed., *Pioneers in Criminology*, 2nd ed., Patterson Smith, Montclair, N.J., 1972. Contains an excellent, thorough discussion of the work of Lombroso (by Marvin E. Wolfgang, pp. 232–91) and briefer accounts of Raffaele Garofalo (by Francis Allen, pp. 318–40) and Enrico Ferri (by Thorsten Sellin, pp. 361–83).

Francis A. Allen, "Garofalo's Criminology and Some Modern Problems," in his *The Borderland of Criminal Justice*, University of Chicago Press, Chicago, 1964. Garofalo's concepts of "natural crime," of criminal characteristics, and of social defense are discussed.

Alfred A. Lindesmith and Yale Levin, "The Lombrosian Myth in Criminology," *American Journal of Sociology* 42: 653–71 (1937). A detailed attack on Lombroso's work and his position in criminology, with a Comment by Thorsten Sellin on pp. 896–97.

Enrico Ferri, *The Positive School of Criminology*, edited with an introduction by Stanley E. Grupp, University of Pittsburgh Press, Pittsburgh, 1968. Three lectures by Ferri on a critique of the classical school, the causes of criminal behavior, and remedies for crime.

# CHAPTER FOUR

# Theories Related
# to Physical Characteristics

One of the oldest "scientific" approaches in criminological theory has emphasized physical and biological abnormality as the distinguishing mark of the criminal. In this approach criminals are viewed as somehow characteristically different, abnormal, defective, and therefore inferior biologically. This biological inferiority is thought to produce in criminals certain physical characteristics that make their appearance different from that of noncriminals. Early criminologists studied the physical appearance of criminals in an attempt to identify these characteristics. The real explanation of criminal behavior, in this view, is biological defectiveness and inferiority—physical and other characteristics are only symptoms of the more fundamental inferiority.

## 1. FORERUNNERS OF PHYSICAL-TYPE THEORIES: PHYSIOGNOMY AND PHRENOLOGY

The belief that unusual physical characteristics mark off the evil and socially obnoxious person is of ancient origin. For example, Homer described the thoroughly despicable Thersites as follows:

One eye was blinking, and one leg was lame;
His mountain shoulders half his breast o'erspread,
Thin hairs bestrew'd his long misshapen head.

*The Iliad*—Pope's translation

The venerable Socrates was examined by a Greek physiognomist, who found that his face revealed him as brutal, sensuous, and inclined to drunkenness. Socrates admitted that such was his natural disposition but said he had learned to overcome these tendencies.[1]

Physiognomy—judging character from facial features—was a recognized study in the Europe of Cesare Beccaria. Eleven years after Beccaria's *Essay on Crimes and Punishment* (1764), Johan Caspar Lavater (1741–1801), the Swiss scholar and theologian, published a four-volume work on physiognomy entitled *Physiognomical Fragments* (Zurich, 1775), which in its way received perhaps fully as favorable attention as the now better-known work of legal reform produced by Beccaria. This work of Lavater systematized many popular observations and made many extravagant claims about the alleged relation between facial features and human conduct. The unfavorable trait indicator of beardlessness in men, or the opposite, the bearded woman, was noted, as was the significance of a "shifty" eye, a "weak" chin, an "arrogant" nose, and so on. Details of these classifications are of little importance now.[2] The principal significance of physiognomy lies in the impetus it gave to the better-organized and logically more impressive view that came to be known as phrenology.

Writers on phrenology were concerned with elaborating Aristotle's idea of the brain as the organ of the mind. Three basic propositions underlie their formulations:

1. The exterior of the skull conforms to the interior and to the shape of the brain.

2. The "mind" consists of faculties or functions.

3. These faculties are related to the shape of the brain and skull; hence, just as the brain is the "organ of the mind," these "bumps" are indicators of the "organs" of the special faculties.

The eminent European anatomist Franz Joseph Gall (1758–1828) is generally given credit for the systematic development of the doctrines of phrenology, though he did not originate or make much use of that term. In 1791 he started publishing materials on the relations between head conformations and the personal characteristics of individuals. Closely allied with Gall in the development of phrenology was his student and onetime collaborator, John Gaspar Spurzheim (1776–1832). It was Spurzheim rather than Gall who carried their

---

1. Havelock Ellis, *The Criminal*, 2nd ed., Scribner, New York, 1900, p. 27.
2. Cf. Erik Nordenshiöld, *The History of Biology*, Knopf, New York, 1928.

doctrines to England and America, lecturing before scientific meetings and stimulating interest in their ideas.

Gall listed 26 special faculties of the brain; Spurzheim increased the number to 35.[3] Their lists included faculties described as amativeness, conjugality, philoprogenitiveness (love of offspring), friendliness, combativeness, destructiveness, acquisitiveness, cautiousness, self-esteem, firmness, benevolence, constructiveness, ideality, and imitativeness. These were said to be grouped into three regions or compartments, one the "lower" or active propensities, another the moral sentiments, and the third the intellectual faculties. Crime was said to involve the lower propensities, notably amativeness, philoprogenitiveness, combativeness, secretiveness, and acquisitiveness. These propensities, however, could be held in restraint by the moral sentiments or the intellectual faculties, in which case no crime would be committed. Character and human conduct were thus conceived of as an equilibrium in the pull of these opposite forces. Animal propensities might impel the individual to crime, but they would be opposed by the higher sentiments and intelligence. Just as other organs were strengthened by exercise and enfeebled by disuse, so were the "organs" of the mind. Careful training of the child, and even of the adult, in right living would strengthen the "organs" of desirable faculties and inhibit through disuse the lower propensities with their concomitants of crime and vice.[4]

The obvious scientific criticism of the phrenological theory of crime is that it is hypothetical. Phrenology disappeared as a scientific discipline because no one was able to substantiate with verifiable data its conceptions of physiological "organs" of the mind or their relation to particular types of behavior. The most serious obstacle to its acceptance by the public, however, was the deterministic nature of its analysis. If human conduct were the result of the organs of the mind, then people's fate was in the hands of their anatomy and physiology. This view was rejected and opposed by teachers, preachers, judges, and other leaders who influenced public opinion, because it contradicted one of their most cherished ideas, namely that humans are masters of their own conduct and capable of making of themselves

3. For a history of phrenology, as well as a defense of its use in modern times, see Sybil Leek, *Phrenology*, Macmillan, New York, 1970. For a discussion of Gall and Spurzheim, see Leonard Savitz, Stanley H. Turner, and Toby Dickman, "The Origin of Scientific Criminology: Franz Joseph Gall as the First Criminologist," in Robert F. Meier, ed., *Theory in Criminology*, Sage, Beverly Hills, Cal., 1977, pp. 41–56.

4. Arthur E. Fink, *The Causes of Crime: Biological Theories in the United States, 1800–1915*, University of Pennsylvania Press, Philadelphia, 1938, pp. 8–9.

what they will.[5] It was the need to show that humans were still masters of their fate (as well as to respond to criticisms of the fatalistic position implied by his earlier work) that led Gall to publish his *Des Dispositions innées de l'âme et de l'esprit du matérialisme* (1811), in which he argued that phrenology was not fatalistic, that *will* and *spirit* were basic and supreme in the direction and control of human behavior.[6]

### 2. CRIMINAL ANTHROPOLOGY: LOMBROSO TO HOOTON

Cesare Lombroso (1835–1909) is the conspicuous illustration of a writer who made the idea of the physical criminal type an important part of his earlier theory of crime causation. The general theory was one of degeneracy; the physical characteristics were simply indicators of inadequacy and degeneracy. The evolutionary theory of the time gave a further indication as to the nature of the degeneracy: It was atavistic, that is, a reversion to an earlier form of animal life. In other words, the criminal type resembled lower or more apelike ancestors, and their physical characteristics were assumed to belong to these earlier evolutionary forms. Some of those physical characteristics, thought to indicate the atavistic type of person who became a criminal, were the following:[7]

1. Deviation in head size and shape from the type common to the race and region from which the criminal came.

2. Asymmetry of the face.

3. Excessive dimensions of the jaw and cheekbones.

4. Eye defects and peculiarities.

5. Ears of unusual size, or occasionally very small, or standing out from the head as do those of the chimpanzee.

6. Nose twisted, upturned, or flattened in thieves, or aquiline or beaklike in murderers, or with a tip rising like a peak from swollen nostrils.

7. Lips fleshy, swollen, and protruding.

8. Pouches in the cheek like those of some animals.

---

5. See, for example, the discussion of the nature vs. nurture debate in Anthony M. Platt, *The Child Savers*, University of Chicago Press, Chicago, 1969, pp. 28–36.

6. *Encyclopedia of the Social Sciences*, Macmillan, New York, 1931, vol. VI, p. 548.

7. This is a partial listing adapted from the basic work by Gina Lombroso Ferrero, *Criminal Man According to the Classification of Cesare Lombroso*, Putnam, New York, 1911, pp. 10–24; reprinted by Patterson Smith, Montclair, N.J., 1972; and summarized by John Lewis Gillin, *Criminology and Penology*, 3rd ed., Appleton-Century-Crofts, New York, 1945, p. 79. Reprinted by permission of Helen N. Gillin.

9. Peculiarities of the palate, such as a large central ridge, a series of cavities and protuberances such as are found in some reptiles, and cleft palate.

10. Abnormal dentition.

11. Chin receding, or excessively long, or short and flat, as in apes.

12. Abundance, variety, and precocity of wrinkles.

13. Anomalies of the hair, marked by characteristics of the hair of the opposite sex.

14. Defects of the thorax, such as too many or too few ribs, or supernumerary nipples.

15. Inversion of sex characters in the pelvic organs.

16. Excessive length of arms.

17. Supernumerary fingers and toes.

18. Imbalance of the hemispheres of the brain (asymmetry of cranium).

In an examination of a group of 383 Italian criminals, Lombroso found that 21 percent had one such anomaly while 43 percent had five or more. Thus he argued that five or more anomalies would indicate that the individual was a "born criminal." Lombroso also compared the anomalies of the skull found among criminals with those found among noncriminal Italian soldiers, with the results given in Table 4-1.[8] This table illustrates the evolving methodology of scientific research in criminal anthropology. Lombroso deserves credit for utilizing the method of control group comparisons in the application of statistical methods to his problem. He was no statistical expert, even for his day, and it remained for others to make more exact and

TABLE 4–1  Percentage Distribution of Skull Anomalies Found by Lombroso

| Conditions as to Anomalies of Skull | Criminals Guilty of Homicide and Sentenced to: | | Noncriminal Italian Soldiers |
|---|---|---|---|
| | Penal Servitude | Imprisonment | |
| | $N = 346$ | $N = 363$ | $N = 711$ |
| No anomalies of skull | 11.9 | 8.2 | 37.2 |
| One or two anomalies | 47.2 | 56.6 | 51.8 |
| Three or four anomalies | 33.9 | 32.6 | 11.0 |
| Five or six anomalies | 6.7 | 2.3 | 0.0 |
| Seven or more anomalies | 0.3 | 0.3 | 0.0 |
| | 100.0 | 100.0 | 100.0 |

8. Cesare Lombroso, *L'uomo delinquente (The Criminal Man)*, 4th ed., Bocca, Torino, 1889, p. 273, as quoted by Enrico Ferri, *Criminal Sociology*, D. Appleton, New York, 1900, p. 12.

careful application of more adequate statistical methodology to the problem of physical differences between criminals and noncriminals.

Such a study was made in England by a group of investigators usually identified with the name of Charles Goring and the famous book entitled *The English Convict: A Statistical Study*.[9] Begun in 1901, it involved carefully measured comparisons of approximately 3,000 English convicts and large groups of noncriminal Englishmen. The study covered a period of eight years, and involved the assistance and cooperation of many persons such as wardens, prison physicians, and other professionals. Notable among the last-named was the statistical expert Karl Pearson. Because of the enormous amount of work involved (this was before the day of computers or calculators) in making the extensive computations and necessary interpretations, the study was not completed and published until 1913.

The convicts studied were all recidivists (and therefore assumed to constitute a thoroughly criminal type of person), and there were comparisons with university undergraduates (Oxford and Cambridge), hospital patients, and the officers and men of units of the British army, notably the Royal Engineers.

The study had originally been conceived in response to a challenge by Lombroso to have an impartial committee study 100 "born criminals," 100 persons with criminal tendencies, and 100 normal persons.[10] Lombroso offered to retract his theories if the physical, mental, and psychological characteristics of the three groups were found to be identical. This challenge was never really met, since Lombroso's opponents said it was impossible to distinguish between the three groups accurately.

Goring's study, begun a number of years later, was strictly a comparison between a group of convicts—persons convicted of crimes and imprisoned—and a group of unconvicted persons, so that no attempt was made to distinguish between "born criminals," persons with criminal tendencies, and normal persons. Also, the methodology relied totally on the use of objective measurements of physical and mental characteristics. Lombroso himself had objected to total reliance on measurements, maintaining that many anomalies were "so small as to defy all but the most minute research."[11] He argued

9. Charles Goring, *The English Convict: A Statistical Study*, His Majesty's Stationery Office, London, 1913. This has been reprinted by Patterson Smith, Montclair, N.J., 1972.

10. Edwin D. Driver, Introductory Essay in Charles Goring, *The English Convict*, Patterson Smith, Montclair, N.J., 1972, p. vii.

11. Cesare Lombroso, *The Female Offender*, Unwin, London, 1895; quoted in Goring, op. cit., p. 16.

that these could be detected by the eye of the trained observer, but could not be measured. Finally the study, as it evolved, went well beyond any attempt to prove or disprove Lombroso's theories, as Goring advanced his own theory of hereditary inferiority. (Goring's theory will be presented in a later chapter; in this chapter we will concentrate on his attempt to disprove Lombroso's theory that criminals were a distinct physical type.)

Lombroso had asserted that criminals, compared with the general population, would show anomalies (i.e., differences or defects) of head height, head width, and degree of receding forehead, as well as differences in head circumference, head symmetry, and so on. Goring, in comparing prisoners with the officers and men of the Royal Engineers, found no such anomalies. There were no more protrusions or other peculiarities of the head among the prisoners than among the Royal Engineers. Goring also compared other characteristics, such as nasal contours, color of eyes, color of hair, and left-handedness, but found only insignificant differences. He compared groups of different kinds of criminals (burglars, forgers, thieves, etc.) on the basis of 37 specific physical characteristics. He concluded that there were no significant differences between one kind of criminal and another that were not more properly related to the selective effects of environmental factors.[12]

The one general exception to his conclusion was a consistent "inferiority in stature and in body weight." The criminals were one to two inches shorter than noncriminals of the same occupational groups, and weighed from three to seven pounds less.[13] Goring was satisfied that these differences were real and significant, and he interpreted them as indicating a general inferiority of a hereditary nature. This interpretation agreed with his general thesis of hereditary inferiority (as measured by comparisons of mental ability and various other indices of hereditary influence) as the basis for criminal conduct.[14]

Goring has been criticized for being too anxious to disprove Lombroso's theories.[15] Supporters of Lombroso maintained that Goring had actually found significant differences between criminal and noncriminal groups for a variety of measures, but that he minimized these differences by "correcting" them for such variables as age and stature. When the differences were still significant after "corrections"

12. Goring, op. cit., pp. 196–214.

13. Ibid., p. 200.

14. Ibid., p. 287, especially Table 119.

15. Edwin D. Driver, "Charles Buckman Goring," in Hermann Mannheim, ed., *Pioneers in Criminology*, Patterson Smith, Montclair, N.J., 1973, p. 440.

had been made, Goring impugned the validity of the original data. Other assessments of Goring's work had generally found more support for Lombroso's theories than Goring admitted.[16]

Goring considered Lombroso's work unscientific. He argued that "the whole of Lombroso's enterprise was conducted . . . with the unconscious intention of stamping a preconceived idea with the hall mark of science"[17] and that it could not be considered an impartial investigation into the truth or falseness of Lombroso's theory. He also criticized Lombroso's willingness to declare that people who had never been involved with the law were criminals solely on the basis of their physical appearance.[18] Goring himself maintained that the use of the term *criminal* should reflect a legal reality—a person who has broken the law and been convicted—rather than any vague ethical or moral conception of "the kind of men who, whether they have or have not committed crime, we believe to be criminal at heart."[19] Finally, he argued that even if specific differences did exist between the criminal and the noncriminal, this would not indicate that the criminal was abnormal. Rather, the criminal was "a selected class of normal man" whose "qualities may present extreme degrees from the normal average."[20] Goring's point is similar to saying that professional basketball players are not tall because they are an abnormal anthropological type, but because they are selected at least partially on the basis of their height.

In spite of numerous and extensive efforts to show that criminals were somehow physically different from noncriminals, the weight of expert and informed opinion was against the proposition.[21] The general conclusions of Goring on the matter came to be accepted by most modern criminologists. Goring wrote:[22]

We have exhaustively compared, with regard to many physical characters, different kinds of criminals with each other, and criminals, as a class, with

16. Driver, Introductory Essay, op. cit., p. v.

17. Goring, op. cit., p. 16.

18. For example, he states that "on one occasion [Lombroso] pointed out, as an example of the criminal type, a youth who had never appeared in a court of justice: 'he may not be a legal criminal,' was the airy utterance, 'but he is a criminal anthropologically.' " Ibid., p. 15. Lombroso's lofty attitude is still with us. See Chapter 7, "Nonarrestable Phases in the Criminal," in Samuel Yochelson and Stanton E. Samenow, *The Criminal Personality*, vol. 1, Jason Arsonson, New York, 1976.

19. Goring, op. cit., p. 21.

20. Ibid., p. 24.

21. For example, Fink, op. cit., pp. 99–150, reviewed the work of more than 35 authors who published a much larger number of studies on the subject.

22. Goring, op. cit., p. 173. (Italics in the original.)

the law-abiding public. . . . Our results nowhere confirm the evidence [of a physical criminal type], nor justify the allegation of criminal anthropologists. They challenge their evidence at almost every point. In fact, both with regard to measurements and the presence of physical anomalies in criminals, our statistics present a startling conformity with similar statistics of the law-abiding class. Our inevitable conclusion must be that *there is no such thing as a physical criminal type.*

Goring's conclusions stood essentially unchallenged until E. A. Hooton, a Harvard anthropologist, undertook an extensive research project on physical type that reached different findings. He reexamined Goring's work and extensively criticized his methodology and conclusions. Hooton's language was positive and to the point:[23]

Criminals are organically inferior. Crime is the resultant of the impact of environment upon low grade human organisms. It follows that the elimination of crime can be effected only by the extirpation of the physically, mentally, and morally unfit; or by their complete segregation in a socially aseptic environment.

The Hooton study was well financed and involved large numbers as well as an elaborateness of detail in measurement and analysis which, on the surface at least, seemed very impressive. Hooton's total group included over 17,000 people from ten states; about 14,000 were prisoners and the rest a noncriminal control group. Among his findings the following may be conveniently summarized as representative of his conclusions:[24]

1. In 19 out of 33 measurements there was "a significant difference between criminals and civilians." (p. 229)

2. "Criminals are inferior to civilians in nearly all their bodily measurements." (True for every offense group.) (p. 229)

3. "Low foreheads, high pinched nasal roots, nasal bridges and tips varying to both extremes of breadth and narrowness, excess of nasal deflections, compressed faces and narrow jaws, fit well into the picture of general constitutional inferiority." (p. 306)

4. Physical inferiority is significant principally because it is associated with mental inferiority. (pp. 307–8)

23. E. A. Hooton, *The American Criminal: An Anthropological Study*, Harvard University Press, Cambridge, Mass., 1939, vol. I, p. 309. This edition has been reprinted by Greenwood Press, Westport, Ct.

24. Hooton, op. cit. Page references in the text are to vol. I.

5. The basic cause of the inferiority (probably) is due to heredity and not to situation or circumstance. (p. 306)

6. Dark eyes and blue eyes are deficient in criminals, and blue-gray and mixed eyes are in excess; homogeneous irides relatively rare, zoned and speckled irides in excess; eyefolds are in excess, but eyebrows that are thin to very thin occur more frequently. (p. 301)

7. Tattooing is more common among criminals than among civilian controls. (p. 301)

8. Thin lips and compressed jaw angles occur more frequently; marked overbite less frequently among criminals than among civilians. (p. 302)

9. The ear of the criminal tends to a slightly rolled helix, and a more perceptible Darwin's point than that of the civilian; also more extreme variations of ear protrusion, and the criminal ear tends to be small. (p. 304)

10. Low and sloping foreheads, long, thin necks, and sloping shoulders are similarly in excess among criminals in comparison with civilians. (p. 304)

A very extensive portion of Hooton's work is devoted to the elaborate comparison of one group of criminals with another on the basis of type of offense. Thus he describes in great anthropological detail the characteristics of different types of criminals, such as murderers, thieves, robbers, and rapists. He concludes that his data show that tall thin men tend to be murderers and robbers; tall heavy men are killers and also commit forgery and fraud; undersized men are thieves and burglars; short heavy persons commit assault, rape, and other sex crimes; whereas men of "mediocre" physique flounder around among the crimes (as in everything else) with no specialty.[25]

Hooton's work immediately stirred up controversy and critical reaction. The reviews were mostly unfavorable, though some were in at least partial agreement.[26] One criticism centered on his rationale for translating physical differences between the criminal and the

25. E. A. Hooton, *Crime and the Man*, Harvard University Press, Cambridge, Mass., 1931, pp. 376–78. This is a one-volume popularization of the more elaborate three-volume work cited above; it has also been reprinted by Greenwood Press, Westport, Ct., 1968.

26. See the following particularly pertinent reviews: E. H. Sutherland in *Journal of Criminal Law and Criminology*, Mar.—Apr. 1939, pp. 911–14; J. Shalloo in *Annals of the American Academy of Political and Social Science*, Sept. 1939; E. B. Reuter in *American Journal of Sociology*, July 1931; Waldemar Kaempffert in the *New York Times*, Oct., 1, 1939; T. C. McCormick, in *American Sociological Review*, April 1940. More extended assessments of Hooton's work are found in Robert K. Merton and M. F. Ashley-Montagu, "Crime and the Anthropologist," *American Anthropologist* 42: 384–408 (Aug. 1940); James S. Wallerstein and Clement J. Wyle, " 'Biological Inferiority' as a Cause for Delinquency," *Nervous Child* 6: 467–72 (Oct. 1947); N. S. Timasheff, "The Revival of Criminal Anthropology," *University of Kansas Law Review* 9: 91–100 (Feb. 1941); and William H. Tucker, "Is There Evidence of a Physical Basis for Criminal Behavior," *Journal of Criminal Law and Criminology* 31: 427–37 (Nov.–Dec. 1940).

noncriminal groups into evidence of inferiority in the criminal group. Unless there is independent evidence of the inferiority of certain kinds of physical characteristics (for example, low foreheads), conclusions regarding inferiority must be drawn from the association with criminality. This is a nice illustration of circular reasoning—use criminality to discover the inferiority, then turn around and use the inferiority to explain or account for the criminality.[27]

A second criticism was that Hooton obtained but tended to disregard many differences just as great, or greater, than those between criminals and noncriminals. Thus there were differences between samples taken in different states, between different occupational groups, between groups measured by different investigators, and so on, which were just as great, or even greater, than those found between criminals and noncriminals or between some of the different types of criminals he discussed at length. He ignored or failed to correct for most of these differences.

Hooton also argued that physical inferiority is inherited, but presented little or no evidence for his claims. As is well known, the state of physical development is greatly influenced by previous conditions of nourishment and other environmental factors. Thus the 11-pound difference in weight he found between the civilians and the prisoners can take on significance only under conditions of a known, standardized diet. This necessary control was ignored.

Finally, in his description of criminal types Hooton ignored the fact that at least one-half of his prisoners had been in prison before and that in their previous commitment a very large proportion had been convicted of a different type of crime than the one involved when he studied them. Thus Hooton found a group of men convicted of robbery (in several degrees); they were his robbers. But had he looked back to the records of the crimes committed at an earlier sentence, many of his present robbers would have been sex offenders or forgers or something else. Had he carried out this elementary step, most of his type differences would have been compromised, if not dissipated entirely.

## 3. BODY TYPE THEORIES: KRETSCHMER TO CORTÉS

Some of the more interesting attempts at relating criminal behavior to physical characteristics are the so-called body type theories. The

---

27. Other scientists of the time engaged in the same type of circular reasoning, cloaking their own social prejudices in the guise of objective science. See Stephen Jay Gould, *The Mismeasure of Man*, Norton, New York, 1981.

body type theorists argue that there is a high degree of correspondence between body type and mental type, or temperament. It should be recalled that Lombroso had attempted to establish some relation between mental disorder and physical characteristics. Many others, before and after Lombroso, have made similar attempts.

One of the best known of the body type theorists is Ernst Kretschmer;[28] he identified three body types: the *leptosome* or *asthenic* type was tall and thin; the *athletic* type had well-developed muscles; and the *pyknic* type was short and fat. The 1955 German edition of Kretschmer's book[29] has an entire chapter, "Konstitution und Verbrechen" ("Constitutional Types and Crime"), in which his interpretations and conclusions are said to be based on a statistical analysis of 4,414 cases. The treatment, nevertheless, is in the form of verbal generalizations and assertions without specific reference to statistical information. No detailed statistical analysis is presented. There is said to be a preponderance of the athletic type in connection with crimes of violence; of the asthenic (leptosome) type in connection with petty thievery and fraud; the pyknic type tends to deception and fraud most generally or, next in frequency, crimes of violence. The *dysplastic*, or *mixed* type, is said to tend to offenses against decency and morality, though this type is also involved in crimes of violence. No mutually exclusive relationships are claimed, only general tendencies to the predominance of certain types in certain general classes of offenders.[30] No specific comparisons appear to have been made with samples of the noncriminal population not under treatment for mental illness. It is therefore impossible to determine what differences or peculiarities of type, if any, characterize the criminals studied.

The later work of William Sheldon,[31] especially his book on delin-

28. Ernst Kretschmer, *Körperbau und Charakter*, Springer-Verlag, Berlin, 1921; 2nd ed., same publisher, 1922. English translation of second edition by W. J. H. Sprott, under the title *Physique and Character*, Kegan Paul, Trench, Trubner, London, 1925, and Harcourt, Brace, New York, 1926. A slight revision and enlargement of this English edition was published in 1936 by The Humanities Press, New York. This revision of the English edition was reprinted in 1973 by Cooper Square, New York. In the meantime there have also appeared several editions in German that so far have not been translated into English. In 1955 there appeared what is listed as the "twenty-first and twenty-second" edition, published by Springer-Verlag, Berlin, Göttingen, and Heidelberg. This edition has been extensively revised and enlarged. New material has been introduced, past criticisms of the method and theory involved are met, and quantitative and statistical findings on the prevalence of the various types are included whenever possible.

29. Ernst Kretschmer, *Körperbau und Charakter*, 21/22 Auflage, Springer-Verlag, Berlin, Göttingen, and Heidelberg, 1955, Ch. 17, pp. 331–57.

30. Ibid., pp. 338, 346–49.

31. William H. Sheldon (with various associates), *Psychology and the Promethean Will*, 1936; *Varieties of Human Physique*, 1940; *The Varieties of Temperament*, 1942; *Varieties of Delinquent Youth*, 1949; *Atlas of Man*, 1954. All published by Harper, New York and London.

quent youth, represents a considerable methodological improvement. Sheldon took his underlying ideas and terminology of types from the fact that a human begins life as an embryo that is essentially a tube made up of three different tissue layers, namely, an inner layer (or endoderm), a middle layer (or mesoderm), and an outer layer (or ectoderm). Sheldon then constructed a corresponding physical and mental typology consistent with the known facts from embryology and the physiology of development. The endoderm gives rise to the digestive viscera; the mesoderm, to bone, muscle, and tendons of the motor-organ system; the ectoderm, to connecting tissue of the nervous system, skin, and related appendages. Sheldon's basic type characteristics of physique and temperament are briefly summarized in the following scheme: [32]

|  *Physique* | *Temperament* |
|---|---|
| 1. *Endomorphic:* relatively great development of digestive viscera; tendency to put on fat; soft roundness through various regions of the body; short tapering limbs; small bones; soft, smooth, velvety skin. | 1. *Viscerotonic:* general relaxation of body; a comfortable person; loves soft luxury; a "softie" but still essentially an extrovert. |
| 2. *Mesomorphic:* relative predominance of muscles, bone, and the motor organs of the body; large trunk; heavy chest; large wrists and hands; if "lean," a hard rectangularity of outline; if "not lean," they fill out heavily. | 2. *Somotonic:* active, dynamic, person; walks, talks, gestures assertively; behaves aggressively. |
| 3. *Ectomorphic:* relative predominance of skin and its appendages, which includes the nervous system; lean, fragile, delicate body; small, delicate bones; droopy shoulders; small face, sharp nose, fine hair; relatively little body mass and relatively great surface area. | 3. *Cerebrotonic:* an introvert; full of functional complaints, allergies, skin troubles, chronic fatigue, insomnia; sensitive to noise and distractions; shrinks from crowds. |

Each person possesses the characteristics of the three types to a greater or lesser degree. Sheldon therefore used three numbers, each between 1 and 7, to indicate the extent to which the characteristics of the three types were present in a given individual. For example, a person whose somatotype is 7–1–4 would possess many endomorphic characteristics, few mesomorphic characteristics, and about an average number of ectomorphic characteristics. Throughout, the

32. The schematic arrangement of basic types has been constructed from the discussion in Sheldon, *Varieties of Delinquent Youth*, pp. 14–30.

avowed purpose was to develop the methodology of an "operational psychiatry."[33]

Sheldon presented individual case histories, uniformly written according to a rigorous case outline, of 200 young males who had had a period of contact, during the decade 1939–49, with the Hayden Goodwill Inn, a small (capacity 80), somewhat specialized, and unusual type of rehabilitation home for boys in Boston, Massachusetts. He found that these youths were decidedly high in mesomorphy and low in ectomorphy, with the average somatotype being 3.5–4.6–2.7. Sheldon had earlier studied 200 college students who were apparently nondelinquents, and had found that the average somatotype was 3.2–3.8–3.4. The difference between these two groups with respect to mesomorphy and ectomorphy is significant ($p = .001$).[34]

The definition of delinquency used in this study, however, specifically related to the problem of developing a methodology for a more objective psychiatric classification and had only an incidental (and superficial) resemblance to the customary use of the term in criminology. Sheldon speaks of "biological delinquency,"[35] "mental delinquency,"[36] and "primary criminality"[37] not as aspects of behavior judged to be criminal in the usual legal sense, but as factors to be rated in accordance with the extent to which observed behavior conforms to that which a particular constitutional type might be expected to produce. Thus one of his cases,[38] an extreme mesomorphic athlete, "a really healthy looking tomcat,"[39] whose sexual activity resulted in numerous cases of "trouble," is not judged delinquent, but rather the opposite, because "he seemed to transmit a fairly good physical stock."[40] Subsequently Sutherland reexamined Sheldon's figures, classifying each youth according to the seriousness and consistency of his delinquent behavior, as reported in the case history.[41] This classification showed that the most delinquent of the youths were significantly more mesomorphic than the least delinquent.[42]

33. Sheldon, *Varieties of Delinquent Youth*, p. 96.

34. Juan B. Cortés, *Delinquency and Crime*, Seminar Press, New York, 1972, p. 14.

35. Sheldon, *Varieties of Delinquent Youth*, op cit., pp. 782–819.

36. Ibid., pp. 820–83.

37. Ibid., p. 679.

38. Ibid., pp. 476–79.

39. Ibid., pp. 477.

40. Ibid., p. 478.

41. E. H. Sutherland, "Critique of Sheldon's *Varieties of Delinquent Youth*," *American Sociological Review* 18: 142–48 (1951).

42. Cortés, op. cit., p. 17.

As is to be expected, Sheldon accepts with but few reservations, and quotes with approval, the more spectacular findings of the Hooton study.[43] His general approval of the basic premise of the Hooton interpretation is explicit and emphatic:[44]

Hooton . . . considers it a datum of common sense that there are structurally superior and inferior human organisms, and that a relationship must exist between structural and behavioral inferiority. Hooton has searchingly looked for, seen and tried to objectify his report on such a relationship. . . . His report is couched in a somewhat different frame of language from that used in the present project, but without question the general impression he gathered from his 15,000 criminals was similar to our impressions from ten years of observation at the Hayden Goodwill Inn. *It can be summarized in a single sentence: Where essential inadequacy is present the inadequacy is well reflected in the observable structure of the organism.*

The association between mesomorphy and delinquency was also found in a study by the Gluecks, who compared 500 persistent delinquents with 500 proven nondelinquents.[45] The two groups were matched in terms of age, general intelligence, ethnic-racial derivation, and residence in underprivileged areas. Photographs of the boys were mixed together and then visually assessed for the predominant body type.[46] By this method 60.1 percent of the delinquents, but only 30.7 percent of the nondelinquents, were found to be mesomorphs.[47] The analysis included a study of 67 personality traits and 42 sociocultural factors, in order to determine which of these were associated with delinquency.[48] The Gluecks found that mesomorphs, in general, were "more highly characterized by traits particularly suitable to the commission of acts of aggression (physical strength, energy, insensitivity, the tendency to express tensions and frustrations in action), together with a relative freedom from such inhibitions to antisocial adventures as feelings of inadequacy, marked submissiveness to authority, emotional instability, and the like."[49] They also found that those mesomorphs who became delinquent were characterized by a number of personality traits not normally found

43. Sheldon, *Varieties of Delinquent Youth*, op. cit., pp. 751–52.

44. Ibid., p. 752. (Italics in the original.)

45. S. Glueck and E. Glueck, *Physique and Delinquency*, Harper, New York, 1956.

46. This procedure is discussed in S. Glueck and E. Glueck, *Unraveling Juvenile Delinquency*, Harvard University Press, Cambridge, Mass., 1950, pp. 192–96.

47. Glueck and Glueck, *Physique and Delinquency*, p. 9.

48. For a complete list of these traits and factors, see Glueck and Glueck, *Physique and Delinquency*, pp. 27–31.

49. Ibid., p. 226.

in mesomorphs, including susceptibility to contagious diseases of childhood, destructiveness, feelings of inadequacy, emotional instability, and emotional conflicts.[50] In addition, three sociocultural factors—careless household routine, lack of family group recreations, and meagerness of recreational facilities in the home—were strongly associated with delinquency in mesomorphs.[51]

The Glueck study has been criticized because there was no control for the rapid body changes that occur in adolescence, because the method of somatotyping involved only visual assessment and not precise measurements, and because the delinquent population included only institutionalized youth.[52] In an attempt to overcome these problems Cortés used a precise measurement technique to somatotype 100 delinquents, of whom 70 were institutionalized and 30 were on probation or under suspended sentence. He also somatotyped 100 private high school seniors who had no record of any delinquency, and 20 institutionalized adult felons. He found that 57 percent of the delinquents were high in mesomorphy, as compared to only 19 percent of the nondelinquents.[53] The mean somatotype of the nondelinquents was 3.9–3.5–3.5, the mean somatotype of the delinquents was 3.5–4.4–3.1, and the mean somatotype of the criminals was 2.8–5.4–3.1.[54]

In order to determine whether body type was associated with temperament, Cortés had 73 boys who were clearly classified as to body type (i.e., whose predominant rating was at least 4.5 and exceeded the other two ratings by at least one-half unit) describe themselves in terms of a set of traits associated with the three temperaments. Table 4-2[55] presents the results of this experiment, and shows that physique is clearly associated with self-description of temperament. This procedure was repeated with 100 college girls and with the 20 convicted adult felons, and similar results were obtained. Finally, using McClelland's Test for Need for Achievement, Cortés found that mesomorphy was associated with need for achievement (n Ach) and with need for power (n Power), as revealed in Table 4-3.[56]

The standard sociological criticism to findings such as these is that

50. Ibid., p. 221.
51. Ibid., p. 224.
52. These criticisms are reviewed in Cortés, op. cit., pp. 19–21.
53. Ibid., p. 28.
54. Ibid., p. 30.
55. Ibid., p. 53. Reproduced by permission of the author and publisher.
56. Ibid., pp. 88, 101. Reproduced by permission of the author and publisher.

TABLE 4–2   Intercorrelations among the Primary Components of Physique (Parnell's Method) and Self-description of Temperament

| Components of Physique | Components of Temperament | | |
| --- | --- | --- | --- |
| | Viscerotonia | Somatotonia | Cerebrotonia |
| | $(N=47)$ | $(N=38)$ | $(N=51)$ |
| Endomorphy | $+.510^b$ | $-.138$ | $-.269$ |
| Mesomorphy | $-.389^a$ | $+.694^b$ | $-.369^a$ |
| Ectomorphy | $-.150$ | $-.256$ | $+.430^a$ |

[a, b] significant at $p=.01$ and $p=.001$, respectively

differences in behavior reflect the effects of social selection processes and that differences in attitude reflect the effects of social stereotyping. For example, Gibbons is quoted as criticizing the Gluecks' study as follows:[57]

These findings were the result of careful measurement, so that there is little question as to their accuracy. However, a sociologist would be quick to point out that a process of *social selection*, rather than biological determinism, probably explains the results. In other words, it is not unlikely that recruits to delinquent conduct are drawn from the group of more agile, physically fit boys, just as "Little League" baseball or "Pop Warner" league football players tend toward mesomorphy. Fat delinquents and fat ball players are uncommon, because social behavior involved in these cases puts fat, skinny, or sickly boys at a disadvantage. If so, the findings reflect the workings of social factors, not biology.

TABLE 4–3   Correlations between Physique, Need for Achievement, and Need for Power

| Motive | Condition | N | Endomorphy | Mesomorphy | Ectomorphy |
| --- | --- | --- | --- | --- | --- |
| n Ach | Nondelinquents | 91 | $+.150$ | $+.537^d$ | $-.195$ |
| | Nondelinquents | 100 | $+.165$ | $+.353^c$ | $-.273^c$ |
| | Delinquents | 100 | $+.012$ | $+.200^a$ | $-.056$ |
| n Power | Nondelinquents | 100 | $-.083$ | $+.092$ | $+.080$ |
| | Delinquents | 100 | $-.061$ | $+.230^b$ | $+.032$ |

[a, b, c, d] significant at $p=.05$, .02, .01, and .001, respectively

57. Don C. Gibbons, *Delinquent Behavior*, Prentice-Hall, Englewood Cliffs, 1970, pp. 75–76, quoted in Cortés, op. cit., pp. 39–40. (Italics in original.)

Cortés reacts strongly to this type of criticism:[58]

It is exasperating to find this type of objection again and again (in practically all books written by sociologists). For one thing, nobody nowadays
speaks of biological *determinism;* but, second, the fact that there may be a
process of social selection, does not detract in the least from the relevance
of many other variables. Who makes this selection? Why is this particular
selection made and not an entirely different one? Is it not, as Gibbons con-
cedes, because fat, skinny, or sickly boys are at a disadvantage? Do physique and constitutional factors play no role whatsoever in baseball, boxing,
or football? It is his last sentence that shows more clearly the one-sidedness
of this point of view: "the findings reflect the workings of social factors, not
biology." The proper and logical conclusion for the entire paragraph, after
the explanation he advances, should rather be: "the findings may reflect
the workings of *both* social *and* biological factors". Human behavior, as most
scholars in the field do not hesitate to recognize, is biosocial in nature, that
is, it has *both* biological and social causes. As Eysenck has written, "It is
time the pendulum started swinging back from an exclusive preoccupation
with social causes to an appropriate appreciation and understanding of biological causes."

His own conclusion is equally strong:[59]

Delinquents and possibly criminals differ from nondelinquents and noncriminals in being *physically* more mesomorphic, more energetic and potentially aggressive *temperamentally,* and in showing higher need for achievement and power *motivationally.*

Cortés's conclusion may be criticized on several counts. The small
number of subjects in the experiments makes such a broad generalization at least somewhat questionable. The differences in mesomorphy between the groups in this study may reflect differences in socioeconomic class rather than in criminality, since the nondelinquent
group was from a private high school, and thus probably upper class,
whereas most criminal and delinquent groups are predominantly lower
class.[60] The experiments did not actually measure the temperament
of the different body types, but measured self-perception of temperament, and no theoretical case is made that those who perceive
themselves as energetic (mesomorphs) are more potentially aggres-

58. Cortés, ibid., p. 40. (Italics in original.) Quoted by permission of the author and publisher.

59. Ibid., p. 348. (Italics in original.)

60. Ibid., p. 89. The author states that the nondelinquents "belong to higher social backgrounds, possess greater intelligence, and are more favored by many other variables. . . ."

sive than those who perceive themselves as tense and anxious (ectomorphs). The study does not directly relate delinquency and criminality to temperament and motivation. Rather, delinquency and criminality are shown to be related to mesomorphy, and mesomorphy is shown to be related to certain temperaments and motivations. The experiments linking mesomorphy to the "energetic" temperament included only 7 delinquents and 20 adult criminals, an extremely small sample. It was found that mesomorphy was related to a higher need for achievement, but no significant differences between the delinquent and nondelinquent groups were observed.[61] Delinquents were significantly higher in need for power than nondelinquents, but no significant differences were found between body types of the nondelinquents.[62] This appears to be rather a mixed bag of results to support such a strong conclusion.

### 4. CONCLUSION

Theories that focus on physical characteristics turn out to be a more or less sophisticated form of shadowboxing with a more subtle and difficult problem, namely the extent to which biological differences explain differences in human behavior. This more difficult problem will be explored in a later chapter, but for the present it can be said that there is no clear evidence that physical appearance, as such, has any consistent relation to legally defined crime. Improved research techniques may help clarify this issue in the future, but present findings tend to be negative.

### RECOMMENDED READINGS

Charles Goring, *The English Convict: A Statistical Study*, 1913, reprinted by Patterson Smith, Montclair, N.J., 1972. Of particular interest is the excellent Introductory Essay written for the reprint edition by Edwin D. Driver, as well as the Introduction to the Abridged Edition of 1919 by Karl Pearson.

Edwin D. Driver, "Charles Buckman Goring," in Hermann Mannheim, ed., *Pioneers in Criminology*, Patterson Smith, Montclair, N.J., 1972. An overview of Goring's principal ideas and methods in their historical context.

Stephen Jay Gould, *The Mismeasure of Man*, Norton, New York, 1981. Lombroso's theory of atavism is presented in Chapter 4 in its historical and scientific context. Gould demonstrates that scientists, desiring to prove their own superiority and the inferiority of other racial and ethnic groups, cloaked their prejudices in the veil of objective science.

61. Ibid., p. 89.
62. Ibid., p. 102.

Gina Lombroso-Ferrero, *Lombroso's Criminal Man*, Patterson Smith, Montclair, N.J., 1972. Lombroso's daughter presents his principal ideas. See also the introductions by Leonard D. Savitz and by Cesare Lombroso.

Leonard Savitz, Stanley H. Turner, and Toby Dickman, "The Origin of Scientific Criminology: Franz Joseph Gall as the First Criminologist," in Robert F. Meier, *Theory in Criminology*, Sage, Beverly Hills, Cal., 1977, pp. 41–56. Gall's and Lombroso's work are compared.

Juan B. Cortés, *Delinquency and Crime: A Biopsychosocial Approach*, Seminar Press, New York, 1972. Presents the author's studies and reviews other investigations into the influence of body type on criminality.

Ysabel Rennie, *The Search for Criminal Man*, Heath, Lexington, Mass., 1978. A thoughtful and insightful analysis that places early criminological theories in a broader historical context.

# CHAPTER FIVE

# Theories Related to Intelligence

Next to physical appearance, mental deficiency probably has been the concept most often used to explain criminal behavior. As the simple but bold hypotheses of the physical-type theorists crumbled one by one (e.g., physiognomy, phrenology, atavism), the idea persisted that there was one constant element that characterized criminals: low intelligence. The shift in emphasis from physical differences to mental differences was easy to make, for both portrayed the criminal as an inferior person. Thus the general logic of the theory remained unchanged.

Early testing of the intelligence of prisoners generally supported the hypothesis that criminals (or at least those who were incarcerated) were mentally inferior. Later studies found that most criminals had normal intelligence, and for a time the hypothesis that there was a relationship between criminality and low intelligence fell into disrepute. In the 1970s, however, there was renewed support for this hypothesis, particularly with respect to juvenile delinquents. The object of the present chapter is to explore critically these changing ideas about intelligence and crime.

## 1. BACKGROUND IDEAS AND CONCEPTS

The language and literature of all peoples have words to describe and stories to illustrate the conduct of "dull-witted" or "slow" individuals whose intelligence is no more than that of a young child. Under the general explanatory principle of demonology, such mentally deficient or retarded individuals were thought to be possessed by

the devil. They were often banished as "unclean" and forced into
exile and almost certain death.

In the rationalist transition from demonological explanations to
naturalistic ones, ideas about this affliction were modified. Instead
of being explained as curses of God, they were explained as curses
of nature. Inheritance and family line of descent became the naturalistic way of accounting for such misfortunes. This view was associated with the evolutionary theories of Charles Darwin and others
in the late nineteenth century. Darwin argued that the evolution of
a species proceeds through natural variations that occur among the
offspring.[1] The weaker and the less capable offspring die off or fail
to, reproduce, while the stronger and more capable survive and
flourish. Through this process of "natural selection" by "the survival
of the fittest," the characteristics of the more capable offspring come
to dominate the species, and the species itself evolves to a more advanced state.

These were the ideas of the time, and it was natural that they would
be applied to the problems of crime. One person who did this was
Lombroso, as discussed in the preceding chapter. But Lombroso relied on a minor point in Darwin's theory, that certain individuals might
be atavistic throwbacks to an earlier evolutionary stage. More important was the implication that, in addition to the development of
superior strains of individuals who were destined to dominate the
species, natural selection would result in the development of inferior strains of people who were destined to die out. While the superior strains of individuals would be characterized by many desirable traits, inferior strains would be characterized by many undesirable
traits.

Richard Dugdale used this basic idea to explain the history of a
family he called the "Jukes."[2] As part of his work for the Prison Association of New York, Dugdale found six members of this family in
a county jail in 1874. He traced the genealogy of the family back
over 200 years and found a history of "pauperism, prostitution, ex-
haustion, disease, fornication, and illegitimacy." He attributed this
melancholy history to the "degenerate" nature of the family. His study
had a striking impact on the thinking at the time, despite the fact
that it was based on unreliable, incomplete, and obscure information

1. Charles R. Darwin, *On the Origin of Species*, Penguin, New York, 1968 (originally published in 1859).

2. Richard L. Dugdale, *The Jukes: A Study in Crime, Pauperism and Heredity*, Putnam, New
York, 1877; reprinted by Arno, New York, 1977.

and was filled with value judgments and unsupported conclusions. For example, Henderson, writing in 1899, cited the Jukes as typical of families of degenerates and argued that private charitable work to alleviate the suffering of these people was actually allowing them to reproduce in great numbers, resulting in "the rising tide of pauperism, insanity, and crime which threatens to overwhelm and engulf our civilization."[3] He argued that this "deterioration of the common stock" must be resisted by segregating such inferior people in institutions and not allowing them to reproduce.

These popular studies of degenerate families supported the popular opinion that criminals are what they are because they do not know enough to understand the hazardous nature of criminality or the satisfying rewards of a law-abiding life. But critical scientific judgment requires more exact and systematic procedures than were possible in such case studies before any considered conclusions can be drawn. Accurate comparisons call for exact measurements, and therefore the critical investigation of the relationship between crime and mental ability could come only after the development of intelligence tests and their applications to this problem.

## 2. INTELLIGENCE TESTING AND CRIME

The systematic observation and recording of individual differences has been a principal concern of experimental psychologists. The exact measurement of individual differences in "reaction time" has long been a commonplace in the psychological laboratory. Other and often more subtle differences have also been studied, such as the ability to memorize, to complete or to straighten out sentences, to complete pictures, to recognize the meanings of words, and to do mental arithmetic. A variety of attempts have been made to measure these differences. For example, in 1880 a German psychologist, H. Ebbinghaus (1850–1909), devised a test of the ability to memorize so that the differences observed among individuals in this respect could be expressed on a numerical scale. This is the essential idea of an intelligence test, the object of which is to express numerically differences among persons in their ability to perform a variety of "men-

---

3. C. R. Henderson, "The Relation of Philanthropy to Social Order and Progress," *Proceedings of the National Conference of Charities and Correction* 26: 1–15 (1899); partially reprinted in Frederic L. Faust and Paul J. Brantingham, eds., *Juvenile Justice Philosophy*, 2nd ed., West, St. Paul, 1979, pp. 48–57.

tal" operations that, taken together, are considered "intelligence" or an indicator of intelligence.[4]

The distinguished French psychologist Alfred Binet (1857–1911) first took intelligence testing out of the laboratory and applied it to the persisting problem of retardation in the Paris schools. In 1892 he became assistant director of the then recently founded psychological laboratory at the Sorbonne (he became director in 1894, holding that position until his death) and began his lifelong quest for a way to measure intelligence, conceived of as native ability rather than learned behavior.[5] He first tried to assess intelligence by measuring the volume of the skull, following the method of his countryman Paul Broca, but quickly became convinced that such methods were useless. After writing a report on his findings, he abandoned the effort.

In 1904 Binet became a member of a commission to formulate policy for the administration of special classes in the public schools of Paris and returned to the effort to measure intelligence. This time, however, he decided to take a practical approach. He assembled a large number of small tasks related to everyday life but which involved the basic reasoning processes. These were then arranged in ascending difficulty so that the first tasks could be performed by very young children while the last could be performed only by adults. In this task he had the valuable assistance and collaboration of Theodore Simon, the medical officer of the Paris schools. Their first scale of tests appeared in 1905 and was called the *Binet-Simon Scale of Intelligence*.

This scale was revised in 1908, when the concept of *mental age* was added.[6] Binet decided to assign an age level to each task on the test. The typical nine-year-old, for example, would be able to perform the tasks graded for age nine or younger but not for age ten or

4. For a short factual account of the development of intelligence tests, see the article by Robert L. Thorndike, "Intelligence and Intelligence Testing," in *International Encyclopedia of the Social Sciences*, Macmillan and the Free Press, New York, 1968, vol. VII, pp. 421–29. Also, see textbooks on psychological testing and chapters on this subject in general psychology texts, such as Lee J. Cronbach, *Essentials of Psychological Testing*, 3rd ed., Harper & Row, New York, 1970, pp. 197–226; Philip H. DuBois, *A History of Psychological Testing*, Allyn and Bacon, Boston, 1970; David A. Goshin, *The Search for Ability*, Russell Sage, New York, pp. 19–44; Frank S. Freeman, *Theory and Practice of Psychological Testing*, Holt, Rinehart and Winston, New York, 1962, pp. 1–23; Gardner Lindzey, Calvin S. Hall, and Richard F. Thompson, *Psychology*, 2nd ed., Worth Publishers, New York, 1978, Ch. 12, pp. 351–78.

5. The following account is derived principally from Stephen Jay Gould, *The Mismeasure of Man*, Norton, New York, 1981, pp. 146–58.

6. This method of determining IQ has now been discarded in favor of one employing means and standard deviations. For a discussion of the present method, as well as a discussion of the problems of the mental age method, see Cronbach, op. cit., pp. 215–18.

older. The age level of the last tasks the child could perform would then be described as his or her mental age and could be compared with his or her chronological age. In 1912 the psychologist W. Stern suggested that mental age be divided by chronological age and the results multiplied by 100. This would then be called the *intelligence quotient*, or IQ (a quotient being the answer in a division problem). Thus the typical nine-year-old who had a mental age of nine would have an IQ of 100, smarter nine-year-olds would have IQs above 100, while duller ones would have IQs below 100.

This test was revised again shortly before Binet's death in 1911. At that time Binet expressed his reservations about the ways in which his test might be used. The test had been designed to identify children who were doing poorly in school so that they could receive special help. Binet argued that the test should not be used to identify children of superior intelligence, since it was not designed for that purpose. He also warned against using the test to label slower students as unteachable so that, instead of being helped, they would be ejected from the schools. Binet was strongly committed to the view that these slower students could improve their performance if properly helped, and he set up special classes in the Paris schools for the children who did poorly on his tests. He wrote with pleasure of the success of these classes, arguing that the pupils increased not only their knowledge but their intelligence as well: "It is in this practical sense, the only one accessible to us, that we say that the intelligence of these children has been increased. We have increased the intelligence of a pupil: the capacity to learn and to assimilate instruction."[7] Thus Binet rejected the idea that intelligence is a fixed and inborn quantity that cannot be changed through instruction.

With the success of the Binet-Simon scale in Paris, numerous revisions, extensions, and adaptations were made in many lands. In the United States Binet's tests and articles were translated into English and popularized by H. H. Goddard of the New Jersey Training School for the Feeble Minded at Vineland. Somewhat later Lewis M. Terman of Stanford University published what became the best-known and most widely used form of the test, called the *Stanford Revision and Extension of the Binet-Scale*. Binet's 1908 scale consisted of 54 individual tests arranged in order of difficulty so that the easiest test might be passed by a child of three, with the most diffi-

7. Quoted in Gould, op. cit., p. 154.

cult requiring the ability of an average adult. The Stanford Revision consisted of 90 tests, similarly arranged in order of difficulty from the three-year-old level to that of the "superior adult."

Unlike Binet, the Americans were convinced that intelligence was a fixed and inborn quantity, so that their primary purpose in giving intelligence tests was to sort people into appropriate social roles.[8] Those with IQs above 115 or 120 were said to be appropriate for the professions, while IQ 75 to 85 was appropriate for semiskilled labor. Terman, for example, mentioned that "anything above 85 IQ in a barber probably represents dead waste."[9]

They were particularly concerned with identifying those whose intelligence was "subnormal." Their purpose, however, was the opposite of Binet's: They wished to institutionalize these people and prevent them from reproducing, much like Henderson had suggested earlier. This required that some IQ score be determined to be the dividing line between normal intelligence and feeblemindedness. Goddard gave intelligence tests to all the inmates at his institution at Vineland and to all new inmates on admission. This testing program disclosed no inmate with a mental age over 13. Goddard therefore concluded that mental age 12 (IQ 75 on the then commonly held assumption that full mental ability is reached at chronological age 16) marked the upper limit of feeblemindedness, so that mental age 13 marked the lower limit of normal intelligence.

With that standard as the basis for comparison, Goddard and many other psychologists gave intelligence tests to the inmates of prisons, jails, hospitals, and various other public institutions. Goddard examined a large number of such studies on the intelligence of criminals.[10] The proportion of criminals diagnosed as feebleminded in these studies ranged from 28 to 89 percent, with the median study finding that 70 percent of criminals were feebleminded. Goddard therefore concluded that most criminals were feebleminded.

Goddard also discovered a large group of "defectives" living in the pine barrens of New Jersey and traced their heritage back to a man who had had an illegitimate child by a "feebleminded" barmaid.[11] Of 480 decendants of this union, Goddard claimed that 143 were

8. Lewis M. Terman, *The Measurement of Intelligence*, Houghton Mifflin, Boston, 1916, p. 17; cited in Gould, op. cit., p. 181.

9. Terman, op. cit., p. 288; quoted in Gould, op. cit., p. 182.

10. H. H. Goddard, *Feeblemindedness: Its Causes and Consequences*, Macmillan, New York, 1914; reprinted by Arno, New York, 1972.

11. H. H. Goddard, *The Kallikak Family, A Study in the Heredity of Feeble-Mindedness*, Macmillan, New York, 1912. Goddard called this family the "Kallikaks" because the name combined the Greek words for "beauty" (*kallos*) and "bad" (*kakos*). Gould, op. cit., pp. 168–

feebleminded, 36 illegitimate, 33 sexually immoral, 24 confirmed alcoholics, 3 epileptics, 3 criminals, and 8 keepers of houses of prostitution. The man later married a righteous Quaker woman, a union ultimately resulting in 496 "normal" descendants who "married into the best families of their state."

Goddard mourned the "havoc that was wrought by one thoughtless act"[12] and concluded that criminality and feeblemindedness were two aspects of the same degenerate state, so that all feebleminded people were potential criminals. Feeblemindedness was said to be caused by a recessive gene that obeyed the normal rules of inheritance originally formulated by Gregor Mendel.[13] Thus Goddard argued that feeblemindedness could be eliminated through selective breeding. This led to his recommendation that the feebleminded be institutionalized and not allowed to reproduce.

These ideas dominated the thinking of mental testers for a time but were directly challenged by the results of intelligence testing administered to draftees during World War I. Following Goddard, the Army Psychological Corps at first made the conventional assumption that those of mental age 12 or below were feebleminded and therefore not fit for military service. This procedure led to a diagnosis of feeblemindedness for 37 percent of the whites and 89 percent of the blacks tested.[14] The patent fallacy of assuming that nearly one-half of the population was feebleminded was generally recognized. Thus Goddard wrote, soon after the war, "The most extreme limit that anyone has dared to suggest is that one percent of the population is feebleminded."[15] He later concluded that feeblemindedness might be remedied by education and that it was not necessary to segregate the feebleminded in institutions and to prevent them from reproducing.[16] Goddard was frank about his own change of mind: "As for myself, I think I have gone over to the enemy."[17]

---

71, points out that Goddard had diagnosed feeblemindedness among this family by sight and did not administer any intelligence tests to them. Goddard also included pictures of them in his book that had been retouched to make them appear evil and retarded.

12. Goddard, *The Kallikaks*, p. 103.

13. Goddard, *Feeblemindedness*, p. 539. See the discussion in Gould, op. cit., pp. 158–64.

14. Robert M. Yerkes, ed., "Psychological Examining in the United States Army," *Memoirs of the National Academy of Sciences*, U.S. Government Printing Office, Washington, D.C., 1921, vol. 15, p. 791.

15. H. H. Goddard, "Feeblemindedness and Delinquency," *Journal of Psycho-Asthenics* 25: 173 (1921).

16. H. H. Goddard, "Feeblemindedness: A Question of Definition," *Journal of Psycho-Asthenics* 33: 225 (1928).

17. Ibid., p. 224.

Publication of the results of World War I testing also provided a new perspective on the relationship between intelligence and crime. A number of studies were done comparing the performance of prisoners with that of draftees on intelligence tests. These studies generally found insignificant differences between the two groups,[18] and several studies found that prisoners actually scored higher than draftees.[19] As a result of such studies feeblemindedness largely disappeared as a basis for explaining criminal behavior.

### 3. LATER STUDIES: DELINQUENCY, RACE, AND IQ

Although it is no longer believed that large numbers of criminals are feebleminded, the IQ of criminals and delinquents has become embroiled in a more recent controversy concerning the relationship of intelligence to race. Blacks, on the average, score about 15 points lower than whites on IQ tests. Some scholars have used the difference in IQ scores to explain the difference in crime and delinquency rates between the races. Their arguments have generally focused on the issue of delinquency rather than crime in general, and it is there that the stronger case has been made.

However, these arguments must be considered in the context of the overall controversy about the meaning of IQ scores. The controversy concerns such issues as whether IQ measures intelligence or whether it measures such other factors as academic achievement or "test-wiseness"; if it actually does measure intelligence, whether the tests are "culturally biased" so that the intelligence of minority groups is underreported; and if there is a real difference between the intelligence of blacks and whites, whether this difference is the result of genetic or environmental influence.[20]

The seeds of this controversy are found in a 1967 speech before the National Academy of Sciences by William Shockley, a winner of

---

18. For example, see Simon H. Tulchin, *Intelligence and Crime*, University of Chicago Press, Chicago, 1939; reprinted 1974.

19. For example, see Carl Murchison, *Criminal Intelligence*, Clark University Press, Worcester, Mass., 1926, Ch. 4.

20. Some recent works discussing this controversy include Paul L. Houts, ed., *The Myth of Measurability*, Hart, New York, 1977; Paul R. Ehrlich and S. Shirley Feldman, *The Race Bomb*, Quadrangle, New York, 1977; N. J. Block and Gerald Dworkin, eds., *The IQ Controversy*, Pantheon, New York, 1976; J. C. Loehlin, G. Lindzey, and J. N. Spuhler, *Race Differences in Intelligence*, Freeman, San Francisco, 1975; Ashley Montagu, ed., *Race and IQ*, Oxford University Press, New York, 1975; Carl Senna, ed., *The Fallacy of I.Q.*, Third Press, New York, 1973; R. J. Herrnstein, *I.Q. in the Meritocracy*, Little, Brown, Boston, 1973; and H. J. Eysenck, *The IQ Argument*, Library Press, New York, 1971.

the Nobel Prize for physics for his role in the invention of the transistor.[21] Shockley speculated that the differences in IQ between blacks and whites might be solely the result of genetic differences and that these genetic differences might also explain the differences in poverty and crime rates between these groups. He also suggested that "IQ test results may actually be a deeper measure, at least on a statistical basis, of a distribution of some more fundamental social capacity." He did not actually argue that the all-genetic model was correct, but he did urge that a National Study Group be set up to research the problem and to make recommendations if the IQ-Poverty-Crime problem was found to be related to genetic differences.[22]

In 1969 Arthur Jensen published a lengthy article in which he positively argued many of the points on which Shockley had only speculated.[23] Specifically, he contended that IQ tests do measure a factor that is important for performance in Western industrialized societies, and that about 80 percent of the individual differences on this score are determined by genetic rather than environmental differences. He concluded that remedial education programs had failed for precisely this reason. This article set off the large IQ controversy just mentioned.

Jensen's article was used by Gordon to argue that variations in delinquency rates are best explained by variations in IQ.[24] Gordon focused on the concept of the prevalence of delinquency, which he defined as the proportion of an age cohort that become delinquent according to a specified criterion by a given age. An example of a prevalence question would be: What is the proportion of boys who have ever been to a juvenile court among boys who are now 18.0 years of age? In a review of the literature, Gordon found nine stud-

21. W. Shockley, "A 'Try Simplest Cases' Approach to the Heredity-Poverty-Crime Problem," *Proceedings of the National Academy of Sciences* 57 (6): 1767–74 (June 15, 1967). Shockley has founded a sperm bank for geniuses, with himself as the first donor, as part of his efforts to increase the genetic endownment of the human race.

22. Several such committees were set up. They concluded that this problem merited study, but denied that it was especially urgent. See "Recommendations with Respect to the Behavioral and Social Aspects of Human Genetics," *Proceedings of the National Academy of Sciences* 69: 1–3 (1972). By 1977, however, the question had become so volatile that one scholar, Herbert C. Kelman of Harvard, argued that it would seem advisable "to forgo research at this time on genetic differences in intelligence among racial groups." See Herbert C. Kelman, "Privacy and Research with Human Beings," *Journal of Social Issues* 33 (3): 169–95 (1977).

23. A. R. Jensen, "How Much Can We Boost IQ and Scholastic Achievement?" *Harvard Educational Review* 39: 1–123 (1969).

24. Robert Gordon, "Prevalence: The Rare Datum in Delinquency Measurement and Its Implications for the Theory of Delinquency," in Malcolm W. Klein, ed., *The Juvenile Justice System*, Sage Publications, Beverly Hills, Ca., 1976, pp. 201–84.

ies that gave 56 prevalence rates for white boys and girls.[25] These rates ranged in seriousness from rates for commitment to training school down to rates for all youths found in police records for at least one minor difficulty, including traffic violations such as overtime parking. When arranged according to their seriousness, these rates were remarkably consistent, with the exception that areas with populations somewhere below 44,000 had considerably lower rates. That is, cities with populations over 44,000 apparently have similar delinquency prevalence rates among white youths for all levels of seriousness.

From this finding Gordon made the following analysis. First, he disagreed with the widely held belief that urbanization should be considered a cause of delinquency. Gordon argued that city size probably acts as a "releaser" of delinquent behavior, rather than as a stimulant of it, so that the potential for delinquency is inherent in the youths themselves. The delinquency is held in check in smaller, tightly knit communities but is "released" once a certain level of anonymity within a larger city is reached. That would explain why delinquency rates do not increase as cities become larger. Second, Gordon argued that delinquency prevalence rates for black youths probably are also consistent within cities with populations over a certain size and that these rates have been shown in several studies to be substantially higher than the rates for whites. He maintained that the higher delinquency rates in larger cities can be adequately explained by the higher proportion of blacks in the population.[26]

Third, Gordon suggested that IQ level might account for the consistency of delinquency prevalence rates for white youths, as well as for the differences between the rates for white and black youths. He

25. These studies are T. P. Monahan, "On the Incidence of Delinquency," *Social Forces* 39: 66–72 (Oct. 1960); J. W. B. Douglas et al., "Delinquency and Social Class," *British Journal of Criminology* 6: 294–302 (July 1966); J. C. Ball et al., "Incidence and Estimated Prevalence of Recorded Delinquency in a Metropolitan Area," *American Sociological Review* 29: 90–93 (Feb. 1964); J. C. Ball, *Social Deviancy and Adolescent Personality*, University of Kentucky Press, Lexington, Ky, 1962; R. J. Havighurst et al., *Growing Up in River City*, John Wiley, New York, 1962; S. R. Hathaway and E. D. Monachesi, *Adolescent Personality and Behavior*, University of Minnesota Press, Minneapolis, 1963; R. A. Gordon, "An Explicit Estimation of the Prevalence of Commitment to a Training School, to Age 18, by Race and by Sex," *Journal of the American Statistical Association* 68: 547–53 (Sept. 1973); A. J. Reiss, Jr. and A. L. Rhodes, "The Distribution of Juvenile Delinquency in the Social Structure," *American Sociological Review* 26: 720–32 (Oct. 1961); and Center for Studies of Crime and Delinquency, *Teenage Delinquency in Small Town America*, Research Report 5, Publication No. (ADM) 75-138, U.S. Government Printing Office, Washington, D.C., 1974.

26. A similar result was obtained in John Laub, "Urbanism, Race, and Crime," *Journal of Research in Crime and Delinquency*, July 1983, pp. 183–97. Using victimization data, Laub found little variation in delinquency rates in cities above about 10,000 population when race is controlled. Thus Laub argued that the higher delinquency rates in large cities is due to their greater concentrations of black youths.

cited Jensen to the effect that IQ is largely a biological factor, and quoted several studies that support the hypothesis that delinquency is related to the biology of the individual. He pointed to the similarity between the distribution of IQ scores and the distribution of delinquency, and demonstrated that court record data from Philadelphia and national rates for commitment to training schools could be duplicated merely by assuming that all youths (both black and white) with IQs below a certain level, and no youths above it, became delinquent. He did not argue that such a relationship between IQ and delinquency actually exists, but that this coincidence "virtually necessitate(s) that there be some more reasonable functional relationship within sex between IQ and delinquency that is common or nearly common to both races." He went on to argue, without supporting data, that the delinquency rates of several other racial groups are also related to IQ. Japanese, Chinese, and Jews have maintained low delinquency rates despite their minority group status and generally low economic position, and these groups are said to have somewhat higher IQs than whites. Mexican-Americans are said to have both delinquency rates and average IQs somewhere in between those of blacks and whites.

Additional support for the association between IQ and delinquency was presented by Travis Hirschi and Michael Hindelang, who reviewed a number of studies on the subject.[27] They found that low IQ was at least as important as social class or race in predicting official delinquency and that it was more important in predicting self-reported delinquency;[28] that delinquency is consistently related to low IQs within races and within social classes so that, for example, lower-class delinquents are more likely to have low IQs than lower-class nondelinquents;[29] and that the principal sociological theories of

27. Travis Hirschi and Michael J. Hindelang, "Intelligence and Delinquency: A Revisionist Review," *American Sociological Review* 42: 572–87 (1977).

28. The term *official delinquency* refers to delinquent behaviors that have been recorded in the official records of criminal justice agencies and thus have become part of official delinquency statistics. *Self-reported delinquency* refers to delinquent behaviors reported by juveniles anonymously on questionnaires, and includes much behavior that is not known to criminal justice agencies.

29. The studies cited with respect to delinquency within social classes are Reiss and Rhodes, op. cit.; Travis Hirschi, *Causes of Delinquency*, University of California Press, Berkeley, 1969. Marvin Wolfgang, Robert M. Figlio, and Thorsten Sellin, *Delinquency in a Birth Cohort*, University of Chicago Press, Chicago, 1972; and D. J. West, *Who Becomes Delinquent?*, Heinemann, London, 1972. The studies cited for delinquency within races are Wolfgang et al., op. cit.; Hirschi, *Causes of Delinquency*; James F. Short, Jr., and Fred L. Strodtbeck, *Group Process and Gang Delinquency*, University of Chicago Press, Chicago, 1965; and Jackson Toby and Marcia L. Toby, "Low School Status as a Predisposing Factor in Subcultural Delinquency," Mimeo, Rutgers University, New Brunswick, N.J., 1961.

delinquency "have been saying for some time that IQ should be related to delinquency for the same reason social class is, or should be,
related to it."[30] They argue that IQ as an explanation of crime and
delinquency has been ignored in criminology because a strong bias
against it arose in the early part of this century. At that time IQ as
an explanation of crime and delinquency was strongly associated with
the physicians (such as Goring and Goddard) who had dominated the
field of criminology since the time of Lombroso. The sociologists who
were beginning to take over the field were eager to focus attention
on the effects of social conditions and away from the characteristics
of the individual. Over the previous 20 years decreasing proportions
of criminals and delinquents had been reported as feebleminded because of the repeated lowering of the "normal" mental age. Hirschi
and Hindelang state that Sutherland "called attention to this twenty-
year trend—which, in fact, continued for another 30 years—and allowed his readers to conclude that it would continue until the initial
claims of difference between delinquents and nondelinquents had no
foundation in fact."[31] The difference between these two groups never
entirely disappeared, however, and seemed to stabilize at about eight
IQ points.


## 4. IMPLICATIONS AND CONCLUSIONS

It seems clear that, whatever it measures, IQ is correlated with juvenile delinquency. But it is still necessary to explain why persons
with low IQ scores become delinquent more frequently than those
with high scores. The explanation one accepts will depend to a large
degree on one's view of what IQ measures.

Gordon, for example, assumes that IQ measures some form of abstract reasoning or problem-solving ability and that this ability is
largely inherited. Given this perspective, he suggested that inappropriate and ineffective child-rearing practices by low-IQ parents might

30. Hirschi and Hindelang, op. cit, p. 579. Support for this statement is derived largely from
a review of Albert Cohen's *Delinquent Boys*, The Free Press, New York, 1955. Cloward and
Ohlin's theory (*Delinquency and Opportunity*, The Free Press, New York, 1960) is said to
predict that higher-IQ youths are more likely to become delinquent; labeling and conflict theories are said to be consistent with the low-IQ argument, since the system is seen as discriminating against these youth; Sutherland's "differential association" theory (Edwin H. Sutherland and Donald R. Cressey, *Criminology*, Lippincott, Philadelphia, 1978, pp. 80–83) is "strictly
silent" on the matter; and "social control" theories are consistent with this view, although they
have not emphasized it in the past.

31. Hirschi and Hindelang, op. cit., p. 580. The reference is to Edwin H. Sutherland, "Mental Deficiency and Crime," pp. 357–75 in Kimball Young, ed., *Social Attitudes*, Henry Holt,
New York, 1931; partially reprinted in Stephen Schafer and Richard D. Knudten, eds., *Criminological Theory*, D. C. Heath, Lexington, Mass., 1977, pp. 157–60.

be the cause of delinquency among their low-IQ children.[32] Hirschi and Hindelang also believe that IQ measures innate ability, but argue that IQ influences delinquency through its effect on school performance. That would imply that low IQ may be correlated with juvenile delinquency, but not with adult criminality. It is possible that youths who perform poorly in schools become truants, have more time on their hands for vandalism, and drift into criminal activities. On the other hand, it may be that adult criminality requires planning, cunning, knowledge, even abstract reasoning, to a far greater extent than do juvenile depredations.

Other interpretations based on the assumption that IQ measures innate ability might also be mentioned. For example, it is reasonable to expect that the more foolish and stupid practitioners of crime will be less able to avoid detection than their more clever associates. It is also possible that brighter criminals and delinquents receive more lenient treatment from the police and the courts.[33] Finally, it is also possible that the antisocial actions of persons with generally lower IQs (such as street crimes) are more likely to be defined as crimes and vigorously prosecuted than the antisocial actions of persons with generally higher IQs (such as white-collar crimes).

In an alternate approach it could be argued that IQ does not measure innate ability, but instead measures qualities that are related to the dominant culture. That would hold that IQ tests are culturally biased—that is, the type of information and skills that are required for a child to do well on an IQ test are much more likely to have been acquired by urban, white children than by rural or black children.[34] Jane Mercer illustrated the meaning of cultural bias by constructing a test of simple behavioral tasks related to intelligence, such as being able to tie one's own shoes by the age of seven.[35] The test

32. Gordon, op. cit., p. 269.

33. Hirschi and Hindelang, op. cit., pp. 582–83, argue that there is no empirical support for either of these contentions. But a recent study of 50 delinquents with superior intelligence found that they received more lenient treatment from the courts. See Gavin Tennent and Dennis Gath, "Bright Delinquents: A Three Year Follow-up Study," *British Journal of Criminology*, 15(4):386–90 (1975).

34. In order to demonstrate this bias, mock IQ tests have been constructed that are explicitly biased in favor of, rather than against, these groups. For a test favoring rural children, see M. E. Shimberg, "An Investigation into the Validity of Norms with Special Reference to Urban and Rural Groups," *Archives of Psychology*, 104 (1929). Some questions from this test are reprinted in Loehlin et al., op. cit., p. 67. For a test favoring black children, see Adrian Dove, "The Chitling Test of Intelligence," partially reprinted in Ehrlich and Feldman, op. cit., pp. 72–73.

35. Jane Mercer, "IQ: The Lethal Label," *Psychology Today*, Sept. 1972, pp. 44–47ff. For a critique of Mercer, see Robert A. Gordon, "Examining Labelling Theory: The Case of Mental Retardation," in Walter R. Gove, ed., *The Labelling of Deviance: Evaluating a Perspective*, Halsted-Wiley, New York, 1975, pp. 35–81.

was given to samples of lower-class blacks and Chicanos, and middle-class whites, all of whom had IQs below 70. Of the blacks, 91 percent were able to pass the test, of the Chicanos, 61 percent passed, whereas none of the whites did. This would indicate that many blacks and Chicanos may be more intelligent than would appear from their IQ scores.

Another approach would be to argue that IQ measures general abilities, but that those abilities are largely determined by the person's environment. Simons severely criticized Hirschi and Hindelang's interpretation of the relationship between IQ and delinquency by citing this literature.[36] He argued that a review of studies of twins raised apart revealed that IQs were different for twins raised in dissimilar environments.[37] That suggests that the environment has a substantial impact on IQ. Simons also cited a number of studies that reported IQ gains averaging about 15 points when low-IQ, lower-class children were placed in special classes, where most of those gains were produced in about one year's time. Hirschi and Hindelang had reported an average gap of only 8 points between delinquents and nondelinquents. Simons concluded that IQ is best viewed as "a broad set of verbal and problem-solving skills which are better labeled academic aptitude or scholastic readiness." He pointed out that the questions on standard verbal intelligence tests are virtually indistinguishable from those on reading comprehension tests, and that the score distributions from the two types of tests are virtually identical. He also cited a study that showed that children in the early grades of lower-class black schools and of middle-class black schools had similar reading comprehension test scores, but by the eighth grade there were large differences between the two groups. That suggests that the lower-class children's interactions with their schools stagnated their growth, and that they were not mentally inferior to begin with. Finally, Simons pointed out that delinquents are almost always described as unmotivated students, and asked why anyone would think that these students would be motivated to perform to the best of their ability on the day the IQ tests are administered when they are not motivated to do so on any other school day.

An argument can also be made against the genetic basis of IQ as an explanation of delinquency by considering the history of the dominant delinquent groups. In their monumental study of delinquency

36. Ronald L. Simons, "The Meaning of the IQ-Delinquency Relationship," *American Sociological Review* 43: 268–70 (April 1978).

37. The study was Urie Bronfenbrenner, "Nature with Nurture: A Reinterpretation of the Evidence," in Montagu, *Race and IQ*, pp. 114–44.

in Chicago,[38] Clifford Shaw and Henry McKay found that, in successive waves of immigration,

one European ethnic group after another moved into the areas of first settlement, which were for the most part inner-city areas, where their children became delinquent in large numbers. As these groups became assimilated and moved out of the inner-city areas, their descendants disappeared from the Juvenile Court and their place was taken by offenders from the groups which took over the areas which had been vacated. . . . During the first decades of this century a large proportion of the offenders were the children of German or Irish immigrants. Thirty years later a large proportion of the offenders were the children of the Polish and Italian immigrants who replaced the German and the Irish in the inner-city areas. . . . More recently large segments of the second- and third-generation Polish and Italian population have been moving out from the inner-city areas and are being replaced by Spanish-speaking peoples and some of the new Negro and white migrants from the South.

If blacks and Hispanics are merely the latest in a long line of ethnic groups whose children have been overrepresented in the juvenile courts, then it seems unlikely that the apparently higher delinquency rates are due to any genetically determined inferiority, whether in IQ or anything else. It is interesting to note that other attempts have been made to identify as racially inferior those groups whose children had high delinquency rates. This practice goes back at least as far as the 1820s, when delinquency in New York was seen primarily as the result of inferior racial stock of the Irish.[39] After IQ tests were developed at the beginning of this century, they were used in an attempt to demonstrate the racial inferiority of the Southern and Eastern European peoples who were then immigrating to the United States. For example, in six separate studies Italian-American children were found to have a median IQ of 84, or 16 points below the U.S. average; this is almost identical to the median IQ of black children today.[40] As a result of these and other similar studies the Johnson-Lodge Immigration Act of 1924 was passed, with the ex-

38. Clifford R. Shaw and Henry D. McKay, *Juvenile Delinquency and Urban Areas*, University of Chicago Press, Chicago, 1969, pp. 374–75.

39. Harold Finestone, *Victims of Change*, Greenwood Press, Westport, Ct., 1976, pp. 17–36.

40. R. Pinter, *Intelligence Testing: Methods and Results*, Holt, New York, 1923, cited in Ehrlich and Feldman, op cit., pp. 50–51. Of course, in 1923 mental age was still being used in IQ testing, and the various newer and more sophisticated testing techniques had not yet been developed, but this does not affect the point made above, that IQ has long been used in the United States to demonstrate racial inferiority.

plicit intention of limiting the immigration of these "biologically inferior" people.[41]

Thus the use of IQ tests in the attempt to demonstrate the genetic
inferiority of certain groups is nothing new. The current studies will
require reinterpretation if black and Hispanic peoples, like their immigrant predecessors, are eventually assimilated into the nation's
population and their children are no longer overrepresented in the
juvenile courts. The most that can be said at the present time is that
IQ tests have functioned, since their development, as a somewhat
accurate predictor of delinquency. Youths who did poorly on these
tests have had higher probabilities of becoming delinquent. But
whether delinquents are actually less intelligent than nondelinquents is not at all clear.

Certainly adult criminals are not severely or mildly retarded; they
are not feebleminded. Some adult criminals no doubt have low IQs,
but as an explanation of crime in general "low intelligence" has a
number of problems. It does not account for fluctuations in crime
rates in the population at large or within a specific group, and it fails
to take into account white-collar crime, organized crime (particularly
its leadership), and political crime, all of which require considerable
intellectual ability.

If there is no significantly large proportion of criminal feeble-minded
or of criminals with excessively low intelligence, then we must look
for other factors for a general explanation of criminality. Some of these
other factors that may affect criminality and may be relevant in the
formulation of criminological theories will be discussed in later chapters.


RECOMMENDED READINGS

Jane Mercer, "IQ: The Lethal Label," *Psychology Today*, Sept. 1972, pp. 44–47ff.
A discussion of the meaning of cultural bias on IQ tests.

Robert Gordon, "Prevalence: The Rare Datum in Delinquency Measurement and
Its Implications for the Theory of Delinquency," in Malcolm W. Klein, ed., *The
Juvenile Justice System*, Sage, Beverly Hills, Cal., 1976, pp. 201–84. Differences
in IQ are said to explain differences in crime rates between racial groups.

Travis Hirschi and Michael J. Hindelang, "Intelligence and Delinquency: A Revisionist Review," *American Sociological Review* 42: 571–87 (Aug. 1977). A review of
current literature arguing the importance of intelligence in the causation of delinquency.

41. Leo J. Kamin, "The Politics of IQ," in Houts, op. cit., p. 60. This article contains a good
discussion of this way of thinking.

Ronald L. Simons, "The Meaning of the IQ–Delinquency Relationship," *American Sociological Review* 43: 268–70 (April 1978). Hirschi and Hindelang are all wet.

Scott Menard and Barbara J. Morse, "A Structuralist Critique of the IQ–Delinquency Hypothesis: Theory and Evidence," *American Journal of Sociology* 89 (6): 1347–78 (May 1984). IQ exerts no causal influence on delinquent behavior but is a criterion used for differential treatment in certain institutional settings.

Edward Sagarin, ed., *Taboos in Criminology*, Sage, Beverly Hills, Cal., 1980. Several articles and responses on the subject of IQ, race, and delinquency, within the context of a discussion of values and science.

Stephen Jay Gould, *The Mismeasure of Man*, Norton, New York, 1981. Chapters 5 and 6 present a history of intelligence testing, including discussions of Binet, Goddard, Terman, Burt, and Jensen. Gould demonstrates how IQ tests have been diverted from Binet's purpose of helping slow students, and have been used instead to justify racism and inequality.

Susan L. Farber, *Identical Twins Raised Apart: A Reanalysis*, Basic Books, New York, 1981. Reviews all Western, nonfraudulent cases of identical twins raised apart. See especially Chapter 7 on IQ, as well as Appendix E, which reproduces available IQ data.

CHAPTER SIX

# Biological Factors
# and Criminal Behavior

The theories covered in the last two chapters were based in part on the idea that criminal behavior might be related to the physical and biological properties of the individual. This chapter focuses directly on the role that biological factors play in the origins of criminal behavior, independent of any association with physical appearance or mental deficiency. Some of these biological factors can be described as hereditary, the result of the genes the individual receives from his or her parents. Others may be the result of genetic mutations that occur at the time of conception or may develop while the fetus is in the uterus. Still others may occur after birth as the result of factors such as injury or inadequate diet.[1]

Early biological theories took the view that structure determines function—that is, individuals behave differently because of the fundamental fact that they are somehow structurally different. Presumably, if there could be complete observations or measurements, all differences between individuals would reduce to some kind of biological difference, and all differences in behavior would be due to some kind of structural difference. These theories tended to focus heavily on inherited factors and to ignore other biological factors.

Modern biological theories, in contrast, generally argue that the presence of certain biological factors increases the likelihood that an individual will engage in criminal behaviors but does not determine that he or she will do so. Criminal behaviors can be fully understood

1. Saleem A. Shah and Loren H. Roth, "Biological and Psychophysiological Factors in Criminality," in Daniel Glaser, ed., *Handbook of Criminology*, Rand McNally, Chicago, 1974, pp. 103–6.

only by considering the interaction between the person's biology and his or her environment. Thus these theories are more appropriately described as *biosocial* theories. The present chapter will examine both older and more recent theories focusing on biological factors as part of the explanation of criminal behavior.

## 1. CRIME AS A HEREDITARY DEFECT

Explanations of human behavior in terms of heredity go far back in antiquity and are based on the commonsense observation that children tend to resemble their parents in appearance, mannerisms, and disposition. Scientific theories of heredity originated around 1850 and were more extensively worked out over the next 50 or 75 years.[2] In connection with the development of the theory of heredity, new statistical methods were devised by Francis Galton and his students (notably Karl Pearson) to measure degrees of resemblance or correlation. Charles Goring[3] used these new statistical techniques in the analysis of criminality, arriving at the conclusion that crime was inherited in much the same way as are ordinary physical traits and features.

Goring assumed that the seriousness of criminality could be measured by the frequency and length of imprisonments.[4] He therefore attempted to find out what physical, mental, and moral factors were correlated with that measure. Goring found that serious criminals (those with frequent and lengthy imprisonments) were physically smaller than other people and were mentally inferior.[5] Although there could be an environmental component to these factors, Goring believed that they both were primarily inherited characteristics.

Goring also found that there were high correlations between the

2. A review of the development of theories of heredity can be found in most textbooks on genetics. See, for example, Eldon J. Gardner and D. Peter Snustad, *Principles of Genetics*, 7th ed., John Wiley, New York, 1984.

3. Charles Goring, *The English Convict*, His Majesty's Stationery Office, London, 1913; reprinted by Patterson Smith, Montclair, N.J., 1972. For discussions of Goring's work, see Thorsten Sellin, "Charles Buckman Goring," *Encyclopedia of the Social Sciences*, Macmillan, New York, 1931, vol. 6, p. 703; Edwin D. Driver, "Charles Buckman Goring," in Hermann Mannheim, ed., *Pioneers in Criminology*, Patterson Smith, Montclair, N.J., 1972, pp. 429–42; and Driver, Introductory Essay in Goring, *The English Convict*, reprint edition, pp. v–xx.

4. Goring treated crime as a strictly legal category, and thus preferred the term *convict* to *criminal*. See Driver, "Charles Buckman Goring," pp. 431–33, and Introductory Essay, pp. ix–x.

5. The fact that no other physical characteristics were associated with criminality was taken as a refutation of Lombroso's theory. See the discussion of Lombroso and Goring in Chapter 4, above.

criminality of one parent and that of the other, between the criminality of parents and that of their children, and between the criminality of brothers. Goring argued that these findings could not be explained by the effect of social and environmental conditions, since he found little or no relationship between the seriousness of criminality and such factors as poverty, nationality, education, birth order, and broken homes. He also argued that these findings could not be explained by the effect of example among people who were closely associated with each other. The criminality of one spouse could not be explained by the example of the other spouse, since most of them were already engaged in crime at the time they got married. The criminality of the children could not be explained by the example of the parents, since the correlation coefficient for stealing (where parents presumably set an example and try to teach their children) was about the same as that for sex crimes (where parents presumably try to conceal the offense). In addition, if criminal parents are removed from the home by imprisonment when the children are young, the children become criminals as frequently, or even more frequently, as children who had reached a more mature age when their criminal parents were removed. In other words, a longer period of contact with a criminal parent did not produce a greater occurrence of criminality among children. Goring therefore concluded that criminality was associated with inherited, but not with environmental, characteristics and recommended that, in order to reduce crime, people with those inherited characteristics not be allowed to reproduce.[6]

There are serious problems with each of Goring's arguments.[7] The most important problem concerns the fact that Goring attempted to establish the effect of heredity by controlling for and eliminating the effect of environment. To accomplish that, it is necessary to have accurate measurements of all the environmental factors involved, which he obviously did not have. Goring dealt with only a few environmental factors, quite imperfectly, and these were roughly measured. Though these particular ones may have shown low correlation with his measure of criminality, other environmental factors might still be very important. By his method of reasoning, the failure to measure environmental influence adequately has the result of overemphasizing the significance of the influence of heredity.

Later studies of the families of criminals have been faced with a similar problem. Ellis reviewed these studies and found remarkably

---

6. Driver, "Charles Buckman Goring," pp. 439–40.

7. See Edwin H. Sutherland and Donald R. Cressey, *Criminology*, 10th ed., Lippincott, Philadelphia, 1978, p. 120.

little evidence for the widespread belief that crime tends to "run in the family."[8] What evidence there is suggests that it is less rampant than is commonly believed.

In spite of these shortcomings, the significance of Goring's work should not be underestimated. Whereas others had argued that crime was caused either by environment or by heredity, Goring was the first to postulate that it might be the result of the interaction between the two, a view that is held by many criminologists today. Although his findings support an emphasis on hereditary factors, Goring did not reject the influence of the environment as a cause of crime. He maintained only that empirical evidence was required to support this view, and that such evidence was not found in his study.[9]

His major contribution, however, was his use of statistical methods in a comparative study of criminals and noncriminals. As Karl Pearson said,[10]

The present writer reckons that one of the chief merits of Goring's work will be that by its very nature it compels those who would controvert it from the scientific side to collect better material and to adopt practically Goring's methods of procedure. They may or may not be successful. Strange as it may seem, the contradiction of his conclusions would be a small matter compared with the fundamental fact that Goring's methods have ploughed deeply the ground, and traced firmly the lines on which the scientific criminologist of the future will be compelled to work.

### 2. THE STUDY OF TWINS

Goring had sought to deal with the problem of the interrelation of heredity and environment by utilizing specialized statistical methods that would eliminate the effect of environmental factors. Another method for dealing with the same problem would be to control the hereditary factor. The study of the relative criminality of twins suggests this possibility, since in genetics there is a clear-cut distinction between identical and fraternal twins. Identical twins are the product of a single fertilized egg and have identical heredity; fraternal twins are the product of two eggs simultaneously fertilized by two sperms, and therefore have the same relation as ordinary siblings. Differences in the behavior of identical twins therefore may not be attributed to differences in heredity, and presumably similarities of behavior could be attributed to their identical inheritance. Ob-

8. Lee Ellis, "Genetics and Criminal Behavior," *Criminology* 20 (1): 43–66 (May 1982).

9. Driver, Introductory Essay, p. xiii.

10. Karl Pearson, Introduction to the Abridged Edition of 1919, in Goring, op. cit., p. xix.

viously this need not be true, since the similarities could be due to similarities in training. But any general tendency to greater similarity of behavior when heredity is identical sets up a strong presumption that the similarity is due to the influence of heredity.

A number of investigators have used this approach in trying to determine the role of heredity in criminality. One of the earlier and more dramatic of these studies was that of the German physiologist Johannes Lange, whose results became generally known with the publication of his famous *Verbrechen als schicksal* in 1929.[11] He found that, in a group of 13 pairs of adult male identical twins, when one twin had a record of imprisonment, the other similarly had been imprisoned in 77 percent of the cases; whereas in a comparable group of 17 pairs of fraternal twins, when one twin had been imprisoned, the other had a prison record in only 12 percent of the cases. In a matched control group of 214 pairs of ordinary brothers of nearest age, when one brother had a prison record, the other brother of the matched pair had a prison record in only 8 percent of the cases. Though the relations suggested are not identical, the implication is nevertheless clear and consistent, and Lange's conclusion is seen in the dramatic title he gave his book, which translates as "crime as destiny."

Even more striking were the results reported in a later American study:[12] In a group of 42 pairs of identical twins, when one had been adjudged a juvenile delinquent, the other was a delinquent in 93 percent of the cases. In a corresponding group of 25 pairs of fraternal twins, when one was a juvenile delinquent, the other was a delinquent in only 20 percent of the cases. In similar studies[13] a variety of results have been reported, though all tend to show greater similarity of criminal behavior among identical than among fraternal twins.

Each of these studies begins with criminals who are known to have twins and determines whether the twins are also criminals. Such a procedure is open to subtle bias, however, since the investigator may attribute criminality in borderline cases only when it is convenient

11. Johannes Lange, *Verbrechen als schicksal: Studien an Kriminellen Zwillingen*, Georg Thieme, Leipzig, 1929. English translation by Charlotte Haldane, as *Crime and Destiny*, Charles Boni, New York, 1930.

12. Horatio H. Newman, Frank H. Freeman, and Karl J. Holzinger, *Twins: A Study of Heredity and Environment*, University of Chicago Press, Chicago, 1937, p. 352; reprinted 1966.

13. See a summary of such studies in Juan B. Cortes, *Delinquency and Crime*, Seminar Press, New York, 1972, pp. 31–35; David Rosenthal, *Genetic Theory and Abnormal Behavior*, McGraw-Hill, New York, 1970, pp. 225–36; and Karl O. Christiansen, "A Review of Studies of Criminality Among Twins," in Sarnoff Mednick and Karl O. Christiansen, eds., *Biosocial Bases of Criminal Behavior*, Gardner Press, New York, 1977, pp. 45–88.

to do so.[14] To avoid the possibility of bias Christiansen used the official *Twins Register* of Denmark to study all twins born in the Danish Islands between 1881 and 1910 when both twins lived at least until the age of 15.[15] They totaled about 6000 pairs. He then used the official *Penal Register* to determine whether either twin, or both, had been found criminal or delinquent. He found 67 cases in which at least one of a pair of male identical twins was registered as a criminal, and in 24 of these cases (35.8 percent) the other twin was also registered. For male fraternal twins he found this to be true in only 14 out of 114 cases (12.3 percent). For females he found criminal concordance in 3 out of 14 cases of identical twins (21.4 percent) and in 1 out of 23 cases of fraternal twins (4.3 percent). Christiansen later demonstrated that concordance was higher for more serious criminality than for less serious.[16]

The principal difficulty with this method is that the greater similarity of behavior noted in the case of the identical twins may be due to the greater similarity of training and environmental experience just as well as to their identical hereditary makeup. There is no certain way of separating environment and heredity as contributing factors in this situation. Referring to his own study, Christiansen pointed out:[17]

Nothing in these results, however, can be interpreted as indicating that a higher twin coefficient in [identical] than in [fraternal] twins, or in pairs with more serious than in pairs with less serious forms of criminality, is due to what Lange called the quite preponderant part played by heredity in the causation of crime.

Dalgaard and Kringlen went even farther in their study of 139 pairs of male Norwegian twins.[18] They found a criminal concordance rate

14. Sutherland found this bias in a study by Rosanoff, who had concluded that there was three times as much criminal concordance among identical twins as among fraternal twins. Sutherland pointed out that all of the "fraternal" delinquents had been brought before the juvenile court, but that 9 of the 29 "identical" delinquents had not. If these 9 were omitted, then the concordance rates for fraternal and identical twins were approximately the same. Sutherland and Cressey, op. cit., p. 116.

15. K.O. Christiansen, "Threshold of Tolerance in Various Population Groups Illustrated by Results from the Danish Criminologic Twin Study," in A. V. S. de Reuck and R. Porter, eds., *The Mentally Abnormal Offender*, Little, Brown, Boston, 1968.

16. K. O. Christiansen, "Seriousness of Criminality and Concordance among Danish Twins," in Roger Hood, ed., *Crime, Criminology, and Public Policy*, The Free Press, New York, 1974.

17. Ibid, p. 77. For the opposite view, see Saleem A. Shah and Loren H. Roth, "Biological and Psychophysiological Factors in Criminality," in Daniel Glaser, ed., *Handbook of Criminology*, Rand McNally, Chicago, 1974, pp. 133–34.

18. Steffen Odd Dalgaard and Einar Kringlen, "A Norwegian Twin Study of Criminality," *British Journal of Criminology* 16: 213–32 (1976). For a criticism of this study, see R. A. Forde, "Twin Studies, Inheritance and Criminality," *British Journal of Criminology* 18 (1): 71–74 (Jan. 1978).

of 25.8 percent for identical twins, but only 14.9 percent for fraternal twins. However, they suggested that the higher rate for identical twins might be due to the similarity of their upbringing. When the twins were grouped according to their mutual closeness, all differences between identical and fraternal twins disappeared. They concluded that "the significance of hereditary factors in registered crime is non-existent."

### 3. THE STUDY OF ADOPTEES

Another method for determining the effects of heredity on criminality is to study the records of adoptees. The first such study was carried out by Schulsinger[19] in a study of psychopathy, which he defined as a consistent pattern of impulse-ridden or acting-out behavior lasting beyond the age of 19 years. Here 57 psychopathic adoptees were selected and matched with 57 nonpsychopathic adoptees on the basis of age, sex, age at transfer to adoptive homes, and social class of adoptive parents. Hospital records were then searched, and it was determined that 14.4 percent of the biological relatives of the psychopathic adoptees had suffered from disorders related to psychopathy, such as alcoholism, drug abuse, or criminality. That compared to only 6.7 percent of the biological relatives of the nonpsychopathic adoptees.

Crowe studied the children of 41 female criminal offenders in Iowa who had given their babies up for adoption during the years 1925 to 1956.[20] These 52 adopted babies were matched with a control group on the basis of age, sex, race, and approximate age at the time of the adoptive decree. The records of the state of Iowa were then searched, and it was found that 8 of the 52 children of the offenders had been arrested, with a total of 18 arrests among them, 7 had been convicted, and 5 incarcerated for a total of 3½ years. In contrast only 2 of the 52 children of the control group had been arrested, each only once, and only one was convicted. None had been incarcerated.

In a more recent study Hutchings and Mednick[21] examined the records of all nonfamilial male adoptions in Copenhagen in which the adoptee had been born between 1927 and 1941. Of these adoptees

19. Fini Schulsinger, "Psychopathy: Heredity and Environment," *International Journal of Mental Health* 1: 190–206 (1972); reprinted in Mednick and Christiansen, op. cit., pp. 109–25.

20. Raymond R. Crowe, "The Adopted Offspring of Women Criminal Offenders," *Archives of General Psychiatry* 27 (5): 600–603 (Nov. 1972).

21. Barry Hutchings and Sarnoff A. Mednick, "Criminality in Adoptees and Their Adoptive and Biological Parents: A Pilot Study," in Mednick and Christiansen, op. cit., pp. 127–41.

TABLE 6–1  Distribution of the Criminality of the Adoptees according to the
Criminality of the Adoptive and Biological Fathers (N = 965)

| Biological Father | Adoptive Father | Percent Adoptees Criminal | N |
|---|---|---|---|
| Not registered | Not registered | 10.5 | 333 |
| | Minor offender only | 13.3 | 83 |
| | Criminal offense | 11.5 | 52 |
| Minor offender only | Not registered | 16.5 | 103 |
| | Minor offender only | 10.0 | 30 |
| | Criminal offense | 41.1 | 17 |
| Criminal offense | Not registered | 22.0 | 219 |
| | Minor offender | 18.6 | 70 |
| | Criminal offense | 36.2 | 58 |

36.4 percent had biological fathers with criminal records.[22] The authors then grouped the boys according to their own criminal records. Of the boys who had no criminal record, only 31.1 percent had biological fathers with criminal records, whereas 37.7 percent of the boys with minor offenses and 48.8 percent of the boys with criminal records had biological fathers with criminal records.[23] These figures indicate that criminality is more likely to occur in an adopted boy when the biological father has a criminal record.

Next, the biological and adoptive fathers of the adoptees were grouped according to their criminal records, and the percentage of sons who had criminal records was determined for each group of fathers. Table 6-1[24] shows the results of this investigation. This table indicates an interactive effect between the criminality of the biological and the adoptive father. When only one is criminal, the effect is not as significant as when both are criminal. In addition, the effect of the criminality of the adoptive father is not as great as the effect of criminality of the biological father.[25]

22. Computation from ibid., p. 131, Table 4.

23. Ibid., p. 131, Table 4.

24. Hutchings and Mednick, op. cit., p. 132, Table 6. See also ibid., p. 137, Table 8. Reprinted by permission of the publisher.

25. Similar findings were reported in a later study based on all adoptions in Denmark between 1924 and 1947. This study also found that the associations between criminality in biological parents and adoptive children were highest for chronic offenders. See Sarnoff A. Mednick, William F. Gabrielli, Jr., and Barry Hutchings, "Genetic Influences in Criminal Behavior: Evidence from an Adoption Cohort," *Science* 224: 891–94 (May 1984). See also William F.

Hutchings and Mednick then selected all the criminal adoptees whose fathers (both biological and adoptive) had been born after 1889, in order to maximize the reliability of police records. The 143 adoptees who met this criterion were matched with 143 noncriminal adoptees on the basis of age and occupational status of adoptive fathers. The criminal adoptees were found to have a higher percentage of criminal adoptive fathers (23 percent vs. 9.8 percent), of criminal biological fathers (49 percent vs. 28 percent), and of criminal biological mothers (18 percent vs. 7 percent).[26]

The authors acknowledged that the basic limitation on adoption studies is that the adopting agency may attempt to match the adoptive home with that of the biological parents, and that this in fact occurred with a large number of the adoptions in their study.[27] Through the use of multiple regression analysis, however, they found that the criminality of the biological father continued to have an effect even when the effects of the adoptive father had been removed.[28]

The authors conclude that "it is not intended here to postulate a simple genetic model for criminality." But they point out that it would not be inconsistent with modern genetics to argue that such differences as were found in this study reflected basic genetic factors. They also speculate that criminality may be related to "a cumulative genetic disadvantage. Some individuals, because of their genetic endowment, find themselves physically and psychologically in a position in society in which they are more likely than their more fortunate fellow members to succumb to crime."[29]

4. XYY CHROMOSOMAL COMPLEMENT

The studies of twins and adoptees, as well as Goring's earlier study of family resemblances, examine whether crime might be related to inherited, genetic characteristics. It is also possible to examine whether crime might be related to uninherited genetic characteristics, those due to mutations at the time of conception. The XYY

Gabrielli, Jr., and Sarnoff A. Mednick, "Urban Environment, Genetics, and Crime," *Criminology* 22 (4): 645–52 (Nov. 1984) and William F. Gabrielli, Jr., and Sarnoff A. Mednick, "Genetic Correlates of Criminal Behavior: Implications for Research, Attribution, and Prevention," *American Behavioral Scientist* 27 (1): 59–74 (1983).

26. Hutchings and Mednick, op. cit., p. 134.

27. Ibid., p. 140.

28. Ibid., pp. 138–39.

29. Ibid., p. 140.

chromosomal complement is one such genetic characteristic that has stimulated a great deal of research about whether it is associated with criminal behavior.

Chromosomes are complex structures in the nuclei of plant and animal cells that determine the particular characteristics of the organism. Every cell of the normal human contains 23 pairs of chromosomes, for a total of 46. One pair of these are the sex chromosomes, which determine the primary and secondary sexual characteristics of the individual. In the normal female these chromosomes are of similar size and are referred to as XX, after their shape. One of the two sex chromosomes of the normal male, however, is smaller and of a different shape, so that the male sex chromosomes are referred to as XY. At conception an ovum and a sperm, each containing 23 chromosomes, unite to form a single cell, which will then develop into the embryo. At times an abnormal cell division occurs before conception, so that the sperm or the ovum contains more than one sex chromosome. The resulting embryo will then have an unusual number of sex chromosomes.

The first of these sex chromosome abnormalities to be investigated was that of the XXY individual (Klinefelter's syndrome). Although the findings are widely disputed, Klinefelter's syndrome is reported to be associated with degeneration of the testes and sterility, breast enlargement, and moderate mental retardation. It has also been linked with alcoholism and homosexuality, and with overrepresentation in institutions for the subnormal.

Interest in the possibility of chromosomal abnormalities in other institutionalized persons led to an investigation of prisoners. Since the presence of the Y chromosome determines maleness, it was hypothesized that a person with an extra Y chromosome (XYY) might be a "supermale" and, as such, be more aggressive and inclined to criminality. Patricia Jacobs did the first study to test this hypothesis in a maximum security mental hospital in Scotland.[30] Her preliminary report showed that 12 of the 196 men on the subnormal wing of the hospital had chromosomal abnormalities, including 7 with the XYY abnormality. Another 2 XYY males were found among the 119 men on the wing for the mentally ill.[31] This finding was statistically significant, since estimates for the rate of XYY abnormalities in the general population are usually no more than 1.5 per 1000.

30. P. A. Jacobs, M. Brunton, and M. M. Melville, "Aggressive Behavior, Mental Subnormalty and the XYY Male," *Nature* 208: 1351–52 (Dec. 1965).

31. W. H. Price, J. A. Strong, P. B. Whatmore, and W. R. McClemont, "Criminal Patients with XYY Sex-Chromosome Complement," *The Lancet* 1:565–566 (Mar. 1966).

The outstanding physical characteristic of these men was that they were exceptionally tall, their mean height being 6 ft., 1 in., whereas the mean height of the other patients was 5 ft., 7 in. In many subsequent research projects on the XYY syndrome, therefore, the subjects were screened on the basis of height, and only taller men were tested. The only other characteristic that clearly has been shown to be associated with the abnormality is an increased tendency to be institutionalized. Originally it was thought that this tendency reflected an increased propensity to violence or other forms of crime. Jacobs and her colleagues, for example, described XYY males as having "dangerous, violent or criminal propensities."[32] This description was reinforced by a number of spectacular crimes committed by persons who were later found to have the XYY characteristic.[33] Further studies, however, showed that XYY inmates were considerably less violent than other inmates. For example, the criminal records of the original group of 9 XYY inmates at the Scottish maximum security hospital were compared with a control group of 18 chromosomally normal inmates at the same institution.[34] The control group not only had a higher average number of criminal convictions, but 21.9 percent of their convictions were for offenses against the person, as compared to only 8.7 percent of the convictions of the XYY group. Based on this and other studies, Sarbin and Miller have concluded:[35]

Contrary to the expectations generated by popular reports and mass media, the studies done thus far are largely in agreement and demonstrate rather conclusively that males of the XYY type are not predictably aggressive. If anything, as a group they are somewhat less aggressive than comparable XY's.

It might be mentioned here that no researcher has maintained that all persons with an XYY chromosomal abnormality will become criminals. All that has been argued is that the XYY male has an increased risk of developing an antisocial personality, compared to the XY male. This has been supported by the location of a significant number of noncriminal XYY males in the general population.

32. Jacobs et al., op. cit., p. 1351.

33. For a discussion of these crimes, see Richard S. Fox, "The XYY Offender: A Modern Myth?" *The Journal of Criminal Law, Criminology and Police Science* 62: 59–73 (Mar. 1971).

34. W. H. Price and P. B. Whatmore, "Behavior Disorders and Pattern of Crime among XYY Males Identified at a Maximum Security Hospital," *British Medical Journal* 1:533 (1967).

35. T. R. Sarbin and J. E. Miller, "Demonism Revisited: The XYY Chromosomal Anomaly," *Issues in Criminology* 5 (2): 199 (Summer 1970).

Several explanations have been offered to explain the high rates of institutionalization among XYY males. Hunter[36] has pointed out that

it might be that because of their great height and build they would present such a frightening picture that the courts and psychiatrists would be biased to direct them to special hospitals for community safety. The bias might be further aggravated by the associated intellectual abnormality.

Thus speculation would seem to be supported by the fact that XYY males generally have less serious records than other comparable institutionalized males. In addition, XYY males tend to be more concentrated in juvenile and mental institutions, where they are "likely to be confined . . . for a wider range of behavior than would normally be seen as justifying strict imprisonment."[37] Kessler and Moos have suggested that chromosomal abnormalities may occur more frequently in lower-class families because of difficult living conditions. If this were the case, the higher rates of chromosomal abnormalities in institutions might only reflect the predominance of lower-class individuals there.[38]

An attempt to resolve these questions was undertaken by Witken and his associates, who obtained blood samples from over 4,000 men born in Copenhagen between 1944 and 1947 and who were at least 184 centimeters in height (approximately 6 feet).[39] They discovered 12 XYY and 16 XXY men in this group. Five of the 12 XYY's (41 percent) had been convicted of one or more criminal offenses, as compared to 3 of the 16 XXY's (19 percent) and 9.3 percent of the normal XY's. However, almost all of the crimes committed by the XYY's were petty property offenses, and neither they nor the XXY's were significantly more likely to commit crimes against the person than the normal XY's. Witkin found no support for the speculation that height or social class might be the reason for the overrepresentation of XYY's in institutions, but he did find evidence to support the view that low intellectual functioning might be involved. He concluded that, because these men are not particularly aggressive, there was no reason to continue attempting to identify them.

36. H. Hunter, "YY Chromosomes and Klinefelter's Syndrome," *The Lancet* 1: 984 (Apr. 1966).

37. Fox, op. cit., p. 68.

38. S. Kessler and R. H. Moos, "The XYY Karyotype and Criminality: A Review," *Journal of Psychiatric Research* 7: 164 (Feb. 1970).

39. Herman A. Witkin et al., "XYY and XXY Men: Criminality and Aggression," in Mednick and Christiansen, op. cit., pp. 165–87.

5. BIOCHEMICAL IMBALANCE

Ever since the demonstration, in 1828, by the German chemist
Frederich Wöhler that he could synthesize the organic compound
urea in the laboratory, there has been speculation about the implications of the idea of the human as a chemical being. Around 1850
some of the physiological and psychological effects of the secretions
of the endocrine glands (hormones) began to be identified. Presently
it was found that some of the secretions themselves could be produced synthetically in the laboratory and would have the same effects as those from the natural functioning of the living glands. The
chemistry of endocrine glands began to lend an attractive color to
certain "objective" theories of personality. Implications of hormonal
balance and imbalance became part of the language of biology and
of human physiology.[40] One of the more exciting popular interpretations of this chemical-glandular theory of personality differences
appeared in the writings of Louis Berman.[41]

Inevitably, too, body chemistry and hormonal imbalance became
central concepts in a so-called new criminology based on biochemistry. A textbook in criminology based on this approach appeared in
1928.[42] The argument advanced was that crime is due to emotional
disturbance growing out of hormonal imbalance. Schlapp and Smith's
book was little more than armchair speculation, in which they rea-
soned by analogy to extend some of the findings in biochemistry (e.g.,
threshold of functional activity) to allegations of causation in connection with a few more or less spectacular or bizarre cases.[43]

A somewhat more systematic approach to the problem was taken
by Berman, who performed a "systematic glandular survey, physical
and chemical, with various adjustive special tests of metabolism and
nerve reactions" on a group of 250 Sing Sing criminals compared with
a control group of normal noncriminal males from New York City.
The criminals "showed a frequency of distribution of glandular defects and disturbances that was two to three times as great as that

40. See the early, challenging expositions by Walter B. Cannon, *Bodily Changes in Pain,
Hunger, Fear, and Rage*, D. Appleton, New York, 1915; George W. Crile, *The Origin and
Nature of the Emotions*, Saunders, Philadelphia, 1915, reprinted by Consortium Press, Wil-
mington, Del., 1970; or Charles Darwin, *The Expression of Emotion in Man and Animals*,
University of Chicago Press, Chicago, 1965.

41. Louis Berman, *The Glands Regulating Personality*, Macmillan, New York, 1921; and *New
Creations in Human Beings*, Doubleday, Doran, New York, 1938.

42. Max G. Schlapp and Edward H. Smith, *The New Criminology*, Boni & Liveright, New
York, 1928. This book should not be confused with a more recent, unrelated book of the same
title by Ian Taylor, Paul Walton, and Jock Young, Harper & Row, New York, 1973.

43. Schlapp and Smith, op. cit., pp. 197–98.

found in the control group."[44] A group of juvenile delinquents included in the study exhibited a similar proportion of glandular disturbances in comparison with normal, nondelinquent juveniles.

Berman, however, does not report in detail how his comparisons were made, how his controls were selected, or the statistical findings of the study. More carefully reported research has not supported his conclusions.

A series of carefully conducted and fully reported research studies at the New Jersey State Home for Boys gave mostly negative results when a group of delinquents with endocrine disorders were compared with a group of normal delinquents. That is, if Berman's claims had been substantiated, there should have been characteristic relationships between the type of gland disturbance involved and the behavior problems of the delinquent. The New Jersey studies found no consistent evidence of such relationships, and no particular difference between the delinquencies of those with gland dysfunction as distinguished from those with normal gland function.[45] Also of interest was the fact that, in the judgment of the investigators, there was no excessive proportion of the delinquents with gland dysfunction.[46]

Though there is an obviously logical and observable relation between gland function and normal sexuality, there is, nevertheless, no clear demonstration of any consistent relationship between gland dysfunction and most sex crimes or other sexual aberrations.[47] The problem is enormously complicated by the general absence of good information on what is normal or natural in human sex behavior. That which is forbidden by law is a crime, but this has no necessary relation to the biology, or endocrinology, of sex as such.[48] There does, however, appear to be a relationship between general criminal activity by women offenders and a common minor endocrine disorder,

44. Louis Berman, *New Creations in Human Beings*, Doubleday, Doran, New York, 1938, pp. 248–49.

45. Matthew Molitch, "Endocrine Disturbance in Behavior Problems," *American Journal of Psychiatry*, March 1937, p. 1179.

46. See the series of two articles by Matthew Molitch and Sam Poliakoff, "Subclinical Hypothyroidism in Children," *Endocrinology*, November 1936, p. 820; "Pituitary Disturbances in Behavior Problems," *American Journal of Orthopsychiatry*, January 1936, pp. 125–33.

47. For the influence of the endocrine hormones on sexual behavior, see Shah and Roth, op. cit., pp. 125–33. For general information on biology and the differences between the sexes, see John Money and Anke A. Erhardt, *Man and Woman, Boy and Girl*, Johns Hopkins Press, Baltimore, 1973.

48. This is well documented in the celebrated "Kinsey Reports"—that is, A. C. Kinsey, W. B. Pomeroy, and C. E. Martin, *Sexual Behavior in the Human Male*, Saunders, Philadelphia, 1948; and same authors with Paul H. Gebhard, *Sexual Behavior in the Human Female*, Saunders, Philadelphia, 1953.

caused by unusually wide variations in hormone levels just before or during menstruation; this is known as premenstrual or menstrual tension. Several studies have shown that women commit a disproportionate amount of crime during that time, and exhibit a variety of other behavioral problems.[49] These studies do not suggest that the variations in hormone levels themselves cause crime, but only that the disorder may be a contributing factor, along with a number of other factors. There also seems to be a relationship between testosterone, the male sex hormone, and increased levels of aggressiveness in males.[50] The increased aggressiveness in boys seems to begin at a very early age, prior to when imitation of same-sex adults would be possible. A number of studies have also found that more violent males have higher levels of testosterone in their system.[51] Differences in testosterone level may account for at least some of the differences in crime rates between males and females.

Most of the research linking gland activity, personality, and behavior problems is based on observations about relatively spectacular changes achieved in particular cases through treatment with hormones. While these cases make very interesting reading, researchers have not demonstrated any systematic connection between crime and hormone imbalance. Consequently, with the exception of the sex hormones discussed above, endocrine hormones today are generally not considered to have any direct relationship to criminal behavior.[52]

Biochemical imbalances in the body may also arise because of an inadequate or improper diet. A number of studies have maintained that delinquents and criminals suffer from vitamin deficiencies, cerebral allergies, or hypoglycemia (low blood sugar).[53] However, like the earlier studies of hormone imbalance, much of this research is based on case histories, with reports of spectacular changes in behavior attributed to changes in the person's diet. These case histories make very interesting reading, but they do not tell us the extent to which nutritional conditions are related to criminal and delin-

---

49. These studies are reviewed in Shah and Roth, op. cit., pp. 124–25.

50. E. E. Maccoby and C. N. Jacklin, "Sex Differences in Aggression," *Child Development* 51:964–80 (1980).

51. Ibid.

52. Shah and Roth, op. cit., p. 122.

53. Leonard J. Hippchen, ed., *Ecologic-Biochemical Approaches to the Treatment of Delinquents and Criminals*, Van Nostrand Reinhold, New York, 1978; Hippchen, ed., *Holistic Approaches to Offender Rehabilitation*, C. C. Thomas, Springfield, Ill., 1982. Hypoglycemia is also discussed in Shah and Roth, op. cit., pp. 125–26; and Mednick et al., "Biology and Violence," pp. 63–64.

quent behavior, or the extent to which those behaviors can be reduced through nutritional therapy. Programs using nutritional therapies may report positive results but generally do not include carefully controlled statistical measures. Proponents argue that these programs offer great promise for the future treatment of criminals and delinquents, but at the present time it is not possible to conclude one way or the other.

## 6. CENTRAL NERVOUS SYSTEM FUNCTIONING

The central nervous system is located in the brain and spinal column and is involved in conscious thought and voluntary motor activities. Electrochemical processes in the brain can be detected through the scalp with an instrument called an electroencephalograph (EEG). Abnormal brain wave patterns recorded by this instrument are thought to be associated with various abnormal behavior patterns in individuals. A large number of studies have been done, beginning in the early 1940s, to determine whether criminal populations have an excess of abnormal patterns. These studies have generally found that between 25 and 50 percent of criminal groups have EEG abnormalities, whereas studies of noncriminal populations generally find between 5 and 20 percent have EEG abnormalities.[54] The differences are even greater for repeatedly violent offenders.

Most of these studies have found that offenders are characterized by an excessive amount of slow brain wave activity, although others have found an excessive amount of fast activity. Since slow brain wave activity is characteristic of younger children, some researchers have speculated that delinquents and criminals are characterized by slow brain development. Others, however, have argued that delinquents and criminals have a low level of cortical stimulation, and tend to be drowsy in the rather dull experimental setting.

In order to test these controversies Mednick and his colleagues recorded the EEGs of a group of 10- to 13-year-old Danish boys who had not committed any delinquent acts.[55] Six years later official records were checked and the EEGs of boys who later committed delinquent acts were compared with the EEGs of boys who did not. They found an excessive amount of slow brain wave activity, but no

54. These studies are reviewed in Sarnoff A. Mednick et al., "Biology and Violence," in Marvin E. Wolfgang and Neil Alan Weiner, eds., *Criminal Violence*, Sage, Beverly Hills, Cal., 1982, pp. 46–52.

55. Sarnoff A. Mednick, Jan Volavka, William F. Gabrielli, Jr., and Turan M. Itil, "EEG as a Predictor of Antisocial Behavior," *Criminology* 19 (2): 219–29 (Aug. 1981).

excessive amount of fast activity, among the delinquent group. Because of the pattern of the brain activity, Mednick maintained that the data did not support the theory of brain immaturity, but rather supported a theory of low cortical stimulation.

A second area of central nervous system functioning that has been widely studied with respect to its effect on criminal behavior is epilepsy. The general public may associate epilepsy with criminality because a person having a *grand mal* seizure may appear to be violent and out of control. In addition, epileptics have been reported in a number of studies to be overrepresented in prisons. Recent research indicates, however, that violence during seizures is a most unlikely event and rarely, if ever, occurs,[56] and that at least some of the reported overrepresentation in prisons is due to very doubtful claims made at plea bargaining as a way of suggesting diminished responsibility for the crime.[57] More scientific attention has been focused on the relationship between criminal behaviors and a milder form of epilepsy known as temporal lobe epilepsy or psychomotor seizures. Persons having these seizures do not lose consciousness or fall to the ground; rather, they may behave in a somewhat mechanical fashion and experience emotions such as fear and anxiety. The evidence on the association between this form of epilepsy and criminal behavior is very unclear and has been interpreted both in support of and against it.[58]

A third area of central nervous system function that may be related to criminal behavior includes various forms of brain damage or dysfunction.[59] Such damage can be detected by medical tests such as X rays, CAT scans, and spinal taps. A variety of studies have found that prisoners and violent patients suffer from an excessive number of brain dysfunctions, particularly in the frontal and temporal lobe regions. They also report a large number of head injuries involving loss of consciousness. Mednick found some support for a relationship between brain damage and violent behavior among juveniles in a study

---

56. Antonio Delgado-Escueta et al., "Special Report: The Nature of Aggression During Epileptic Seizures," *New England Journal of Medicine* 305 (12): 711–716 (1981). See also Dietrich Blumer, "Epilepsy and Violence," in Denis J. Madden and John R. Lion, eds., *Rage, Hate, Assault, and Other Forms of Violence*, Spectrum, New York, 1976, pp. 207–21.

57. M. J. Oliver, "Epilepsy, Crime and Delinquency, A Sociological Account," *Sociology* 14 (3): 417–40 (1980).

58. Mednick et al., "Biology and Violence," pp. 49–50. See also the discussion in Shah and Roth, op. cit., pp. 117–22; and Vernon H. Mark and Frank R. Ervin, *Violence and the Brain*, Harper & Row, New York, 1970.

59. Mednick et al., "Biology and Violence," pp. 52–58.

of children born at a hospital in Copenhagen between 1959 and 1961.[60] Those who later became violent delinquents had generally good medical, physical, and neurological reports during pregnancy and delivery, despite relatively poor social conditions. However, they had significantly worse physical and neurological status at one year of age. Similar findings were reported by Dorothy Lewis and her colleagues.[61] Lewis also found a strong association between parental criminality and the presence of serious medical problems in their children. She suggested that delinquency among children with criminal parents may reflect the combined physical and psychological effects of parental neglect and battering, rather than any genetic factors.[62]

## 7. LEARNING DISABILITIES

One type of central nervous system dysfunction that has been the subject of a considerable amount of recent research is the so-called learning disability.[63] This disability is thought to be a type of minimal brain dysfunction among otherwise normal and intelligent children who are unable to learn in a normal classroom setting. The National Advisory Committee on Handicapped Children has issued the following definition:[64]

Children with special learning disabilities exhibit a disorder in one or more of the basic psychological processes involved in understanding or using spoken or written languages. These may be manifested in disorders of listening, thinking, talking, reading, writing, spelling, or arithmetic. They include conditions which have been referred to as perceptual handicaps, brain

60. Ibid., p. 55

61. Dorothy Otnow Lewis et al., "Perinatal Difficulties, Head and Face Trauma, and Child Abuse in the Medical Histories of Seriously Delinquent Children," *American Journal of Psychiatry* 136 (4): 419–23 (April 1979). See also Lewis et al., "Violent Juvenile Delinquents: Psychiatric, Neurological, Psychological, and Abuse Factors," *Journal of the American Academy of Child Psychiatry* 18 (2): 307–19 (1979); and Lewis, ed., *Vulnerabilities to Delinquency*, Spectrum, New York, 1981.

62. Dorothy Otnow Lewis et al., "Parental Criminality and Medical Histories of Delinquent Children," *American Journal of Psychiatry* 136 (3): 288–92 (March 1979).

63. For a general discussion of learning disabilities, see H. Myklebust, "Learning Disabilities: Definitions and Overview" in H. R. Myklebust, ed., *Progress in Learning Disabilities*, vol. I, Grune & Stratton, New York, 1968. See also articles in *Journal of Learning Disabilities*, and in R. E. Weber, ed., *Handbook of Learning Disabilites*, Prentice-Hall, Englewood Cliffs, N.J., 1974.

64. National Advisory Committee on Handicapped Children, *Special Education for Handicapped Children, First Annual Report*, U.S. Government Printing Office, Washington, D.C., 1968, p. 4.

injury, minimal brain dysfunction, dyslexia, developmental aphasia, etc. They do not include learning problems which are due primarily to visual, hearing, or motor handicaps, to mental retardation, emotional disturbance, or to environmental disadvantage.

There has been considerable speculation that delinquents are disproportionately afflicted with learning disabilities, since a great many of them have severe learning problems in school. In order to determine whether learning disabilities and delinquency are related, the Law Enforcement Assistance Adminstration commissioned a research agency to review the literature and to make policy recommendations based on what was found.[65]

Theoretically, learning disabilities could be related to delinquency either through a biological or a social chain of events.[66] Those who argue for the biological link hold that children with learning disabilities are generally impulsive and have poor reception of social cues and poor ability to learn from experience. These factors decrease the effectiveness of the usual social rewards and sanctions, and can result in an increased susceptibility to delinquency.

The social link is more complicated. A learning-disabled child has a poor academic record and may be perceived by adults as a disciplinary problem in the schools. These two factors may cause the child to be labeled a problem child and grouped with other problem children, so that he begins to associate with peers who are hostile to school and prone to delinquency. These circumstances may ultimately lead to increased absenteeism and to dropping out of school. A learning-disabled child is frequently socially awkward and unattractive, and when this is combined with difficulties in school, it can lead to a negative self-image, with an increased need for compensating success. All these factors can combine to produce delinquent behavior.

A review of empirical studies was undertaken, and six studies were found in which it was possible to estimate the incidence of learning disabilities in a delinquent population. The estimates ranged from 22 to 90 percent. The differences between these estimates resulted primarily from different definitions of learning disabilities. The study reporting the highest percentage had stated that "our philosophy [is] that a learning disability or dysfunction is anything which prevents a child from achieving successfully in a normal educational setting,"

---

65. This research is reported in Charles A. Murray, *The Link Between Learning Disabilities and Juvenile Delinquency*, U.S. Government Printing Office, Washington, D.C., 1976.

66. Ibid., pp. 23–28.

a much broader definition than the one quoted above. Only two of the studies used the narrower definition, and neither of these studies reported incidence rates. In one of these studies it was concluded that unusually high levels of learning disabilities among delinquents were unlikely; the other study was not completed because of lack of funds.

In two other studies the performance of institutionalized delinquent groups was compared with the performance of nondelinquent groups on 18 separate learning-disability-related tasks. The nondelinquent groups outperformed the delinquent groups on 10 of these tasks, but the delinquents did not perform significantly better than the nondelinquents on any of the tasks. This finding is consistent with the presence of more learning disabilities in the delinquent groups, but other explanations are also possible.

The authors conclude that "the existence of a causal relationship between learning disabilities and delinquency has not [been] established; the evidence for a causal link is feeble."[67] They go on to say, however, that "with few exceptions, the quantitative work to date has been so poorly designed and presented that it cannot be used even for rough estimates of the strength of the link." They argue that the major motivation behind the attempt to establish a relationship between learning disabilities and delinquency is that people who have worked with delinquents have become convinced that a large number of their clients are unable to learn in the normal classroom setting, for reasons beyond their control. This conviction has been supported by a wide variety of data, but it would appear that the causes for these "learning handicaps" are social rather than biological.

## 8. AUTONOMIC NERVOUS SYSTEM FUNCTIONING

In all mammals there is a relatively separate part of the nervous system which controls many of the body's involuntary functions. Called the autonomic nervous system, it is especially active in a "fight or flight" situation, when it prepares the body for maximum efficiency by increasing the heart rate, rerouting the blood from the stomach to the muscles, dilating the pupils, increasing the respiratory rate, and stimulating the sweat glands. Lie detectors measure these functions and use them to determine whether the subject is telling the truth. The theory is that, as a child, the average person has been conditioned to anticipate punishment when he tells a lie. This antic-

---

67. Ibid., p. 65.

ipation produces the involuntary fight or flight response, which results in a number of measurable changes in heart, pulse, and breathing rate, and, because sweat itself conducts electricity, in the electric conductivity of the skin.

The anxiety reaction in anticipation of punishment has been described by some researchers as the primary socializing agent for children.[68] The child is conditioned by his parents to anticipate punishment in certain types of situations, and the anxiety he feels in those situations (usually called conscience or guilt) often leads him to avoid them. Because the anxiety reaction in anticipation of punishment is essentially an autonomic nervous system function related to the fight or flight response, the level of socialization in children may depend at least in part on the functioning of that system. Specifically, if the fight or flight response is activated slowly or at low levels in situations in which punishment is anticipated, or if it fails to deactivate quickly when the situation changes, then the child will be difficult to socialize.

The first to examine this question was Eysenck, who based his discussion on Jung's concepts of introversion and extroversion as the major attitudes or orientations of the personality.[69] The introvert is oriented toward the inner, subjective world, and tends to be more quiet, pessimistic, retiring, serious, cautious, reliable, and controlled. The extrovert is oriented toward the external, objective world, and is more sociable, impulsive, carefree, optimistic, and aggressive. He craves excitement, like to take chances, tends to be undependable, and loses his temper more easily. Eysenck notes that the diagnosis of this personality dimension is highly reliable, with self-ratings, ratings by others, and ratings by objective tests all highly consistent.

Eysenck also utilized Pavlov's concepts of excitation and inhibition.[70] Excitation means simply that the stimulus that was presented to the organism has successfully passed through the autonomic nervous system to be registered in the cortex. Obviously this concept is central to the explanation of all learning and behavior. But in order to explain the patterns of conditioning, Pavlov also found it necessary to postulate that something like cortical fatigue occurs after a

68. H. J. Eysenck, *Crime and Personality*, Houghton Mifflin, Boston, 1964, pp. 100–19; Gordon Trassler, "Criminal Behavior," in H. J. Eysenck, ed., *Handbook of Abnormal Psychology*, Putnam, London, 1972; Sarnoff A. Mednick, "A Biosocial Theory of the Learning of Law-Abiding Behavior," in Mednick and Christiansen, op. cit., pp. 1–8.

69. Eysenck, *Crime and Personality*, pp. 34–36.

70. Ibid., pp. 68–87.

period of excitation. Conditioning was found to slow down after a period of time, but would resume at a higher level after a rest period. Pavlov called this phenomenon inhibition.

Eysenck hypothesized that these two sets of concepts were connected, and that introverts were characterized by higher levels of excitation and/or lower levels of inhibition, whereas extroverts were characterized by the opposite. Because extroverts have lower levels of stimulation coming into the cortex, they experience "stimulus hunger," whereas introverts, whose cortices receive stronger stimulation for longer periods of time, will be oriented toward "stimulus avoidance."[71] The possibility of punishment is therefore much more threatening to the introvert. He will experience high anxiety reactions in these situations and will seek to avoid them. Extroverts, on the other hand, will experience less anxiety both because they are less sensitive to pain and because they will more readily seek out prohibited activities in their search for stimulation. Eysenck further argued that psychopaths are extreme extroverts and that they fail to develop adequate consciences because of the way their autonomic nervous systems function.[72]

In a number of more recent studies autonomic nervous system functioning has been examined by measuring the same peripheral functions that are monitored by a lie detector. For example, Mednick[73] maintains that the rate of skin conductance response (SCR) recovery—the time between the peak skin conductance amplitude and the return of that amplitude to normal levels—can be taken to measure the general rate of recovery in the autonomic nervous system. If so, it would measure the rate at which the anxiety reaction in anticipation of potential punishment is diminished following removal from the threatening situation. Mednick argues that the rate at which the anxiety dissipates is crucial, since fear reduction is the most powerful reinforcer known to psychology. When fear is dissipated quickly, the individual receives a large reinforcement for avoiding the situation of potential punishment, and conditioning is much more likely to occur. After reviewing studies on the subject, Siddle concluded:[74]

The results concerning SCR recovery and antisocial behavior appear to be quite consistent. Subjects who display antisocial behavior (psychopaths, adult

71. Ibid., p. 99.
72. Ibid., pp. 39–43.
73. Mednick, "A Biosocial Theory," op. cit., pp. 2–4.
74. David A. T. Siddle, "Electrodermal Activity and Psychopathy," in Mednick and Christiansen, op. cit., pp. 206–7.

criminals, and adolescent delinquents) also display significantly slower SCR recovery than do matched controls.

Siddle's conclusion was not supported by others, however. In 1971 Passingham reviewed ten studies generally cited as supporting the view that criminals condition less well than noncriminals.[75] He found that all the studies suffered methodological problems such as irrelevant or crude measures of conditioning, inadequate or no control groups, or atypical samples. He concluded that Eysenck's and Mednick's theories were not at that time supported by any data. Nine years later, Bartol presented an extensive and favorable review of Eysenck's theory, concluding that it "offers promising possibility as a generalized, testable theory of criminality."[76] However, he found that most of the research about the theory was inconclusive, while the remaining research was divided between that which was supportive and that which was damaging to the theory. He suggested that "Eysenck's heavy reliance on classical conditioning principles as a primary explanation for criminality, while avoiding other forms of learning, may prove to be one of his theory's damaging weaknesses."[77]

9. IMPLICATIONS AND CONCLUSIONS

Biological theories must be viewed in terms of a "multiple factor" approach to criminal behavior—that is, the presence of those biological factors is said to increase the likelihood but not determine absolutely that an individual will engage in criminal behaviors. These factors generate criminal behaviors when they interact with psychological or social factors. Mednick, for example, has suggested an interaction between biological and social factors:[78]

Where the social experiences of an antisocial individual are not especially antisocial, biological factors should be examined. The value of the biological factors is more limited in predicting antisocial behavior in individuals who have experienced criminogenic social conditions in their rearing.

75. R. E. Passingham, "Crime and Personality: A Review of Eysenck's Theory," in V. D. Nebylitsyn and J. A. Gray, eds., *Biological Bases of Individual Behavior*, Academic Press, London, 1972. See also Adrian Raine and Peter H. Venables, "Classical Conditioning and Socialization—An Interaction," *Personality and Individual Differences* 2 (4): 273–83 (1981).

76. Curt R. Bartol, *Criminal Behavior, A Psychosocial Approach*, Prentice-Hall, Englewood Cliffs, N.J., 1980, pp. 32–49.

77. Ibid., p. 48.

78. Mednick et al., "Biology and Violence," pp. 55, 68. A similar conclusion is reached in Mednick et al., "An Example of Biosocial Interaction Research," in Mednick and Christiansen, op. cit, pp. 9–23.

Within the context of this multiple factor approach, biological theories of criminal behavior can be judged in terms of the extent to which there are demonstrable biological differences between criminals and noncriminals. Such differences must also be shown to be causally related to criminal behaviors. The evidence to date is not sufficient to conclude that biological differences can be found in a majority of criminals, and where those differences are found, the causal linkages to criminal behavior are still weak.

## RECOMMENDED READINGS

Frank H. Marsh and Janet Katz, *Biology, Crime and Ethics*, Anderson, Cincinnati, 1985. An excellent book of readings addressing all aspects of the relationship between biology and crime.

Sarnoff A. Mednick et al., "Biology and Violence," in Marvin W. Wolfgang and Neil Alan Weiner, eds., *Criminal Violence*, Sage, Beverly Hills, Cal., 1982. A thorough review of biological research as applied specifically to the problem of violence.

Sarnoff Mednick and Jan Volvka, "Biology and Crime," in Norval Morris and Michael Tonry, eds. *Crime and Justice*, vol. 2, University of Chicago Press, Chicago, 1980. A detailed overview of biological research on criminal behavior.

Walter R. Gove and G. Russell Carpenter, eds., *The Fundamental Connection Between Nature and Nurture*, D. C. Heath, Lexington, Mass., 1981. A review of the evidence about biological, psychological, and social influences on human behavior.

C. Ray Jeffery, ed., *Biology and Crime*, Sage, Beverly Hills, Cal., 1979. A book of readings about the individual offender and political implications of biological theories.

Edward Sagarin, ed., *Taboos in Criminology*, Sage, Beverly Hills, Cal., 1980. Biological research in criminology is discussed in the context of values and science.

Susan L. Farber, *Identical Twins Raised Apart: A Reanalysis*, Basic Books, New York, 1981. Reviews all Western, non-fraudulent cases of identical twins raised apart, with a brief discussion of criminality on pp. 228–30. In general, concludes that the data support environmental rather than biological causes of behavior.

# CHAPTER SEVEN

# The Personality of the Offender

The term *personality* refers to the complex set of emotional and behavioral attributes that tend to remain relatively constant as the individual moves from situation to situation. This chapter examines theories that explain criminal behavior primarily in terms of the enduring personality attributes of the individual. In general, psychological and psychiatric theories include the personality of the offender within their explanations of criminal behavior. Thus, these theories are the focus of the present chapter.

Psychological and psychiatric theories also consider biological and situational factors in their explanations of criminal behavior. Much of the biological research presented in Chapter 6 has been done by psychologists and psychiatrists and can be considered as part of psychological or psychiatric theories of crime. Those theories also consider the impact of the situation on the individual, and they explain behavior by interrelating the situation with individual's biological and psychological characteristics. Situational factors, however, will be discussed in the chapters on sociological theories of criminal behavior. In addition, some psychological theories argue that criminal behavior is the result of normal learning processes. These theories will be discussed in Chapter 12 on criminal behavior as normal learned behavior.

The present chapter considers only those psychological and psychiatric theories that argue that criminal behavior originates primarily in the personalities of offenders rather than in their biology or in situation. This includes psychoanalytic theories that argue that the causes of criminal behavior are found in unconscious elements of the personality. It also includes research on the conscious personality, using a type of psychological test called the *personality inventory*. Finally, the present chapter discusses specific personality types thought to be associated with criminality, such as the *antisocial personality*.

## 1. HISTORICAL BACKGROUND: PSYCHIATRY AS A SPRINGBOARD FOR PSYCHOANALYTIC THEORY

Before looking at the psychoanalytic view of the causes of criminal behavior, it is necessary to consider the differences between psychiatry in general and the psychoanalytic movement. Psychiatry grew out of the experience of medical doctors in dealing with the basic problem of mental disease. Control of the dangerous and often outrageous behavior of the mentally and emotionally disturbed has been a problem in organized societies from the earliest times. Historically it has often been indistinguishable from the control of the dangerous and often outrageous behavior of the criminal. In early societies demonology as a system of thought provided what was considered the most adequate explanation for both crime and insanity, the influence of evil spirits or the Devil.[1]

Yet there was an objective, naturalistic school of medical thought in ancient Greece that goes back to roughly 600 B.C. This medical thought rested on the science of Pythagoras (580–510 B.C.), Alcmaeon (550–500 B.C.), and Empedocles of Agrigentum (490–430 B.C.), and had as its most distinguished member Hippocrates (460?–?377 B.C.), the Father of Medicine. This last name is, of course, well known and honored for the Hippocratic oath, which is solemnly assumed by all practitioners of medicine and the healing arts.

Pythagoras and his pupil Alcmaeon identified the brain as the organ of the mind, and conceived of mental illness as a disorder of that organ. Empedocles introduced certain explanatory principles of personality (namely, the qualities of heat, cold, moisture, and dryness; and the humors—blood, phlegm, black bile, and yellow bile) that were to be in use for hundreds of years, through the Middle Ages into almost modern times.

In this conception delirium and various other kinds of mental dis-

---

1. For good accounts of principal historical developments, see Erwin H. Ackerknecht, M.D., *A Short History of Medicine*, rev. ed., Johns Hopkins Press, Baltimore, 1982; Brian Inglis, *A History of Medicine*, World, Cleveland, 1965; Charles Singer and E. Ashworth Underwood, *A Short History of Medicine*, Oxford University Press, New York, 1962; or George Rosen, *Madness in Society*, University of Chicago Press, Chicago, 1968.

orders were explained as aspects of special functions of the brain. Hysteria, mania, and melancholia were recognized, described, and prescribed for just as objectively and scientifically as were the medications suggested for a long list of wounds and other human afflictions.[2] In this sense psychiatry constituted an important division of the developing field of medical knowledge from the very beginning.[3]

As medical knowledge slowly grew, recognition and identification of insanity as a disease became more general. By the time of Sigmund Freud (1856–1939), all of the ordinary concepts of abnormal psychology had been developed out of experience in dealing with disturbed persons. Difficulties due to *organic disorders*—for example, head injuries that leave the mind blank or that distort vision or hearing or cause a ringing in the ears, or those due to disease or degeneration, such as syphilitic paresis or the senility of old age— were well known. They had long been distinguished from the *functional disorders* in which there is strange behavior but no known organic disease. There have always been people who would hear voices when no one was speaking, or who could see what no one else could see; or those who fail to see, even as the blind, yet apparently have physically undamaged eyes. Even the central concept of psychoanalysis, the *unconscious*, made its appearance and served useful purposes before Freud. The concept of the unconscious is said to have been developed by von Hartman (1842–1906), and was extensively utilized and further developed by Morton Prince (1854–1929) in several non-Freudian studies of dissociation or split-personality phenomena.[4] Somewhat the same circumstance is true of several other ideas or concepts that have been used extensively in psychoanalysis. Thus repression, projection, symbolic behavior, and various notions of substitute responses were well documented in elaborate case histories and classified under a changing system of "type" names. This

2. "To those women suffering from hysteria, Hippocrates recommended marriage and pregnancy as general treatment, while the immediate attacks were to be met with substances causing unpleasant tastes and odors combined with purges and pessiaries." N. D. C. Lewis, *A Short History of Psychiatric Achievement*, Norton, New York, 1941, p. 35.

3. For a good short review of the history and general development of contemporary psychiatry, see ibid., or Winfred Overholser, "An Historical Sketch of Psychiatry," *Journal of Clinical Psychopathology* 10 (2) (Apr. 1949), reprinted in Richard C. Allen, Elyce Z. Ferster, and Jesse G. Rubin, *Readings in Law and Psychiatry*, Johns Hopkins University Press, Baltimore, 1975.

4. Lewis, op. cit., p. 134; Morton Prince, *The Dissociation of a Personality: A Biographical Study in Abnormal Psychology*, Longmans, Greens, New York, 1906, reprinted by Greenwood Press, Westport, Ct., 1969; Morton Prince, *The Unconscious*, Macmillan, New York, 1914, reprinted (1921 edition) by Arno, New York.

was the descriptive and typological psychiatry of pre-Freudian practice.[5]

## 2. SIGMUND FREUD AND PSYCHOANALYSIS

While psychiatry is as old as medicine, psychoanalysis is a relatively recent development associated with the life and work of Sigmund Freud and some of his pupils, notably Alfred Adler (1870–1937), Carl Jung (1875–1961), and Wilhelm Stekel (1868–1940). Psychoanalysis is an extremely complicated and not particularly unified set of ideas, due to the fact that Freud himself revised his most fundamental ideas at several points in his life, and his followers continued to propose revisions and extensions after his death. Nevertheless it has had a profound impact on almost all modern thought, including philosophy, literature, and conceptions of human (and, consequently, criminal) behavior. The following is only a very brief overview of some basic ideas associated with psychoanalysis, meant to give a sense of what it is about.[6]

Sigmund Freud lived most of his life in Vienna and published most of his important ideas during the first 40 years of this century. Like other psychiatrists before him, he was a physician who was concerned with the medical treatment of a variety of functional disorders that seemed to be unrelated to any organic causes. He more or less asked the question "What do we have to assume about the human personality in order to explain the facts with which we are presented?"[7]

Freud first adopted the idea of the unconscious, as used by earlier psychiatrists, arguing that the behaviors could be explained by traumatic experiences in early childhood that left their mark on the individual despite the fact that the individual was not consciously aware of those experiences. Freud invented the technique of psychoanalysis to treat these problems. The idea was one of free association;

5. See J. R. Whitwell, *Historical Notes on Psychiatry*, H. K. Lewis, London, 1936; E. A. Strecker, *Fundamentals of Psychiatry*, Lippincott, Philadelphia, 1943; Lewis, op. cit., pp. 66–159; E. C. Mann, *Manual of Psychological Medicine and Allied Nervous Disorders*, Blakiston, Philadelphia, 1883.

6. For an overview of psychoanalytic theory as applied to the explanation of crime, see Fritz Redl and Hans Toch, "The Psychoanalytic Explanation of Crime," in Hans Toch, ed., *Psychology of Crime and Criminal Justice*, Holt, Rinehart and Winston, New York, 1979. See also Hermann Mannheim, *Comparative Criminology*, Houghton Mifflin, New York, 1965, pp. 312ff.

7. Redl and Toch, op. cit.

the patient relaxed completely and talked about whatever came to mind. By exploring these associations the individual was able to reconstruct the earlier events and bring them to consciousness. Once the patient was conscious of these events, the theory held that the events would lose their unconscious power and the patient would gain a degree of conscious control and freedom.

Freud later revised his conceptions of the conscious and unconscious, in a sense redefining the conscious as ego, and splitting the unconscious into the id and superego. *Id* was a term used to describe the great reservoir of biological and psychological drives, the urges and impulses that underlie all behavior. That includes the libido, the full force of sexual energy in the individual, as diffuse and tenacious as the "will to live" found in all animals. The id is permanently unconscious, and responds only to what Freud called "the pleasure principle"—if it feels good, do it. The *superego*, in contrast, is the force of self-criticism and conscience and reflects requirements that stem from the individual's social experience in a particular cultural milieu. The superego may contain conscious elements in the form of moral and ethical codes, but it is primarily unconscious in its operation. The superego arises out of the first great love attachment the child experiences, that with his or her parents. The child experiences them as judgmental, and ultimately internalizes their values as an *ego-ideal*—that is, as an ideal conception of what he or she should be. Finally, what Freud called the *ego* is the conscious personality. It is oriented toward the real world in which the person lives (termed by Freud the "reality principle"), and attempts to mediate between the demands of the id and the prohibitions of the superego.[8]

Given this basic organization of the personality, Freud explored how the ego handles all the conflicts between the superego and the id. The basic problem is one of guilt: The individual experiences all sorts of drives and urges coming from the id, and feels guilty about them because of the prohibitions of the superego. There are a variety of ways the individual may handle this situation. In *sublimation* the drives of the id are diverted to activities approved of by the superego. For example, aggressive and destructive urges may be diverted to athletic activity. Sublimation is the normal and healthy way

8. Something of the flavor of Freud's theory can be acquired by comparing his categories of id, ego, and superego to the transactional analysis categories of child, adult, and parent. See Eric E. Berne, *Games People Play*, Grove Press, New York, 1964; Thomas A. Harris, *I'm OK—You're OK*, Harper and Row, New York 1967; Richard C. Nicholson, "Transactional Analysis: A New Method for Helping Offenders," *Federal Probation* 34 (3): 29–38 (Sept. 1970).

the ego handles the conflicts between the drives of the id and the prohibitions of the superego. In *repression*, in contrast, those drives are stuffed back into the unconscious and the individual denies that they exist. This may result in a variety of strange effects on behavior. One possible result is a *reaction formation*, as when a person with repressed sexual drives becomes very prudish about all sexual matters. Another result might be *projection*, in which, for example, a person with repressed homosexual urges frequently sees homosexual tendencies in others.

Freud believed that these basic conflicts were played out in different ways at different points of the life cycle. Of particular interest to him were the experiences of early childhood. He argued that each infant goes through a series of phases in which the basic drives were oriented around, first, oral drives, then anal drives, and finally genital drives. During the genital stage (around the ages of three and four) the child is sexually attracted to the parent of the opposite sex and views the same-sex parent as competition. This is the famous Oedipus complex in boys, and the comparable Electra complex in girls. If the guilt produced by these urges is not handled adequately by the ego, it leaves a lasting imprint on the personality that affects later behavior.

One of the major tools Freud used to treat these problems was *transference*, the tendency for past significant relationships to be replayed during current significant relationships. As the relationship with the analyst takes on increasing significance in the patient's life, the patient will tend to replay with the analyst the earlier relationships in his life that are presently generating his problems. For example, if the patient's problems stem from an earlier relationship with his father, the patient will tend to create a similar relationship with the analyst. Treatment then consists of straightening out the current relationship between analyst and patient, which has the effect of also straightening out the earlier relationship the patient had with his father.

### 3. PSYCHOANALYTIC EXPLANATIONS OF CRIMINAL BEHAVIOR

While the above is only a brief presentation of psychoanalytic theory, it provides the basic orientation for psychoanalytic explanations of criminal behavior. Within the psychoanalytic perspective criminal and delinquent behaviors are attributed to disturbances or malfunctions in the ego or superego. The id, in contrast, is viewed as a constant and inborn biologically based source of drives and urges; it does not vary substantially among individuals.

Freud himself did not discuss criminal behavior to any great extent. He did, however, suggest that at least some individuals performed criminal acts because they possessed an overdeveloped superego, which led to constant feelings of guilt and anxiety.[9] There is a consequent desire for punishment to remove the guilt feelings and restore a proper balance of good against evil. Unconsciously motivated errors (i.e., careless or imprudent ways of committing the crime) leave clues so that the authorities may more readily apprehend and convict the guilty party, and thus administer suitably cleansing punishment. This idea has been extensively developed by later Freudians.[10] Criminality of this type is said to be appropriate for treatment through psychoanalysis, since it can uncover the unconscious sources of guilt and free the person from the compulsive need for punishment.

While excessive guilt from an *overdeveloped* superego is one source of criminal behavior within the psychoanalytic framework, August Aichhorn, a psychoanalytically oriented psychologist, suggested alternate sources for crime and delinquency, based on his years of experience running an institution for delinquents.[11] He found that many children in his institution had *underdeveloped* superegos, so that the delinquency and criminality were primarily expressions of an unregulated id. Aichhorn attributed this to the fact that the parents of these children were either absent or unloving, so that the children failed to form the intimate attachments necessary for the proper development of their superegos. Aichhorn based his treatment techniques for these children on providing a happy and pleasurable environment, so as to promote the type of identification with adults that the child failed to experience earlier. He commented that most training

---

9. See Sigmund Freud, "Criminals from a Sense of Guilt," in *The Standard Edition of the Complete Psychological Works of Sigmund Freud*, Hogarth Press, London, vol. 14, pp. 332–33.

10. This idea is elaborated in such works as Walter Bromberg, *Crime and the Mind: A Psychiatric Analysis of Crime and Punishment*, Macmillan, New York, 1965; Seymour L. Halleck, *Psychiatry and the Dilemmas of Crime*, Harper & Row, New York, 1967; David Abrahamsen, *The Psychology of Crime* (1960) and *Crime and the Human Mind* (1944), both published by Columbia University Press, New York; also his *Who are the Guilty?*, Rinehart, New York, 1952; Kate Friedlander, *The Psychoanalytic Approach to Juvenile Delinquency*, Kegan Paul, Trench & Trubner, London, 1947; Erich Fromm, *Escape from Freedom*, Farrar & Rinehart, New York, 1941; Ben Karpman, *The Individual Criminal*, Nervous and Mental Disease Publishing Co., Washington, D.C., 1935; William A. White, *Crimes and Criminals*, Farrar & Rinehart, New York, 1933; August Aichhorn, *Wayward Youth*, Viking, New York, 1963; and Theodor Reik, *The Compulsion to Confess*, Farrar, Straus, and Cudahy, New York, 1945.

11. August Aichhorn, op. cit.

schools "attempted through force, through fear of punishment, and without rewards of love to make the delinquent socially acceptable. Since most of their charges belong to the type just described, they only exaggerated what the parents had already begun and consequently they were doomed to failure."[12] Freud approved of these techniques in his Foreword to Aichhorn's book, and concluded that they, rather than psychoanalysis per se, were appropriate in the case of young children and of adult criminals dominated by their instincts.[13]

Aichhorn also suggested that other types of delinquents existed, including those who, from an overabundance of love, were permitted to do anything they wanted by overprotective and overindulgent parents.[14] He did not find that there were many of these, but they required different treatment techniques than the delinquents created by the absent or excessively severe parents described above. Finally, there also were a few delinquents who had well-developed superegos but who identified with criminal parents.[15] Again, these required very different treatment techniques.

Much of later psychoanalytic theorizing with respect to criminal behavior is consistent with the types of delinquents suggested by Aichhorn. Healy and Bronner, for example, examined 105 pairs of brothers, where one brother was a persistent delinquent and the other was a nondelinquent.[16] They concluded that the delinquent brother had failed to develop normal affectional ties with his parents due to a variety of situational factors. Delinquency, they argued, was essentially a form of sublimation in which the delinquent attempted to meet basic needs that were not being met by his family. Bowlby focused on early maternal deprivation as the origin of delinquency, arguing similarly that the basic affectional ties had failed to form.[17] Redl and Wineman found that "children who hate" lacked factors leading to identification with adults, such as feelings of being wanted, loved, encouraged, and secure.[18] They said that these children not only

---

12. Ibid., p. 209.

13. Sigmund Freud, Foreword in ibid.

14. Aichhorn, op. cit., pp. 200–202.

15. Ibid., pp. 224–25.

16. William Healy and Augusta Bronner, *New Light on Delinquency and Its Treatment*, Yale University Press, New Haven, Ct., 1931.

17. John Bowlby, *Child Care and the Growth of Love*, Penguin, Baltimore, 1953. A review of research about his theory is presented in J. E. Hall-Williams, *Criminology and Criminal Justice*, Butterworths, London, 1982, pp. 59–68.

18. Fritz Redl and David Wineman, *Children Who Hate*, The Free Press, New York, 1951. See also Redl and Wineman, *Controls from Within*, Free Press, New York, 1952.

lacked adequate superegos, but their egos had been organized to defend the unregulated expression of their id desires. Redl and Wineman called this the "delinquent ego." Like Aichhorn, they recommended that these children be treated with unconditional love, to promote the identification with adults they lacked in earlier childhood.

Psychoanalytic theory has been tremendously influential in modern psychiatry and has also had a massive impact on the modern world. Despite its remarkable success, however, fundamental criticisms have been leveled against it. The major criticism, and it is frequently made, is that the theory is untestable. Psychoanalytic theory is a set of interrelated concepts, which, taken together, explain both criminal and noncriminal behavior, provided the system is valid. The question raised by these critics is whether it is possible to determine whether that system is valid.

Several authors have argued that Freud's ideas can be reduced to testable hypotheses, that these hypotheses have been tested in a great deal of empirical research, and that the results of the research have generally supported the theory.[19] Despite such research on the general validity of Freudian concepts, the psychoanalytic explanation of any particular individual's behavior seems particularly subjective and out of reach of objective measuring devices. Cleckley, for example, made the following comments:[20]

When teaching young physicians in psychiatric residency training I was often also impressed by the influence of the examiners convictions on items of experience reported by such patients. I found that some of these patients could be led on in almost any direction to report almost any sort of infantile recollection one sought to produce. . . . I have become increasingly convinced that some of the popular methods presumed to discover what is in the unconscious cannot be counted upon as reliable methods of obtaining evidence.

Psychoanalytic explanations of behavior are made after the behavior has already occurred, and rely heavily on interpretations of unconscious motivations.[21] These interpretations may make a great deal

19. Seymour Fisher and Roger P. Greenberg, *The Scientific Credibility of Freud's Theories and Therapy*, Basic Books, New York, 1977; Paul Kline, *Fact and Fantasy in Freudian Theory*, 2nd ed., Methuen, New York, 1981.

20. Hervey Cleckley, *The Mask of Sanity*, Mosby, St. Louis, 1976, pp. 406–7.

21. Curt R. Bartol, *Criminal Behavior: A Psychosocial Approach*, Prentice-Hall, Englewood Cliffs, N.J., 1980, p. 7.

of sense, but there is generally no way to determine the accuracy of the analyst's interpretation of an individual case within the framework of accepted scientific methodology. A methodology in which only the analyst understands the meaning of the facts of the case—the patient may understand neither the facts nor the meaning of those facts—does not lend itself to third-person, impersonal verification or to generalization beyond the particular case.

An alternate way to evaluate the psychoanalytic perspective would be to argue that the "truth" of the psychoanalytic interpretation of events is not important.[22] Rather, the important point is whether psychoanalysis, as a process, is able to cure people of their afflictions. Unfortunately, patients who receive psychiatric and psychoanalytic treatment generally have no greater chances of being cured than those who receive no treatment at all.[23] The usefulness of this perspective within criminology is therefore in some doubt.

## 4. RESEARCH USING PERSONALITY TESTS

Commonsense notions of what constitutes personality generally have sought to specify qualities of the individual other than intellectual ability. Words such as *aggressive, belligerent, suspicious, timid, withdrawn, friendly, cooperative, likable, argumentative,* and *agreeable* have long been used to describe or express impressions of some of these qualities. Psychological tests or measurements of personality differences have been developed more or less in parallel to intelligence tests. Inevitably, too, as in the case of intelligence tests, delinquents and criminals have been tested with personality scales or inventories to discover how their personalities differ from those of nondelinquents when comparisons are made in terms of test scores or standardized quantitative scales.

22. The "truth" of psychoanalytic interpretations of events is currently at the center of a major controversy in psychoanalytic circles. Jeffrey Masson, *Assault on the Truth: Freud's Suppression of the Seduction Theory,* Farrar, Straus & Giroux, New York, 1984, argues that psychoanalysis was "born" at the point when Freud stopped believing the literal truth of what his patients told him. The case involved a woman who remembered being sexually abused by her father, and Freud concluded that this was an imaginary rather than a real event. Present evidence suggests that these and many other similar events reported to Freud had actually happened but that Freud refused to believe them for a variety of personal reasons. Freud's conclusion in this particular case also had the effect of covering up a rather outrageous example of medical malpractice by his intimate friend Wilhelm Fliess. For a readable account of this controversy, see Janet Malcolm, *In the Freud Archives,* Knopf, New York, 1984. A similar charge had been leveled against Freud in Judith Lewis Herman, *Father-Daughter Incest,* Harvard University Press, Cambridge, Mass., 1981.

23. R. K. Schwitzgebel, "The Right to Effective Treatment," *California Law Review* 62: 936–56 (1974).

In 1950 Schuessler and Cressey[24] published the results of a survey of studies made in the United States during the preceding 25 years, in which comparisons between delinquents and nondelinquents were made in terms of scores on objective tests of personality. At least 30 different personality scales were used. Their conclusion was that "of 113 such comparisons, 42 per cent showed differences in favor of the non-criminal, while the remainder were indeterminate. The doubtful validity of many of the obtained differences, as well as the lack of consistency in the combined results, makes it impossible to conclude from these data that criminality and personality elements are associated."[25]

This negative conclusion would be more impressive if it had been drawn from a comparison of carefully controlled studies, so that the percentages computed on the total are of quite uncertain meaning. It appears, however, that even when studies are carefully controlled, the results do not demonstrate a clearly delineated difference between the personality makeup of criminals and noncriminals. It is apparently more a matter of interrelatedness of characteristics than of any great differences in their presence or absence. This would seem to be a major conclusion that properly may be drawn from the many carefully controlled comparisons made by the Gluecks in their intensive study of 500 delinquent boys compared with 500 nondelinquent boys and reported in considerable detail in the book *Unraveling Juvenile Delinquency*.[26]

The Gluecks summarize their impression of this interrelationship of characteristics in the following passage:[27]

A meaningful pattern does tend to emerge from the interweaving of separately-spun strands: On the whole, delinquents are more extroverted, vivacious, impulsive, and less self-controlled than the non-delinquents. They are more hostile, resentful, defiant, suspicious, and destructive. They are less fearful of failure or defeat than the non-delinquents. They are less concerned about meeting conventional expectations, and are more ambivalent toward or far less submissive to authority. They are, as a group, more socially assertive. To a greater extent than the control group, they express feelings of not being recognized or appreciated.

24. Karl F. Schuessler and Donald R. Cressey, "Personality Characteristics of Criminals," *American Journal of Sociology* 55: 476–84 (Mar. 1950).

25. Ibid., p. 476.

26. Sheldon Glueck and Eleanor Glueck, *Unraveling Juvenile Delinquency*, Commonwealth Fund, New York, 1950.

27. Ibid., p. 275.

This is, on the whole, a verbal picture of what, in other connections, would not be called an undesirable combination of personality traits. Any theory based on personality traits must recognize and explain the fact that the delinquent often is, or may be, as attractive and as socially acceptable a sort of person as the nondelinquent.

As contradictory and confusing as some of the Gluecks' findings are, from the standpoint of theory making, the difference between delinquents and nondelinquents nevertheless lend themselves to statistical formulations as prediction tables. The Gluecks developed three such tables,[28] one based on factors in the social background, one based on character traits as determined by the Rorschach test, and one based on personality traits as determined in the psychiatric interview. All three are said to give impressive results. For example, in the best-score class only about 10 percent may be expected to become delinquent, as opposed to about 90 percent in the worst-score class.[29]

Similar results have been obtained with the Minnesota Multi-phasic Personality Inventory (MMPI), which is a list of 550 statements developed to aid in psychiatric diagnosis.[30] The person taking the test decides whether the statements are true or false. Ten different scales are then scored and assumed to measure different aspects of the personality. These scales were originally identified by the names of the psychiatric symptoms or pathologies they were assumed to measure, such as hypochondriasis, depression, or hysteria. Since the MMPI is now often used with normal individuals, there is a tendency to identify the scales by number only (Scale 1, Scale 2, etc.). These ten scores are arranged into a "profile" of the individ-

---

28. Ibid., pp. 257–71, for detailed tables.

29. Ibid., Table XX-3, p. 262. The predictive validity of a revised table was supported in studies by M. M. Craig and S. J. Glick ["Ten Years' Experience with the Glueck Social Prediction Table," *Crime and Delinquency* 9: 249–61 (1963); and "Application of the Glueck Social Prediction Table on an Ethnic Basis," *Crime and Delinquency* 11: 175–78 (1965)] and N. B. Trevvett ["Identifying Delinquency-Prone Children," *Crime and Delinquency* 11: 186–91 (1965)]. Kurt Weis ["The Glueck Social Prediction Table: An Unfulfilled Promise," *Journal of Criminal Law, Criminology and Police Science* 65: 397–404 (1974)], however, has argued that its results are only slightly better than chance.

30. For a full discussion of the use of the MMPI, see S. R. Hathaway and P. E. Meehl, *An Atlas for the Clinical Use of the MMPI*, University of Minnesota Press, Minneapolis, 1951; for an account of its application and use in the study of delinquency, see S. R. Hathaway and E. D. Monachesi, *Analyzing and Predicting Juvenile Delinquency with the MMPI* (1953) and *Adolescent Personality and Behavior* (1963), both published by the University of Minnesota Press, Minneapolis. A more recent review of studies using the MMPI on criminals can be found in Edwin I. Megargee and Martin J. Bohn, Jr., *Classifying Criminal Offenders*, Sage, Beverly Hills, Cal., 1979.

ual, so that no single score indicates an individual's performance on the MMPI.[31]

Waldo and Dinitz examined 94 personality studies performed between 1950 and 1965 in an update of Schussler and Cressey's study, and found that about 80 percent of these studies reported statistically significant personality differences between criminals and noncriminals.[32] The most impressive results were found with the MMPI, where Scale 4, previously called the "psychopathic deviate" scale, consistently produced significant results. These studies generally concluded that delinquents and criminals were more "psychopathic" than nondelinquents and noncriminals.

Waldo and Dinitz, however, were very cautious in their interpretation of these studies. They pointed out that the items on Scale 4 include the statement "I have never been in trouble with the law," and that this statement alone would distinguish between delinquents and nondelinquents. Scale 4 also includes other statements that delinquents and nondelinquents might answer differently, such as "I like school," "My relatives are nearly all in sympathy with me," and "My sex life is satisfactory." Waldo and Dinitz also pointed out that at least some of the differences between delinquents and nondelinquents may have been due to differences in socioeconomic class between the two groups, that many of the studies did not use random samples, and that differences *within* delinquent groups were often greater than differences *between* delinquents and nondelinquents. Finally, they pointed out that Scale 4 had originally been constructed by listing statements with which "psychopaths" tend to disagree and "normal" persons tend to agree. The original psychopathic group consisted largely of young delinquents, so that the scale was constructed as a set of statements with which nondelinquents are more likely to agree than delinquents. A person who scores high on Scale 4 is one whose responses are similar to those of a group consisting primarily of young delinquents. It should not be surprising, therefore, if that person is also a delinquent.

On the average, delinquents and criminals disagreed with only 4 more statements out of the 50 statements on the scale than did nondelinquents and noncriminals. When the actual statements on the scale are reviewed, it seems likely that differences in the Scale 4 scores

31. For a full discussion of the profiles, see Hathaway and Meehl, *An Atlas;* a short account may be found in Hathaway and Monachesi, *Analyzing and Predicting . . . ,* pp. 19–23.

32. Gordon P. Waldo and Simon Dinitz, "Personality Attributes of the Criminal: An Analysis of Research Studies, 1950–1965," *Journal of Research in Crime and Delinquency* 4(2):185–202 (July 1967).

do not reflect any personality differences, but simply reflect differences in the situations in which delinquents and criminals find themselves. Thus, results of tests with the MMPI may tell us little or nothing that is relevant to understanding the causes of criminal and delinquent behavior. Like the findings of the Gluecks, however, the differences between criminals and noncriminals may be arranged into statistical tables that may have some usefulness in criminal justice policy. One such use for the MMPI has been presented by Megargee and Bohn, who argue that prisoners can be classified into ten distinct groups based on their MMPI profiles.[33] They do not present any theoretical arguments about the origin of these "personality types," and state only that sorting prisoners into these groups is a useful tool for prison management.

Reviews of the use of personality tests sometimes conclude that most criminals fall into one of three personality types: the neurotic or conflicted offender, who is characterized by some form of mental illness; the unsocialized or psychopathic offender, who lacks any feelings of guilt; and the normal offender, whose criminality is derived from close social ties to other offenders.[34] Yet this classification of criminals seems extremely weak. Regarding the first personality type, it is certainly true that some criminals are "neurotic" and "conflicted," but some noncriminals are also. Research indicates that, when proper controls are introduced for age, sex, social class, and other life history factors, criminals as a group experience no more mental illness than do other groups in society.[35] Regarding the second personality type, it has been pointed out above that the finding that some offenders have psychopathic personalities means that their responses to a set of statements were similar to the responses of a group of criminals and delinquents. When those statements are actually examined, it seems unlikely that the different responses reflect differences in personality. Regarding the third personality type, the finding that some criminals are "normal" means that no differences are found between them and noncriminals on personality tests. It seems the best conclusion to draw is that the differences that appear be-

33. Megargee and Bohn, op. cit.

34. Bartol, op. cit., pp. 14–15; Daniel Glaser, *Crime in Our Changing Society*, Holt, Rinehart and Winston, New York, 1978, pp. 113–15. These three types are very similar to the three types suggested by August Aichhorn (see above). For a similar classification from the psychoanalytic perspective, see Franz Alexander and Hugo Staub, *The Criminal, The Judge, and the Public*, rev. ed., The Free Press, New York, 1956.

35. John Monahan and Henry J. Steadman, "Crime and Mental Disorder: An Epidemiological Approach," in Michael Tonry and Norval Morris, eds., *Crime and Justice*, vol. 4, University of Chicago Press, Chicago, 1983. See also Bartol, op. cit., pp. 142–77.

tween criminals and noncriminals on personality tests do not seem to have any theoretical relevance to understanding the causes of criminal behavior.

## 5. PSYCHOPATHY, SOCIOPATHY, AND THE ANTISOCIAL PERSONALITY

In addition to appearing on personality inventories, the term *psychopath* is used by psychiatrists to describe individuals who exhibit a certain group of behaviors and attitudes. When used in this way, the term *psychopath* can be considered synonymous with the more recent terms *sociopath* and *antisocial personality*. The three terms will be used interchangeably in this section. The *Diagnostic and Statistical Manual of Mental Disorders* defines the antisocial personality as follows.[36]

The term is reserved for individuals who are basically unsocialized and whose behavior pattern brings them repeatedly into conflicts with society. They are incapable of significant loyalty to individuals, groups, or social values. They are grossly selfish, callous, irresponsible, impulsive, and unable to feel guilt or to learn from experience and punishment. Frustration tolerance is low. They tend to blame others or offer plausible rationalization for their behavior.

Cleckley points out that "The term psychopath (or antisocial personality) as it is applied by various psychiatrists and hospital staffs sometimes becomes so broad that it might be applied to almost any criminal."[37] He argues, however, that psychopathy is distinctly different from criminality, that the majority of psychopaths are not criminals, and the majority of criminals are not psychopaths. Psychopaths may be found in any profession, including business, science, medicine, and psychiatry.[38] The typical psychopath differs from the typical criminal in that his actions are less purposeful and his goals more incomprehensible, he causes himself needless sorrow and shame, and he usually does not commit major crimes or crimes of violence.[39]

These terms are not merely descriptions of behavior patterns but

36. *Diagnostic and Statistical Manual of Mental Disorders*, 2nd ed., American Psychiatric Association, Washington, D.C., 1968, p. 41.

37. Cleckley, op. cit., p. 263.

38. Ibid., pp. 188–221.

39. Ibid., pp. 261–63.

also imply that those behaviors originate in the personality of the individual. It is possible, however, that the behaviors may be explained by factors other than personality. For example, Yablonsky argued that "core" members of violent gangs were sociopaths, and led the gang in moblike violence as a way of acting out their own hostility and aggression.[40] Other gang researchers described the behavior of core gang members in a similar way, but argued that the behavior resulted from the need to create and maintain a leadership position in the gang.[41]

One major problem with the use of these terms has been that operational definitions have sometimes focused solely on the person's history of antisocial behaviors and have ignored the many personality characteristics mentioned in the definition given above. For example, Guze[42] diagnosed sociopathy

if at least two of the following five manifestations were present in addition to a history of police trouble (other than traffic offenses): a history of excessive fighting . . . school delinquency . . . poor job record . . . a period of wanderlust, or being a runaway. . . . For women, a history of prostitution could be substituted for one of the five manifestations.

Guze found that sociopathy, along with alcoholism and drug addiction, were the only psychiatric conditions consistently associated with criminality.[43] Given his definition of sociopathy, this conclusion might be considered merely a matter of terminology. Guze, however, went on to question whether sociopathy should be considered a psychiatric disorder that would qualify the offender for a plea of diminished responsibility at his trial. In fact, following the *Leach* case in 1957 sociopaths were classified as mentally diseased in the District of Columbia, and persons who were so diagnosed would be acquitted by reason of insanity.[44] These persons were then committed to a mental hospital where they were treated and released when their illness had been cured. Guze himself believes that psychiatry has no consistently effective methods for treating sociopathy, so he recom-

40. Lewis Yablonsky, *The Violent Gang*, Penguin, New York, 1970, pp. 236–47.

41. James F. Short, Jr., and Fred L. Stodtbeck, *Group Process and Gang Delinquency*, University of Chicago Press, Chicago, 1974, especially pp. 248–64. This material had been previously published in *Social Problems* 12: 127–40 (Fall 1964).

42. Samuel B. Guze, *Criminality and Psychiatric Disorders*, Oxford University Press, New York, 1976, pp. 35–36.

43. Ibid., p. 124.

44. *U.S.* v. *Leach*, Crim. No. 450–57 D.D.C.; in re Rosenfield, D.C.D.C. 1957, 157 F. Supp. 18; *Blocker* v. *U.S.*, 1959, 107 U.S. App. D.C. 63 at pp. 65–71; 274 F. 2d 572 at pp. 574–80; and 288 F.2d 853 at pp. 860–61.

mended that sociopaths be locked up until they reach middle age.[45]

Guze's recommendation illustrates one of the principal problems with the use of this diagnosis. The reason for locking the person up is an assumption that he or she will continue to participate in anti-social activities if allowed to remain free. Thus the person is to be confined not for acts done in the past but for acts that might be done in the future. When one considers the actual criteria used by Guze to diagnose sociopathy, it is apparent that his recommendation would apply to a great many people who have never committed serious crimes but who are more or less marginal members of society. By normal standards of justice it would seem extremely inappropriate to send these people to prison for extended lengths of time.

Guze's assumption that these offenders will continue committing crimes until middle age is not supported by a recent study by William McCord, who has done extensive work on psychopaths and crime.[46] McCord found that delinquents who had been diagnosed as psychopathic at two juvenile institutions had only slightly worse recidivism rates than other delinquents at those institutions, and that several years after release the recidivism rates were identical. Such a finding makes Guze's recommendation especially frightening.

The terms *psychopath, sociopath,* and *antisocial personality* are psychiatric classifications that describe constellations of behaviors and attitudes that tend to appear together within given individuals. As such, these terms may have some usefulness for psychiatrists who want a shorthand way to describe a certain type of person with whom they come in contact in the practice of their profession. But when those terms are applied to criminals, they seem to be simply labels that psychiatrists attach to more serious offenders and which do not seem to add anything to our ability to identify these offenders in the first place, to understand why they behave this way, or to do anything about them in the long run.

Recent research shows that a relatively small group of offenders is responsible for a disproportionate amount of serious criminal activity.[47] It may be a reasonable and effective policy to lock up these offenders for extended periods of time, and a considerable amount of research is presently going on about how to carry out such a pol-

45. Guze, op. cit., p. 137.

46. William McCord, *The Psychopath and Milieu Therapy,* Academic Press, New York, 1982. See also William McCord and Jose Sanchez, "The Treatment of Deviant Children: A Twenty-Five-Year Follow-Up Study," *Crime and Delinquency* 29 (2): 238–53 (April 1983).

47. See, for example, Marvin E. Wolfgang, Robert F. Figlio, and Thorsten Sellin, *Delinquency in a Birth Cohort,* University of Chicago Press, Chicago, 1972.

icy.[48] To some extent psychiatrists such as Guze are simply recommending such a policy, and arguing that they are able to identify such offenders through psychiatric means. If that is their claim, then their track record so far has been a poor one. This track record is examined further in the next section, which directly addresses the attempt by psychiatrists to predict dangerous behavior.

## 6. THE PREDICTION OF FUTURE DANGEROUSNESS

Guze's recommendation to lock up sociopaths until they reach middle age raises the issue of whether the law should attempt to prevent the future occurrence of crimes by confining dangerous or antisocial people. In fact, a large number of "dangerous offender," "habitual criminal," and "sexual psychopath" laws have been passed by various states. Most of these laws rely at least in part on psychiatric evaluation in the attempt to predict the future criminality of particular individuals, and they provide extended sentences on the basis of that prediction.

Morris and Hawkins argue that these laws have been complete failures, producing chaotic and unjust results, sweeping up nuisances and social misfits and leaving untouched the truly dangerous and serious offenders.[49] The failure of these laws was strikingly in evidence when a Supreme Court decision in 1966 required the transfer to regular mental hospitals of 967 patients in New York State hospitals for the criminally insane because proper procedure had not been followed in their commitments. All of these patients had been considered "dangerous." In the following five years only 26 of these were returned to the hospitals for the criminally insane. One-half of the original group were later discharged from the mental hospital altogether, and of these, 83 percent had no further arrests.[50] They had been held an average of 13 years.

Although attempting to predict dangerous behavior would seem to be extremely important, in practice it is confounded by so many difficulties that it often does more harm than good. Brodsky notes that "there seems to be no such behavioral entity as dangerousness" and that "to predict the likely commission of a specific offense, such

48. This research and the empirical and ethical problems associated with it is extensively reviewed in Jacqueline Cohen, "Incapacitation as a Strategy for Crime Control: Possibilities and Pitfalls," in Michael Tonry and Norval Morris, eds., *Crime and Justice*, pp. 1–84.

49. Norval Morris and Gordon Hawkins, *The Honest Politician's Guide to Crime Control*, University of Chicago Press, Chicago, 1970, pp. 185–92.

50. H. J. Steadman, "The Psychiatrist as a Conservative Agent of Social Control," *Social Problems* 20 (2): 263–71 (1972).

as murder, is very difficult."[51] Shah points out that the definition of *dangerousness* is generally left unspecified in the law and is interpreted within a particular social context.[52] For example, drunk drivers can easily be shown to be more dangerous to both themselves and to others than paranoid schizophrenics, psychotics, or sexual psychopaths, yet these persons are never considered under the "dangerous offender" laws. At the same time many would state that an exhibitionist, who is generally included under these laws, is not dangerous to anyone. Sarbin argues that the underlying meaning of *dangerousness* in these laws involves its threat to the social morality of the existing power structure, rather than to physical danger itself.[53]

The most extensive attempt to predict violent behavior was a 10-year study in Massachusetts by Kozol and his associates,[54] which involved the use of extensive psychiatric and social casework services in the attempt to predict the future likely dangerousness of a group of high-risk offenders prior to their release from prison. Morris summarized the results of this study in Table 7-1.[55] Although it might be said that they had a relatively good batting average, it still should be pointed out that they were unable to predict nearly two-thirds of the violent crime that ultimately occurred (31 crimes out of 48), and that nearly two-thirds of the persons whom they predicted would be violent (32 persons out of 49) were not. Because of the probable occurrence of such errors, Morris argues that it is fundamentally unjust to detain anyone on the basis of a prediction of his future behavior.[56] In addition, the idea that a person can be punished for what he *might* do rather than for what he has actually done seriously threatens the basic notions of freedom of the individual from unwarranted governmental control.[57]

Monahan extensively reviewed the clinical techniques for predicting violent behavior and concluded that it can only be done within

51. Stanley L. Brodsky, *Psychologists in the Criminal Justice System*, University of Illinois Press, Urbana, Ill., 1973, p. 142.

52. Saleem A. Shah, "Crime and Mental Illness: Some Problems in Defining and Labeling Deviant Behavior," *Mental Hygiene* 53 (1): 31 (Jan. 1969).

53. Theodore R. Sarbin, "The Dangerous Individual," *British Journal of Criminology* 22: 285–295 (1967).

54. Harry L. Kozol, Richard J. Boucher, and Ralph F. Garofalo, "The Diagnosis and Treatment of Dangerousness," *Crime and Delinquency* 18: 371–92 (1972).

55. Norval Morris, *The Future of Imprisonment*, University of Chicago Press, Chicago, 1974, p. 71. Reprinted by permission of the publisher.

56. Ibid., p. 73.

57. Ibid., pp. 83–84.

TABLE 7–1    Results of the Kozol Study

| Prediction | Result | | Total |
| --- | --- | --- | --- |
| | No Violent Crime | Violent Crime | |
| Safe | 355 | 31 | 386 |
| Violent crime | 32 | 17 | 49 |
| Total | 387 | 48 | 435 |

very restricted circumstances.[58] Specifically he concluded that it is possible to estimate the probability of a violent act in the immediate future when the person is going to remain in a situation that is essentially similar to ones in which he or she had committed violent acts in the past. Monahan presented a complex procedure for estimating this probability, which included (1) a comparison of the circumstances the offender was likely to encounter in the near future with the circumstances in which the offender had committed violent acts in the past; (2) the recency, severity, and frequency of violent acts the individual had committed in the past; and (3) general statistics on the probability of violence for individuals who are similar in age, sex, race, class, history of drug abuse, residential and employment stability, and educational attainment. Monahan stated that it is not possible to predict violence over a long period of time, or to predict it when a person was moving from one situation to a very different one (e.g., on being released from prison). He also maintained that this type of prediction is entirely separate from the diagnosis of mental disease, and that if mental disease is also of interest, a separate examination must be undertaken. Finally Monahan argued that psychologists should confine themselves to estimating the probability of a violent act and should not recommend whether any official action should be taken in a given case. According to Monahan, criminal justice officials are responsible for deciding whether or not to take official actions while the role of psychologists and psychiatrists is to provide accurate information on which to base those decisions.

## 7. IMPLICATIONS AND CONCLUSIONS

Bartol has made the following comment about sociologists and psychologists who search for the causes of criminal behavior:[59]

58. John Monahan, *Predicting Violent Behavior*, Sage, Beverly Hills, Cal., 1981.
59. Bartol, op. cit., p. 5.

Sociologists have often looked for strictly social-situational clues, assuming that situational factors exert overwhelmingly powerful influences on the individual. More often than not, sociological criminologists have treated the individual as if he or she were "empty headed" and invariably swayed one way or the other by persons and events. Psychologists, on the other hand, have generally searched for evasive personality variables to over-ride the situational variables. . . . Which is more important in criminal activity, the person or the situation? The answer does not crucially concern us here. Why? Because it depends on the person and the situation. In some cases, personality is the major determinant of whether or not a person engages in criminal action, while in other cases the situation might exert the more powerful influence. We should shift our focus from examining the situation-free person or the situation-bound person and analyze instead the specific interactions between the situation and the person's cognitions and behavior patterns.

To some extent Bartol's statement represents an appropriate conclusion to this chapter. However, an additional point must also be made, which is that the research so far has failed to establish a very large role for the personality as a cause of criminal behavior. Certainly there are exceptions to this rule. There is no question that for some individuals personality is the major determinant of criminal behavior, but those individuals appear to be relatively infrequent exceptions. In order to understand the behavior of most criminals and delinquents, it is more profitable to start by analyzing their life situation rather than their personality characteristics.

### RECOMMENDED READINGS

Curt R. Bartol, *Criminal Behavior: A Psychosocial Approach*, Prentice-Hall, Englewood Cliffs, N.J., 1980. A broad review of psychological theories of crime, including biological and situational aspects.

Curt R. Bartol, *Psychology and American Law*, Wadsworth, Belmont, Cal., 1983. Applies psychological principles to the criminal justice system. Includes one chapter on the psychology of criminal behavior.

David J. Tennenbaum, "Personality and Criminality: A Summary and Implications of the Literature," *Journal of Criminal Justice* 5 (3): 225–35 (1977). A more recent update of the studies by Schuessler and Cressey and by Waldo and Dinitz, reaching similar conclusions.

John Monahan and Henry J. Steadman, "Crime and Mental Disorder: An Epidemiological Approach," in Michael Tonry and Norval Morris, eds., *Crime and Justice*, vol. 4, University of Chicago Press, Chicago, 1983. Rates of mental illness are no higher among criminals than among comparable groups in the general population.

Hans Toch, ed., *Psychology of Crime and Criminal Justice*, Holt, Rinehart and Winston, New York, 1979. Includes excellent chapters on psychoanalytic explanations of crime (by Fritz Redl and Hans Toch), the antisocial personality (by Albert Rabin), personality tests and delinquency (by Charles Hanley), insanity (by Thomas Szasz), and many others.

Kent S. Miller, *The Criminal Justice and Mental Health Systems: Conflict and Collusion*, Oelgeschlager, Gunn & Hain, Cambridge, Mass., 1980. The two systems have very similar functions and are rapidly being merged.

William S. Laufer and James M. Day, eds., *Personality Theory, Moral Development and Criminal Behavior*, Lexington Books, Lexington, Mass., 1983. A collection of original writings on the psychology of personality and moral development, including cognitive-developmental, biosocial, social-learning, social-psychological, and psychodynamic perspectives.

Hans Toch, *Violent Men: An Inquiry Into the Psychology of Violence*, Aldine, Chicago, 1969. Violent men have propensities for violence that are built into their personalities and modes of functioning.

Nancy Andreasen, *The Broken Brain: The Biological Revolution in Psychiatry*, Harper and Row, New York, 1984. Serious forms of mental illness are mainly due to abnormalities in brain structure and chemistry, not to emotional trauma.

# CHAPTER EIGHT

# Crime, Poverty, and Economic Inequality

In sharp contrast to the explanations of criminal behavior that focus on the characteristics of the individual are those theories that minimize or ignore entirely the significance of the individual's biological or psychological makeup. Perhaps the oldest and most elaborately documented of the theories with a nonindividual orientation are those that explain criminal behavior in terms of economic differences or influence. Discussions of the sad state of the poor, with arguments about the undesirable consequences of poverty such as sickness, vagrancy, crime, and hopeless despair, go far back into antiquity.[1] These discussions have generated a great many empirical studies concerning the relationship between poverty and crime.

There are several possible relationships between poverty and crime. It is possible, for instance, that poverty is related to another factor, such as resentment or malnutrition, that is the actual cause of crime, or that a factor such as low intelligence causes both crime and poverty. But the most commonly held view is that poverty itself causes crime. Some of the studies attempting to test this view focus on variations in economic conditions to see if they correspond to variations in crime rates. If crime is caused by poverty, so the reasoning goes, then there should be more crime in places and at times where there are more poor people. Thus these studies have compared times of economic depression with times of economic prosperity, and wealthy areas of a country with poverty-stricken areas, to see if there are any systematic differences in their crime rates. The present chapter ex-

1. For a brief history of these arguments as they relate to crime, see Lynn McDonald, *The Sociology of Law and Order*, Faber and Faber, London, 1976.

amines those studies, along with more recent studies that examine whether crime is associated with inequality rather than poverty, that is, with poverty that exists next to wealth.

## 1. HISTORICAL BACKGROUND: GUERRY AND QUETELET

The first attempts to test the connection between general economic conditions and crime rates came with the development in Europe of relatively accurate official records, as part of the development of stable social and political organization. Systematic registries of births and deaths, for example, developed in European cities and states in the 1500s.[2] In the 1600s various items in the official records began to be counted and compared as part of an analysis of economic conditions and their consequences. In England such studies came to be called "political arithmetic,"[3] while in Germany they were called "moral statistik."[4] Edmund Halley (1656–1742), the astronomer for whom Halley's comet was named, compiled and published, in 1692–93, the first systematic "life expectancy tables."[5] Adam Smith made cogent use of these same official data on social and economic conditions in his great work, *Inquiry into the Nature and Causes of the Wealth of Nations* (1776), as did Malthus in his controversial studies on population growth.[6]

The first modern national crime statistics were published in France in 1827,[7] and shortly after that, Guerry published what is considered by many to be the first work in "scientific criminology."[8] He used shaded ecological maps to represent differing crime rates in relation to various social factors. After preliminary publication in 1829, his work appeared in expanded book form in 1833 under the title *Essai sur la statistique morale de la France*. Guerry tested the commonly

2. Walter F. Wilcox, "History of Statistics," in *Encyclopedia of the Social Sciences*, vol. 14, Macmillan, New York, 1931, p. 356.

3. Bernard Lécuyer and Anthony R. Oberschall, "The Early History of Social Research," *International Encyclopedia of the Social Sciences*, vol. 15, pp. 36–37.

4. Yale Levin and Alfred Lindesmith, "English Ecology and Criminology of the Past Century," *Journal of Criminal Law and Criminology* 27: 801–16 (Mar.–Apr. 1937), p. 815; reprinted in Harwin L. Voss and David M. Peterson, eds., *Ecology, Crime, and Delinquency*, Appleton-Century-Crofts, New York, 1971, pp. 47–64.

5. Lécuyer and Oberschall, op. cit., p. 37.

6. Cf. Thomas R. Malthus, *Essay on Principle of Population as it Affects the Future Improvement of Society*, London, 1798. For a discussion of Malthus, see the article by Mark Blaug in *International Encyclopedia of the Social Sciences*, vol. 9, pp. 549–52.

7. Alfred Lindesmith and Yale Levin, "The Lombrosian Myth in Criminology," *American Journal of Sociology* 42: 653–71 (March 1937), p. 655.

8. Terence Morris, *The Criminal Area*, Routledge and Kegan Paul, New York, 1957, pp. 42–53; reprinted in Voss and Peterson, op. cit., pp. 65–76.

held belief that crime was associated with poverty, but he found instead that the wealthiest region of France had a higher rate of property crimes but only about half the rate of violent crime. However, Guerry had measured wealth and poverty by the amount of direct taxation, and he pointed out that the wealthiest sections had a great deal of poverty in them. Although he did not directly measure the poverty in those wealthier provinces, he concluded that poverty itself did not cause property crime, but rather the main factor was opportunity: In the wealthier provinces there was much more to steal.

An elaborate analysis of crime in France, Belgium, and Holland appeared in 1831, by Adolphe Quetelet (1796–1874), the distinguished Belgian mathematician, astronomer, and developer of social statistics.[9] Quetelet had been called "the first social criminologist" whose view was that "society prepares the crime and the guilty is only the instrument by which it is accomplished."[10] Quetelet examined the relationship between crime and poverty, and found a pattern similar to the one Guerry had noted. Like Guerry, Quetelet suggested that opportunities might have something to do with explaining this pattern in that wealthier cities "might attract vagabonds who hope to find impunity by losing themselves in the crowd."[11] He also pointed to an additional factor: the great inequality between wealth and poverty in the same place excites passions and provokes temptations of all kinds.[12] This problem is especially severe in those places where rapidly changing economic conditions can result in a person suddenly passing from wealth to poverty while all around him still enjoy wealth. In contrast, provinces that were generally poor and had little wealth had less crime as long as people were able to satisfy their basic needs.

## 2. CRIME AND UNEMPLOYMENT

Since that time there have been literally hundreds of studies on this subject, published in Europe and in the United States.[13] Almost from

9. Adolphe Quetelet, *Research on the Propensity for Crime at Different Ages*, translated by Sawyer F. Sylvester, Anderson, Cincinnati, 1984.

10. C. Bernaldo de Quiros, *Modern Theories of Criminality*, Little, Brown, Boston, 1911, p. 10.

11. Quetelet, op. cit., p. 40.

12. Ibid., pp. 37–38.

13. European and American studies up to 1935 are reviewed in Thorsten Sellin, *Research Memorandum on Crime in the Depression*, Social Science Research Council Bulletin No. 27, New York, 1937; reprinted by Arno Press, New York, 1972. A number of these studies are also reviewed in the first and second editions of the present book. See George B. Vold, *The-*

the first, however, there has been disagreement about the findings and debate about whether the conclusions being drawn were justified. A few of the more recent studies, focusing on the relationship of unemployment to crime and delinquency, are described here to give a sense of these controversies. Unemployment is one indicator of general economic conditions, since it increases in times of depression and decreases in times of prosperity.

Consider first the studies that focus on the relationship between unemployment and juvenile delinquency. A study by Glaser and Rice found that delinquency is inversely related to unemployment; that is, delinquency is high when unemployment is low and vice versa.[14] Glaser and Rice suggested that this might be because in times of unemployment parents are more available to their children. Two econometric studies, however, concluded that delinquency is directly related to unemployment, and that a 1 percent increase in unemployment results in an approximately .15 percent increase in delinquency.[15] A third econometric study found that unemployment had no effect on the criminality of urban males in the age group 14 to 24.[16] Danser and Laub used victimization data rather than official police statistics, and concluded that there was no relationship between juvenile delinquency and adult unemployment, contradicting Glaser and Rice's findings.[17] They also found that there was no relationship between delinquency and juvenile unemployment rates,

*oretical Criminology*, 2nd ed., prepared by Thomas J. Bernard, Oxford University Press, New York, 1979, pp. 168–71. Abstracts of more recent studies may be found in Thomas C. Castellano and Robert J. Sampson, "Annotations and References of the Literature on the Relationship between Economic Conditions and Criminality," in Kenneth R. Danser and John H. Laub, *Juvenile Criminal Behavior and Its Relation to Economic Conditions*, Criminal Justice Research Center, Albany, 1981.

14. Daniel Glaser and Kent Rice, "Crime, Age, and Employment," *American Sociological Review* 24:679–86 (Oct. 1959). Additional support for this study can be found in Jack P. Gibbs, "Crime, Unemployment and Status Integration," *The British Journal of Criminology* 6 (1): 49–58 (Jan. 1966). The study was criticized as a statistical artifact in Marcia Guttentag, "The Relationship of Unemployment to Crime and Delinquency," *Journal of Social Issues* 24 (1): 105–14 (Jan. 1968).

15. Larry D. Singell, "An Examination of the Empirical Relationship Between Unemployment and Juvenile Delinquency." *The American Journal of Economics and Sociology* 26 (4): 377–86; and Belton M. Fleischer, "The Effect of Unemployment on Juvenile Delinquency," *Journal of Political Economy* 71: 543–55 (Dec. 1963). Related works by Fleischer are "The Effect of Income on Delinquency," *The American Economic Review*, March 1966, pp. 118–37, and *The Economics of Delinquency*, Quadrangle Books, Chicago, 1966. This position is supported in Harold L. Votey, Jr., and Llad Phillips, "The Control of Criminal Activity: An Economic Analysis," in Daniel Glaser, ed., *Handbook of Criminology*, Rand McNally, Chicago, 1974, pp. 1065–69.

16. Isaac Ehrlich, "Participation in Illegitimate Activities: A Theoretical and Empirical Investigation," *Journal of Political Economy*, May–June 1973, pp. 521–64.

17. Danser and Laub, op. cit.

even within specific age, sex, and racial groups. Calvin, in contrast, argues that there is a close relationship between unemployment and crime for black youths, and that those who argue that there is no relationship are using incorrect data or faulty interpretations.[18]

There have also been contradictory findings on the question of the relationship between unemployment and adult crime. Nagel found a strong correlation between crime rates and unemployment rates when he ranked each of the 50 states on those two measures.[19] Brenner concluded, on the basis of a study of national crime and unemployment statistics from 1940 to 1973, that a sustained 1 percent increase in unemployment results in a 5.7 percent increase in murder.[20] Berk and his colleagues studied programs that provide unemployment benefits to released prisoners, and concluded: "For ex-offenders at least, unemployment and poverty do cause crime."[21] In contrast, a number of other authors have concluded that there is either no relationship between unemployment and crime or that the relationship (sometimes found to be positive and sometimes negative) is insignificant.[22] Orsagh reviewed a number of these studies, concluding: "Unemployment may affect the crime rate, but even if it does, its general effect is too slight to be measured. Therefore, the proper inference is that the effect of unemployment on crime rates is minimal at best."[23]

18. Allen D. Calvin, "Unemployment Among Black Youths, Demographics, and Crime," *Crime and Delinquency* 27 (2): 234–44, (1981).

19. William G. Nagel, "A Statement on Behalf of a Moratorium on Prison Construction," *Crime and Delinquency* 23 (2): 154–72 (Apr. 1977).

20. Harvey Brenner, *Estimating the Social Costs of National Economic Policy*, U.S. Government Printing Office, Washington, D.C., 1976. See also a summary of his testimony before the House Judiciary Committee's Subcommittee on Crime in *Criminal Justice Newsletter*, Oct. 10, 1977, p. 5.

21. Richard A. Berk, Kenneth J. Lenihan, and Peter H. Rossi, "Crime and Poverty: Some Experimental Evidence from Ex-Offenders," *American Sociological Review* 45: 766–86 (Oct. 1980). See also their *Money, Work, and Crime: Experimental Evidence*, Academic Press, New York, 1980.

22. See, for example, Sharon K. Long and Ann D. Witte, "Current Economic Trends," in Kevin N. Wright, ed., *Crime and Criminal Justice in a Declining Economy*, Oelgeschlager, Gunn & Hain, Cambridge, Mass., 1981, pp. 69–143; D. Jacobs, "Inequality and Economic Crime," *Sociology and Social Research* 66: 12–28 (Oct. 1981); Alan Booth, David R. Johnson, and Harvey Choldin, "Correlates of City Crime Rates: Victimization Surveys Versus Official Statistics," *Social Problems* 25: 187–97 (1977); and Paul E. Spector, "Population Density and Unemployment," *Criminology* 12 (4): 399–401 (1975).

23. Thomas Orsagh, "Unemployment and Crime," *Journal of Criminal Law and Criminology* 71 (2): 181–83 (Summer 1980).

3. COUNTING POOR PEOPLE

Measures of general economic conditions and unemployment are both ways of estimating the extent of poverty at a particular place and time. But it is also possible to measure poverty more directly by counting the number of poor people in an area, to see if areas that have more poor people have greater amounts of crime. Results of such studies, however, have also proved inconsistent and even contradictory.

For example, using 1970 statistics, Cho found that the percentage of people below the poverty line in the 49 largest cities of the United States was not associated with any of the seven index crimes reported by the FBI.[24] Jacobs reached a similar conclusion with respect to the crimes of burglary, robbery, and grand larceny.[25] In contrast Ehrlich found that there was a positive relationship between state property crime rates for 1940, 1950, and 1960 and the percentage of households receiving less than half the median income.[26] An even stronger result was found by Loftin and Hill, who created an index of "structural poverty" including measures of infant mortality, low education, and one-parent families, as well as income.[27] They found very strong correlation between this measure and state homicide rates. Similar results using the same index of structural poverty were found in two additional studies, one of which concluded that it was strongly correlated with homicides involving families and friends but not in homicides involving strangers.[28] To make matters even more confusing, some studies have found that there are different poverty-crime relationships in different regions of the country.[29] One of these studies concluded that the results are

24. Y. H. Cho, *Public Policy and Urban Crime*, Ballinger, Cambridge, Mass., 1974.

25. D. Jacobs, "Inequality and Economic Crime," *Sociology and Social Research* 66: 12–28 (Oct. 1981).

26. Isaac Ehrlich, "Participation in Illegal Activities," in Gary S. Becker and W. M. Landes, eds., *Essays in the Economics of Crime and Punishment*, Columbia University Press, New York, 1974.

27. Colin Loftin and R. H. Hill, "Regional Subculture and Homicide," *American Sociological Review* 39: 714–24 (1974).

28. Steven F. Messner, "Regional and Racial Effects on the Urban Homicide Rate: The Subculture of Violence Revisited," *American Journal of Sociology* 88: 997–1007 (1983); M. Wayne Smith and Robert Nash Parker, "Type of Homicide and Variation in Regional Rates," *Social Forces* 59 (1): 136–47 (Sept. 1980). Smith and Parker argue that structural poverty is related to homicides between families and friends, but not between strangers.

29. Steven F. Messner, "Regional Differences in the Economic Correlates of the Urban Homicide Rate," *Criminology* 21 (4): 477–88, (Nov. 1983); John D. McCarthy, Omer Galle, and William Zimmern, "Population Density, Social Structure, and Interpersonal Violence," *American Behavioral Scientist* 18 (6): 771–89 (July–Aug. 1975); Booth, Johnson, and Choldin, op. cit.

best explained by variations in the way crimes are reported and re-corded, rather than by variations in the incidence of crime.[30]

## 4. INTERPRETING THE STUDIES

All of these studies, extending back over a period of more than 150 years, have given inconclusive if not actually contradictory results. The interpretations of these studies, accordingly, have been based on two contradictory theoretical assumptions. The first is that *the relationship is inverse or negative;* that is, when economic conditions are good, the amount of criminality should be low, while when economic conditions are bad, criminality should be high. That assumption is found throughout history and is still fairly commonly believed by the public. But many studies have contradicted that assumption, and as a result a second theoretical assumption has arisen, that *the relationship is direct or positive;* that is, that criminality is an extension of normal economic activity (a criminal fringe, as it were), and that therefore it increases and decreases in the same manner as other economic conditions. If the second assumption is correct, the amount of crime should increase and be at its highest point when economic conditions are good, and it should decrease when conditions are bad.

The theoretical position represented by the second assumption was stated by Morris Ploscowe in 1931, in an attempt to explain the generally accepted belief that crime had increased throughout much of the Western world during the previous 150 years, despite the obvious increase in the economic well-being of nearly everyone.[31] Ploscowe argued that the unparalleled economic and social progress had given the ordinary worker a much better economic position than he had ever enjoyed in the past, but it also brought new pressures and demands that often resulted in criminality. He concluded: "Where increased incentives and increased occasions for illegitimate activities result from an increased amount of legitimate activity, there is apt to be an increase in crime."[32]

But Ploscowe's assumption about rising crime rates was later contradicted in a study by Gurr and his colleagues, which found that the crime rates of London, Stockholm, and Sydney had actually decreased from the 1840s to the 1930s (Ploscowe wrote his report in

30. Booth et al., op. cit.

31. Morris Ploscowe, "Some Causative Factors in Criminality," *Report on the Causes of Crime,* vol. 1, part 1, no. 13, Report of National Commission on Law Observance and Law Enforcement, Washington, D.C., June 26, 1931, pp. 115–16.

32. Ibid., p. 114.

1931) and at that time were only about one-eighth of their earlier levels.[33] Gurr also found that from the 1930s to the 1970s crime had increased by approximately the same amount as the previous decrease. He speculated that some of the recent increases in crime rates may be due to more complete police reporting of crimes, but argued that, in general, these statistics reflected basic trends in the incidence of criminal behavior.

Gurr considered the relationship between crime and economic conditions, and found support for both assumptions:[34]

The evidence of the city studies is that poverty *and* wealth are correlated with the incidence of common crime, not only theft but crimes against the person as well. In nineteenth century London, Stockholm, and New South Wales both theft and assault increased during periods of economic slump and declined when economic conditions improved again. Economic distress had very little effect on crime rates in either direction in the twentieth century, but as total productivity (wealth) increased, so did common crime. Evidently two separate causal processes were at work at different times.

Some of the confusion in the statistical arguments over the relationship between economic conditions and criminality arises because the same studies can be interpreted as supporting both theoretical positions. That is the result of a problem in specifying the amount of time before economic changes are said to have an effect on criminality. Should one assume that changes in crime rates will occur at the same time as changes in economic conditions, or should one assume that there will be some period of delay, or *lag*, before the crime rates are affected? Some studies find very different relationships between economic conditions and criminality when different time lags are considered.[35] The same study can then be cited as support for both contradictory theoretical assumptions simply by selecting the data at different time lags.

33. Ted Robert Gurr, *Rogues, Rebels, and Reformers*, Sage, Beverly Hills, Cal., 1976. This study also considers crime rates of Calcutta, a non-Western city that had a different pattern of crime rates. For the complete study, see Ted Robert Gurr, Peter N. Grabosky, and Richard C. Hula, *The Politics of Crime and Conflict: A Comparative History of Four Cities*, Sage, Beverly Hills, Cal., 1977. A shorter version is found in Gurr's article "Contemporary Crime in Historical Perspective: A Comparative Study of London, Stockholm, and Sydney," *Annals of the American Academy of Political and Social Science* 434: 114–36 (Nov. 1977).

34. Gurr, *Rogues, Rebels, and Reformers*, p. 179.

35. See, for example, Dorothy Swaine Thomas, *Social Aspects of the Business Cycle*, Routledge & Kegan Paul, London, 1925, p. 143. This point is argued more extensively and with supporting data in earlier editions of the present text. See George B. Vold, *Theoretical Criminology*, Oxford University Press, New York, 1958, pp. 177–81; see also the 2nd ed., prepared by Thomas J. Bernard, 1979, pp. 176–78.

Another problem is that poverty is always in part a subjective condition, relative to what others have, rather than any simple objective fact of the presence or absence of a certain amount of property or other measure of wealth. What one person considers poverty another may view as a level of satisfactory comfort, if not of abundance. Unemployment, too, is somewhat related to the subjective factor of "willingness to work." Thus, despite the fact that poverty and unemployment are genuine kinds of human experience, they nevertheless do not lend themselves readily to the accurate gathering of information.[36]

## 5. POVERTY, ECONOMIC INEQUALITY, AND RELATIVE DEPRIVATION

This discussion raises the possibility that factors such as economic inequality and relative deprivation may be related to crime rather than poverty itself. Poverty and economic inequality are quite different concepts, and both are different from the concept of relative deprivation. It is therefore necessary to distinguish clearly between these three terms before continuing.

Poverty refers to the lack of some fixed level of material goods necessary for survival and minimum well-being. In contrast, economic inequality refers to a comparison between the material level of those who have the least in a society and the material level of other groups in that society. Countries in which everyone has an adequate material level have little or no poverty, but they may still have a great deal of economic inequality if there is a very large gap between those who have the least and those who have the most. On the other hand, countries in which everyone is poor have a great deal of poverty but little or no economic inequality.

Relative deprivation has been extensively discussed by a number of authors.[37] It combines economic inequality with feelings of resentment and injustice among those who have the least in the society.[38] Countries with little or no poverty may have a problem with relative deprivation if those who have the least in the society are angry because they believe the distribution of material wealth is un-

---

36. For some of the problems of counting unemployed persons, see Gwynn Nettler, *Explaining Crime*, 3rd ed., McGraw-Hill, New York, 1984, pp. 127–29.

37. See especially W. G. Runciman, *Relative Deprivation and Social Justice*, University of California Press, Berkeley, Cal., 1966.

38. Steven Stack, "Income Inequality and Property Crime: A Cross-National Analysis of Relative Deprivation Theory," *Criminology* 22 (2): 229–57 (May 1984).

just. Much of the current confusion in evaluating research on the relationship between economic conditions and crime comes from a failure to distinguish among these three quite different concepts.[39]

Arguments about the relationship between crime and relative deprivation are similar to strain theories,[40] which are presented in Chapter 11. But a number of recent studies have attempted to link crime to economic inequality, without considering whether it is associated with feelings of anger or resentment.[41] These studies have produced their most consistent results with respect to the crime of homicide, which is significant both because homicide is the most serious crime and because it generally is the most accurately reported.

Six studies of international crime rates have found that countries with more economic inequality tend to have higher homicide rates, while those with less economic inequality tend to have lower homicide rates.[42] No studies have reached the opposite conclusion, and none has been inconclusive. The consistency of this finding may be attributed in part to the fact that many of these studies used similar data sets, so that they may not have been totally independent replications. However, these same studies reached contradictory conclusions about the relationship between economic inequality and property crime rates, some concluding that there was a relationship and others concluding that there was not.[43] This suggests that there may be some real relationship between a nation's homicide rates and the extent of its economic inequality.

Studies of the relationship between American crime rates and economic inequality have been less consistent but are still impres-

39. See, for example, Nettler, op. cit., pp. 220–38, in which the three types of studies are lumped together.

40. See Steven Box, *Deviance, Reality and Society*, 2nd ed., Holt, Rinehart and Winston, New York, 1981.

41. For example, many of these studies use the Gini coefficient, which is a statistic that measures the extent to which incomes are dispersed in a society relative to the average income in that society. The Gini coefficient is an objective measure of income inequality, but not a measure of poverty nor of relative deprivation. See S. Yitzhaki, "Relative Deprivation and the Gini Coefficient," *Quarterly Journal of Economics* 93: 321–24 (May 1974).

42. Steven F. Messner, "Societal Development, Social Equality, and Homicide," *Social Forces* 61: 225–40 (1982); Steven F. Messner, "Income Inequality and Murder Rates: Some Cross-National Findings," *Comparative Social Research* 3: 185–98 (1980); John Braithwaite and Valerie Braithwaite, "The Effects of Income Inequality and Social Democracy on Homicides: A Cross-National Comparison," *British Journal of Criminology* 20: 45–53 (1980); John Braithwaite, *Inequality, Crime, and Public Policy*, Routledge and Kegan Paul, London, 1979; Marvin D. Krohn, "Inequality, Unemployment, and Crime, *Sociological Quarterly* 17: 303–33 (1976); and Lynn McDonald, *Sociology of Law and Order*, Faber and Faber, London, 1976.

43. In addition to the studies cited in footnote 42, see Stack, op. cit., which fails to support the property crime–inequality link, and K. L. Avio and C. S. Clark, *Property Crime in Canada: An Econometric Study*, University of Toronto Press, Toronto, 1976, which reaches the opposite conclusion.

sive. Five studies have found that economic inequality, but not poverty, was directly correlated with crime rates. Three of those studies considered both violent and property crimes,[44] one considered only property crimes,[45] and one considered only violent crimes.[46] Three additional studies agreed that economic inequality was directly correlated with crime rates but argued that poverty was also correlated. One of these studies considered only homicide rates,[47] one considered only burglary and robbery,[48] and one dealt with aggravated assault, burglary, and robbery.[49] One additional study found that economic inequality was directly correlated with crime rates but did not consider any data on poverty.[50]

Three studies by Messner have presented contradictory results, all focusing on the crime of homicide and all using the same data set. In the first study Messner found that neither poverty nor economic inequality was associated with homicide rates in 204 metropolitan areas in the United States.[51] In the second study Messner found that "structural poverty," as defined by Loftin and Hill,[52] was associated with homicide but that economic inequality was not.[53] In the third study he found that economic inequality had a positive but insignificant relationship to homicide and that poverty was related to homicide outside the South.[54]

44. John Braithwaite, op. cit.; "City Crime: Report of the Council on Municipal Performance," summarized by John Tepper Marlin, *Criminal Law Bulletin* 9 (7): 557–604 (1973); Paul Eberts and Kent P. Schwirian, "Metropolitan Crime Rates and Relative Deprivation, *Criminologica* 5: 43–52 (Feb. 1968). Despite the title of Eberts and Schwirian's article, they consider only a measure of income inequality, not a measure of relative deprivation.

45. David Jacobs, "Inequality and Economic Crime," *Sociology and Social Research* 66: 12–28 (Oct. 1981).

46. Judith R. Blau and Peter M. Blau, "The Cost of Inequality: Metropolitan Structure and Violent Crime," *American Sociological Review* 47: 114–29 (1982). This study was replicated using victimization data rather than official data. The replication found support for the relationship between inequality and homicide but not aggravated assault or rape. See Robert M. O'Brien, "Metropolitan Structure and Violent Crime: Which Measure of Crime?" *American Sociological Review* 48 (3): 434–47 (June 1983).

47. Loftin and Hill, op. cit.

48. Sheldon Danziger, "Explaining Urban Crime Rates," *Criminology* 14: 291–95 (Aug. 1976).

49. Sheldon Danziger and David Wheeler, "The Economics of Crime: Punishment or Income Redistribution," *Review of Sociology and Economics* 33: 113–31 (1975).

50. Kirk Williams and S. Drake, "Social Structure, Crime, and Criminalization: An Empirical Examination of the Conflict Perspective," *Sociological Quarterly* 21: 563–68 (Autumn 1980); Richard Rosenfeld, "Income Inequality and Urban Crime," in G. A. Tobin, ed., *The Changing Structure of the City*, Sage, Beverly Hills, Cal., 1979.

51. Steven F. Messner, "Poverty, Inequality and the Urban Homicide Rate," *Criminology* 20: 103–14 (May 1982).

52. Loftin and Hill, op. cit.

53. Messner, "Regional and Racial Effects," op. cit.

54. Messner, "Regional Differences in Economic Correlates," op. cit.

A number of other researchers have responded to Messner's studies, maintaining that his findings involved statistical errors. These researchers replicated Messner's work in four separate studies that reached differing conclusions.[55] All four studies concluded that poverty was associated with homicide. Two of the studies also concluded that economic inequality was associated with homicide.[56] The third study concluded that economic inequality between racial groups was consistently associated with homicide but that overall economic inequality was not.[57] The fourth study found only a slight and insignificant relationship between economic inequality and homicide.[58]

## 6. IMPLICATIONS AND CONCLUSIONS

The relationship between crime and poverty is a difficult and confusing problem that has embroiled criminology in controversy for almost two centuries. It is easy to believe that there is a relationship between crime and poverty, since the large majority of criminal justice work involves dealing with poor people. But in the end it seems best to conclude that there is no direct causal relationship between crime and poverty since crime rates do not consistently increase and decrease as the number of poor people increases and decreases.

On the other hand, recent studies on economic inequality suggest that criminologists may have been looking at the wrong end of the social scale. These studies suggest that poor people have high crime rates when other people around them are wealthy and that they have low crime rates when other people around them are poor. Thus, the key factor needed to explain the amount of crime in a particular location may be the number of wealthy people, not the number of poor people.[59] The results of these studies have not been uniform, but they have been consistent enough to suggest that economic inequality, when properly conceptualized and measured, may turn out to be an important factor in explaining crime rates.

55. William C. Bailey, "Poverty, Inequality, and City Homicide Rates: Some Not So Unexpected Findings," *Criminology* 22 (4): 531–50 (Nov. 1984); Kirk R. Williams, "Economic Sources of Homicide: Reestimating the Effects of Poverty and Inequality," *American Sociological Review* 49: 283–89 (1984); Robert Nash Parker and Colin Loftin, "Poverty, Inequality, and Type of Homicide: A Reconsideration of Unexpected Results," paper presented at the annual meeting of the American Society of Criminology, Denver, 1983; and Richard Rosenfeld, "Inequality, Relative Deprivation and Crime: Explaining Some Discrepant Findings," paper presented at the Annual Meeting of the American Society of Criminology, Toronto, 1982.

56. Parker and Loftin, op. cit.; Rosenfeld, op. cit.

57. Williams, op. cit.

58. Bailey, op. cit.

59. Eberts and Schwirian, op. cit.; Danzinger and Wheeler, op. cit.; Fleisher, *The Economics of Delinquency*, op. cit.

RECOMMENDED READINGS

John Braithwaite, *Inequality, Crime and Public Policy*, Routledge and Kegan Paul, London, 1979. Reviews criminological theories and research to demonstrate the processes by which income inequality causes crime. Using cross-national and U.S. data, Braithwaite finds that five of seven' index offenses are strongly related to inequality. He then offers thoughtful comments on policy implications of this finding.

Peter M. Blau, *Inequality and Heterogeneity*, The Free Press, New York, 1977. A general theory of the social consequences of structural inequality, without reference to any cultural elements of resentment.

Judith R. Blau and Peter M. Blau, "The Cost of Inequality: Metropolitan Structure and Violent Crime," *American Sociological Review* 47: 114–29 (Feb. 1982). An application of Blau's general theory, finding that murder, rape, robbery, and assault are all associated with inequality but are not associated with poverty, proportion of blacks in the population, or Southern location.

Sharon K. Long and Ann D. Witte, "Current Economic Trends," in Kevin N. Wright, ed., *Crime and Criminal Justice in a Declining Economy*, Oelgeschlager, Gunn & Hain, Cambridge, Mass., 1981, pp. 69–143. Reviews available research and clarifies conceptual problems on economic theories of crime. Concludes that the quality of employment is more important then unemployment as a cause of crime.

Jane R. Chapman, *Economic Realities and the Female Offender*, Lexington Books, Lexington, Mass., 1980. Illustrates the economic nature of much crime by women, and the inability of the criminal justice system to help female offenders achieve economic stability.

James W. Thompson et al., *Employment and Crime: A Review of Theories and Research*, U.S. Government Printing Office, Washington, D.C., 1981. Applies econometric theory to crime, incorporating the idea of a segmented labor market that provides lower-class minorities only with dead-end jobs. Argues that programs to enhance employment can reduce crime.

Matthew G. Yeager, "Unemployment and Imprisonment," *Journal of Criminal Law and Criminology* 70 (4): 586–88 (1979); Ivan Jankovic, "Labor Market and Imprisonment," *Crime and Social Justice* 8: 17–31 (1977). Unemployment is strongly related to imprisonment rates, regardless of crime rates.

Thomas Orsagh and Ann D. Witte, "Economic Status and Crime: Implications for Offender Rehabilitation," *Journal of Criminal Law and Criminology* 2 (3): 1055–71 (1981). Reviews studies on the relationship between crime and employment, income, and economic viability, in the context of an assessment of econometric theories of crime. They suggest programs for improving economic viability for certain groups of offenders.

James DeFronzo, "Economic Assistance to Impoverished Americans: Relationship to Incidence of Crime," *Criminology* 21 (1): 119–36 (Feb. 1983). Using data from 39 metropolitan areas in 1970, the study found that public assistance reduces rates of homicide, rape, and burglary.

Michael Harrington, *The Other America: Poverty in the United States*, rev. ed., Macmillan, New York, 1970. A classic and important work on the subject.

# CHAPTER NINE

# Durkheim, Anomie, and Modernization

The preceding chapter concluded that economic inequality might be associated with crime. In contrast Emile Durkheim viewed inequality as a natural and inevitable human condition that is not associated with social maladies such as crime unless there is also a breakdown of social norms or rules. Durkheim called such a breakdown *anomie* and argued that it had occurred in his own society as a result of the rapid social changes accompanying the modernization process. Like Lombroso's theories, written approximately 20 years earlier, Durkheim's theories were in part a reaction to the classical assumptions that humans were free and rational in a contractual society. But where Lombroso had focused on the determinants of human behavior within the individual, Durkheim focused on society and its organization and development.

Durkheim's theories are complex, but his influence on criminology has been great. The present chapter examines his theories and discusses them in the context of later research on the relationship between crime and modernization. But Durkheim's ideas also appear in several later chapters. In the 1920s a group of Chicago sociologists used his theories, among others, as the basis for an extensive research project linking juvenile delinquency to rapid social changes in urban areas. These studies are presented in Chapter 10. In 1938 Robert K. Merton revised Durkheim's conception of anomie and applied it directly to American society. This and other similar theories are now known as *strain* or *opportunity* theories of crime and delinquency and are presented in Chapter 11. In 1969 Travis Hirschi returned to Durkheim's original conception of anomie and used it as the basis for his *control* theory of delinquency. Control theories are discussed in Chapter 12. Finally, Durkheim's view of "crime as normal" is the basis for social reaction views of the law-enactment process, which are discussed in Chapter 14.

## 1. EMILE DURKHEIM

Emile Durkheim (1858–1917) has been called "one of the best known and one of the least understood major social thinkers."[1] Presenting his thought is no easy task, since "the controversies which surround this thought bear upon essential points, not details."[2] For this reason it is best to approach his work by first considering the political and intellectual climate in which it evolved.

The nineteenth century in France was an age of great turmoil generated by the wake of the French Revolution of 1789 and by the rapid industrialization of French society. Speaking of these two "revolutions," Nisbet has pointed out that "[i]n terms of immediacy and massiveness of impact on human thought and values, it is impossible to find revolutions of comparable magnitude anywhere in human history."[3] The writings of the day were filled with a "burning sense of society's sudden, convulsive turn from a path it had followed for millennia" and a "profound intuition of the disappearance of historic values—and with them, age-old securities, as well as age-old tyrannies and inequalities—and the coming of new powers, new insecurities, and new tyrannies that would be worse than anything previously known unless drastic measures were taken. . . ."[4]

Sociology had been developed by Auguste Comte in the first half of the century largely in response to the effects of these two revolutions; it was part of a more general effort to construct a rational society out of the ruins of the traditional one.[5] Sociologists saw themselves as providing a rational, scientific analysis of the monumental social changes that were occurring, in order to "mastermind the political course of 'social regeneration.'"[6] This regeneration would

---

1. Dominick LaCapra, *Emile Durkheim, Sociologist and Philosopher*, Cornell University Press, Ithaca, N.Y., 1972, p. 5.

2. Ibid., p. 5.

3. Robert A. Nisbet, *Emile Durkheim*, Prentice-Hall, Englewood Cliffs, N.J., 1965, p. 20.

4. Ibid., p. 20.

5. LaCapra, op. cit., p. 41.

6. Julius Gould, "Auguste Comte," in T. Raison, ed., *The Founding Fathers of Social Science*, Penguin, Harmondsworth, U.K., 1969, p. 40.

consist primarily of the reestablishment of social solidarity, which appeared to have substantially disintegrated in French society.

Emile Durkheim was born of Jewish parents in a small French town on the German border, one year after the death of Comte. After completing his studies in Paris he spent several years teaching philosophy at various secondary schools in the French provinces near Paris. He then spent a year in Germany, where he studied social science and its relation to ethics under the famed experimental psychologist Wilhelm Wundt. Durkheim's publication of two articles as a result of these studies led to the creation of a special position for him at the University of Bordeaux, where in 1887 he taught the first French university course in sociology. In 1892 Durkheim received the first doctor's degree in sociology awarded by the University of Paris, and ten years later he returned to a position at the university, where he dominated sociology until his death in 1917.

Durkheim's analysis of the processes of social change involved in industrialization is presented in his first major work, *De la division du travail social (The Division of Labor in Society)*[7], written as his doctoral thesis and published in 1893. In it he describes these processes as part of the development from the more primitive "mechanical" form of society into the more advanced "organic" form. In the mechanical form each social group in society is relatively isolated from all other social groups, and is basically self-sufficient.[8] Within these social groups individuals live largely under identical circumstances, do identical work, and hold identical values. There is little division of labor, with only a few persons in the clan or village having specialized functions. Thus there is little need for individual talents, and the solidarity of the society is based on the uniformity of its members.

Contrasted with this is the organic society, in which the different segments of society depend on each other in a highly organized division of labor. Social solidarity is no longer based on the uniformity of the individuals, but on the diversity of the functions of the parts of the society. Durkheim saw all societies as being in some stage of progression between the mechanical and the organic structures, with no society being totally one or the other. Even the most primitive societies could be seen to have some forms of division of labor, and

7. Emile Durkheim, *The Division of Labor in Society*, tr. by George Simpson, The Free Press, New York, 1965.

8. Raymond Aron, *Main Currents in Sociological Thought*, vol. II, tr. by Richard Howard and Helen Weaver, Basic Books, New York, 1967, p. 12.

even the most advanced societies would require some degree of uniformity of its members.[9]

Law plays an essential role in maintaining the social solidarity of each of these two types of societies, but in very different ways. In the mechanical society law functions to enforce the uniformity of the members of the social group, and thus is oriented toward repressing any deviation from the norms of the time. In the organic society, on the other hand, law functions to regulate the interactions of the various parts of society and provides restitution in cases of wrongful transactions. Because law plays such different roles in the two types of societies, crime appears in very different forms. Durkheim argued that to the extent a society remains mechanical, crime is "normal" in the sense that a society without crime would be pathologically overcontrolled. As the society develops toward the organic form, it is possible for a pathological state, which he called anomie, to occur, and such a state would produce a variety of social maladies, including crime. Durkheim developed his concept of "crime as normal" in his second major work, *The Rules of the Sociological Method,*[10] published in 1895, only two years after *The Division of Labor;* he went on to develop anomie in his most famous work, *Suicide,*[11] published in 1897. These concepts will be explored in the following sections.

## 2. CRIME AS NORMAL IN MECHANICAL SOCIETIES

Mechanical societies are characterized by the uniformity of the lives, work, and beliefs of their members. All of the uniformity that exists in a society, that is, the "totality of social likenesses," Durkheim called the *collective conscience.*[12] Since all societies demand at least some degree of uniformity from their members (in that none are totally organic), the collective conscience may be found in every culture. In every society, however, there will always be a degree of diversity in that there will be many individual differences among its members. As Durkheim said, "There cannot be a society in which the individuals do not differ more or less from the collective type."[13]

9. Ibid., pp. 12–13.

10. Emile Durkheim, *The Rules of the Sociological Method,* tr. by Sarah A. Solovay and John H. Mueller, ed. by Georege E. G. Catlin, The Free Press, New York, 1965.

11. Durkheim, *Suicide,* tr. by John A. Spaulding and George Simpson, ed. by George Simpson, The Free Press, New York, 1951.

12. Durkheim, *Division of Labor,* p. 80, n. 10. In French, the term *conscience* has overtones of both "conscience" and "consciousness," but the term is usually translated as "collective conscience."

13. Durkheim, *Rules,* p. 70.

To the extent that a particular society is mechanical, its solidarity will come from the pressure for uniformity exerted against this diversity. Such pressure is exerted in varying degrees and in varying forms. In its strongest form it will consist of criminal sanctions. In weaker forms, however, the pressure may consist of designating certain behaviors or beliefs as morally reprehensible or merely in bad taste.

If I do not submit to the conventions of society, if in my dress I do not conform to the customs observed in my country and my class, the ridicule I provoke, the social isolation in which I am kept, produce, although in attenuated form, the same effects as a punishment in the strict sense of the word. The constraint is nonetheless efficacious for being indirect.[14]

Durkheim argued that "society cannot be formed without our being required to make perpetual and costly sacrifices."[15] These sacrifices, embodied in the demands of the collective conscience, are the price of membership in society, and fulfilling the demands gives the individual members a sense of collective identity, which is an important source of social solidarity. But, more important, these demands are constructed so that it is inevitable that a certain number of people will not fulfill them. The number must be large enough to constitute an identifiable group, but not so large as to include a substantial portion of the society. This enables the large mass of the people, all of whom fulfill the demands of the collective conscience, to feel a sense of moral superiority, identifying themselves as good and righteous, and opposing themselves to the morally inferior transgressors who fail to fulfill these demands. It is this sense of superiority, of goodness and righteousness, which Durkheim saw as the primary source of the social solidarity. Thus criminals play an important role in the maintenance of the social solidarity, since they are among the group of those identified by society as inferior, which allows the rest of society to feel superior.

The punishment of criminals also plays a role in the maintenance of the social solidarity. When the dictates of the collective conscience are violated, society responds with repressive sanctions not so much for retribution or deterrence, but because without them those who are making the "perpetual and costly sacrifices" would become

14. Ibid., pp. 2–3.

15. Kurt Wolff, ed., *Emile Durkheim et al., Writings on Sociology and Philosophy*, Harper & Row, New York, 1960, p. 338.

severely demoralized.[16] For example, when a person who has committed a serious crime is released with only a slap on the wrist, the
average, law-abiding citizen may become terribly upset. He feels that
he is playing the game by the rules, and so everyone else should
too. The punishment of the criminal is necessary to maintain the allegiance of the average citizen to the social structure. Without it the
average citizen may lose his overall commitment to the society and
his willingness to make the sacrifices necessary for it. But beyond
this, the punishment of criminals also acts as a visible, societal
expression of the inferiority and blameworthiness of the criminal
group. This reinforces the sense of superiority and righteousness found
in the mass of the people, and thus strengthens the solidarity of the
society.

Crime itself is normal in society because there is no clearly marked
dividing line between behaviors considered criminal and those considered morally reprehensible or merely in bad taste. If there is a
decrease in behaviors designated as criminal, then there may be a
tendency to move behaviors previously designated as morally reprehensible into the criminal category. For example, not every type of
unfair transfer of property is considered stealing. But if there is a
decrease in the traditional forms of burglary and robbery, there then
may be an associated increase in the tendency to define various forms
of white-collar deception as crime. These behaviors may always have
been considered morally reprehensible, and in that sense they violated the collective conscience. They were not, however, considered
crimes. Society moves them into the crime category because criminal sanctions are the strongest tool available to maintain social solidarity.

Since the institution of punishment serves an essential function, it
will be necessary in any society.

Imagine a society of saints, a perfect cloister of exemplary individuals. Crimes,
properly so called, will there be unknown; but faults which appear venial
to the layman will create there the same scandal that the ordinary offense
does in ordinary consciousnesses. If, then, this society has the power to
judge and punish, it will define these acts as criminal and will treat them
as such. For the same reason, the perfect and upright man judges his smallest
failings with a severity that the majority reserve for acts more truly in the
nature of an offense.[17]

---

16. Nisbet, op. cit., p. 225. See also Jackson Toby, "Is Punishment Necessary?" *Journal of
Criminal Law, Criminology and Police Science* 55: 332–37 (1964).

17. Durkheim, *Rules*, pp. 68–69.

Thus a society without crime is impossible. If all the behaviors that are presently defined as criminal no longer occurred, new behaviors would be placed in the crime category.[18] Crime, then, is inevitable because there is an inevitable diversity of behavior in society. The solidarity of the society is generated by exerting pressure for conformity against this diversity, and some of this pressure will inevitably take the form of criminal sanctions.[19]

Let us make no mistake. To classify crime among the phenomena of normal sociology is not merely to say that it is an inevitable, although regrettable, phenomenon, due to the incorrigible wickedness of men; it is to affirm that it is a factor in public health, an integral part of all societies.

The abnormal or pathological state of society would be one in which there was no crime. A society that had no crime would be one in which the constraints of the collective conscience were so rigid that no one could oppose them. In this type of situation crime would be eliminated, but so would the possibility of progressive social change. Social change is usually introduced by opposing the constraints of the collective conscience, and those who do this are frequently declared to be criminals. Thus Socrates and Jesus were declared criminals, as were Mahatma Gandhi and George Washington. The leaders of the union movement in the 1920s and 1930s were criminalized, as were the leaders of the civil rights movement of the 1960s. If the demands of the collective conscience had been so rigidly enforced that no crime could exist, then these movements would have been impossible also.

Thus crime is the price society pays for the possibility of progress. As Durkheim wrote,[20]

To make progress, individual originality must be able to express itself. In order that the originality of the idealist whose dreams transcend his century may find expression, it is necessary that the originality of the criminal, who is below the level of his time, shall also be possible. One does not occur without the other.

In a similar way individual growth cannot occur in a child unless it is possible for that child to misbehave. The child is punished for misbehavior, and no one wants the child to misbehave. But a child

18. Ibid., p. 67.
19. Ibid., p. 67.
20. Ibid., p. 71.

who never did anything wrong would be pathologically overcontrolled. Eliminating the misbehavior would also eliminate the possibility of independent growth. In this sense the child's misbehavior is the price that must be paid for the possibility of personal development. Durkheim concluded:[21]

From this point of view, the fundamental facts of criminality present themselves to us in an entirely new light. Contrary to current ideas, the criminal no longer seems a totally unsociable being, a sort of parasitic element, a strange and unassimilable body, introduced into the midst of society. On the contrary, he plays a definite role in social life. Crime, for its part, must no longer be conceived as an evil that cannot be too much suppressed. There is no occasion for self-congratulation when the crime rate drops noticeably below the average level, for we may be certain that this apparent progress is associated with some social disorder.

### 3. ANOMIE AS A PATHOLOGICAL STATE IN ORGANIC SOCIETIES

To the extent that a society is mechanical, it derives its solidarity from pressure for conformity against the diversity of its members. The criminalizing of some behaviors is a normal and necessary part of this pressure. But to the extent that a society is organic, the function of law is to regulate the interactions of the various parts of the whole. If this regulation is inadequate, there can result a variety of social maladies, including crime. Durkheim called the state of inadequate regulation anomie.

Durkheim first introduced this concept in *The Division of Labor in Society*. There he argued that the industrialization of French society, with its resulting division of labor, had destroyed the traditional solidarity based on uniformity. But this industrialization had been so rapid that the society had not yet been able to evolve sufficient mechanisms to regulate its transactions. Periodic cycles of overproduction followed by economic slowdown indicated that the relations between producers and consumers were ineffectively regulated. Strikes and labor violence indicated that the relations between workers and employers were unresolved. The alienation of the individual worker and the sense that the division of labor was turning men into mere "cogs in the wheel" indicated that the relation of the individual to his work was inadequately defined.[22]

Durkheim expanded and generalized his notion of anomie four years

21. Ibid., p. 72.
22. Durkheim, *Division of Labor*, pp. 370–73.

later with the publication of his most famous work, *Le Suicide*. In it he statistically analyzed data that showed that the suicide rate tends to increase sharply both in periods of economic decline and in periods of economic growth. Whereas suicide in a time of economic decline might be easily understood, the key question is why suicide would increase in a time of prosperity. Durkheim proposed that society functions to regulate not only the economic interactions of its various components, but also how the individual perceives his own needs. Durkheim's theory of anomie has been used as the basis for later explanations of crime and a variety of other deviant behaviors.[23] Because of its importance in criminology and sociology, the theory is presented here at some length, and in Durkheim's own words.[24]

a. No living being can be happy or even exist unless his needs are sufficiently proportioned to his means. In other words, if his needs require more than can be granted, or even merely something of a different sort, they will be under continual friction and can only function painfully.

b. In the animal, at least in a normal condition, this equilibrium is established with automatic spontaneity because the animal depends on purely material conditions.

c. This is not the case with man, because most of his needs are not dependent on his body. . . . A more awakened reflection suggests better conditions, seemingly desirable ends craving fulfillment. . . . Nothing appears in man's organic nor in his psychological constitution which sets a limit to such tendencies. . . . They are unlimited so far as they depend on the individual alone. . . . Thus, the more one has, the more one wants, since satisfactions received only stimulate instead of filling needs.

d. A regulative force must play the same role for moral needs which the organism plays for physical needs. . . . [S]ociety alone can play this moderating role; for it is the only moral power superior to the individual, the authority of which he accepts. . . . [I]t alone can estimate the reward to be prospectively offered to every class of human functionary, in the name of the common interest.

e. As a matter of fact, at every moment of history there is a dim perception, in the moral consciousness of societies, of the respective value of different social services, the relative reward due each, and the consequent degree of comfort appropriate on the average to workers in each occupation. . . . Under this pressure, each in his sphere vaguely realizes the extreme

23. Marshall B. Clinard, ed., *Anomie and Deviant Behavior*, The Free Press, New York, 1964.

24. Reprinted with permission of Macmillan Publishing Co., Inc., from *Suicide* by Emile Durkheim, pp. 246–53. © The Free Press, a Corporation, 1952.

limit set to his ambitions and aspires to nothing beyond. . . . Thus, an end and goal are set to the passions. . . .

f. But when society is disturbed by some painful crisis or by beneficent but abrupt transitions, it is momentarily incapable of exercising this influence; thence come the sudden rises in the curve of suicides which we have pointed out above.

g. In the case of economic disasters, indeed, something like a declassification occurs which suddenly casts certain individuals into a lower state than their previous one. Then they must reduce their requirements, restrain their needs, learn greater self-control. . . . So they are not adjusted to the condition forced on them, and its very prospect is intolerable. . . .

h. It is the same if the source of the crisis is an abrupt growth of power and wealth. Then, truly, as the conditions of life are changed, the standard according to which needs were regulated can no longer remain the same; for it varies with social resources. . . . The scale is upset; but a new scale cannot be immediately improvised. Time is required for the public conscience to reclassify men and things. So long as the social forces thus freed have not regained equilibrium, their respective values are unknown and so all regulation is lacking for a time. The limits are unknown between the possible and the impossible, what is just and what is unjust, legitimate claims and hopes and those which are immoderate. Consequently, there is no restraint upon aspirations. . . . Appetites, not being controlled by a public opinion, become disoriented, no longer recognize the limits proper to them. Besides, they are at the same time seized by a sort of natural erethism simply by the greater intensity of public life. With increased prosperity desires increase. At the very moment when traditional rules have lost their authority, the richer prize offered these appetites stimulates them and makes them more exigent and impatient of control. The state of de-regulation or anomy is thus further heightened by passions being less disciplined, precisely when they need more disciplining.

Durkheim went on to argue that French society, over the previous 100 years, had deliberately destroyed the traditional sources of regulation for human appetites.[25] Religion had almost completely lost its influence over both workers and employers. Traditional occupational groups, such as the guilds, had been destroyed. Government adhered to a policy of laissez-faire, or noninterference, in business activities. As a result human appetites were no longer curbed. This freedom of appetites was the driving force behind the French industrial revolution, but it also created a chronic state of anomie, with its attendant high rate of suicide.

25. Ibid., pp. 254–58.

## 4. ASSESSING DURKHEIM'S THEORY OF CRIME

Durkheim presented his theory of crime in the context of an overall theory of modernization—the progression of societies from the mechanical to the organic form. One of the problems with assessing his theory is that he predicted that different things would happen at different times. Specifically he argued that (1) the punishment of crime would remain fairly stable in mechanical societies, independent of changes in the extent of criminal behavior; (2) as those societies made the transition to organic societies in the process of modernization, a greater variety of behaviors would be tolerated, there would be a vast expansion of "functional" law to regulate the interactions of the emerging organic society, and punishments would become less violent as their purpose changed from repression to restitution; and (3) in organic societies, the extent of criminal behavior would increase during periods of rapid social change. Each of these ideas has generated additional theories and research in more recent times.

Erikson reformulated Durkheim's theory about the stability of punishment in mechanical societies, based on a study of the Puritan colony in seventeenth-century Massachusetts.[26] This society had a relatively constant level of punishment throughout the century despite three "crime waves" attributed to Antinomians, Quakers, and witches. Erikson concluded:[27] "When a community calibrates its control machinery to handle a certain volume of deviant behavior it tends to adjust its . . . legal . . . definitions of the problem in such a way that this volume is realized." Erikson's reformulation has stimulated a number of other studies testing whether societies tend to have relatively constant punishment rates. Nils Christie demonstrated a remarkable stability in the imprisonment rates for Norway from 1880 to 1964, while Blumstein and his colleagues have done several studies demonstrating the stability of punishment in the United States over extended periods of time.[28] However, several other studies either have failed to find a similar effect or have criticized the re-

26. Kai T. Erikson, *Wayward Puritans*, John Wiley, New York, 1966.

27. Ibid., p. 26.

28. Nils Christie, "Changes in Penal Values," in Christie, ed., *Scandinavian Studies in Criminology*, vol. 2, Scandinavian University Books, Oslo, 1968, pp. 161–72; Alfred Blumstein and Jacqueline Cohen, "A Theory of the Stability of Punishment," *Journal of Criminal Law and Criminology* 64: 198–207 (June 1973); Alfred Blumstein, Jacqueline Cohen, and Daniel Nagin, "The Dynamics of a Homeostatic Punishment Process," *Journal of Criminal Law and Criminology* 67: 317–34 (Sept. 1977); and Alfred Blumstein and Soumyo Moitra, "An Analysis of the Time Series of the Imprisonment Rate in the States of the United States: A Further Test of the Stability of Punishment Hypothesis," *Journal of Criminal Law and Criminology* 70: 376–90 (Sept. 1979).

search methods of studies that do find an effect.[29] Thus the evidence to date must be said to be equivocal.

It might be pointed out, however, that these more recent studies have all used data from nineteenth- and twentieth-century Western nations, mostly the United States. Durkheim's theory does not predict that punishment levels in such societies will remain constant, since those cannot be considered mechanical societies. The Puritan colony in Massachusetts can reasonably be considered such a society, so that Erikson's study supports Durkheim's theory while the others neither support nor challenge it. On the other hand, Erikson's interpretation has been challenged by Chambliss, who suggests that "his conclusion is hardly supported by the data he presents."[30] Erikson, following Durkheim, had described the three crime waves as being generated by the need to establish the moral boundaries of the community. Chambliss pointed out that each of these crime waves occurred when the power and authority of the ruling groups were threatened. He concluded:

Deviance was indeed created for the consequences it had. But the consequences were not "to establish moral boundaries"; rather, they aided those in power to maintain their position. . . . Erikson gives no evidence that any of these crime waves actually increased social solidarity except through the elimination of alternative centers of authority or power.

Durkheim made three arguments about crime during the process of transition from mechanical to organic societies. Wolfgang has stated that contemporary American society illustrates Durkheim's first argument about the increasing tolerance for diversity in more advanced societies: "My major point is that we are currently experiencing in American culture, and perhaps in Western society in general, an expansion of acceptability of deviance and a corresponding contraction of what we define as crime."[31] However, Spitzer found

29. M. Calahan, "Trends in Incarceration in the United States," *Crime and Delinquency* 25: 9–41 (1979); David F. Greenberg, "Penal Sanctions in Poland," *Social Problems* 28: 194–204 (1980); David Rauma, "Crime and Punishment Reconsidered: Some Comments on Blumstein's Stability of Punishment Hypothesis," *Journal of Criminal Law and Criminology* 72: 1772–98 (1981); Richard A. Berk, David Rauma, Sheldon L. Messinger, and T. F. Cooley, "A Test of the Stability of Punishment Hypothesis," *American Sociological Review* 46: 805–29 (1981); and Richard A. Berk, David Rauma, and Sheldon L. Messinger, "A Further Test of the Stability of Punishment Hypothesis," in John Hagan, ed., *Quantitative Criminology*, Sage, Beverly Hills, Cal., 1982, pp. 39–64.

30. William J. Chambliss, "Functional and Conflict Theories of Crime," in Chambliss and Milton Mankoff, eds., *Whose Law? What Order?*, John Wiley, New York, 1976, pp. 11–16.

31. Marvin E. Wolfgang, "Real and Perceived Changes in Crime," in Simha F. Landau and Leslie Sebba, *Criminology in Perspective*, D. C. Heath, Lexington, Mass., 1977, pp. 27–38.

that more developed societies were characterized by severe punishments, while simple societies were characterized by lenient punishments, which is the opposite of Durkheim's second argument.[32] Spitzer's findings are consistent with several studies that have found that rural areas in Western societies before modernization were characterized by fairly high levels of violence, and also by a considerable degree of tolerance for it.[33] It was only after modernization, with the concentration of populations in anonymous cities, that societies began to punish violence consistently and severely. Durkheim may have derived his idea from the fact that punishments in European societies were becoming much less severe at the time, due to the reforms introduced by Beccaria and other classical theorists. But the extremely harsh punishments that had been imposed prior to those reforms were not associated with simple, undeveloped societies, but rather with absolute monarchies. Those types of punishments were not found in earlier, simpler societies.[34]

Durkheim also predicted a great expansion in functional law as modern societies attempt to regulate all their new functions. In his case study of four cities from 1800 to the present, Gurr found "the veritable explosion of laws and administrative codes designed to regulate day-to-day interactions, in domains as dissimilar as trade, public demeanor, and traffic."[35] While some of this was generated by "the functional necessity of regulating the increased traffic and commercial activities of growing cities," as Durkheim had argued, Gurr also found that a great deal of other legislation was passed defining and proscribing new kinds of offenses against morality and against "collective behavior" such as riots and protests.[36] Gurr argued that the new offenses against morality arose primarily from the effort to apply middle-class values to all social groups, while the offenses against collective behavior arose from efforts of the elite groups to maintain their power.[37]

Durkheim argued, finally, that the source of high crime rates in

32. Steven Spitzer, "Punishment and Social Organization," *Law and Society Review* 9: 613–37 (1975).

33. See, for example, Howard Zehr, *Crime and Development of Modern Society*, Rowman & Litlefield, Totowa, N.J., 1976.

34. Michel Foucault, *Discipline and Punish*, Pantheon, New York, 1977, pp. 3–69. See also Philippe Ariès, *Centuries of Childhood*, Knopf, New York, 1962, Chapter 1, for a discussion of the tendency to idealize the past as harmonious and peaceful.

35. Ted Robert Gurr, *Rogues, Rebels, and Reformers*, Sage, Beverly Hills, Cal., 1976, p. 180.

36. Ibid., p. 177.

37. Ibid., pp. 93–115.

organic societies lay in normlessness or anomie generated by the rapid social changes associated with modernization. Durkheim's theory of anomie led to the later ecological, strain, and control theories of crime, so that the assessment of this argument must to a certain extent await the presentation of those theories in Chapters 10, 11, and 12. But those theories do not directly link the breakdown of social norms to the processes of modernization, as did Durkheim's theory. Durkheim's theory of anomie is therefore assessed here in the context of his overall theory of modernization.

Durkheim attributed the high rates of crime and other forms of deviance in his own society to the normlessness generated by the French and Industrial revolutions. One very basic criticism of this argument is that crime in France was not rising at the time. Lodhi and Tilly conclude that between 1831 and 1931 the incidence of theft and robbery declined in France, citing a massive decline in the statistics for serious property crime during that period.[38] The statistics for violent crime remained approximately stable over the same period, with some tendency toward a decline. Durkheim had formulated his theory of anomie in the context of a study of suicide rates, not crime rates. Having done so, he simply presumed that crime was also increasing, although he nowhere presented data to support his conclusion. McDonald argues that the statistics showing decreases in crime rates were available to Durkheim, as well as to other prominent criminologists of the time who also presumed that crime rates were increasing, but that none of them took any notice:[39]

These facts suggest, to me at least, that there was more interest in work that was wrong, but fitted in with accepted theory, than in work, however thorough, that was right but that did not. That crime was rising was part of all criminological theory in the nineteenth century, from left to right. Marxists of that time were no more willing to admit that social and economic conditions were improving than Durkheimians that industrialization and urbanization did not inevitably lead to higher crime.

In a separate study of French statistics, Zehr reached different conclusions than Lodhi and Tilly, finding that "crime rates in general, but especially property crime rates, rose during the nineteenth

38. A. Q. Lodhi and Charles Tilly, "Urbanization, Crime and Collective Violence in Nineteenth Century France," *American Journal of Sociology* 79: 297–318 (1973). See also A. V. Gatrell and T. B. Hadden, "Criminal Statistics and Their Interpretations," in E. A. Wrigley, ed., *Nineteenth-Century Society*, Cambridge University Press, Cambridge, U.K., 1972, pp. 336–96.

39. Lynn McDonald, "Theory and Evidence of Rising Crime in the Nineteenth Century," *British Journal of Sociology* 33: 404–20 (Sept. 1982), p. 417

century; on the whole, crime was more frequent by 1910 than it had been in 1830."[40] However, he also argued that rates for homicide and assault were dropping by the end of the century, when Durkheim was writing, and that theories such as Durkheim's that focus on the disorganizing effects of urban growth could not explain the patterns of theft that he found:[41] "Theft rates should have been higher in new and growing cities than in older, more stable cities and theft rates in expanding cities should have risen at first, then dropped as the conditions of urban social life stabilized. No such phenomenon is apparent."

Zehr found that most crime that occurred in rural areas was violent rather than property crime, and that in the initial stages of industrialization both violent and property crimes rose in urban areas. He interpreted this initial rise in urban violent crime to the stresses and tensions of city life, combined with the rural traditions of dealing with stressful situations in violent ways. Thus this initial burst of violence "seems to have represented the retention, not the breakdown, of traditional values and relationships."[42] These rates stabilized and began to decline after adjustment to urban life.[43]

## 5. CONCLUSION

Durkheim's influence has been extremely broad in criminology and sociology. His primary impact was that he focused attention on the role that social forces play in determining human conduct at a time when the dominant thinking held either that people were free in choosing courses of action or that behavior was determined by inner forces of biology and psychology. Although this is now the dominant view used to explain crime, it was considered quite radical at the time.[44]

While there is no clear agreement on whether his theory of the relationship between crime and modernization is accurate, there is at least some evidence that the basic patterns of crime found in the

---

40. Howard Zehr, "The Modernization of Crime in Germany and France, 1830–1913," in Louise I. Shelley, ed., *Readings in Comparative Criminology,* Southern Illinois University Press, Carbondale, Ill., 1981, pp. 136–37. For the complete study, see Zehr, *Crime and Development,* op. cit. Zehr criticized Lodhi and Tilly for failing to consider cases dropped or diverted to lower courts, but Lodhi and Tilly argue that these rates fluctuated differently.

41. Ibid., p. 137.

42. Ibid.

43. Ibid., p. 140.

44. See the chapter on Durkheim in Ian Taylor, Paul Walton, and Jock Young, *The New Criminology,* Harper, New York, 1973, pp. 67–90.

modern world can only be accounted for by such a theory. Shelley
reviewed studies of crime and modernization and found that the same
changes in crime patterns that occurred first in Western Europe have
reoccurred in Eastern European socialist nations and in the emerging nations of Asia, Africa, and Latin America as they have undergone modernization.[45] She concluded: "The evidence . . . suggests
that only the changes accompanying the developmental process are
great enough to explain the enormous changes that have occurred in
international crime patterns in the last two centuries."[46]

At least some of the changes that have accompanied the modernization process, however, do not seem to be those predicted by
Durkheim's theory. Premodern societies were characterized by high
levels of violent crime, in contrast to Durkheim's arguments about
their stability. There appears to have been a long-term decline in
crime over the last several hundred years as the process of modernization has occurred, something that Durkheim's theory does not
predict.[47] Short-term increases in that long-term decline occurred in
the early stages of urbanization and industrialization, but those short-
term increases seem to have been associated with the retention, not
the breakdown, of rural culture. Gurr argues that other sources of
short-term increases in crime rates include wars and growths in the
size of the youth population.[48] Thus Durkheim may have been right
in pointing to modernization as a fundamental factor in the explanation of crime, but he may not have accurately described the effect
that it has.

On the other hand, Durkheim's basic argument was that modernization is linked to crime through the breakdown of social norms and
rules—that is, he associated crime with the absence of social controls. It may be that this argument is correct but that Durkheim was
mistaken in characterizing premodern societies as having strong social controls and low crime rates. The long-term decline in crime rates
may then be explained by the continuously increasing level of social
controls associated with increasing modernization.[49] The relation-

45. Louise I. Shelley, *Crime and Modernization*, Southern Illinois University Press, Carbondale, Ill., 1981, pp. 141–42.

46. Ibid.

47. See Steven F. Messner, "Societal Development, Social Equality, and Homicide," *Social
Forces* 61: 225–40 (1982).

48. Ted Robert Gurr, "Historical Forces in Violent Crime," in Michael Tonry and Norval Morris,
eds., *Crime and Justice*, vol. 3, University of Chicago Press, Chicago, 1981, pp. 340–46. See
also Gurr, "On the History of Violent Crime in Europe and America," in Hugh David Graham
and Ted Robert Gurr, eds., *Violence in America*, 2nd ed., Sage, Beverly Hils, Cal., 1979.

49. This is basically Gurr's interpretation. See the sources in footnote 48, above.

ship between crime and social controls will be further explored in Chapter 13.

## RECOMMENDED READINGS

Robert A. Nisbet, *The Sociology of Emile Durkheim*, Oxford University Press, New York, 1974. A concise introduction to Durkheim's fundamental ideas, with an especially good chapter on deviance.

Dominick LaCapra, *Emile Durkheim, Sociologist and Philosopher*, Cornell University Press, Ithaca, N.Y., 1972. A comprehensive interpretation and assessment of the thought of Durkheim, seen in its historical context.

Robert A. Nisbet, *Emile Durkheim*, Prentice-Hall, Englewood Cliffs, N.J., 1965. A long essay examining Durkheim's contributions to modern sociology, followed by a series of articles by other authors on various aspects of Durkheim's work.

Walter A. Lunden, "Emile Durkheim," in Hermann Mannheim, *Pioneers in Criminology*, Patterson Smith, Montclair, N.J., 1972, pp. 385–99. A brief review of Durkheim's life and contributions to criminology.

Ian Taylor, Paul Walton, and Jock Young, *The New Criminology*, Harper, New York, 1973. Contains a long and excellent chapter on Durkheim from a radical perspective.

Theodore Mills, "Equilibrium and the Processes of Deviance and Control," *American Sociological Review* 24: 671–79 (Oct. 1959). Identifying and punishing criminals increases social solidarity only in simple societies; in complex societies it is more likely to have the opposite effect.

Louise I. Shelley, *Crime and Modernization*, Southern Illinois University Press, Carbondale, Ill., 1981. A review and synthesis of the literature on the impact of industrialization and urbanization on crime. See also the companion volume, *Readings in Comparative Criminology*.

Robert B. Seidman, *The State, Law, and Development*, St. Martin's Press, New York, 1978. A study of how law can be used to initiate development and modernization.

# CHAPTER TEN

# The Ecology of Crime

One of Durkheim's arguments was that rapid social change was associated with increases in crime due to the breakdown of social controls. This idea was one of several used by members of the Department of Sociology at the University of Chicago in the 1920s in their attempt to pinpoint the environmental factors associated with crime and to determine the relationship among those factors. Their procedure involved correlating the characteristics of each neighborhood with the crime rates of that neighborhood. This first large-scale study of crime in America produced a mass of data and a large number of observations about crime that led directly to much of the later work in American criminology. Since this research was based on an image of human communities taken from plant ecology, it became known as The Chicago School of Human Ecology.

## 1. THE THEORY OF HUMAN ECOLOGY

The term *ecology*, as it is used today, is often linked to the idea of protecting the natural environment. In its original meaning, however, it is a branch of biology in which plants and animals are studied in their relationships to each other and to their natural habitat. Plant life and animal life are seen as an intricately complicated whole, a web of life in which each part depends on almost every other part for some aspect of its existence. Organisms in their natural habitat exist in an ongoing balance of nature, a dynamic equilibrium in which each individual must struggle to survive. Ecologists study this web of interrelationships and interdependencies in an attempt to discover the forces that define the activities of each part.

Human communities, particularly those organized around a free-market economy and a laissez-faire government, could be seen to resemble this biotic state in nature. Each individual struggles for his or her survival in an interrelated, mutually dependent community. The Darwinian law of survival of the fittest applies here as well.

Robert Park proposed a parallel between the distribution of plant life in nature and the organization of human life in societies.[1] He had been a Chicago newspaper reporter for 25 years and had spent much of that time investigating social conditions in the city. Chicago was at that time a massive city of over 2 million; between 1860 and 1910 it had doubled in population every 10 years, with wave upon wave of immigrants. Park was appointed to the Sociology Department at the University of Chicago in 1914. From the study of plant and animal ecology he derived two key concepts that formed the basis of what he called the "theory of human ecology."

The first concept came from the observations of the Danish ecologist Warming, who noted that a group of plants in a given area might have many characteristics that, in combination, were similar to those of an individual organism.[2] Warming called such groups "plant communities." Other ecologists argued that the plant and animal life in a given habitat tended to develop a "natural economy" in which different species are each able to live more prosperously together than separately. This is called "symbiosis," or the living together of different species to the mutual benefit of each. Since each plant and animal community was said to resemble an organism, the balance of nature in the habitat was said to resemble a super-organism.

Park's work as a newspaperman had led him to view the city in a similar way—not merely as a geographic phenomenon, but as a kind of social organism[3]:

The city may . . . be regarded as a functional unit in which the relations among individuals that compose it are determined, not merely by the city's

1. Park's background and a review of the theory of human ecology are presented in Terence Morris, *The Criminal Area*, Humanities Press, New York, 1966, pp. 1–18. See also Winifred Raushenbush, *Robert E. Park: Biography of a Sociologist*, Duke University Press, Durham, 1979; and Amos H. Hawley, "Human Ecology," *International Encyclopedia of the Social Sciences*, vol. 4, Macmillan and the Free Press, New York, 1968, pp. 328–37.

2. Eugenius Warming, "Plant Communities," in Robert E. Park and Ernest W. Burgess, *Introduction to the Science of Sociology*, University of Chicago Press, Chicago, 1969, pp. 175–82.

3. Robert E. Park, *Human Communities*, The Free Press, Glencoe, Ill., 1952, p. 118.

physical structure, nor even by the formal regulations of a local government, but rather more by the direct and indirect interaction of individuals
upon one another. Considered from this point of view, the urban community turns out to be something more than a mere congeries of peoples and
institutions. On the contrary, its component elements, institutions, and
persons are so intimately bound up that the whole tends to assume the
character of an organism, or to use Herbert Spencer's term, a super-
organism.

Within this super-organism called the city, Park found many "natural areas" where different types of people lived. These natural areas,
like the natural areas of plants, had an organic unity of their own.
Some of them were racial or ethnic communities, such as China-
town, Little Italy, or the "Black Belt." Other natural areas were
peopled by individuals in certain income or occupational groups, or
they were industrial or business areas. Still other areas were physically cut off from the rest of the city by railroad tracks, rivers, major
highways, or unused space. Symbiotic relationships existed not only
among the people within a natural area (where the butcher needed
the baker for bread and the baker needed the butcher for meat), but
also among the natural areas within the city. Each natural area was
seen as playing a part in the life of the city as a whole.

The second basic concept Park took from plant ecology involved
the process by which the balance of nature in a given area might
change. A new species may invade the area, come to dominate it,
and drive out other life forms. For example, a cleared field in one
of the southern states will first be covered with tall weeds. Later this
field will be invaded and dominated by broomsedge and, even later,
by pine trees. Finally the field will stabilize as an oak-hickory forest.
Ecologists call this process "invasion, dominance, and succession."

This process can also be seen in human societies. The history of
America is a process of invasion, dominance, and succession by the
whites into the territory of the Indians. And in cities one cultural or
ethnic group may take over an entire neighborhood from another
group, beginning with the shift of only one or two residents. Similarly, business or industry may move into and ultimately take over a
previously residential neighborhood.

The processes of invasion, dominance, and succession were further explored by Park's associate, Ernest Burgess, who pointed out
that cities do not merely grow at their edges. Rather, they have a
tendency to expand radially from their center in patterns of concen-

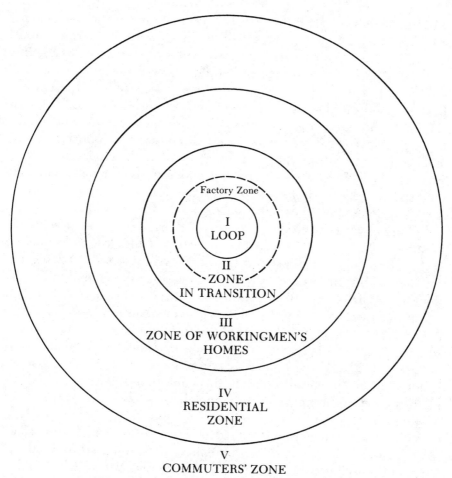

FIGURE 10–1   The growth of the city. *Source:* Ernest W. Burgess, "The Growth of the City," in Robert E. Park, Ernest W. Burgess, and Roderick D. McKenzie, *The City*, The University of Chicago Press, Chicago, 1928, p. 51. Reproduced by permission of the publisher.

tric circles, each moving gradually outward. This tendency was portrayed by Burgess in Figure 10–1.

Zone I is the central business district or "Loop." Zone II is the area in transition, being invaded by the central business district and industrial areas. This is generally the oldest section of the city. The residential districts in this zone are already deteriorating, and will be allowed to deteriorate further because it is anticipated that they will be torn down in the foreseeable future to make way for incoming business and industry. Since this is the least desirable residential section of the city, it is usually occupied by the poorest classes, including the most recent migrants to the city.

Zone III is the zone of workers' homes, occupied by those who have escaped the deteriorating conditions in Zone II. Beyond this is Zone IV, the residential districts of single-family houses and more expensive apartments. Beyond the city limits are the suburban areas and the satellite cities, which constitute Zone V, the commuter zone. Each of these five zones is growing and thus is gradually moving outward into the territory occupied by the next zone, in a process of invasion, dominance, and succession.

No one city totally conforms to this pattern, since it is influenced by a variety of natural and historical factors. Chicago, for example, is most dramatically influenced by the presence of Lake Michigan, and more subtly influenced by such other factors as the Chicago River, the railroad lines, and the location of industry and highways.

Natural areas occur within each zone. For example, Burgess notes the location in Chicago's Zone II of the so-called Ghetto, where Jewish immigrants initially settled. In Zone III was "Deutschland," an area of Jewish workers' homes, which was constantly receiving new residents from the Ghetto, and at the same time was constantly losing residents to the more desirable neighborhoods in the residential zone.[4]

Within the framework of these ideas Park and his colleagues studied the city of Chicago and its problems. They attempted to discover "the processes by which the biotic balance and the social equilibrium are maintained once they are achieved, and the processes by which, when the biotic balance and the social equilibrium are disturbed, the transition is made from one relatively stable order to another."[5]

## 2. RESEARCH IN THE "DELINQUENCY AREAS" OF CHICAGO

Park's theories were used as the basis for a broadly ranging study of the problem of juvenile delinquency in Chicago by Clifford R. Shaw. The problem of crime and delinquency had become of increasing concern to social scientists in the 1920s because the country was

---

4. Ernest W. Burgess, "The Growth of the City," in Park, Burgess, and McKenzie, *The City*, University of Chicago Press, Chicago, 1928, p. 62.

5. Robert E. Park, "Human Ecology," *American Journal of Sociology* 42: 158 (1936).

gripped in a crime wave generated by resistance to Prohibition, a problem that was particularly severe in Chicago.

Shaw worked as a probation and parole officer during this period and became convinced that the problem of juvenile delinquency had its origin in the juvenile's "detachment from conventional groups" rather than in any biological or psychological abnormalities.[6] Following his appointment to the Institute for Juvenile Research in Chicago, Shaw devised a strategy, based on the theory of human ecology, to study the process by which this "detachment from conventional groups" occurred.

Because he saw delinquents as essentially normal human beings, he felt that their illegal activities were somehow bound up with their environment. Therefore the first stage of his strategy involved analyzing the characteristics of the neighborhoods that, according to police and court records, had the most delinquents. But even in the worst of these neighborhoods only about 20 percent of the youth were actually involved with the court. Shaw therefore compiled extensive "life histories" from individual delinquents to find out exactly how they had related to their environment.

Shaw first published his neighborhood studies in 1929 in a volume entitled *Delinquency Areas,* and he subsequently published more of his research in two studies coauthored with Henry D. McKay, *Social Factors in Juvenile Delinquency* (1931) and *Juvenile Delinquency and Urban Areas* (1942). In these studies Shaw and McKay constructed a series of *spot maps* such as Figure 10–2, which pinpointed the residences of those juveniles involved at various stages of the criminal justice system. Other spot maps showed various other community characteristics, such as the location of demolished buildings, the incidence of tuberculosis, and the residences of truants. *Rate maps,* such as Figure 10–3, were then constructed on the basis of 140 "square mile areas." These maps showed the percentage of the total juvenile population of the area who were involved in the criminal justice system, based on data from the preceding census. In a comparison of the two maps it can be seen that areas with the highest rates of delinquency are not necessarily those with the greatest number of delinquents. That is because some of the high-rate areas had smaller total juvenile populations. Finally, *zone maps,* such as Figure 10–4, were constructed to show that in spite of wide varia-

6. James F. Short, Jr., "Introduction to the Revised Edition," in Clifford R. Shaw and Henry D. McKay, *Juvenile Delinquency and Urban Areas,* University of Chicago Press, Chicago, 1969, p. xlvii. Additional background material on Shaw and his colleague Henry McKay can be found in Jon Snodgrass, "Clifford R. Shaw and Henry D. McKay: Chicago Criminologists," *British Journal of Criminology* 16: 1–19 (Jan. 1976).

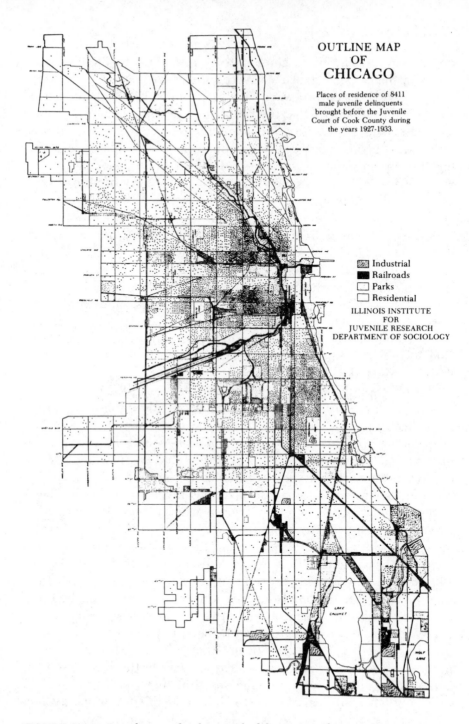

FIGURE 10–2    Distribution of male juvenile delinquents, Chicago, 1927–33. *Source:*
Clifford R. Shaw and Henry D. McKay, *Juvenile Delinquency and Urban Areas,*
University of Chicago Press, Chicago, 1969, p. 51. Reproduced by permission of
the publisher.

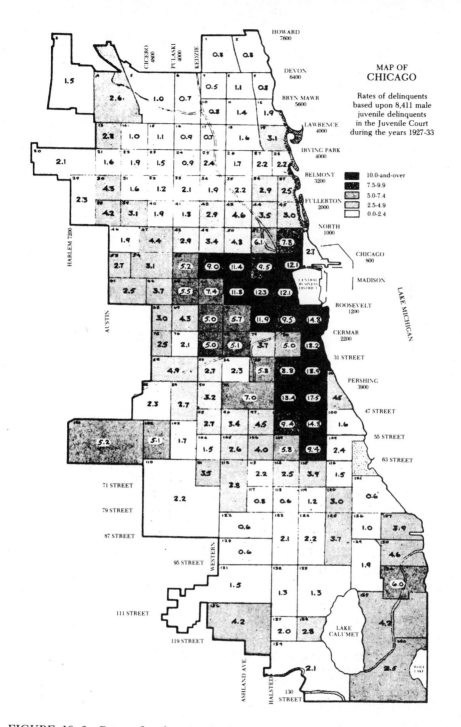

FIGURE 10-3  Rates of male juvenile delinquents, Chicago, 1927-33. *Source:* Clifford R. Shaw and Henry D. McKay, *Juvenile Delinquency and Urban Areas,* University of Chicago Press, Chicago, 1969, p. 54. Reproduced by permission of the publisher.

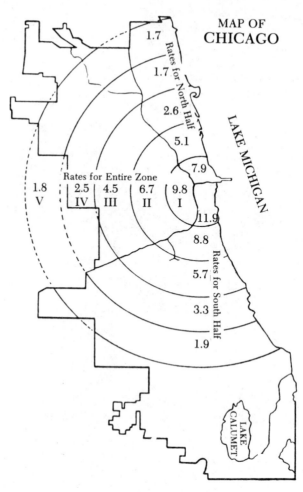

MAP OF
**CHICAGO**

1.7

Rates for North Half

1.7

2.6

5.1

7.9

Rates for Entire Zone

| 1.8 | 2.5 | 4.5 | 6.7 | 9.8 |
|-----|-----|-----|-----|-----|
| V   | IV  | III | II  | I   |

11.9

8.8

Rates for South Half

5.7

3.3

1.9

LAKE MICHIGAN

LAKE CALUMET

FIGURE 10–4   Zone rates of male juvenile delinquents, Chicago, 1927–33. *Source:*
Clifford R. Shaw and Henry D. McKay, *Juvenile Delinquency and Urban Areas,*
University of Chicago Press, Chicago, 1969, p. 69. Reproduced by permission of
the publisher.

tions in specific locations there was a general tendency for community problems to be concentrated close to the center of the city.

Shaw and McKay reached the following conclusions as a result of
their statistical analysis:

1. Physical Status: The neighborhoods with the highest delinquency rates were found to be located within or immediately adja-
cent to areas of heavy industry or commerce. These neighborhoods
also had the greatest number of condemned buildings, and their

TABLE 10–1   Rates of Delinquents for Areas Grouped According to Percentage
Increase or Decrease of Population: 1927–33

| Percentage Increase or Decrease of Population, 1920–30 | Rate of Delinquents 1927–33 |
|---|---|
| Decreasing: | |
| 20–39 | 9.5 |
| 0–19 | 6.3 |
| Increasing: | |
| 0–19 | 4.1 |
| 20–39 | 3.0 |
| 40 and over | 2.0 |

*Source:* Shaw and McKay, *Juvenile Delinquency and Urban Areas*, p. 145.

population was decreasing. The population change was assumed to
be related to an industrial invasion of the area, which resulted in
fewer buildings being available for residential occupation. Table
10–1[7] shows the relationship between rates of population change
and delinquency.

2. Economic Status: The highest rates of delinquency were found
in the areas of lowest economic status as determined by a number
of specific factors, including the percentage of families on welfare,
the median rental, and the percentage of families owning homes.[8]
These areas also had the highest rates of infant deaths, active cases
of tuberculosis, and insanity. But Shaw and McKay concluded that
economic conditions did not in themselves *cause* these problems. This
conclusion was based on the fact that the rates of delinquency, of
adult criminality, of infant deaths, and of tuberculosis for the city as
a whole remained relatively stable between 1929 and 1934, when the
Great Depression hit, and there was a tenfold increase in the number of families on public or private assistance. Median rentals, welfare rates, and other economic measures continued to show that the
areas with the highest concentrations of these problems were in the
lowest economic status relative to other areas of the city. These
problems appeared to be associated with the least privileged groups
in society, regardless of the actual economic conditions of that society as a whole.

3. Population Composition: Areas of highest delinquency were

7. Clifford R. Shaw and Henry D. McKay, *Juvenile Delinquency and Urban Areas*, University of Chicago Press, Chicago, 1969, p. 145. Reprinted by permission of the publisher.
8. Ibid., pp. 147–52.

TABLE 10–2   Rates of Delinquents for Areas Grouped by Percentage of
Foreign-born and Negro Heads of Families: 1930

| Percentage of Foreign-born and Negro Heads of Families, 1930 | Rate of Delinquents 1927–33 |
|---|---|
| 70.0 and over | 8.2 |
| 60.0–69.9 | 4.8 |
| 50.0–59.9 | 3.9 |
| 40.0–49.9 | 2.8 |
| Under 40.0 | 1.7 |

consistently associated with higher concentrations of foreign-born and
Negro heads of families, as seen in Table 10–2.[9] In order to determine the precise role of racial and ethnic factors in the causation of
delinquency, Shaw and McKay further analyzed these data. They
found that certain inner-city areas in Zone II remained among those
with the highest delinquency rates in the city despite shifts of almost
all the population of these areas. In 1884 approximately 90 percent
of the population in these areas was German, Irish, English, Scottish, or Scandinavian. By 1930 approximately 85 percent of the population was Czech, Italian, Polish, Slavic, or other. In spite of this
dramtic shift in ethnic populations, these eight areas continued to
have some of the highest delinquency rates in the city. At the same
time there was no increase in delinquency rates in the areas into which
the older immigrant communities moved.

They also found that, within similar areas, each group, whether
foreign-born or native, recent immigrant or older immigrant, black
or white, had a delinquency rate that was proportional to the rate of
the overall area. No racial, national, or nativity group exhibited a
uniform characteristic rate of delinquency in all parts of the city. Each
group produced delinquency rates that ranged from the lowest to the
highest in the city, depending on the type of area surveyed. Although some variation associated with the group could be seen, it
was apparent that the overall delinquency rate of a particular group
depended primarily on how many individuals of that group resided
in "delinquency areas." Shaw and McKay concluded:[10]

In the face of these facts it is difficult to sustain the contention that, by
themselves, the factors of race, nativity, and nationality are vitally related

9. Ibid., p. 155. Reprinted by permission of the publisher.
10. Ibid., pp. 162–63.

to the problem of juvenile delinquency. It seems necessary to conclude, rather, that the significantly higher rates of delinquents found among the children of Negroes, the foreign born, and more recent immigrants are closely related to existing differences in their respective patterns of geographical distribution within the city. If these groups were found in the same proportion in all local areas, existing differences in the relative number of boys brought into court from the various groups might be expected to be greatly reduced or to disappear entirely.

In addition to this research, Shaw compiled and published a series of "life histories" of individual delinquents, including *The Jackroller* (1930), *The Natural History of a Delinquent Career* (1931), and *Brothers in Crime* (1938). The basic findings of these histories are summed up in the following points.

1. Delinquents, by and large, "are not different from large numbers of persons in conventional society with respect to intelligence, physical condition, and personality traits."[11]

2. In delinquency areas "the conventional traditions, neighborhood institutions, public opinion, through which neighborhoods usually effect a control over the behavior of the child, were largely disintegrated."[12] In addition, parents and neighbors frequently approved of delinquent behavior, so that the child grew up "in a social world in which [delinquency] was an accepted and appropriate form of conduct."[13]

3. The neighborhoods included many opportunities for delinquent activities, including "junk dealers, professional fences, and residents who purchased their stolen goods" and "dilapidated buildings which served as an incentive for junking." There was also a "lack of preparation, training, opportunity, and proper encouragement for successful employment in private industry."[14]

4. Delinquent activities in these areas began at an early age as a part of play activities of the street.[15]

5. In these play activities, there is a continuity of tradition in a given neighborhood from older boys to younger boys.[16] This tradition includes

11. Clifford R. Shaw, *Brothers in Crime*, University of Chicago Press, Chicago, 1938, p. 350. See also Shaw's *The Jackroller*, University of Chicago Press, Chicago, 1930, p. 164; and *The Natural History of A Delinquent Career*, University of Chicago Press, Chicago, 1931, p. 226.

12. Shaw, *Natural History*, p. 229. See also *The Jackroller*, p. 165, and *Brothers in Crime*, p. 358.

13. Shaw, *Brothers in Crime*, p. 356. See also Shaw and McKay, op. cit., p. 172; *The Jackroller*, p. 165; and *Natural History*, p. 229.

14. Ibid., p. 356.

15. Shaw, *Brothers in Crime*, pp. 354, 355; *Natural History*, p. 227; *The Jackroller*, p. 164. See also Short, op. cit., p. xli.

16. Shaw and McKay, op. cit., pp. 174–75.

the transmission of such different criminal techniques as jackrolling, shop-lifting, stealing from junkmen, or stealing automobiles, so that different neighborhoods were characterized by the same types of offenses over long periods of time.[17]

6. The normal methods of official social control could not stop this pro-cess.[18]

7. It was only later in a delinquent career that the individual began "to identify himself with the criminal world, and to embody in his own philos-ophy of life the moral values which prevailed in the criminal groups with which he had contact."[19] This was due both to the continuous contact the delinquent had with juvenile and adult criminals on the street and in cor-rectional institutions, and to rejection and stigmatization by the commu-nity.

Shaw concluded that delinquency and other social problems are closely related to the process of invasion, dominance, and succession that determines the concentric growth patterns of the city.[20] When a particular location in the city is "invaded" by new residents, the established symbiotic relationships that bind that location to a natu-ral area are destroyed. Ultimately this location will be incorporated as an organic part of a new natural area, and the social equilibrium will be restored. Meanwhile the natural organization of the location will be severely impaired.

These "interstitial areas" (so called because they are *in-between* the organized natural areas) become afflicted with a variety of social problems that are directly traceable to the rapid shift in populations. The formal social organizations that existed in the neighborhood tend to disintegrate as the original population retreats. Because the neighborhood is in transition, the residents no longer identify with it, and thus they do not care as much about its appearance or repu-tation. There is a marked decrease in "neighborliness" and in the ability of the people of the neighborhood to control their youth. For example, in an established neighborhood, a resident who is aware that a child is getting into trouble may call that child's parents or may report that child to the local authorities. But because new peo-ple are continuously moving into the interstitial area, residents no

17. Ibid., p. 174.

18. Shaw, *Natural History*, p. 233; *Brothers in Crime*, p. 260; Shaw and McKay, op. cit., p. 4.

19. Shaw, *Natural History*, p. 228. See also *The Jackroller*, pp. 119, 165; *Brothers in Crime*, p. 350.

20. Morris, op. cit., pp. 77, 78; Ian Taylor, Paul Walton, and Jock Young, *The New Crimi-nology*, Harper & Row, New York, 1973, pp. 110–14.

longer know their own neighbors or their neighbors' children. Thus children who are out of their parents' sight may be under almost no control, even in their own neighborhood. The high mobility of the residents also means that there is a high turnover of children in the local schools. This is disruptive both to learning and to discipline. Finally, the area tends to become a battleground between the invading and retreating cultures. This can generate a great deal of conflict in the community, which tends to be manifested in individual and gang conflicts between the youth of the two cultures.

Although other areas only periodically undergo this process, areas in Zone II are continually being invaded both by the central business district and by successive waves of new immigrants coming into the city from foreign countries and from rural areas. These new immigrants already have many problems associated with their adjustment to the new culture. In addition, the neighborhood into which the immigrant moves is in a chronic state of "social disorganization." This presents the immigrant with many additional problems, and there is almost no help available to solve any of them. Thus recent immigrants tend to have a wide range of social problems, including delinquency among their youth. These problems are resolved as recent immigrants acquire some of the resources necessary both to solve their own problems and to move into the better-established neighborhoods of Zone III, with its natural processes of social control.

## 3. LATER CRITICISMS AND REPLICATIONS

Shaw and McKay's work has been extremely influential in criminology, to the extent that Short has argued that "in the quarter of a century since its original publication, little has happened to alter the factual picture presented, and theoretical advances and more recent programs of delinquency control are in large part extensions or modifications of those suggested here."[21] Despite this long-term significance, a number of serious criticisms have been raised about both the theory and the research methods Shaw and McKay used.

In 1936 Robison criticised Shaw and McKay's reliance on official police and court records to measure delinquency in a given area.[22]

21. Short, op. cit., p. xxvi. A detailed assessment of Shaw's impact on criminology can be found in Harold Finestone, "The Delinquent and Society: The Shaw and McKay Tradition," in James F. Short, ed., *Delinquency, Crime and Society*, University of Chicago Press, Chicago, 1976, pp. 23–49; and Finestone, *Victims of Change: Juvenile Delinquency in American Society*, Greenwood, Westport, Ct., 1977, pp. 77–150.

22. Sophia M. Robison, *Can Delinquency Be Measured?*, Columbia University Press, New York, 1936.

In her study based on the records of both criminal justice and social welfare agencies, she found that juvenile "maladjustment" was evenly distributed throughout the city. A large number of more recent self-report surveys (where researchers ask both delinquent and nondelinquent youths if they have ever committed certain offenses) have found that delinquency is not concentrated in lower-class groups as Shaw and McKay reported, but rather is fairly evenly distributed among the social classes.[23] However, self-report surveys have been criticized in several major studies where researchers found that official police and court records accurately portray the distribution of delinquency among social groups, if one considers only those forms of delinquency that are likely to result in official police or court actions.[24] Thus this criticism of Shaw and McKay's work may not be valid.

In 1938 Alihan criticized the theory of human ecology on which Shaw had based his empirical investigations.[25] She argued that it was based on a series of false analogies with plant ecology, and that the field of ecology had discarded the concepts that plant communities have an organic unity of their own and that the balance of nature is a super-organism. In addition, she argued that Shaw's work was not really based on ecological theory anyway:[26]

[Shaw] neither investigates symbiotic and competitive relations, nor does he probe into the organic, natural reactions of the delinquents. In fact, there is little in Shaw's study to suggest Park's and other ecologists' interpreta-

---

23. These studies are reviewed in Lamar T. Empey, *American Delinquency*, Dorsey, Homewood, Ill., 1982, pp. 103–27. A summary of the criticisms of official data can be found in Gary E. Jensen and Dean G. Rojek, *Delinquency: A Sociological View*, D. C. Heath, Lexington, Mass., 1980, pp. 74–81.

24. See, for example, Delbert S. Elliott and Suzanne S. Ageton, "Reconciling Race and Class Differences in Self Reported and Official Estimates of Delinquency," *American Sociological Review* 45: 95–110 (Feb. 1981); Donald Clelland and Timothy J. Carter, "The New Myth of Class and Crime," *Criminology* 18: 319–36 (1980); John Braithwaite, "The Myth of Social Class and Criminality Reconsidered," *American Sociological Review* 46: 36–57 (1981). The controversy is by no means resolved. For the opposite view, see Charles R. Tittle, Wayne J. Villemez, and Douglas A. Smith, "The Myth of Social Class and Criminality," *American Sociological Review* 43: 643–56 (Oct. 1978). Another recent study that reaches a similar conclusion is Michael J. Hindelang, Travis Hirschi, and Joseph Weiss, *Measuring Delinquency*, Sage, Beverly Hills, Cal., 1981.

25. M. A. Alihan, *Social Ecology: A Critical Analysis*, Columbia University Press, New York, 1938.

26. Ibid., p. 83. For other criticisms of the theory of human ecology, see B. T. Robson, *Urban Analysis: A Study of City Structure*, Cambridge University Press, Cambridge, U.K., 1969, pp. 8–38. For criticisms of how this framework has restricted the development of criminology, see Paul J. Brantingham and C. Ray Jeffery, "Afterword: Crime, Space, and Criminological Theory," in Paul J. Brantingham and Patricia L. Brantingham, eds., *Environmental Criminology*, Sage, Beverly Hills, Cal., 1981, pp. 227–37.

tion of the biotic substructure. Instead, Shaw confined himself to the finding of correlations between the frequency of a social phenomenon, delinquency, in various areas and the relative distance of these areas from the center of the city, following the ideal zonal pattern into which every city supposedly tends to fall. This done, he interprets delinquency primarily in terms of social, cultural, and economic factors. He does not submit any evidence to show that the different frequencies of delinquency in different areas are ecological adaptions to the particular area.

Shaw and McKay's argument that different racial and ethnic groups have similar rates of delinquency in similar neighborhoods also has been criticized.[27] In 1933 Hayner found that Japanese living in deteriorated areas had very low rates of delinquency. Shaw and McKay made a similar finding in neighborhoods in three cities in the western United States which had high percentages of Oriental residents.[28] And in 1949 Jonassen argued that Shaw and McKay's conclusion that different racial and ethnic groups possessed similar delinquency rates when they were living in similar neighborhoods was not supported by their data.[29] This raised the possibility that delinquency rates may be directly related to racial and ethnic factors rather than being indirectly related through areas of residence.

Bursik and Webb addressed the issue of the relationship of racial factors to delinquency rates by testing Shaw and McKay's argument about *residential succession,* that neighborhoods retain their delinquency rates despite total turnovers in population.[30] Using data on Chicago neighborhoods directly comparable to that of Shaw and McKay, they found that the residential succession argument was supported by data from 1940 to 1950. However, after 1950 all neighborhoods undergoing racial change were characterized by high delinquency rates, regardless of their delinquency rates before the change. Bursik and Webb interpret their finding in terms of community stability. At the time Shaw and McKay wrote, the zones of transition were found exclusively in the inner-city areas, and the

27. Norman S. Hayner, "Delinquency Areas in the Puget Sound Region," *American Journal of Sociology* 39: 314–28 (Nov. 1933). See also Helen G. MacGill, "The Oriental Delinquent in the Vancouver Juvenile Court," *Sociology and Social Research* 22: 428–38 (May–June 1938).

28. Shaw and McKay, *Juvenile Delinquency and Urban Areas,* 1942 ed. pp. 359, 369–71, 376.

29. Christen T. Jonassen, "A Re-evaluation and Critique of the Logic and Some Methods of Shaw and McKay," *American Sociological Review* 14: 608–14 (Oct. 1949); reprinted in Harwin L. Voss and David M. Peterson, *Ecology, Crime, and Delinquency,* Appleton-Century-Crofts, New York, 1971, pp. 133–46.

30. Robert J. Bursik, Jr., and Jim Webb, "Community Change and Patterns of Delinquency," *American Journal of Sociology* 88 (1): 24–42 (1982).

process of dispersion to outlying residential areas was gradual. This "natural" process was disrupted in more recent times as blacks attempted to follow in the footsteps of other ethnic groups. Strong white resistance to any blacks moving into the neighborhood would be followed by total white flight and total racial turnover in a very short time. In such situations social institutions may disappear entirely or may persevere but be resistant to including the new residents, resulting in the high delinquency rates associated with social disorganization. Bursik and Webb found that, after the neighborhoods had stabilized, they "had delinquency rates not much different than would have been expected from their previous patterns."[31] This finding was consistent with several other studies which found that delinquency rates were increasing in black neighborhoods that had recently undergone residential changes but were decreasing in black neighborhoods that had been stable for some time.[32]

A fourth major criticism concerned the so-called ecological fallacy. The above-mentioned delinquency rates of Oriental groups demonstrate the point that one cannot make inferences about individuals and subgroups on the basis of information about the total population of the area in which those people live. For example, many Orientals in cities in the western United States lived in high-delinquency areas but did not themselves have high delinquency rates. That point had been argued earlier by both Robison and Alihan in their criticisms of Shaw and McKay's work, but it was demonstrated mathematically in 1950 by Robinson, using data on the literacy of racial and ethnic groups.[33] He concluded that "an ecological correlation is almost certainly not equal to its corresponding individual correlation." While the ecological fallacy is now considered well-known and obvious, a surprising number of researchers still fall into its trap.[34]

All of these criticisms led to a number of reformulations of Shaw and McKay's theory and/or research methods. The first of those reformulations was by Bernard Lander, in a study of Baltimore pub-

31. Ibid., p. 39.

32. Robert E. Kapsis, "Residential Succession and Delinquency," *Criminology* 15 (4): 459–86 (Feb. 1978). See also more recent findings by McKay reported in the 1969 edition of Shaw and McKay, op. cit., p. 345, and interesting comments by Snodgrass, op. cit., pp. 5–6.

33. W. S. Robinson, "Ecological Correlations and the Behavior of Individuals," *American Sociological Review* 15: 351–57 (June 1950); reprinted in Voss and Peterson, op. cit., pp. 147–58.

34. For recent examples of the ecological fallacy, see John Baldwin, "Ecological and Areal Studies in Great Britain and the United States," in Norval Morris and Michael Tonry, eds. *Crime and Justice: An Annual Review of Research*, vol. 1, University of Chicago Press, Chicago, 1979, pp. 43–44.

lished in 1954.[35] Lander used several modern statistical techniques not available to Shaw and McKay, and reached a number of quite different conclusions. Data on seven population and housing variables available on census tracts from the 1940 U.S. census were compared to delinquency rates in those tracts. After using partial correlations to control for the influence of other variables, Lander argued that there was no relationship between delinquency and either substandard housing or residential overcrowding. He then used factor analysis to demonstrate that the eight variables in his study were clustered into two general factors—he described them as a "socioeconomic" factor including low rent and low education, and an "anomic" factor including percentage of owner-occupied homes, percentage of blacks in an area, and delinquency rate. The term *anomic* was taken from Durkheim's theory and was interpreted as a weakening or breakdown of the social norms that regulated an individual's behavior. Lander argued that it was the anomic factor that was related to delinquency, not the socioeconomic factor. Lander's study was replicated by several other researchers, but criticisms that he had misused statistical techniques ended this line of research.[36] A second reformulation of Shaw and McKay's studies met a similar fate. Called "social area analysis," it rejected the theory of human ecology and substituted the urbanization theories of another Chicago sociologist, Lewis Wirth. A number of studies were carried out within this framework, but they have been severely criticized as being faulty in both theory and research methodology.[37]

Despite these false starts, ecological research remains alive and well

35. Bernard Lander, *Towards an Understanding of Juvenile Delinquency*, Columbia University Press, New York, 1954. Lander's conclusions are reprinted in Voss and Peterson, op. cit., pp. 161–174. See also the extended discussion of this study and the reactions to it in the Introduction to Voss and Peterson, op. cit., pp. 23–33.

36. The replications include David J. Bordua, "Juvenile Delinquency and 'Anomie': An Attempt at Replication," *Social Problems* 6: 230–38 (Winter 1959–59), and Roland J. Chilton, "Continuity in Delinquency Area Research," *American Sociological Review* 29: 71–83 (Feb. 1964). The major criticisms are in Robert A. Gordon, "Issues in the Ecological Study of Delinquency," *American Sociological Review* 32: 927–44 (Dec. 1967), with commentaries and a reply in 33: 594–620 (Aug. 1968). The articles are all reprinted in Voss and Peterson, op. cit., where they are also discussed in the Introduction (pp. 28–33). For another discussion of these criticisms, see Baldwin, op. cit., pp. 45–54.

37. These studies include Kenneth Polk, "Juvenile Delinquency and Social Areas," *Social Problems* 5: 214–17 (Winter 1957–58), and "Urban Social Areas and Delinquency," *Social Problems* 14: 320–25 (1967); Charles V. Willie, "The Relative Contribution of Family Status and Economic Status to Delinquency," *Social Problems* 14: 326–35 (Winter 1967); and Richard Quinney, "Crime, Delinquency, and Social Areas," *Journal of Research in Crime and Delinquency* 1: 149–54 (July 1964). The major criticisms are found in Gordon, op. cit., and Baldwin, op. cit., pp. 40–45.

and has split into several directions. In England ecological research has focused on questions of public housing policy.[38] As much as half of the housing in large English cities is now publicly owned, and the large-scale entrance of the government into the housing market has drastically altered the ecological patterns of cities. These studies have attempted to determine how delinquency areas are created and maintained, and have generally been associated with labeling, conflict, and radical theories which will be presented in Chapters 14, 15, and 16.

In the United States ecological research has become largely divorced from theory and focuses instead on the description of spatial aspects of crime and justice. Initially these studies examined the differences in crime rates between urban and rural areas, between different cities, between different areas within cities, and between different regions of the country.[39] Later studies turned to a wider variety of questions related to crime sites (the places where offenses are committed), such as the distance between the crime site and the offender's residence;[40] the relationship between specific offenses and various characteristics of the crime site, such as land-use policy, climate and seasonality, population density, city size, and so on;[41] the reasons offenders select certain crime sites;[42] and the way these sites can be designed so as to prevent the occurrence of crime.[43] Spatial distributions of various aspects of the criminal justice system have

---

38. See Baldwin, op. cit., pp. 37–40, and A. E. Bottoms and Polii Xanthos, "Housing Policy and Crime in the British Public Sector," in Brantingham and Brantingham, *Environmental Criminology*, pp. 206–8, for brief reviews of this work. A more complete review can be found in John Baldwin, "British Areal Studies of Crime: An Assessment," *British Journal of Criminology* 15: 211–27 (1975).

39. See Keith D. Harries, *The Geography of Crime and Justice*, McGraw-Hill, New York, 1974; and Judith A. Wilks, "Ecological Correlates of Crime and Delinquency," in President's Commission on Law Enforcement and Administration of Justice, *Task Force Report: Crime and Its Impact—An Assessment*, U.S. Government Printing Office, Washington, D.C., 1967, pp. 138–56. Wilks comments on why ecological research has become divorced from theory.

40. See Simon Hakim and George F. Rengert, *Crime Spillover*, Sage, Beverly Hills, Cal., 1981.

41. K. D. Harries, *Crime and the Environment*, Charles C. Thomas, Springfield, Ill. 1980. See also various studies in Daniel E. Georges-Abeyie and Keith D. Harries, eds., *Crime: A Spatial Perspective*, Columbia University Press, New York, 1980.

42. Paul J. Brantingham and Patricia L. Brantingham, "A Theoretical Model of Crime Site Selection," in Marvin D. Krohn and Ronald L. Akers, eds. *Crime, Law, and Sanctions*, Sage, Beverly Hills, Ca., 1978, pp. 105–18; further discussed in Patricia L. Brantingham and Paul J. Brantingham, "Notes on the Geography of Crime," in Brantingham and Brantingham, *Environmental Criminology*, pp. 27–54.

43. C. Ray Jeffery, *Crime Prevention Through Environmental Design*, Sage, Beverly Hills, Cal., 1971; Oscar Newman, *Defensible Space*, Macmillan, New York, 1972. For an assessment of defensible space theory and research, see Ralph B. Taylor, Stephen D. Gottfredson, and Sidney Brower, "The Defensibility of Defensible Space," in Travis Hirschi and Michael Gottfredson, eds., *Understanding Crime*, Sage, Beverly Hills, Cal., 1980, pp. 53–71.

also been examined.[44] These are more accurately described as "geographical" or "environmental" studies of crime and justice rather than as ecological studies.[45]

While Shaw and McKay's theory is no longer associated with ecological research, it has retained a vitality all its own and continues to influence criminology. The theory itself is called the cultural transmission theory, and it has been broken down into two basic components: the idea that high-delinquency areas are characterized by a breakdown of the normal kinds of social relations and organizations, so that criminal and delinquent behaviors are allowed to emerge, and the idea that those behaviors become supported over time by values and norms, so that the area develops a criminal or delinquent subculture.[46] The first of those ideas is associated with the later control theories of crime, which will be presented in Chapter 13. It is also similar to arguments that Durkheim made about crime as a result of the breakdown of social controls, which was discussed in Chapter 9. The second idea is similar to differential association and subcultural theories of crime, which will be presented in Chapter 12.

After considerable deliberation, Shaw and McKay concluded that the second of these ideas was more important and that it accounted for the "preponderance" of slum delinquency. Kornhauser, however, criticized this aspect of their theory:[47]

Shaw and McKay's mixed model is untenable. Their conclusion that the "preponderance" of slum delinquency is accounted for by the autonomous delinquent subculture must be false if their control model is true. If the delinquent tradition exists, the community must, according to Shaw and McKay, be disorganized. . . . If the community were disorganized but devoid of a delinquent tradition, it would still produce a new crop of delinquency and crime . . . or else social disorganization theory is false.

Kornhauser therefore extracted a "community control" model from Shaw and McKay's theory, arguing that communities characterized

44. Keith D. Harries and Stanley D. Brunn, *The Geography of Laws and Justice*, Praeger, New York, 1978.

45. For distinctions between ecological, geographic, and environmental studies of crime and justice, see Daniel E. Georges, *The Geography of Crime and Violence*, Association of American Geographers, Washington, D.C., 1978; and Paul J. Brantingham and Patricia L. Brantingham, Introduction in Brantingham and Brantingham, eds., *Environmental Criminology*, pp. 18–24.

46. Ruth Rosner Kornhauser, *Social Sources of Delinquency*, University of Chicago Press, Chicago, 1978, pp. 61–69. The theory has also been presented in propositional form in Kapsis, op. cit., pp. 461–64.

47 Kornhauser, op. cit., pp. 67–68.

by ethnic and racial heterogeneity, frequent residential mobility, and low economic status are unable to achieve effective social controls. She then reviewed a large number of empirical studies to demonstrate support for that model.[48]

## 4. POLICY IMPLICATIONS

Because Shaw felt[49] that juvenile delinquency was generated by social disorganization in interstitial areas, he did not believe that treatment of individual delinquents would have much effect in reducing overall delinquency rates.

It would appear from the findings of this study that successful treatment of the problem of delinquency in large cities will entail the development of programs which seek to effect changes in the conditions of life in specific local communities and in whole sections of the city. Diagnosis and supervision of the individual offender probably will not be sufficient to achieve this end.

In Shaw's view these programs could only come from organizations of neighborhood residents, so that the natural forces of social control could take effect. Thus, in 1932, he launched the Chicago Area Project, which established 22 neighborhood centers in six areas of Chicago.[50] Control of these centers rested with committees of local residents rather than with the central staff of the project, and local residents were employed as staff.

These centers had two primary functions. First, they were to coordinate such community resources as churches, schools, labor unions, industries, clubs, and other groups in addressing and resolving community problems. Second, they were to sponsor a variety of activity programs including recreation, summer camping and scouting activities, handicraft workshops, discussion groups, and community projects.[51] Through these activities the project sought "to develop a positive interest by the inhabitants in their own welfare, to establish democratic bodies of local citizens who would enable the whole community to become aware of its problems and attempt their solution by common action."[52]

48. Ibid., pp. 69–138; model summarized in table on p. 73.

49. Shaw and McKay, op. cit., p. 4.

50. See Solomon Kobrin, "The Chicago Area Project—A 25-Year Assessment," *Annals of the American Society of Political and Social Science*, Mar. 1959, pp. 19–29; or Anthony Sorrentino, "The Chicago Area Project After 25 Years," *Federal Probation*, June 1959, pp. 40–45.

51. Shaw and McKay, op. cit., p. 324.

52. Morris, *The Criminal Area*, p. 83.

The Chicago Area Project operated continuously for 25 years, until Shaw's death in 1957. Although its effect on the juvenile delinquency in these areas was never precisely evaluated,[53] it has been stated that "in all probability delinquency was substantially reduced."[54] A similar project in Boston was carefully evaluated by Walter B. Miller over a three-year period.[55] Here it was found that the project was effective in achieving many admirable goals. It established close relationships with local gangs and organized their members into clubs, it increased their involvement in recreational activities, it provided them with access to occupational and educational opportunities, it formed citizens' organizations, and it increased interagency cooperation in addressing community problems.

The goal of all these activities, however, was to reduce the incidence of delinquent behavior. To assess the impact of the project on the behavior of the youth, Miller analyzed the daily field reports of the outreach workers, which included a description of the activities of each youth. The behaviors were then classified as "moral" or "immoral" (where "immoral" meant disapproval by the community, but not necessarily a violation of the law) and as "legal" or "illegal." It was found that the ratio of moral to immoral behaviors remained relatively constant throughout the project, and that, although the total number of illegal acts decreased slightly during the project, the number of major offenses by boys increased. In addition, data were compiled on the number of court appearances made by each youth before, during, and after contact with the project, and these data were compared with the number of court appearances by a control group. There was almost no difference in these statistics. Miller concluded that the project had had a "negligible impact" on delinquency.[56]

This finding would have been anticipated by Morris, who earlier had remarked:[57]

The rationale of the Project makes the assumption that delinquency is a direct result of conditions in the community, though it pointed out that there was no conclusive evidence to suggest that local conditions in themselves *caused* delinquency. Rather, the suggestion was that they, like delinquency, were symptomatic of a common problem. It might well be that the

53. Short, op. cit., p. xlvi.

54. Martin R. Haskell and Lewis Yablonsky, *Juvenile Delinquency*, Rand McNally, Chicago, 1974, p. 423.

55. Walter B. Miller, "The Impact of a 'Total-Community' Delinquency Control Project," *Social Problems* 10: 168–91 (Fall 1962).

56. Ibid., p. 187.

57. Morris, op. cit., p. 84.

most communal action can do is to cure the symptoms, leaving the malady untouched.

Snodgrass asserts that Shaw and McKay figured out what that malady was, although they did not ever attempt to do anything about it. The problem lay in the economic activities of the civic leaders whose businesses and industries were invading and disorganizing the inner-city areas. These were the same civic leaders who were on the board of directors of the Chicago Area Project. Snodgrass quotes McKay as saying that[58]

the businessmen who are on the boards want to be told that they are doing something important by their contributions and hours of conferences and that their philanthropy is curing the evil. . . . [I]t makes no difference to them that the conditions which they are trying in this trivial manner to correct are largely due to their own every-day behavior.

Shaw was said to have reached a similar conclusion, and is quoted as saying: "There may be only one way to settle things, that is, by organized power." Snodgrass passed a harsh judgment on the Chicago Area Projects:[59]

The CAP was actually a measure designed to curb delinquency, not industry, in the interim between initial invasion and compete succession. It was a palliative attempting to bring temporary stability to the areas to control delinquency until the area was no longer in transition. There was no quarrel with the invasion, only with the ensuing disorganisation. . . . Beneath it all lay the assumption that the expansion and prosperity of industry took ultimate precedence over the preservation of the community. . . . While searching for what might create community, [Shaw and McKay] ignored what they knew full well destroyed it.

Shaw and McKay noted, but did explore, the implications of the fact that Chicago's Gold Coast was also located in the so-called zone of transition. It was an exclusive area that was protected from invasion by business and industry by the power, wealth, and prestige of its residents.[60] This suggests that the ultimate reason for the social disorganization that Shaw and McKay found in the slums was the powerlessness of their residents to protect themselves and their neighborhoods from that invasion.

58. Jon Snodgrass, "Clifford R. Shaw and Henry D. McKay: Chicago Sociologists," *British Journal of Criminology* 16 (1): 1–19 (1979), p. 16.

59. Ibid., pp. 16–17.

60. Ibid., p. 11.

## 5. CONCLUSIONS

Shaw and McKay's theory and the policy implications derived from it were essentially conservative because they ignored the processes by which delinquency areas were created, and focused instead on the characteristics of those areas. Shaw and McKay were apparently aware of those processes, but they lacked a theoretical framework within which they could explore them. Various theoretical frameworks were later developed in criminology to explore such questions, and the British studies mentioned above are carrying out such explorations. These studies can probably be considered the most direct descendants of Shaw and McKay's work in present-day criminology.

Despite the many severe criticisms that have been leveled at the work of the Chicago School of Human Ecology, it can be described as a gold mine that continues to enrich criminology today. The individual case studies remain classic portrayals of delinquents and their social worlds, the urban research methods have led to a wide variety of empirical studies, and the cultural transmission theory underlies much of contemporary theoretical criminology.

## RECOMMENDED READINGS

Clifford R. Shaw and Henry D. McKay, *Juvenile Delinquency and Urban Areas*, rev. ed., University of Chicago Press, Chicago, 1969. Shaw and McKay's basic work, with an excellent Introduction to the Revised Edition by James F. Short, Jr.

Clifford R. Shaw, *The Jackroller*, University of Chicago Press, Chicago, 1930; reprinted by the University of Chicago Press, 1966, with an Introduction by Howard S. Becker. A delinquent boy's own story.

The Jackroller and Jon Snodgrass, *The Jackroller at 70*, D. C. Heath, Lexington, Mass., 1982. The rest of the Jackroller's life story, as told shortly before his death. Additional sections on related issues by James Short, Gilbert Geis, and Solomon Kobrin.

Jon Snodgrass, "Clifford R. Shaw and Henry D. McKay: Chicago Criminologists," *British Journal of Criminology* 16: 1–19 (Jan. 1976). A review of Shaw's and McKay's lives and works, along with some of their opinions about their work, based on interviews and previously unpublished materials.

James F. Short, ed., *Delinquency, Crime and Society*, University of Chicago Press, Chicago, 1976. A book of readings focusing on the contributions of Shaw and McKay. See especially the reading by Finestone.

Harwin L. Voss and David M. Peterson, eds., *Ecology, Crime, and Delinquency*, Appleton-Century-Crofts, New York, 1971. A book of readings with an excellent introduction that traces ecological studies up to about 1970.

K. D. Harries, *Crime and the Environment*, C. C. Thomas, Springfield, Ill., 1980. A small, readable work reviewing many of the more recent American studies.

Owen Gill, *Luke Street: Housing Policy, Conflict and the Creation of the Delinquent Area*, Macmillan, London, 1977. One of the recent British area studies which concludes that the delinquency area was created by the decision of local authorities to dump problem clients into a specific location.

David L. Decker, David Schichor, and Robert M. O'Brien, *Urban Structure and Victimization*, D. C. Heath, Lexington, Mass., 1982. An ecological study comparing the victimization rates in 26 cities, with 9 structural characteristics of those cities.

Marshall Clinard, *Cities With Little Crime: The Case of Switzerland*, Cambridge University Press, Cambridge, U.K., 1978. Crime is affected by the spatial ecology of cities, the degree of political centralization, and the involvement of youth in sports and recreation programs.

Robert E. L. Faris, *Chicago Sociology: 1920—1932*, Chandler, San Francisco, 1967. A general account of the development of the Sociology Department at Chicago, and the theory and research that emerged from it.

# CHAPTER ELEVEN

# Strain Theories

Strain theories propose that there are certain socially generated pressures or forces that drive people to commit crimes. These so-called strains are not evenly distributed in society. Rather, they are most severe among the groups with the highest crime rates. Robert K. Merton proposed the first strain theory in a paper revising Durkheim's theory of anomie. While Merton attempted to explain crime in general, later strain theories focused on urban gang delinquency. Strain theories gained widespread acceptance during the 1960s and provided the ideological underpinning for President Lyndon Johnson's War on Poverty. More recently a number of theoretical and empirical criticisms have been leveled against these theories. This chapter begins with a review of the most important strain theories and then discusses the recent objections that have been made to them.

## 1. ROBERT K. MERTON AND ANOMIE IN AMERICAN SOCIETY

Durkheim had analyzed anomie as a breakdown in the ability of society to regulate the natural appetites of individuals. Merton, in an article first published in 1938, pointed out that many of the appetites of individuals were not necessarily "natural," but rather were "culturally induced." At the same time he argued that the social structure could limit the ability of certain groups to satisfy those appetites. This would mean that the social structure itself might "exert a definite pressure on certain persons in the society to engage in nonconformist rather than conformist conduct"[1] and would explain why crime is more concentrated in some groups than in others. In 1964 Merton's revision of anomie theory was called "the most influential single formulation in the sociology of deviance in the last 25 years, and . . . possibly the most frequently quoted single paper in modern sociology."[2]

Merton began by pointing out that the culture of any society defines certain goals it deems "worth striving for." [3] There are many such goals in every society, and they vary from culture to culture. Perhaps the most prominent culture goal in American society, however, is to acquire wealth. This might be regarded merely as a "natural aspiration," as Durkheim maintained. But American culture encourages this goal far beyond any intrinsic rewards the goals itself might have. Accumulated wealth is generally equated with personal value and worth and is associated with a high degree of prestige and social status. Those without money may be degraded even if they have personal characteristics that other cultures may value, such as age or spiritual discipline.

In addition, whereas Durkheim said that culture functioned to limit these aspirations in individuals (although at certain times it did not do this well), Merton argued that American culture specifically encourages all individuals to seek the greatest amount of wealth. American culture is based on an egalitarian ideology in which it is maintained that all people have an equal chance to achieve wealth. This ideology is frequently illustrated by "Horatio Alger" stories in which "poor boy makes it big." Although not all individuals are expected to achieve this goal, all are expected to try. Those who do not may be unfavorably characterized as "lazy" or "unambitious."[4]

Cultures also specify the approved norms, or *institutionalized means,* all individuals are expected to follow in pursuing the culture goals. These means are based on values in the culture, and generally will rule out many of the technically most efficient methods of achieving the goal. For example, in American culture the institutionalized means that should be used to achieve wealth can generally be identified as "middle-class values" or "the Protestant work ethic." They include hard work, honesty, education, and deferred

1. Robert K. Merton, *Social Theory and Social Structure*, The Free Press, Glencoe, Ill., 1968, p. 186.

2. Marshall B. Clinard, "The Theoretical Implications of Anomie and Deviant Behavior," in Clinard, ed., *Anomie and Deviant Behavior*, The Free Press, New York, 1964, p. 10.

3. Merton, op. cit., p. 187.

4. Ibid., p. 193.

gratification. The use of force and fraud, which may be more efficient methods of gaining wealth, is forbidden.[5]

Merton argued that because all persons cannot be expected to achieve the goals of the culture, it is very important that the culture place a strong emphasis on the institutionalized means and the necessity of following them for their own value.[6] These means must provide some intrinsic satisfactions for all persons who participate in the culture. This is similar to the situation in athletics, in which the sport itself must provide enjoyment, even if the person does not win. The phrase "It's not whether you win, it's how you play the game" expresses the notion that the primary satisfaction comes from following the institutionalized means (rules) rather than achieving the goal (winning).

In athletics, however, the goal of winning may be unduly emphasized, so that there is a corresponding deemphasis on the rewards provided by the sport itself. In this situation ("It's not how you play the game, it's whether you win") the institutionalized means are placed under a severe strain. Merton argues that this is the situation in American culture regarding the goal of achieving wealth.[7] The goal has been emphasized to the point that the institutionalized means are little reward in themselves. The person who adheres to these methods—that is, hard work, education, honesty, deferred gratification—receives little social reward for it unless he or she also achieves at least a moderate degree of wealth as a result. But the person who achieves wealth, even if it is not by the approved means, still receives the social rewards of prestige and social status. This situation places a severe strain on the institutionalized means, particularly for those persons who cannot achieve wealth through their use.

This strain falls on a wide variety of people in the society, but it tends to be more concentrated among persons in the lower class. In that group the ability to achieve wealth is limited not only by the talents and efforts of the individual, but by the social structure itself. Only the most talented and the most hard-working individuals from this class can ever expect to achieve wealth through the use of the institutionalized means. For the majority of persons this possibility is simply not realistic, and therefore the strain can be most severe. By the same token, the strain is least apparent among those in the upper classes, in which, using the same institutionalized means, a

5. Ibid., p. 187.
6. Ibid., p. 188.
7. Ibid., p. 190.

person of moderate talents can achieve a degree of wealth with only reasonable efforts.

For certain groups, then, a severe strain on the cultural values arises because (1) the culture places a disproportionate emphasis on the achievement of the goal of accumulated wealth and maintains that this goal is applicable to all persons, and (2) the social structure effectively limits the possibilities of individuals within these groups to achieve this goal through the use of institutionalized means. This contradiction between the culture and the social structure of society is what Merton defines as anomie.[8]

Merton's concept of anomie is similar to Durkheim's in that both refer to a condition in the society which results in a breakdown of the regulation of the individual's desires, so that the person wants more than he can obtain within the given structure of a society. There are major differences between the two conceptions, however. Durkheim conceived of anomie as something that occured only during times of rapid economic change and that was relatively evenly distributed throughout the society at those times. Merton conceived of anomie as a relatively permanent feature of American life that had a disproportionate effect on the lowest classes. The differences between the two theories can be clarified by distinguishing between *culture*, which refers to the way the people in a society think, and *structure*, which refers to the way a society is organized, and by considering how the two theories describe the forces that *drive* an individual toward criminal behavior, and those that *restrain* the individual from criminal behavior.

Durkheim argued that the driving forces of criminal behavior were appetites and impulses that were inherent in human nature. Because human nature is something that does not change, the forces driving individuals to crime were said to be relatively constant and not subject to change. Therefore differences in the amount of crime at different times and places could not be explained by differences in the forces driving individuals to commit criminl acts. Differences in the amount of criminal behavior could only be explained by differences in the restraining forces. Durkheim argued that societies restrained human nature either through culture (the consensus of values in mechanical societies) or through structure (the interrelationships among the different functions in organic societies). These restraints broke down during periods of rapid social change, resulting in higher levels of criminal behavior.

8. Ibid., p. 216.

Merton's was a more fully social theory in that the drive to crime was said to lie in culture and not in human nature. He argued that in American society the forces driving individuals toward criminal behaviors were stronger than in other societies due to the overemphasis on the goal of accumulating wealth. The forces restraining the individual from committing a crime were also cultural—adherence to the institutionalized means. Those restraining forces were weakened in American society, since there was no strong emphasis on adhering to the institutionalized means as long as you achieved wealth. Merton explained the high level of crime in American society in terms of *cultural imbalance,* the imbalance between the cultural forces driving the individual toward criminal behavior and the cultural forces restraining the individual from criminal behavior.

However, Merton described American culture as relatively uniform throughout the class structure, so that everyone is similarly pressured to achieve wealth and everyone has a relatively weak allegiance to the institutionalized means. Thus cultural imbalance does not explain why the lower classes in America have higher crime rates than the upper classes. Merton therefore used social structure, not culture, to explain why lower-class people in America have higher crime rates than upper-class people. That explanation focused on the distribution of legitimate opportunities in the social structure—that is the ability to achieve wealth through institutionalized means. Merton argued that those opportunities were relatively concentrated in the higher classes and relatively absent in the lower classes. The distribution of criminal behavior is said to be a sort of mirror image of the distribution of legitimate opportunities, being relatively concentrated in the lower classes and relatively absent in the upper classes.[9]

Merton's theory therefore presents a more complex relationship between driving and restraining forces, and between structure and culture, than does Durkheim's theory. Although he did not explicitly acknowledge it, Merton's reformulation of anomie theory changed Durkheim's most fundamental conceptions of the role of human nature and of social forces in the origin of criminal behavior.

There are various ways in which an individual can respond to this

9. Many interpretations of Merton's theory, particularly those by control theorists, describe his theory solely in terms of variations in the driving forces. See, in particular, Travis Hirschi, *Causes of Delinquency,* University of California Press, Berkeley, 1969, pp. 4–8; and Ruth Rosner Kornhauser, *Social Sources of Delinquency,* University of Chicago Press, Chicago, 1978, pp. 21–50, 139–50, and 165–67. That interpretation entirely ignores Merton's structural arguments. It is ironic that Kornhauser (op. cit., p. 146) then criticizes Merton's theory for its failure to restore the importance of social structure in the explanation of criminal behavior.

TABLE 11–1   Merton's Typology of Modes of Individual Adaptation*

| Modes of Adaptation | Culture Goals | Institutional Means |
| --- | --- | --- |
| I. Conformity | + | + |
| II. Innovation | + | − |
| III. Ritualism | − | + |
| IV. Retreatism | − | − |
| V. Rebellion | ± | ± |

*Key: + signifies "acceptance," − signifies "rejection," and ± signifies "rejection of prevailing values and substitution of new values."

problem of anomie, depending on his attitude toward the culture goals and the institutionalized means. Merton describes these options as conformity, innovation, ritualism, retreatism, and rebellion (Table 11–1).[10]

To the extent that a society is stable, most persons in it will choose conformity, which entails acceptance of both the culture goals and the institutionalized means. These persons strive to achieve wealth through the approved methods of middle-class values and will continue to do so whether or not they succeed.

Most crime that exists in society, however, will probably take the form of innovation. Persons who innovate retain their allegiance to the culture goal of acquiring wealth (since this is so heavily emphasized), but they find that they cannot succeed at this through the institutionalized means. Therefore they figure out new methods by which wealth can be acquired. Businessmen may devise different forms of white-collar crime entailing fraud and misrepresentation, or they may cheat on their income tax. Workers may systematically steal from their place of employment. Poor people may develop illegal operations, such as gambling, prostitution, or drug dealing, or they may burglarize and rob. In each of these cases the individual has retained his commitment to the culture goal, but is pursuing it through unapproved means.

This situation is very similar to that described by the classical thinkers, who maintained that since humans were hedonistic, they would always choose the most technically efficient methods of achieving their goals, unless limited by punishments, imposed by society.[11] Although the classical thinkers thought this was the nor-

10. Reprinted with permission of Macmillan Publishing Co., Inc., from *Social Theory and Social Structure*, by Robert K. Merton. Copyright © 1968, 1967, by Robert K. Merton.

11. Merton, op. cit., p. 211.

mal condition of people, Merton argued that it was the condition only when the cultural goals were overemphasized to the point that the norms broke down.

A third possible adaptation involves rejecting the possibility of ever achieving wealth, but retaining allegiance to the norms of hard work, honesty, etc. This is the adaptation of those persons who wish to "play it safe." They will not be disappointed by failure to achieve their goals, since they have abandoned them. At the same time they will never find themselves in any trouble since they abide by all the cultural norms. This is the perspective of "the frightened employee, the zealously conformist bureaucrat in the teller's cage"[12] and tends to be found most frequently among persons in the lower middle class. These persons have achieved a minimum level of success through the institutionalized means, but have no real hope of achieving anything more. The fear of losing even this minimum level locks them into their adaptation.

The fourth adaptation—retreatism—involves simply dropping out of the whole game. Dropouts neither pursue the cultural goals nor act according to the institutionalized means. Those who choose this adaptation include "psychotics, autists, pariahs, outcasts, vagrants, vagabonds, tramps, chronic drunkards and drug addicts."[13] Merton points out that this adaptation does not necessarily arise from a lack of commitment to the culture. It can also occur when there is a strong commitment to both the goals and the means, but no real possibility of achieving success.

There results a twofold conflict: the interiorized moral obligation for adopting institutional means conflicts with pressures to resort to illicit means (which may attain the goal) and the individual is shut off from means which are both legitimate and effective. The competitive order is maintained, but the frustrated and handicapped individual who cannot cope with this order drops out.

Rebellion is the last of the possible adaptations to the problem of anomie. Here the person responds to his frustrations by replacing the values of the society with new ones. These new values may be political, in which the goals are, for example, the achievement of a socialist society, and the approved means might involve violent revolution. On the other hand these values might be spiritual, in which the goals entail the achievement of certain states of consciousness,

12. Ibid., p. 204.
13. Ibid., p. 207.

and the means involve fasting and meditation. Or the values might
be in one of any number of other areas. The basic point is that this
person ceases to function as a member of the existing society and
begins to live within an alternate culture.

These adaptations do not describe personality types. Rather they
describe an individual's choice of behaviors in response to the strain
of anomie. Some individuals may consistently choose one adaptation, such as the low-level bureaucrat who responds to her situation
through ritualism. But this same bureaucrat may occasionally innovate by stealing small amounts from her employer, or she may occasionally retreat through the use of alcohol. Other persons develop
patterns of behavior involving the use of several adaptations simultaneously. For example, a professional criminal (innovation) may also
consistently use narcotics (retreatism) while at the same time promoting a militant, revolutionary philosophy (rebellion). These behaviors might not be seen as consistent with each other unless it is
understood that they are all responses to the anomic stresses the individual faces.

These same adaptations may be seen in other situations in which
there is a discrepancy between the emphasis placed on the goals and
the means to achieve them. In athletics, if the goal of winning is
overemphasized, those who cannot win within the institutionalized
means (rules) may be strongly motivated to cheat (innovate), they
may merely continue playing without hope of winning (ritualism), they
may quite playing altogether (retreatism), or they may attempt to get
a different game going (rebellion). Students are often faced with a
strong overemphasis of the goal of achieving high grades, and may
resort to similar adaptations. Deviant behavior among scientists has
been analyzed in terms of an overemphasis on the goal of originality
in scientific research.[14] Those who cannot achieve this goal may resort to various adaptive behaviors such as "reporting only the data
which support an hypothesis, making false charges of plagiarism,
making self-assertive claims, being secretive lest one be forestalled,
occasionally stealing ideas, and in rare cases, even fabricating data."[15]

Although Merton regarded all these adaptations (except conformity) as deviant, they do not all entail criminality. The ritualist adaptation in particular, with its rigid adherence to the norms of society,

14. Robert K. Merton, "Priorities in Scientific Discovery: A Chapter in the Sociology of Science," *American Sociological Review* 22: 635–59 (Dec. 1957). See also Harriet Zuckerman,
"Deviant Behavior and Social Control in Science," in Edward Sagarin, ed., *Deviance and Social Change*, Sage, Beverly Hills, Cal., 1977, pp. 87–138.

15. Clinard, op. cit., p. 23. For a recent example, see Claudia Wallis, "Fraud in a Harvard
Lab," *Time*, Feb. 28, 1983, p. 49.

does not involve any crime at all. Retreatism involves crime to the extent that society criminalizes the process of dropping out with laws against vagrancy, public drunkenness, and drug use. Rebellion, when it is politically oriented, may involve such criminal activities as assassinations and bombings, or the expression of the militant beliefs may itself be criminalized. Innovation itself is not necessarily criminal: [16]

On the top economic levels, the pressure toward innovation not infrequently erases the distinction between business-like strivings this side of the mores and sharp practices beyond the mores. As Veblen observed, "It is not easy in any given case—indeed it is at times impossible until the courts have spoken—to say whether it is an instance of praiseworthy salesmanship or a penitentiary offense."

Finally, Merton makes the point that "the foregoing theory of anomie is designed to account for some, not all, forms of deviant behavior customarily described as criminal or delinquent." The intention of the theory is to focus attention on one specific problem, "the acute pressure created by the discrepancy between culturally induced goals and socially structured opportunities," and does not attempt to explain all the diverse behaviors that at one time or another are prohibited by the criminal law.

A number of theorists have attempted to extend and refine Merton's theories. The most significant of these attempts was by Richard Cloward, writing in 1959.[17] Whereas Merton focuses on the fact that lower-class people had limited access to legal means of achieving success goals, Cloward pointed out that these same people often had very broad access to illegal means that existed in their neighborhoods. The local pawn shop, which would fence stolen goods; the junkyard, which would take that hot car off your hands; the numbers racket; the drug and prostitution rings all provided illegal opportunities to achieve the success goals of society. Cloward also pointed out that the mere presence of an opportunity is not enough unless you have been introduced to the ways of taking advantage of it.[18] This "learning structure" had been described by Shaw and McKay in their studies of delinquency areas and by Sutherland in his theory that crime is normal, learned behavior; and Cloward regarded his

16. Merton, *Social Theory and Social Structure*, p. 195.

17. Richard A. Cloward, "Illegitimate Means, Anomie, and Deviant Behavior," *American Sociological Review* 24: 164–76 (Apr. 1959).

18. Ibid., p. 168.

formulation as a consolidation of these three approaches. Merton agreed with Cloward's theory, regarding it as a substantial extension of his own theory.[19]

## 2. STRAIN AS THE EXPLANATION OF GANG DELINQUENCY

Merton's reformulation of anomie theory focused on the special strains under which certain segments of the population are placed, and used those strains to explain criminality. This type of argument has been also used in two major theories to explain urban, lower class, male gang delinquency, one by Albert Cohen and the other by Richard Cloward and Lloyd Ohlin.

In his work with juveniles, Cohen found that most delinquent behavior occurred in gangs rather than individually, and that most of it was "non-utilitarian, malicious, and negativistic."[20] This type of delinquency, in contrast to most adult crime, seemed to serve no useful purpose. Juvenile gangs stole things they did not want or need, vandalized and maliciously destroyed property, and participated in gang wars and unprovoked assaults. Purposeless crimes could not be explained by Merton's theory, which argued that crimes had the purpose of acquiring money, although by illegitimate means. Cohen believed that these actions were methods of gaining status among the delinquent's peers, but then he had to ask why these behaviors were "a claim to status in one group and a degrading blot in another."[21] He concluded that gangs have a separate culture from the dominant culture, with a different set of values for measuring status. The question that Cohen then addressed was why and how this separate culture had evolved.

Merton described people as seeking the cultural goal of success. In a similar way Cohen saw youths as seeking the goal of status among their peers. He utilized the classic distinction between achieved status, which is earned in competition with one's own age and sex group, and ascribed status, which is acquired by virtue of one's family, such as when one's father is an important person. Competition for achieved status normally takes place within the school. Cohen saw the school as a solidly middle-class institution, permeated by the values of its middle-class teachers and administrators. Status in school was judged

19. Robert K. Merton, "Social Conformity, Deviation and Opportunity Structures: A Comment on the Contributions of Dubin and Cloward," *American Sociological Review* 24: 188 (Apr. 1959).

20. Albert K. Cohen, *Delinquent Boys: The Culture of the Gang*, The Free Press, New York, 1955.

21. Ibid., p. 27.

on the basis of such values as ambition, responsibility, achievement (especially in the areas of academic work and athletics), deferred gratification, rationality, courtesy, ability to control physical aggression, constructive use of time, and respect for property.[22]

A youth who has no ascribed status by virtue of his family, and who typically loses in the competition for achieved status, is placed under a severe strain. He can continue to conform to middle-class values, but he must then be content with a low-status position among his peers. Or he can rebel against middle-class values and set up a new value structure according to which he can increase his status and self-worth. Youths who rebel in such a way tend to come together to form a group in order to validate their choices and reinforce their new values. The delinquent gang is such a group. It is a spontaneous development in which a number of youths, each of whom faces a similar problem (low status), together create a common solution to that problem.

Lack of status may affect youths in different social classes, but, like Merton's anomie, it disproportionately affects youths from the lower class. These youths generally have no ascribed status from their families, since their parents normally have low-status occupations. At the same time they are at a disadvantage in competing for achieved status in schools. Lower-class children often have internalized values different from those of middle-class children prior to entering the school. When measured against these values, they perform poorly and must either adjust to these new values or reject them. Thus members of delinquent gangs will generally be lower-class children. And because the gang is primarily rebelling against middle-class values, it takes on the "negativistic" character noticed by Cohen.

Merton's and Cohen's theories differ in several respects. Merton emphasized the utilitarian nature of crime, focusing on innovation as a response to the social structural pressures, whereas Cohen sought to explain the nonutilitarian character of much delinquency. Cohen's theory is similar to the "rebellion" adaptation proposed by Merton, but it differs in that the particular form the rebellion takes is determined by a reaction against middle-class values. In Merton's theory rebellion may take any one of a number of different forms. Finally, Cohen saw the choice of rebellion as linked to the choices of other members of the group, whereas Merton portrayed the choice of an adaptation as an individual response.

Cloward and Ohlin sought to resolve the conflicts between the

22. Ibid., pp. 88–91.

TABLE 11–2   Cloward and Ohlin's Classification of Lower-Class Youth

|                                          | Orientation of Lower-Class Youth | |
| ---------------------------------------- | -------------------------------- | -------------------------------- |
| Categories of Lower-Class Youth          | Toward Membership in Middle Class | Toward Improvement in Economic Position |
| Type I                                   | +                                | +                                |
| Type II                                  | +                                | −                                |
| Type III                                 | −                                | +                                |
| Type IV                                  | −                                | −                                |

theories of Merton and Cohen, and also to integrate with these two theories the ideas of the Chicago Ecologists and of Edwin Sutherland.[23] Whereas Merton had argued that lower-class youths strive for monetary success and Cohen that they strive for status, Cloward and Ohlin argued that these were separate strivings which could operate independently of each other. They proposed four categories of lower-class youths, as shown in Table 11–2.[24] Youths who seek an increase in status are seen as striving for membership in the middle class, while other youths seek an improvement in their economic position without seeking to change their class association.

Cohen claimed that most delinquency is committed by boys of Type I and Type II, who are striving to increase their status. Cloward and Ohlin agreed that when pressures toward delinquency arose among these boys, they were likely to be of the type described by Cohen, that is, reactions against the middle-class values in which the boy believes, but with which he is unable to conform due to social structural pressures. But they argue that these boys do not constitute the major group of delinquents, since their values generally are consistent with those of middle-class authorities. Instead, the most serious delinquents are of Type III. These youths are oriented toward conspicuous consumption, "fast cars, fancy clothes, and swell dames," goals that are phrased solely in economic terms and not in terms of middle-class life-styles. These youths experience the greatest conflict with middle-class values, since they "are looked down upon both for what they do *not* want (i.e., the middle-class style of life) and for what they *do* want (i.e., 'crass materialism')."[25] These are the youths,

23.  Richard A. Cloward and Lloyd E. Ohlin, *Delinquency and Opportunity: A Theory of Delinquent Gangs*, The Free Press, New York, 1960.

24.  Reprinted with permission of Macmillan Publishing Co., Inc., from *Delinquency and Opportunity* by Richard A. Cloward and Lloyd Ohlin. © The Free Press, a Corporation, 1960.

25.  Cloward and Ohlin, op. cit, p. 97.

Cloward and Ohlin claim, who have been repeatedly described in the literature of juvenile delinquency. Finally, Cloward and Ohlin argue that Type IV youths, although they may incur criticism from middle-class authorities for their "lack of ambition," generally stay out of trouble because they tend to avoid middle-class institutions and people as much as possible.

Cloward and Ohlin then refer to the earlier extension of Merton's theory by Cloward in order to explain the particular form of delinquency which these Type III youths will commit. It is assumed that there are no legitimate opportunities for these youths to improve their economic position. If illegitimate opportunities are presented, as described by Cloward, then these youths will tend to form "criminal" gangs, in which the emphasis is on production of income. If, however, neither legitimate nor illegitimate opportunities are available, then the youths' frustration and discontent will be heightened. In addition, lack of opportunities is often a symptom of a lack of social organization (whether legitimate or illegitimate) in the community, which means there will be fewer controls on the youths' behavior. In this circumstance the youths will tend to form a violent, or "conflict," gang to express their anger. This is the source of the "non-utilitarian, malicious, and negativistic" activity described by Cohen. Finally, Cloward and Ohlin describe a "retreatist subculture" similar to Merton's "retreatist" adaptation and similarly populated with "double failures." Youths in this subculture were unable to achieve the economic improvement they sought, whether because of lack of opportunity or because of internal prohibitions against the use of illegitimate means. They also fail in the resort to conflict and violence. This group turns to alcohol or to drugs, and drops out.

## 3. ASSESSING STRAIN THEORIES

Strain theories have strongly influenced criminology and sociology, and for a time they dominated both fields. Because they have been so influential, strain theories have been subject to a great deal of scrutiny and to a very large number of criticisms. Some of the criticisms have been theoretical, focusing on the adequacy of their terms and concepts, while others have been empirical, focusing on whether the theories are supported by research.

Virtually everyone who criticizes strain theories begins by acknowledging how appealing and plausible they are. They take a very optimistic view of human nature: criminals are driven to commit crimes, and would be law-abiding citizens if only given a chance. The drive to commit crime is said to originate in culture, so that it is not seen as an inevitable condition of human nature. Crime is concentrated among the lower classes because the structure of society denies them the opportunity to make money in legitimate ways. The solution to the crime problem lies in reform, not revolution or repression. That reform focuses on changing society to live up to the ideals of democracy and egalitarianism, ideals with which most of us agree. Nettler quotes an old saying in his discussion of strain theories: "It may not be true, but it's a good story."[26]

A number of authors have focused their criticisms on theoretical problems with strain theories, arguing that they rely primarily on their intuitive appeal but are difficult to verify or falsify as scientific theories. Nettler, for example, maintains that the two key concepts in Cloward and Ohlin's theory are aspiration and opportunity and that neither term is defined very clearly.[27] Although delinquents may state verbally that they aspire to a goal, they may exhibit no effective motivation toward it, and when presented with a legitimate opportunity to achieve that goal they may fail to take advantage of the opportunity. Kitsuse and Dietrick made a related argument about Cohen's theory.[28] They pointed out that it involves an analysis of the psychological motivations of gang youths at an earlier point in time (when they were in the process of forming a gang) and argue that it is impossible to verify such a theory empirically. Hirschi also discussed the difficulties of testing Cohen's theory.[29] On the one hand, youths are said to agree with middle-class values, but, on the other hand, they are said to rebel against those values and reject them. Thus, research showing that delinquents agree with middle-class values can be said to support Cohen's theory, but so can research showing that delinquents reject middle-class values. Lemert criticized the basic distinction between culture and structure in Merton's theory, arguing that the rigid dichotomy drawn between them may be so artificial as to have little meaning in reality.[30] In addition, he questioned whether any society in the contemporary world can be said to have one set of values, even if the subcultural values of ethnic minorities are excluded.

26. Gwynn Nettler, *Explaining Crime*, 2nd ed., McGraw-Hill, New York, 1978, p. 237.

27. Ibid., pp. 228–30. See also 3rd ed., 1984, pp. 208–12.

28. John I. Kitsuse and David C. Dietrick, "Delinquent Boys: A Critique," in Harwin L. Voss, ed., *Society, Delinquency, and Delinquent Behavior*, Little, Brown, Boston, 1970, pp. 238–45.

29. Hirschi, op. cit., pp. 125–6.

30. Edwin Lemert, "Social Structure, Social Control, and Deviation," in Clinard, ed., op. cit., pp. 57–97.

Other authors have focused their criticisms on empirical research, maintaining that it fails to support the basic arguments that strain theories make. For example, Kitsuse and Dietrick question Cohen's description of gang delinquency as "malicious, negativistic, and non-utilitarian," saying that much gang delinquency is really serious criminal activity.[31] Bordua pointed to the utilitarian nature of much gang delinquency and also argued that delinquency can be fun, so that it is not necessary that youths be "driven" to it by forces beyond their control.[32]

The most extensive criticisms of strain theories have been made by Kornhauser, who charged that they were afflicted with a large number of theoretical and empirical problems.[33] One of her most important criticisms was that Cloward and Ohlin's theory could be conceptualized in terms of a gap between aspirations and expectations—that is, delinquents want a lot but do not expect to get very much.[34] Kornhauser then reviewed the empirical research on the aspirations and expectations of delinquents and argued that it showed that delinquency is associated with both low expectations and low aspirations. She maintained that such youths would not be strained, since there is no gap between what they want and what they expect to get. Essentially Kornhauser agreed that delinquents don't expect to get much, but she argued that they don't want much either, so there is no problem in that regard.

Cloward and Ohlin's theory, however, is designed to explain the behavior of one small group of youths: seriously delinquent urban male gang members. Studies that focus directly on those youths have produced strong and consistent support of the theory, including its argument about the gap between aspirations and expectations.[35] There are two exceptions to the general pattern of empirical support. First, Cloward and Ohlin portrayed gang delinquents as talented youths who have a sense of injustice concerning the absence of legitimate opportunities.[36] Most of the research indicates that gang delinquents have few social abilities, so this aspect of Cloward and Ohlin's theory

31. Kitsuse and Dietrick, op. cit.

32. David J. Bordua, "Delinquent Subcultures: Sociological Interpretations of Gang Delinquency," *Annals of the American Academy of Political and Social Science* 338: 119–36 (Nov. 1961).

33. Kornhauser, op. cit., pp. 139–80.

34. Ibid., pp. 167–80.

35. Thomas J. Bernard, "Control Criticisms of Strain Theories: An Assessment of Theoretical and Empirical Adequacy," *Journal of Research in Crime and Delinquency* 21 (4): 353–72 (Nov. 1984).

36. Cloward and Ohlin, op. cit., p. 117.

is not supported by the data.[37] Second, Cloward and Ohlin described three types of gangs (criminal, conflict, and retreatist) that develop in response to strain, but that typology is not supported by the data and should be discarded. Neither aspect of Cloward and Ohlin's theory is essential to its argument, and both can be discarded without damage to the overall theory.[38]

Most of the theoretical criticisms of strain theories, including those raised by Kornhauser, focus on their cultural elements. But strain theories should be interpreted primarily as structural theories, and the cultural elements in the theories should be considered secondary.[39] This distinction is illustrated in Liebow's study of a group of black men who regularly met on a particular corner in a blighted area of inner-city Washington, D.C.[40] Liebow argued that the values these men held were not cultural in that they were not passed from generation to generation as a valued heritage. Rather, each man experienced the same failures in jobs, marriages, and life in general; each man generated "public fictions" to defend himself against those failures (e.g., "I got divorced because I was too much of a man for any one woman"); and each man supported the others in maintaining those fictions. It is those public fictions that have been interpreted by sociologists as "lower-class culture." Liebow concluded: "What appears as a dynamic, self-sustaining cultural process is, in part at least, a relatively simple piece of social machinery which turns out, in a rather mechanical fashion, independently produced lookalikes."[41]

Liebow's theory is a strain theory since it describes men who are driven by social forces to do things they would rather not do. Those forces are rooted in social structure—the organization of society that, in a way that these men do not understand and cannot control, virtually guarantees that they will fail at almost everything they do. The strain theories of Merton, Cohen, and Cloward and Ohlin should also be viewed as describing a social structural mechanism: individuals

---

37. See Nettler, 3rd ed., op. cit., pp. 212–18, for a discussion of this point.

38. Bernard, op. cit., pp. 366–68. The sense of injustice is necessary for strain theories only if one adheres to a Durkheimian view of a "biological meritocracy" in which individuals who are at their proper social level, given their abilities, will be satisfied. It is also possible to construct strain theories in which individuals at low social levels are strained, even if they have low abilities and do not perceive their station in life as unjust. For a strain theory that does not rely on talented delinquents with a sense of injustice, see Martin Gold, *Status Forces in Delinquent Boys*, Institute for Social Research, Ann Arbor, Mich., 1963.

39. Bernard, op. cit., pp. 357–59.

40. Elliot Liebow, *Tally's Corner*, Little, Brown, Boston, 1967.

41. Ibid., p. 223.

confront similar socially structured situations that they do not necessarily understand and cannot control. These individuals end up
thinking and acting in similar ways, even though each is "independently produced."

## 4. POLICY IMPLICATIONS

Liebow's primary recommendation was that "the Negro man, along
with everyone else, must be given the skills to earn a living and an
opportunity to put these skills to work."[42] Other strain theories have
similar policy implications, and during the 1960s those theories had
a great impact on federal policy toward crime and delinquency.[43] After
Robert Kennedy, who was then attorney general of the United States,
read Cloward and Ohlin's book, he asked Lloyd Ohlin to help develop a new federal policy on juvenile delinquency. The result was
the passage of the Juvenile Delinquency Prevention and Control Act
of 1961, which was based on a comprehensive action program developed by Cloward and Ohlin in connection with their book. The
program included improving education, creating work opportunities, organizing lower-class communities, and providing services to
individuals, gangs, and families. The program was later expanded to
include all lower-class people and became the basis of Lyndon Johnson's War on Poverty. Although billions of dollars were spent on these
programs, the only clear result seems to have been the massive political resistance that was generated against this attempt to extend
opportunities to people without them. The programs, having failed
to achieve their goals, were eventually dismantled by Richard Nixon.

Since no genuine extension of opportunities ever took place, this
failure might be attributed to the opposition the programs encountered. Rose has offered an alternative interpretation of the failure of
these programs.[44] The War on Poverty was based on strain theories,
which argue that crime and poverty have their origins in social
structural arrangements. Therefore, these theories imply that the

42. Ibid., p. 224.

43. For a brief review of the attempt to implement Cloward and Ohlin's ideas in federal policy, see LaMar T. Empey, *American Delinquency*, rev. ed., Dorsey, Homewood, Ill., 1982,
pp. 240–45. For more extended accounts, see Peter Maris and Martin Rein, *Dilemmas of Social Reform*, 2nd ed., Aldine, Chicago, 1973; James F. Short, Jr., "The Natural History of an
Applied Theory: Differential Opportunity and Mobilization for Youth," in N. J. Demerath,
ed., *Social Policy and Sociology*, Academic Press, New York, 1975, pp. 193–210; Joseph J.
Helfgot, *Professional Reforming: Mobilization for Youth and the Failure of Social Science*,
Heath, Lexington, Mass., 1981; and Stephen M. Rose, *The Betrayal of the Poor: The Trans-
formation of Community Action*, Schenkmann, Cambridge, Mass., 1972.

44. Rose, op. cit.

solution to the problems of crime and poverty require social structural change. As originally conceived, the War on Poverty was designed to change social structural arrangements, not to change individual people. That is, its primary purpose was to change what Liebow described as the "relatively simple piece of social machinery" that was producing poor and criminal people. Its primary purpose was not to change the poor and criminal people after they had been produced.

However, most of these programs were taken over by the bureaucracies of poverty-serving agencies, who immediately acted to protect and enhance their own bureaucratic interests. As a consequence, when the poverty programs were actually implemented, virtually all of them were designed to change poor people, and very few were designed to change social structural arrangements. Rose maintains that the War on Poverty failed because its original purpose was subverted as it was transformed to serve the interests of the established poverty-serving bureaucracies. Thus, he entitles his book *The Betrayal of the Poor*.

## 5. CONCLUSION

Strain theories argue that certain social structural arrangements generate forces that drive individuals toward crime and delinquency. Empirical research with seriously delinquent urban male gang members has provided considerable support for this basic contention. However, the failure of the War on Poverty illustrates that the policy implications of strain theories are difficult to achieve in the real world.

Nettler comments that one of the reasons the policy implications of strain theories have not been effective is "the impotence of *teaching* to change what *training* has produced."[45] This comment fails to recognize that strain theories focus on the social structural arrangments that produced the training in the first place. Thus, the policy implications of strain theories focus on changing the "relatively simple piece of social machinery" that is producing criminals and delinquents, rather than changing the criminals and delinquents after they have been produced.

The problem with the policy implications of strain theories is that patterns of self-interest always develop around existing social structural arrangements.[46] People who benefit from those arrangements

45. Nettler, op. cit., 3rd ed., p. 218.
46. Talcott Parsons, *Politics and Social Structure*, The Free Press, New York, 1969, p. 95.

protect their self-interests by resisting social change. There is an old saying: "Reform is like trying to take a bone away from a dog." The lesson from the War on Poverty is that there are many self-interests associated with the way we presently deal with crime and poverty and that the idealistic reformers could not get that bone away from the dog. It was not even a close fight.

There is no question that the problems described by strain theories are complex. It is not merely a matter of talented individuals confronted with inferior schools and discriminatory hiring practices. Rather, a good deal of research indicates that many delinquents and criminals are untalented individuals who cannot compete effectively in complex industrial societies.[47]

When viewed in the light of that research, strain theories can be interpreted as suggesting that untalented people want many of the same things as talented people but find they cannot obtain these things through legitimate means. Some of them therefore attempt to obtain those things through criminal activity. From this perspective, strain theories would seem to pose some disturbing questions for public policy. Do untalented people have the same rights as talented people to want material goods, the respect of their peers, and power and control over their own lives? Does society have an obligation to provide untalented as well as talented people with legitimate opportunities to obtain these things?

## RECOMMENDED READINGS

Robert K. Merton, *Social Theory and Social Structure*, The Free Press, New York, 1968, pp. 185–214. The current version of Merton's anomie theory.

Richard A. Cloward and Lloyd E. Ohlin, *Delinquency and Opportunity*, The Free Press, New York, 1955. The classic theory of delinquent gangs that links the theories of Durkheim and Merton to those of Shaw, McKay, and Sutherland.

Albert K. Cohen, *Delinquent Boys: The Culture of the Gang*, The Free Press, New York, 1955. The classic theory of malicious, nonutilitarian, and negativistic gang delinquency.

Marshall B. Clinard, ed., *Anomie and Deviant Behavior*, The Free Press, New York, 1964. A book of original papers on anomie by leading sociologists in various areas of deviant behavior.

Thomas J. Bernard, "Control Criticisms of Strain Theories: An Assessment of Theoretical and Empirical Adequacy," *Journal of Research in Crime and Delinquency*, 21(4): 353–72 (Nov. 1984). Theoretical objections to strain theories are largely self-

47. Nettler, op. cit., 3rd ed., pp. 212–18.

contradictory, and empirical studies that focus directly on seriously delinquent populations provide considerable support.

Elliott Liebow, *Tally's Corner: A Study of Negro Streetcorner Men*, Little, Brown, Boston, 1967. A vivid portrayal of social structural strain.

John Laub, *Criminology in the Making: An Oral History*, Northeastern University Press, Boston, 1983. Interviews with Albert Cohen and Lloyd Ohlin provide considerable background information about the origin and development of their theories.

# CHAPTER TWELVE

# Criminal Behavior
# as Normal Learned Behavior

Richard Cloward pointed out that the mere presence of an opportunity, whether legitimate or illegitimate, was meaningless unless a person had learned how to take advantage of it. Thus Merton's use of the term *means* necessarily included both *opportunity structures* and *learning structures*. The present chapter focuses on those learning structures and examines theories that argue that learning to take advantage of illegitimate opportunities involves all the same processes as learning to take advantage of legitimate opportunities. These theories describe criminal behavior as normal learned behavior.

## 1. BASIC PSYCHOLOGICAL ASSUMPTIONS

Theories of criminal behavior as normal learned behavior are based on general theories of how learning takes place, and as those general theories have changed, the theories of criminal behavior have changed along with them. Learning refers to habits and knowledge that develop as a result of the experiences of the individual in entering and adjusting to the environment.[1] These are to be distinguished from unlearned or instinctive behavior, which seems in some sense to be present in the individual at birth and determined by biology.

---

1. Basic information about learning theories may be found in Gordon H. Bower and Ernest R. Hilgard, *Theories of Learning*, Prentice-Hall, Englewood Cliffs, N.J., 1981; Stewart H. Hulse, Howard Egeth, and James Deese, *The Psychology of Learning*, 5th ed., McGraw-Hill, New York, 1980; Robert C. Bolles, *Learning Theory*, 2nd ed., Holt, Rinehart and Winston, New York, 1979; Winifred F. Hill, *Learning: A Survey of Psychological Interpretations*, 3rd ed., Crowell, New York, 1977. These theories are briefly reviewed in Gwynn Nettler, *Explaining Crime*, 3rd ed., McGraw-Hill, New York, 1984, pp. 296–300.

One of the oldest formulations about the nature of learning is that we learn by association.[2] Aristotle (384–322 B.C.) argued that all knowledge is acquired through experience and that none is inborn or instinctive. Basic sensory experiences become associated with each other in the mind because they occur in certain relationships to each other as we interact with the object. Aristotle formulated four laws of association that described those relationships: the law of similarity, the law of contrast, the law of succession in time, and the law of coexistence in space. The most complex ideas, according to Aristotle, are all built out of these simple associations between sensory experiences.

Associationism has been the dominant learning theory through the centuries to the present time. It was elaborated by such philosophers as Hobbes, Locke, and Hume, and was the basis for the first experiments on human memory, carried out by Ebbinhaus,[3] as well as for the first experiments on animal learning, carried out by Thorndike.[4] The *behaviorist* revolution substituted observable stimuli and responses for the mental images and ideas of earlier times, but retained the basic idea that learning is accomplished through association. At the present time a major controversy among learning theorists is between such behavioral theorists and the *cognitive* theorists, who retain the original Aristotelian notion that learning takes place because of the association of ideas and factual knowledge.[5] Where behaviorists argue that we acquire habits through the association of stimuli with responses, cognitive theorists argue that we

2. For a detailed account of the development of associationism, see J. R. Anderson and Gordon H. Bower, *Human Associative Memory*, Winston and Sons, Washington, D.C., 1973. Concise accounts can be found in Hulse, Egeth, and Deese, op. cit., pp. 2–4, and Bower and Hilgard, op. cit., pp. 2–4. The major alternative to associationism began with Plato (427?–347 B.C.), who emphasized the rational aspects of human learning. See Bower and Hilgard, op. cit., pp. 4–8; and Hulse, Egeth, and Deese, op. cit., pp. 4–8. Where Aristotle broke complex learning down to its simplest components, Plato argued that the whole was greater than the sum of its parts. He emphasized the inborn capacity of the human mind to organize raw sense data, and his ideas appear in modern times in the form of Gestalt psychology. This school has gained support recently from research on "species specific" behaviors. See Keller Breeland and Marian Breeland, "The Misbehavior of Organisms," *American Psychologist* 16: 681–84 (1961); M. E. P. Seligman, "On the Generality of the Laws of Learning," *Psychological Review* 77: 406–18 (1970); J. Garcia and R. Koelling, "Relation of Cue to Consequence in Avoidance Learning," *Psychonomic Science* 4: 123–124 (1966). However, this view has not been applied to crime, so it is not presented here.

3. H. Ebinghaus, *Memory*, Teachers College, New York, 1913; reprinted by Dover, New York, 1964.

4. E. L. Thorndike, "Animal Intelligence," *Psychological Review Monograph Supplement* 2 (8) (1898).

5. Bower and Hilgard, op. cit., pp. 15–17.

acquire factual knowledge through the association of memories, ideas, or expectations. Behaviorists argue that learning occurs primarily through trial and error, while cognitive theorists describe learning as taking place through insight into problem solving. Despite these and other controversies between behavioral and cognitive learning theories, both can be traced back to Aristotle's original ideas about association as the basis of learning.

There are three basic ways that individuals learn through association. The simplest way is *classical* conditioning, as originally described by Pavlov. Some stimuli will reliably produce a given response without any prior training of the organism. For example, a dog will consistently salivate when presented with meat. Pavlov consistently presented meat to dogs along with some other stimulus that did not by itself produce the salivation—for example, the sound of a bell. He found that after a few pairings the sound of the bell itself was sufficient to produce salivation in the dog. What Pavlov demonstrated was that behaviors could be learned by association: If the sound of a bell is associated consistently with the presentation of the meat, then the dog learns to salivate at the sound of the bell alone.

In classical conditioning the organism is passive and learns what to expect from the environment. In *operant* conditioning the organism is active and learns how to get what it wants from the environment. Operant conditioning is associated with B. F. Skinner and is now probably the dominant learning theory in psychology. Operant conditioning uses rewards and punishments to reinforce certain behaviors. For example, rats may be taught to press a lever by rewarding that behavior with a food pellet or by punishing with an electric shock its failure to push the lever. The rat learns to operate on its environment by associating rewards and punishments with its own behaviors. Thus operant conditioning is another way of learning by association.

While both classical and operant conditioning are associated with the behaviorist school of learning theory, a third theory describing how people learn by association attempts to combine both operant conditioning and elements from cognitive psychology. Called *modeling* or *social learning* theory, it emphasizes the point that behavior may be reinforced not only through actual rewards and punishments, but also through expectations that are learned by watching what happens to other people. Bandura, for example, argues that "virtually all learning phenomena resulting from direct experiences can occur on a vicarious basis through observation of other persons'

behavior and its consequences for them."[6] While classical and operant conditioning are both tested extensively with animal experiments, social learning theory is more focused on human learning,
since it directs attention to higher mental processes.

## 2. TARDE'S LAWS OF IMITATION

An early criminologist who presented a theory of crime as normal
learned behavior was Gabriel Tarde (1843–1904).[7] Tarde rejected
Lombroso's theory that crime was caused by biological abnormality,
arguing that criminals were primarily normal people who, by accident of birth, were brought up in an atmosphere in which they learned
crime as a way of life. He phrased his theory in terms of "laws of
imitation," which were similar to Aristotle's laws of learning except
that they focused on associations among individuals rather than associations among sensations within one individual. Like Aristotle's
original theory, Tarde's theory was essentially a cognitive theory in
which the individual was said to learn ideas through the association
with other ideas, and behavior was said to follow from those ideas.

Tarde's first law was that people imitate one another in proportion
to how much close contact they have with one another. Thus imitation is most frequent, and changes most rapidly, in cities. Tarde described this as "fashion." In rural areas, in contrast, imitation is less
frequent and changes only slowly. Tarde defined that as "custom."
Tarde argued that crime begins as a fashion and later becomes a custom, much like any other social phenomenon.

The second law of imitation was that the inferior usually imitates
the superior. Trade traced the history of crimes such as vagabon-
dage, drunkenness, and murder, and found that they began as crimes
committed by royalty, and later were imitated by all social classes.
Similarly, he argued that many crimes originated in large cities, and
were then imitated by those in rural areas.

The third law of imitation was that the newer fashions displace the
older ones. Tarde argued, for example, that murder by knifings had
decreased while murder by shooting increased.

---

6. Albert Bandura, *Principles of Behavior Modification*, Holt, Rinehart and Winston, New
York, 1969, p. 118.

7. The following account is taken from Margaret S. Wilson Vine, "Gabriel Tarde," in Hermann Mannheim, ed., *Pioneers in Criminology*, 2nd ed., Patterson Smith, Montclair, N.J.,
1972, pp. 292–304. See also Don Martindale, *The Nature and Types of Sociological Theory*,
Houghton Mifflin, Boston, 1960, pp. 305–9; and Jack H. Curtis, "Gabriel Tarde," in Clement
S. Mihanovich, ed., *Social Theorists*, Bruce, Milwaukee, 1953, pp. 142–57.

Tarde's theory was important at the time for its role in opposing Lombroso's theories. It retains some importance for us at the present time, since it was the first attempt to describe criminal behavior in terms of normal learning rather than in terms of biological or psychological defects. From this point of view, the major problem with the theory is that it was based on such a simplistic model of learning. This was the state of learning theory at the time that Tarde wrote. A later theory with some elements of the same basic idea— criminal behavior is the result of normal learning—was presented by Sutherland. Although the model of learning on which the theory was based is also relatively simple, Sutherland's theory continues to have a profound impact on criminology.

## 3. SUTHERLAND'S DIFFERENTIAL ASSOCIATION THEORY

Edwin H. Sutherland (1883–1950) was born in a small town in Nebraska and received his bachelors degree from Grand Island College there.[8] He taught for several years at a small Baptist college in South Dakota before leaving to obtain his Ph.D. from the University of Chicago. While there, he was strongly influenced by *symbolic interactionism,* a theory developed by George Herbert Mead (1863–1931), who was on the faculty at the time.[9] Symbolic interactionism was to play a major role in Sutherland's theory of criminal behavior.

Sutherland's interests were primarily focused on problems of unemployment, and that was the subject of his dissertation. Following his graduation he taught for six years at a small college in Missouri, and then went to the University of Illinois, where his department chairman suggested that he write a book on criminology. The result was the first edition of *Criminology,* published in 1924.[10]

Sutherland's theory of criminal behavior emerged gradually in several editions of this book, as he formulated his thinking on the subject and systematized his presentation of that thinking. He was influenced in this endeavor by a report on criminology written by Jerome Michael and Mortimer J. Adler, which appeared in 1933 and

---

8. See George B. Vold, "Edwin Hardin Sutherland: Sociological Criminologist," *American Sociological Review* 16 (1): 3–9 (Feb. 1951).

9. For a review of Mead's thought, see Herbert Blumer, *Symbolic Interactionism,* Prentice-Hall, Englewood Cliffs, N.J., 1969. The theory is briefly reviewed in George B. Vold, *Theoretical Criminology,* 2nd ed. prepared by Thomas J. Bernard, Oxford University Press, New York, 1979, pp. 255–58.

10. Edwin H. Sutherland, *Criminology,* Lippincott, Philadelphia, 1924.

severely criticized the state of criminological theory and research.[11] Sutherland was extremely annoyed by the report, and responded to it by attempting to create a general theory that could organize the many diverse facts known about criminal behavior into some logical arrangement. The first brief statement of that general theory appeared in the second edition of *Criminology*, published in 1934. In the third edition of the book, published in 1939, Sutherland made a more systematic and formal presentation of his theory, and further expanded and clarified it in the fourth edition, appearing in 1947. The theory has remained unchanged since that edition, and consists of the following nine points:[12]

1. Criminal behavior is learned. . . .

2. Criminal behavior is learned in interaction with other persons in a process of communication. . . .

3. The principal part of the learning of criminal behavior occurs within intimate personal groups. . . .

4. When criminal behavior is learned, the learning includes (a) techniques of committing the crime, which are sometimes very complicated, sometimes very simple; (b) the specific direction of the motives, drives, rationalizations, and attitudes. . . .

5. The specific directions of the motives and drives is learned from definitions of the legal codes as favorable or unfavorable. In some societies an individual is surrounded by persons who invariably define the legal codes as rules to be observed, while in others he is surrounded by persons whose definitions are favorable to the violation of the legal codes. . . .

6. A person becomes delinquent because of an excess of definitions favorable to violation of law over definitions unfavorable to violation of law. This is the principle of differential association. . . .

7. Differential associations may vary in frequency, duration, priority, and intensity. This means that associations with criminal behavior and also associations with anticriminal behavior vary in those respects. . . .

8. The process of learning criminal behavior by association with criminal and anticriminal patterns involves all of the mechanisms that are involved in any other learning. . . .

11. Jerome Michael and Mortimer J. Adler, *Crime, Law, and Social Science*, Patterson Smith, Montclair, N.J., 1971. Sutherland's reaction to this report is discussed in the Introduction to this reprint edition by Gilbert Geis, and in Donald R. Cressey, "Fifty Years of Criminology," *Pacific Sociological Review* 22: 457–80 (1979).

12. Edwin H. Sutherland *Criminology*, 4th ed., Lippincott, Philadelphia, 1947, pp. 6–7. The most recent edition is Edwin H. Sutherland and Donald R. Cressey, *Criminology*, 10th ed., Lippincott, Philadelphia, 1978, where the theory appears on pp. 80–82.

9. While criminal behavior is an expression of general needs and values, it is not explained by those general needs and values, since noncriminal behavior is an expression of the same needs and values. Thieves generally steal in order to secure money, but likewise honest laborers work in order to secure money. The attempts by many scholars to explain criminal behavior by general drives and values, such as the happiness principle, striving for social status, the money motive, or frustration, have been, and must continue to be, futile, since they explain lawful behavior as completely as they explain criminal behavior. They are similar to respiration, which is necessary for any behavior, but which does not differentiate criminal from noncriminal behavior.

Sutherland's theory has two basic elements. The first element identifies the *content* of what is learned. This includes specific techniques for committing crimes; appropriate motives, drives, rationalizations, and attitudes; and more general "definitions favorable to law violation." All of these are cognitive elements; that is, they are all ideas rather than behaviors. The second element of Sutherland's theory identifies the *process* by which the learning takes place. Learning is said to occur through associations in intimate personal groups. Both elements of Sutherland's theory are derived from Mead's symbolic interactionist theory.

Sutherland's description of the content of what is learned is derived from Mead's general argument that "human beings act toward things on the basis of the meanings that the things have for them."[13] In Mead's theory a cognitive factor—"meanings"—determines behavior. Concrete experiences in the person's life, such as social or economic position, unemployment, racial discrimination, peer pressures, physical abuse, or a learning disability can mean very different things to different people. Mead regarded meaning as the central factor in the explanation of behavior and assessed the influence of psychological or social conditions in terms of the meaning those conditions have for the individual.

Mead argued that people construct relatively permanent "definitions" of their situation out of the meanings they derive from their experiences.[14] That is, they derive particular meanings from particular experiences but then generalize them so that they become a set way of looking at things. On the basis of those different definitions, two people may act toward similar situations in very different ways.

13. Bumer, op. cit., p. 2–3.

14. Cf. W. I. Thomas, *The Unadjusted Girl*, Little, Brown, Boston, 1923, pp. 41–53. For a more recent discussion, see Peter McHugh, *Defining the Situation*, Bobbs-Merrill, Indianapolis, 1968.

To cite an old and common example, two brothers may grow up in identical terrible conditions, but one may become a gangster while the other becomes a priest. Sutherland drew on Mead's theory and argued that the key factor determining whether people violate the law was not the social or psychological conditions they experience but the way they define those conditions. In particular, Sutherland argued that people tend to violate the law when "definitions favorable to law violation" outweigh "definitions unfavorable to law violation."

The second element in Sutherland's theory concerned the process by which those definitions were learned and was also derived from Mead's theory. Mead had argued that "the meaning of such things is derived from, or arises out of, the social interaction one has with one's fellows."[15] Following Mead's theory, Sutherland argued that the meaning of criminal acts, whether murder or shoplifting, marijuana smoking or income tax evasion, prostitution or embezzlement, arises primarily from the meanings given those acts by other people with whom the individual associates in intimate personal groups. Sutherland specified the key characteristics of those associations, saying that they may vary in "frequency, duration, priority, and intensity." This was an attempt to explain why some associations were more important and others less important for the learning of these definitions.

Sutherland also discussed the general social conditions underlying the differential association process. In the 1939 version of his theory Sutherland described those general social conditions in terms of *culture conflict*, where that term meant that different groups in a society have different ideas about appropriate ways to behave.[16] *Social disorganization* was then introduced to describe the presence of culture conflict in a society, the term taken from general sociological theories, including the Chicago School of Human Ecology. Sutherland summed up his argument as follows: "Systematic criminal behavior is due immediately to differential association in a situation in which cultural conflicts exist, and ultimately to the social disorganization in that situation."[17]

In the 1949 and final version of his theory Sutherland rejected the

15. Blumer, op. cit.

16. Sutherland, *Criminology*, 1939 ed., p. 7.

17. Ibid., p. 8. Notice that in this edition Sutherland restricted his theory to explaining "systematic" criminal behavior, that is, crime as a way of life. That restriction appeared only in this edition and was removed in the following edition, where the theory again was phrased as a general theory explaining all criminal behavior.

term *social disorganization* and replaced it with the term *differential social organization*. Social disorganization implies that there is an absence of organization. In contrast with that implication, Sutherland argued that there are numerous divergent associations organized around different interests and for different purposes. Under this condition of divergent, differential social organizations, it is inevitable that some of these groups will subscribe to and support criminal patterns of behavior, others will be essentially neutral, and still others will be definitely anticriminal and self-consciously law-abiding. Sutherland concluded: "The criminal culture is as real as lawful culture and is much more prevalent than is usually believed."[18]

Because of some confusion about the term *culture conflict*, Sutherland's coauthor, Donald R. Cressey, substituted the term *normative conflict* after Sutherland's death. Norms are socially accepted rules about how you are supposed to act in specific situations and circumstances.[19] Normative conflict, then, refers to the situation in which different social groups (i.e., differential social organization) hold different views about appropriate ways to behave in specific situations and circumstances. In making this substitution, Cressey stated that he was clarifying, not changing, the meaning of Sutherland's argument.

Sutherland's theory, then, states that in a situation of differential social organization and normative conflict, differences in behavior, including criminal behaviors, arise because of differential associations. That is really only another way of saying that a person who associates with Methodists is likely to become a Methodist, a person who associates with Republicans is likely to become a Republican, and a person who associates with criminals is likely to become a criminal.

A great deal of modern theory and research in criminology can be traced to Sutherland's original formulation. Cultural and subcultural theories are based on Sutherland's arguments about normative conflict and focus on the *content* of what is learned. These theories retain the cognitive orientation of Sutherland's original theory and examine the role of ideas in causing criminal behaviors. Other theories, however, focus on the learning *process* that Sutherland described rather than on the content of the ideas that were said to be learned. These theories tend to be associated with the more modern behav-

18. Ibid.

19. Donald R. Cressey, "Culture Conflict, Differential Association, and Normative Conflict," in Marvin E. Wolfgang, ed., *Crime and Culture*, Wiley, New York, 1968, pp. 43–54.

ioral theories of learning, although at least some of them retain Sutherland's emphasis on differential association. These two branches of modern theory and research are presented in the next two sections.

## 4. CULTURAL AND SUBCULTURAL THEORIES

In Sutherland's theory the actual causes of criminal behavior are *ideas*—the definitions favorable to law violation. Cultural and subcultural theories also focus on the role of ideas in causing criminal behaviors. These theories, like Sutherland's, may explore the sources of those ideas in general social conditions, but they are characterized by the argument that it is the ideas themselves, rather than the social conditions, that directly cause criminal behavior.[20]

Walter B. Miller presented one such cultural theory, focusing on the explanation of gang delinquency.[21] He argued that the lower class has a separate, identifiable culture distinct from the culture of the middle class, and that this culture has a tradition at least as old as that of the middle class. Where the middle class has "values" such as achievement, the lower class has "focal concerns" that include *trouble* (getting into and staying out of trouble are dominant concerns of lower-class people); *toughness* (masculinity, endurance, strength, etc., are all highly valued); *smartness* (skill at outsmarting the other guy; "street sense" rather than high IQ); *excitement* (the constant search for thrills, as opposed to just "hanging around"); *fate* (the view that most things that happen to people are beyond their control, and nothing can be done about them); and *autonomy* (resentment of authority and rules). Miller described this lower-class culture as a "generating milieu" for gang delinquency because it interacts with several social conditions typically found in poor areas. Lower-class families are frequently headed by females, so that male children do not have a masculine role model in the family. These boys may then acquire an exaggerated sense of masculinity. In addition, crowded conditions in lower-class homes means that the boys tend to hang out on the street, where they form gangs. The delin-

20. In contrast, the strain theories of Cohen and of Cloward and Ohlin both use the term *subculture*, but both locate the primary causes of criminal behavior directly in social conditions. There are common thinking patterns that arise among delinquents, but the thinking patterns are not the cause of the criminal behavior. In strain theories, both the thinking patterns and the criminal behaviors are caused by the same social structural forces. See Chapter 11.

21. Walter B. Miller, "Lower Class Culture as a Generating Milieu of Gang Delinquency," *Journal of Social Issues* 14 (3): 5–19 (1958).

quent nature of much gang activity is then a rather obvious consequence of the way the boys think, that is, of the lower-class culture and its focal concerns.

A general theory of criminal violence was presented by Wolfgang and Ferracuti, called the "subculture of violence."[22] This theory relied to some extent on Wolfgang's earlier study of homicide in Philadelphia.[23] Wolfgang had found that a significant number of the homicides that occurred among lower-class people seemed to result from very trivial events that took on great importance because of mutually held expectations about how people would behave. Wolfgang interpreted these events in theoretical terms taken from Sutherland's theory:[24]

The significance of a jostle, a slightly derogatory remark, or the appearance of a weapon in the hands of an adversary are stimuli differentially perceived and interpreted by Negroes and whites, males and females. Social expectations of response in particular types of social interaction result in differential "definitions of the situation." A male is usually expected to defend the name or honor of his mother, the virtue of womanhood . . . and to accept no derogation about his race (even from a member of his own race), his age, or his masculinity. Quick resort to physical combat as a measure of daring, courage, or defense of status appears to be a cultural expression, especially for lower socio-economic class males of both races. When such a culture norm response is elicited from an individual engaged in social interplay with others who harbor the same response mechanism, physical assaults, altercations, and violent domestic quarrels that result in homicide are likely to be common.

Wolfgang and Ferracuti generalized the findings of this and a number of other studies on criminal violence into an overall theory that was designed to explain one type of homicide, the passion crimes that were neither planned intentional killings nor manifestations of extreme mental illness.[25] They described underlying conflicts of values between the dominant culture and this subculture of violence. For example, people in the subculture of violence tend to value honor more highly than people in the dominant culture. On the other hand they tend to value human life less highly. There are also normative

22. Marvin E. Wolfgang and Franco Ferracuti, *The Subculture of Violence*, Sage, Beverly Hills, Cal., 1981.

23. Marvin E. Wolfgang, *Patterns in Criminal Homicide*, University of Pennsylvania Press, Philadelphia, 1958.

24. Ibid., pp. 188–89.

25. Wolfgang and Ferracuti, op. cit., p. 141. The theory itself is presented in seven points on pp. 158–61, and is summarized on pp. 314–16.

conflicts between the subculture of violence and the dominant culture. Those refer to "rules" about what behaviors are expected in
response to the trivial jostles or remarks that were the cause of so
many homicides. Those norms are backed up with social rewards and
punishments: People who do not follow the norms are criticized or
ridiculed by other people in the subculture, and those who follow
them are admired and respected. These norms take on a certain life
of their own, independent of whether they are approved by the individuals who follow them, since the failure to follow the norms may
result in the person becoming a victim of the violence. Thus each
individual may respond to a situation violently because he or she expects the other individual to respond violently, even if neither person approves of the violence. In this sense the subculture of violence is similar to a wartime situation in which "it is either him or
me."[26]

Wolfgang and Ferracuti, like Sutherland, argued that the immediate causes of these passion homicides are ideas—values, norms, and
expectations of behavior. Like Sutherland, they agreed that these ideas
had originated in general social conditions, and suggested that theories such as those by Cohen, Cloward and Ohlin, or Miller might
explain the origin of the subculture. They themselves, however, refused to speculate on how the subculture of violence had arisen.[27]
That question was not vital to their theory, since the cause of the
violent behaviors was said to be the ideas themselves rather than the
social conditions that had generated those ideas in the past. Essentially they argued that the subculture had arisen in the past for specific historical reasons, but that it was transmitted from generation
to generation as a set of ideas after those original social conditions
had disappeared. Thus their policy recommendations did not require dealing with general social conditions, but only required doing
something to break up the patterns of ideas that constituted the subculture of violence. For example, one of their major policy recommendations was to disperse the subculture by scattering low-income
housing projects throughout the city rather than concentrating them
in inner-city areas.[28] Once the subculture was dispersed, individuals
would gradually be assimilated into the dominant culture and the
violent behaviors would cease to occur.

The subculture of violence thesis has generated a large amount of

26. Ibid., p. 156.
27. Ibid., p. 163.
28. Ibid., p. 299.

additional theory and research, especially with respect to explaining higher levels of violent crime in the American South and among blacks. A number of theorists have argued that there is a Southern subculture of violence that has its historical roots in the exaggerated sense of "honor" among Southern gentlemen, the institutionalized violence associated with maintaining a part of the population in slavery, the defeat at the hands of Northerners in the Civil War, the subsequent economic exploitation of Southern states by the North, and so on.[29] As with Wolfgang and Ferracuti's theory, these studies argue that the subculture of violence arose in the South for a variety of historical reasons, but that it continues now because the ideas are passed from generation to generation, although the conditions that originally gave rise to the ideas no longer exist.

Lynn A. Curtis presented a subcultural theory of violence among American blacks that is essentially an adaptation of Wolfgang and Ferracuti's theory.[30] According to Curtis, "the central impulse mechanism" underlying the subculture of violence is an exaggerated view of "manliness."[31] This is combined with a "brittle defensiveness" that leads to heated standoffs in situations that others would find trivial. Some individuals have good verbal skills and may handle these confrontations without resort to physical force. Others, however, lack verbal skills, and resort to physical violence becomes their only option. This results in a high number of murders and assaults among friends and in families.[32] The same exaggerated view of manliness leads to frequent and almost routine sexual demands on women. Men who have good verbal skills will use words to manipulate women in order to obtain sex. Others may simply resort to physical force, resulting in a high incidence of rapes.[33]

Curtis's adaptation of Wolfgang and Ferracuti's theory made an importance change in the basic theoretical orientation in that he tied the subculture of violence more closely to the general social conditions that generate it. The historical conditions that had a role in forming the black subculture of violence include all the factors involved in forming the Southern subculture of violence, since most blacks in northern cities originally migrated from the South. But Curtis

29. See, for example, S. Hackney, "Southern Violence," in Hugh D. Graham and Ted Robert Gurr, eds., *The History of Violence in America*, Bantam, New York, 1969, pp. 505–27; and R. D. Gastil, "Homicide and a Regional Subculture of Violence," *American Sociological Review* 36: 412–27 (June 1971).

30. Lynn A. Curtis, *Violence, Race, and Culture*, Heath, Lexington, Mass., 1975.

31. Ibid., p. 37.

32. Ibid., pp.49–67.

33. Ibid., pp. 69–86.

also argued that current social conditions are involved. He included the use of repressive violence by police in black ghettoes and the general absence of legitimate opportunities. Curtis described culture as a key intervening variable between these current social conditions and the behaviors of each individual.[34] Each individual independently experiences these social conditions, and to a certain extent his or her behavior is a direct response to the social conditions. But each individual also learns ideas and interpretations of these conditions from others who face similar conditions, and to a certain extent his or her behavior is a response to those ideas and interpretations.

Thus, Curtis's theory is partly a cultural theory like Wolfgang and Ferracuti's, describing the direct causal impact of ideas on behaviors, and is partly a structural theory like the strain theories presented in the last chapter, describing the direct causal impact of general social conditions on behaviors. Curtis's policy recommendations reflected this double causation. Unlike Wolfgang and Ferracuti, Curtis argued that the general social conditions that are responsible for producing the subculture of violence must be addressed, in addition to attempts to modify the subculture of violence itself.[35]

Curtis reviewed a large number of empirical studies to demonstrate that the research on the question of race and violent crime was consistent with his argument.[36] Similarly other researchers have tested the subculture of violence thesis with respect to explaining high levels of violent crime in the South.[37] While a fair amount of research has supported this thesis, a number of recent studies have argued that both black and Southern violence are better explained by economic inequality.[38] These studies find that high rates of violent crime are not associated with large black populations or with

34. Ibid., pp. 17–19.

35. Ibid., pp. 119–23.

36. See Lynn A. Curtis, *Criminal Violence: National Patterns and Behavior*, Heath, Lexington, Mass., 1975.

37. See Colin K. Loftin and R. H. Hill, "Regional Subculture and Homicide: An Empirical Examination of the Gastil-Hackney Thesis," *American Sociological Review* 39: 714–24 (Oct. 1974); W. G. Doerner, "The Index of Southernness Revisited," *Criminology* 16: 47–56 (May 1978); H. S. Erlanger, "The Empirical Status of the Subculture of Violence Thesis," *Social Problems* 22: 280–92 (Dec. 1974); H. S. Erlanger, "Is There a 'Subculture of Violence' in the South?" *Journal of Criminal Law and Criminology* 66: 483–90 (Dec. 1976); J. F. O'Connor and A. Lizotte, "The 'Southern Subculture of Violence' Thesis and Patterns of Gun Ownership," *Social Problems* 25: 420–29 (April 1978); J. S. Reed, "To Live—To Die—In Dixie: A Contribution to the Study of Southern Violence," *Political Science Quarterly* 86: 429–43 (Sept. 1971); M. D. Smith and R. N. Parker, "Type of Homicide and Variation in Regional Rates," *Social Forces* 59: 136–47 (Sept. 1980).

38. These studies are discussed briefly in Chapter 8.

Southern location when there is relative equality. These studies link high levels of violence directly to social conditions, so that an intervening cultural variable is unnecessary.

## 5. THE LEARNING PROCESS AND CRIMINALITY

While cultural and subcultural theories are derived from Sutherland's arguments about the content of what is learned, other theory and research has focused on his description of the learning process. In Sutherland's theory learning is said to take place in "intimate personal groups." One of the problems that has always bedeviled the theory is the obvious fact that not everyone in contact with criminals adopts or follows the criminal pattern. What, then, is the difference in the nature or quality of the association that in one instance leads to acceptance of the definition but in another leads only to an acquaintance with it but not acceptance. Sutherland argued that those qualities were "frequency, duration, priority, and intensity," and he supported this argument with case histories and with self-appraisal statements by various individuals who had followed a criminal pattern.[39] Sutherland's coauthor, Cressey, attempted to support the argument in a study of individuals convicted of financial crimes such as embezzlement.[40] However, he was unable to establish any pattern of differential associations to explain these crimes.

A more detailed test of the theory was attempted by Short, who asked groups of delinquents whether they considered their friends to be delinquents.[41] Priority was operationalized as the first friends they could remember, frequency as the friends with whom they had associated most often, duration as the friends with whom they had associated for the longest time, and intensity as "best friends." In a later study Short[42] focused on the quality of intensity, and hypothesized that

those boys and girls who are *most seriously involved in delinquent behavior* will indicate that their best friends are persons whom they characterize in terms hypothesized to be *delinquency producing;* boys and girls who are

39. See, for example, Edwin H. Sutherland, *White Collar Crime*, Dryden, New York, 1949, pp. 222–56.

40. Donald R. Cressey, *Other People's Money*, The Free Press, Glencoe, Ill., 1953.

41. James F. Short, Jr., "Differential Association and Delinquency," *Social Problems*, 4: 233–39 (Jan. 1957); also his "Differential Association with Delinquent Friends and Delinquent Behavior," *Pacific Sociological Review* 1: 20–25 (Spring 1958).

42. James F. Short, Jr., "Differential Association as a Hypothesis: Problems of Empirical Testing," *Social Problems* 8: 14–25 (Summer 1960). (Italics in original.)

*least involved in delinquent behavior* will have characterized their best friends in terms hypothesized to be *delinquency inhibiting;* boys and girls in-between these extremes in delinquency involvement will also fall in-between them in terms of characterizations of best friends.

These studies supported the differential association theory, although Short acknowledged that they were "extremely limited application(s) of a very broadly conceived concept."[43]

Less support for the theory was found in a study by Reiss and Rhodes,[44] in which the "intensity" of criminal associations was also addressed. They investigated the actual delinquent behavior of 299 delinquent boys and each boy's two best friends, and did not rely on the boys' assessments of each other. The conclusion was as follows:[45]

The association of boys with the *same* kind of delinquent behavior in close friendship triads while somewhat greater than chance is well below what one would expect from the learning hypothesis in differential association theory and the results are not independent of social class. Close friendship choices are more closely correlated with delinquency *per se* than with participation in specific patterns of delinquency presumably learned from others.

Several comments can be made about these studies. First, demonstrating that delinquents tend to associate primarily with other delinquents would not demonstrate that delinquency is *caused* by those associations. It may be, as Sheldon and Eleanor Glueck have said, that "birds of a feather flock together"[46]—that is, that a delinquent boy tends to select as his friends those whose values and behaviors are similar to his own. Second, the way the terms were operationalized clearly leaves much to be desired. Short concluded his study by calling for "a restatement of the theory of differential association into a series of 'verifiable' propositions from which verifiable predictions may be derived."[47] Such a restatement was undertaken by De Fleur and Quinney,[48] using symbolic logic. They found that

43. Ibid., p. 24.

44. Albert J. Reiss, Jr., and A. Lewis Rhodes, "An Empirical Test of Differential Association Theory," *Journal of Research in Crime and Delinquency,* 1 (1): 5–18 (Jan. 1964).

45. Ibid., pp. 17–18. (Italics in original.)

46. Sheldon Glueck and Eleanor T. Glueck, *Unraveling Juvenile Delinquency,* Commonwealth Fund, New York, 1950, p. 164.

47. Short, "Differential Association as a Hypothesis," p. 24.

48. Melvin L. De Fleur and Richard Quinney, "A Reformulation of Sutherland's Differential Association Theory and a Strategy of Empirical Verification," *Journal of Research in Crime and Delinquency* 3 (1): 1–22 (Jan. 1966).

the theory was logically consistent with the exception of point 6, which they found to be misleading. Their reformulation, intended to be logically consistent with the rest of the theory, is as follows:[49]

Overt criminal behavior has as its necessary and sufficient conditions a set of criminal motivations, attitudes, and techniques, the learning of which takes place when there is exposure to criminal norms in excess of exposure to corresponding anticriminal norms during symbolic interpretation in primary groups.

They also found that the theory was "at such a high level of abstraction that it is not possible to test it directly with empirical data,"[50] but that logically it generated a large number of specific, testable hypotheses. They conclude that "differential association theory will be supported to the degree to which hypotheses generated from the supersets can be verified in the world of behavioral reality."[51] But, they did not attempt to provide operational definitions of the terms involved, stating only that "until fundamental problems of taxonomy concerning criminal behavior and the various factors associated with its etiology are clarified, empirical testing of the theory will remain a very difficult problem at best."[52]

Sheldon Glueck had originally raised the issue of whether differential association theory could be tested, asking "has anyone actually counted the number of definitions favourable to violation of law and definitions unfavourable to violation of law, and demonstrated that in the predelinquency experience of the vast majority of delinquents and criminals, the former exceed the latter?"[53] Glueck also questioned the assertion that all criminal behavior is learned from others, and that none is invented by the individual.[54]

[Differential association theory] attributes all criminal conduct to indoctrination by other criminals or contagion by criminalistic "patterns" and utterly ignores such primitive impulses of aggression, sexual desire, acquisitiveness, and the like, which lead children to various forms of anti-social conduct before they have learned it from others. What is there to be learned about simple lying, taking things that belong to another, fighting and sex

49. Ibid., p. 9.
50. Ibid., p. 22.
51. Ibid., p. 21.
52. Ibid., p. 22.
53. Sheldon Glueck, "Theory and Fact in Criminology: A Criticism of Differential Association," *British Journal of Delinquency* 7: 92–109 (Oct. 1956).
54. Ibid., p. 94.

play? Do children have to be taught such natural acts? . . . It is rather *non*-delinquent behaviour that is learned. Unsocialized, untamed and un-instructed, the child resorts to lying, slyness, subterfuge, anger, hatred, theft, aggression, attack and other forms of asocial behaviour in its early attempts of self-expression and ego formation.

Finally, he argued that the theory failed to take into account significant individual differences, and maintained that, although criminality is not inherited, some people, "because of certain traits useful to the kind of activities involved in criminal behaviour, probably have a higher delinquency *potential* than others."[55]

### 6. MORE RECENT THEORIES OF THE NORMAL LEARNING PROCESS

Several attempts have been made to broaden Sutherland's theory to meet these and other criticisms.[56] In these attempts it has generally been maintained that criminal behavior is normally learned behavior, but the conception of what is involved in "normal learning" has been updated to include more modern learning theories. In particular, these more recent theories drop Sutherland's argument that the principal part of normal learning takes place in intimate personal groups, although they may retain that as one important source of learning. These theories argue that learning can also take place through direct interactions with the environment, independent of associations with other people, through the principles of operant conditioning. In addition to changing the description of the learning process, the more recent theories also change the description of the content of what is learned. Specifically, these theories switch from Sutherland's original cognitive orientation that only ideas are learned, and adopt the more recent theoretical orientation that behaviors themselves can be directly learned through both operant conditioning and social learning.

The first such reformulation was by Daniel Glaser, who suggested that criminal learning involved identification with criminal roles rather than direct face-to-face association with criminals.[57] Thus a youth might

---

55. Ibid., p. 93. (Italics in original.)

56. For other criticisms, see Juan B. Cortés, *Delinquency and Crime*, Seminar, New York, 1972, pp. 166–78; and L. Reed Adams, "The Adequacy of Differential Association Theory," *Journal of Research in Crime and Delinquency* 11: 1–8 (Jan. 1974).

57. Daniel Glaser, "Criminality Theories and Behavioral Images," *American Journal of Sociology* 61: 433–44 (Mar. 1956).

identify with Al Capone and imitate his behavior even though he had never met him. That reformulation was designed to bring role theory and other aspects of contemporary learning theory into differential association, and to account for the influence of the media on criminal behavior, which Sutherland's theory ignored.

Glaser later revised his theory into what he called "differential-anticipation" theory, the basic assumption of which is that "expectations determine conduct."[58] Glaser argued that a person's expectations are derived from (1) procriminal and anticriminal "social bonds," by which Glaser means the relative rewards and punishments of criminal and legal behavior for each individual person, particularly as it relates to conforming to other people's standards of conduct so as to please rather than alienate them; (2) differential learning of tastes, skills, and rationalizations about whether to expect gratification from criminal or legitimate activities; and (3) perceived opportunities, reflecting expectations about the risks and chances for success of engaging in criminal or legal activities. Glaser concludes: "Differential-anticipation theory assumes that a person will try to commit a crime wherever and whenever the expectations of gratification from it—as a result of social bonds, differential learning, and perceptions of opportunity—exceed the unfavorable anticipations from these sources."[59]

Glaser's theory to some extent is an attempt to integrate three divergent views in criminology—strain theories that focus on perceptions of opportunities, normal learning theories that focus on differential learning, and control theories that focus on social bonds. Despite this attempt at integration, the theory remains essentially similar to Sutherland's. Like Sutherland's theory, Glaser's has a heavily cognitive orientation in that the primary determinant of behavior is an idea—"expectations." In addition, Glaser argues that these ideas are learned primarily in social situations, that is, the rewards and punishments that reinforce these ideas are derived from interactions with other people. Glaser uses the principles of operant conditioning in his theory but applies it primarily to socially generated consequences rather than nonsocial consequences that are directly related to the behavior.[60]

A more substantial step away from Sutherland's theory was made by Burgess and Akers, who rewrote the principles of differential as-

58. Daniel Glaser, *Crime in Our Changing Society*, Holt, Rinehart and Winston, New York, 1978, pp. 126–27.

59. Ibid., p. 127.

60. For example, see ibid., pp. 116–17.

sociation into the language of operant conditioning.[61] This reformulation held that "criminal behavior is learned both in nonsocial situations that are reinforcing or discriminative and through that social interaction in which the behavior of other persons is reinforcing or discriminative for criminal behavior."[62] The addition of "nonsocial situations" constitutes a recognition that the environment itself can reinforce criminality, aside from the person's "social interactions" with other individuals. But Burgess and Akers maintain, with Sutherland, that "the principal part of the learning of criminal behavior occurs in those groups which comprise the individual's major source of reinforcement."[63]

Akers later revised and updated this theory, and expanded the principles of operant conditioning to include modeling, or social learning, theory,[64] which argues that a great deal of learning among humans takes place by observing the consequences that behaviors have for other people. Akers's formulation of social learning theory proposed a specific sequence of events by which the learning of criminal behavior is said to take place.[65] The sequence originates with the differential association of the individual with other individuals who have favorable "definitions" of criminal behavior, who function as role models for criminal behavior, and who provide social reinforcements for those behaviors. The initial participation of the individual in criminal behavior is explained by those factors. After the person has begun to commit criminal behaviors, the actual consequences of those behaviors determine whether the behaviors are continued or not. Those include the rewards and punishments directly experienced by the individual as a consequence of participating in the criminal behavior, and also the rewards and punishments the person experiences vicariously, by observing the consequences that criminal behavior has for others.

A third reformulation of differential association theory was undertaken by Jeffery, which he called the "theory of differential reinforcement."[66] Where Akers had expanded the basic theory of operant conditioning to include modeling and the vicarious experience of

61. Robert L. Burgess and Ronald L. Akers, "A Differential Association—Reinforcement Theory of Criminal Behavior," *Social Problems* 14: 128–47 (Fall 1968).

62. Ibid., p. 146.

63. Ibid., p. 140.

64. Ronald L. Akers, *Deviant Behavior*, Wadsworth, Belmont, Cal., 1977.

65. Ronald L. Akers, Marvin D. Krohn, Lonn Lanza-Kaduce, and Marcia Radosevich, "Social Learning and Deviant Behavior," *American Sociological Review* 44: 636–55 (1979).

66. C. R. Jeffery, "Criminal Behavior and Learning Theory," *Journal of Criminal Law, Criminology and Police Science* 56: 294–300 (Sept. 1965).

watching what happens to other people when they commit criminal behaviors, Jeffery expanded operant conditioning to include biological factors, a perspective he called "biological behaviorism." He then used the theory to make recommendations for crime prevention that relied primarily on changing the physical environment.[67]

## 7. ASSESSING SUTHERLAND'S THEORY

Sutherland's theory has had a massive impact on criminology. At the time it was written criminology was dominated by physicians and psychiatrists who searched for the causes of criminal behavior in biological and psychological abnormalities. Sutherland's theory, more than any other, was responsible for the decline of that view and the rise of the view that crime is the result of environmental influences acting on biologically and psychologically normal individuals.

In order to assess this school of thought it is necessary to distinguish between Sutherland's theory itself and the more modern learning theories that have followed it. To a considerable extent Sutherland's theory was based on an outdated theory of learning. His argument that learning consists entirely in ideas ("definitions") and that the principal part of learning occurs in differential associations in intimate personal groups must be assessed in terms of general research on the nature of human learning. The field of learning theory has its own controversies and to some extent Sutherland's theory, as a cognitive theory, must do its own battle with other cognitive theories and with the more popular behavioral theories. There is no reason to think that Sutherland's theory will emerge triumphant from that battle. Quite to the contrary, there are many reasons to believe that, as a learning theory, Sutherland's theory has virtually no importance whatsoever. Sutherland, after all, was not a learning theorist and was not particularly familiar with the major theory and research on human learning that was going on at the time.[68]

Sutherland's legacy to criminology is not his specific learning theory but his argument that criminal behavior is normal learned behavior. The task Sutherland focused on, and the task still facing criminologists today, is to explore the implications of that argument for criminology. In the first edition of this book Vold argued that the

---

67. See C. Ray Jeffery, *Crime Prevention Through Environmental Design*, rev. ed., Sage, Beverly Hills, Cal., 1977, especially pp. 235–67, 311–18.

68. It is interesting that at the time Sutherland wrote the final version of differential association theory, he was located at the University of Indiana, where in a nearby building B. F. Skinner was conducting the experiments that would revolutionize learning theory.

logical implication of Sutherland's theory is that crime must be viewed in the context of political and social conflict:[69]

> If criminal behavior, by and large, is the normal behavior of normally responding individuals in situations defined as undesirable, illegal, and therefore criminal, then the basic problem is one of social and political organization and the established values or definitions of what may, and what may not, be permitted. Crime, in this sense, is political behavior and the criminal becomes in fact a member of a "minority group" without sufficient public support to dominate and control the police power of the state.

Sutherland seemed to draw a similar implication from his theory. After making the first systematic presentation of the theory in 1939, he turned his attention to white-collar crime and retained that focus until his death.[70] Sutherland argued that white-collar crimes are normal learned behaviors and that there are no essential differences between those behaviors and the behaviors of lower-class criminals when viewed from the perspective of causation. The differences in official crime rates between the upper and lower classes arise because upper-class people have sufficient political power to control the enactment and enforcement of criminal laws. Their antisocial behaviors either are not defined as wrongs at all or are defined as civil wrongs. The antisocial behaviors of lower-class people, in contrast, are defined and processed as crimes, so that they end up with high official crime rates.

Sutherland's theory of white-collar crime is an illustration of Vold's more general point that if criminal behavior is normal learned behavior, then crime must be viewed in the context of political and social conflict. In Sutherland's theory, white-collar criminals can be described as a "majority group" who are able to dominate and control the police powers of the state. They therefore are free to engage in normal learned behaviors, even when those behaviors are antisocial, without fear of being defined as criminals. It is for that reason that they have low official crime rates. Ordinary criminals, in contrast, can be viewed as a "minority group" who lack that same political power. They have high official crime rates because many of their normal learned behaviors are defined and processed as crimes. Further discussion of this implication will be presented in Chapter 15

---

69. George B. Vold, *Theoretical Criminology*, Oxford University Press, New York, 1958,p. 202; see also the 2nd ed. prepared by Thomas J. Bernard, 1979, pp. 247–48.

70. Edwin H. Sutherland, "White Collar Criminality," *American Sociological Review* 5: 1–12 (Feb. 1940); "Is 'White Collar Crime' Crime?" *American Sociological Review* 10: 132–39 (April 1945); and *White Collar Crime*.

on conflict criminology, as well as in the section on white-collar crime in Chapter 17.

Even though it is not necessary to defend Sutherland's theory as an adequate learning theory, it can be mentioned that a number of criticisms are based on fundamental misinterpretations of it. Kornhauser, for example, describes Sutherland's theory as a "cultural deviance" theory.[71] She attributes to Sutherland the view that individuals always act on the basis of values and that values are always defined by the culture to which the individual conforms. Cultures therefore can be deviant (hence the term *cultural deviance*) in that they can contain criminal values, but individuals themselves can never be deviant because individuals always conform to their own culture. Kornhauser maintains that this is circular because it equates culture with behavior. She also argues that criminal behaviors are not generally valued even by criminals, although they may be condemned less forcefully by people who live in a slum, since those people see criminal behaviors as intimately tied up with the terrible conditions of their own lives.[72]

Kornhauser's portrayal of Sutherland's theory has little resemblance to the theory itself. Sutherland did indeed discuss the conflict of "cultures," but Cressey changed that to the conflict of "norms" in order to void the kind of confusion that Kornhauser exhibits. While there is no generally accepted definition of the term *norms*,[73] most definitions contain three elements: rules about how to act in specific situations and circumstances, social acceptance or approval of those rules, and socially generated rewards and punishments associated with those rules to back them up. Kornhauser's criticism focuses on the level of social acceptance associated with criminal norms. Are criminal norms associated with *valued* behaviors, or are they associated with *expectations* about behavior that may not be valued at all?

Kornhauser attributes to Sutherland's theory a very high level of social approval for criminal behavior. In fact, she describes the level of approval in terms of "cultural values," which are a design for living passed as a valued heritage from generation to generation.[74] Thus, she attributes to Sutherland the view that criminals value their criminal behavior in much the same way as religious persons value their

---

71. Ruth Rosner Kornhauser, *Social Sources of Delinquency*, University of Chicago Press, Chicago, 1978, pp. 189–204.

72. Ibid., p. 225.

73. See Jack P. Gibbs, *Norms, Deviance, and Social Control: Conceptual Matters*, Elsevier, New York, 1981, pp. 7–21, for a discussion of the various definitions of norms.

74. Kornhauser, op. cit., pp. 1–20.

religious practices. Given her interpretation, it is not suprising that she concludes that the theory is without foundation.[75]

Cressey, in contrast, identified norms with "expectations for conduct,"[76] and seems to attribute a relatively low level of social approval or valuation to the behavior. A similar low level of social approval is found in Wolfgang and Ferracuti's subculture of violence theory, where the emphasis is heavily on expectations of behavior in certain situations, together with social rewards and punishments backing up those expectations. Wolfgang and Ferracuti describe value conflicts underlying the differences in behavior but do not state that the violent behaviors themselves are necessarily valued behaviors. Rather, they are expected behaviors in specific circumstances. Failure to engage in those behaviors results in socially generated punishments such as ridicule, while engaging in the behaviors results in socially generated rewards such as respect. People in the subculture who engage in violence may feel no guilt about it because it was expected behavior in the circumstances. Other people in the subculture may respond to the same violence with respect rather than revulsion and may view a person who fails to engage in violence in those circumstances as a coward or as stupid.

Another criticism Kornhauser raises is that ideas and beliefs are determined by concrete conditions in the person's life and that they have no independent causal effect on behavior.[77] Kornhauser's criticism attacks the cognitive elements of Sutherland's theory, which asserts that behaviors are directly caused by ideas or beliefs. That cognitive orientation has been eliminated in the more recent adaptations of Sutherland's theory, so the criticism does not apply to those theories. For example, Akers takes a position that is similar to Kornhauser's in that his social learning theory describes the process by which general social structural arrangements are translated into individual behaviors.[78] Akers also describes the learning of ideas and beliefs—"definitions" that are either favorable, neutralizing, or unfavorable to law violation—but does not maintain that these ideas or beliefs have an independent causal effect on behaviors separate from their social structural origins.

The role of ideas in the generation of human behaviors is a controversy that cannot be resolved within criminology, since it per-

75. Ibid., p. 242.
76. Cressey, "Culture Conflict," p. 51.
77. Kornhauser, op. cit., pp. 207–10.
78. Akers, *Deviant Behavior*, pp. 61–68.

tains to the larger controversy between behavioral and cognitive learning theories. Thus, it is not really meaningful to assert on the basis of studies in criminology that one or the other position is correct. There is no question that there are structural sources for beliefs—that is one of the most fundamental propositions in sociology. The question is whether those beliefs attain some life of their own in the causes of behavior in general and in the causes of criminal behavior in particular. The most reasonable position at the present time, considering all the various contradictory research on the subject, seems to be the position that Curtis takes, that culture functions as a crucial intervening variable between social structure and individual behavior. That is, ideas and beliefs—including "definitions" of behavior, expectations about how to behave in particular situations, social approval or valuation of certain behaviors, and social responses that back up those expected and approved behaviors with rewards and punishments—have some direct causal impact on behavior, independent of their social structural sources.

## 8. CONCLUSION

Sutherland described criminal behavior as normal learned behavior and went on to make specific assertions about the nature of normal learning. He asserted that normal learning primarily involves the learning of ideas and beliefs in the process of associating with other people. Behaviors, including criminal behaviors, follow from and are a product of those ideas and beliefs.

The adequacy of Sutherland's assertions can only be assessed in the context of general theories and research about human learning. In general, it seems reasonable to conclude that ideas and beliefs learned in association with other people do have some direct causal impact on criminal behaviors. However, criminal behaviors may also be associated with other types of normal learning. More recent theories of criminal behavior, such as Akers's social learning theory, retain Sutherland's view that criminal behavior is normal learned behavior but more adequately incorporate modern learning principles in the description of the normal learning process.

Sutherland's theory has been extremely important in the recent development of criminology. Its importance is not based on Sutherland's assertions about the nature of human learning. Rather, it is based on the implications of the view that criminal behavior is normal learned behavior. That view suggests a new question for criminology to examine: why are the normal learned behaviors of some groups defined as criminal, while the normal learned behaviors of other groups are defined as legal? Sutherland himself attempted to respond to that new question with his theories about white-collar crime. A substantial portion of modern criminology also responds to that question, which will be discussed in later chapters of this book.

RECOMMENDED READINGS

Ronald L. Akers, *Deviant Behavior: A Social Learning Approach*, 2nd ed., Wadsworth, Belmont, Cal., 1977. A social learning theory of crime, with a broad review of literature demonstrating consistency with the theory.

James F. Short, Jr., "Collective Behavior, Crime, and Delinquency," in Daniel Glaser, ed., *Handbook of Criminology*, Rand McNally, Chicago, 174, pp. 403–49. Provides an excellent discussion, closely based on the empirical literature, of the relationship among norms, social organization, and criminal behavior.

Albert Bandura, *Aggression: A Social Learning Analysis*, Prentice-Hall, Englewood Cliffs, N.J., 1973. Modeling, or observational learning, derived from family influences, subcultural influences, and the mass media, is the most important source of new patterns of aggressive behaviors.

M. Phillip Feldman, *Criminal Behavior: A Psychological Analysis*, John Wiley, London, 1977. An integrative theory that focuses on modern learning theory, including both learning not to offend through early socialization, and learning to offend through differential reinforcement, social modeling, and situational inducements. The theory also incorporates biological and personality differences and the effects of social labeling.

Michael T. Nietzel, *Crime and its Modification: A Social Learning Approach*, Pergamon, New York, 1979. Approaches adult crime from the viewpoint of behavior modification and community psychology. Examines current deficiencies in behavior therapies and recommends behavior techniques in community settings, focusing on early intervention and prevention.

Henry P. Lundsgaard, *Murder in Space City*, Oxford University Press, New York, 1977. A detailed analysis of homicide patterns in Houston, concluding that they are best explained by cultural patterns that proscribe and prescribe acceptable expressions of individual violence. In particular, citizens are rewarded when they kill in defense of honor, property, or personal rights, and they are not viewed as deserving punishment when they kill individuals with whom they have unsatisfactory interpersonal relationships.

John Laub, *Criminology in the Making: An Oral History*, Northeastern University Press, Boston, 1983. Contains a most interesting and entertaining interview with Donald Cressey.

Piers Beirne, "Cultural Relativism and Comparative Criminology," *Contemporary Crises* 7 (4): 371–91 (1983). Criminal behavior can only be understood in the cultural context in which it occurs, and in terms of the cultural and subjective values of those who engage in it.

Craig A. McEwen, *Designing Correctional Organizations for Youths: Dilemmas of Subcultural Development*, Ballinger, Cambridge, Mass., 1978. A comparison of 10 institutional and 13 community programs for youth in Massachusetts, focusing on the effect that different policies and different patterns of interaction have on subcultural elements such as values, norms, expectations, and collectively shared definitions of program situations.

Donald R. Cressey, "Delinquent and Criminal Subcultures," in Sanford H. Kadish, ed., *Encyclopedia of Crime and Justice*, vol. 2, Macmillan, New York, 1983, pp. 584–90. A brief and recent statement by Sutherland's coauthor.

# CHAPTER THIRTEEN

# Social Control Theories

Many theories of criminal behavior argue that there are some special forces—either biological, psychological, or social—that drive individuals to commit crime. Control theories, however, take a different stance. They start with the assumption that the motivation for criminal behavior is a part of human nature and that all individuals would naturally commit crimes if left to their own devices. The key question, then, is why most people do *not* commit crimes. Control theories answer that question by focusing on the restraining, or "controlling," forces imposed on individuals. Those forces are said to break down in certain situations, resulting in crime and other "uncontrolled" behaviors. Thus individuals are said to commit crime because of the weakness of forces restraining them from doing so, not because of the strength of forces driving them to do so.

The control perspective has been found in earlier chapters in this book. For example, Durkheim's theory of anomie described the breakdown of social restraints on behaviors that are motivated by unlimited human needs. This theory falls into the control perspective because it describes the driving forces behind criminal behaviors (unlimited human needs) as the same at all times and places, and explains differences in the amount of crime on the basis of differences in the restraining forces (societal restraints). Aichhorn argued that most delinquency was the result of unrepressed id forces that were freed because of an inadequate superego. This theory explains the differences in behavior on the basis of differences in the controlling forces found in the superego, not differences in the driving forces found in the id. Eysenck's description of variations in the autonomic nervous system also takes the control perspective, since it describes biological conditions under which punishment either inhibits or fails to inhibit the natural drives toward criminal behavior.

The control perspective thus represents a broad point of view espoused by many theorists. All such theorists, however, are not discussed in this chapter. Rather, the chapter examines a number of recent sociological theorists who take the control perspective and describe their work as control theories. Their theories are especially important as explanations of delinquency, since most of the research supporting this view has been done with juvenile populations. Control theories, however, may also be used to explain adult criminality.

## 1. EARLY CONTROL THEORIES: REISS TO RECKLESS

In 1951 Albert J. Reiss published an article in which he examined a number of factors related to the control perspective, to see which might be used to predict probation revocation among juvenile offenders.[1] Reiss reviewed the official court records of 1,110 white male juvenile probationers between the ages of 11 and 17. He found that probation revocation was more likely when the juvenile was psychiatrically diagnosed as having weak ego or superego controls and when the psychiatrist recommended either intensive psychotherapy in the community or treatment in a closed institution. Reiss argued that such diagnoses and recommendations were based on an assessment of the juvenile's "personal controls"—that is, his ability to refrain from meeting his needs in ways that conflicted with the norms and rules of the community. In addition, he found that probation revocation was more likely when juveniles did not regularly attend school, and when they were described as behavior problems by school authorities. Reiss argued that these were a measure of the acceptance or submission of the juvenile to the control of socially approved institutions.[2]

Reiss seems to have derived his theoretical perspective from the psychiatrists who provided the diagnoses and recommendations at the juvenile court. Thus his theory might be traced ultimately to Freud. Nevertheless, it took the form of a sociological theory and was the first of the self-described control theories of delinquency referred to above. Reiss's arguments in support of control theory, however, were

---

1. Albert J. Reiss, "Delinquency as the Failure of Personal and Social Controls," *American Sociological Review* 16:196–207 (April 1951).
2. Ibid., p. 206.

quite weak. A variety of factors related to the strength of family and community controls over the juvenile were not found to be valid predictors of probation revocation. The strongest associations were found between probation revocation and the diagnoses and recommendations of the psychiatrists. Reiss argued that the failure of personal controls explained both phenomena, thus accepting at face value the theoretical framework of the psychiatrists. But such an explanation is tautological unless it is supported by some additional evidence about the strength or weakness of personal controls.[3] The association of probation revocation with truancy and school problems was much weaker, and also can be explained from other perspectives besides control theory.

In 1957 Jackson Toby introduced the concept of having a "stake in conformity" as the basic mechanism by which tendencies toward delinquency are controlled.[4] He argued that all youths are tempted to break the law, but some youths risk a great deal more by giving in to those temptations: youths who do well in school risk not only being punished for breaking the law, but also jeopardize their future careers. Thus they have a high stake in conforming to the laws. But those who do poorly in school have much less to lose. They risk only being punished for their offense, since their future prospects are already dim. Thus they have less incentive to resist the temptations to do what they want to do. Toby also argued that peer support for deviance can develop in communities that have a large number of youths with low stakes in conformity, so that the community develops even higher crime rates than would be expected by considering the stakes in conformity of the individual youths. Conversely, youths in suburbs who have low stakes in conformity normally obtain no support from their peers for delinquency. Thus these youths may be unhappy, but usually do not become delinquent.

Toby focused on how well the youth did in school, but he stated: "In all fairness, it should be remembered that the basis for school adjustment is laid in the home and the community."[5] The following year, F. Ivan Nye published a study that focused on the family as

3. Cf. Travis Hirschi, *Causes of Delinquency*, University of California Press, Berkeley, 1969, pp. 11 and 198, n. 4.

4. Jackson Toby, "Social Disorganization and Stake in Conformity: Complementary Factors in the Predatory Behavior of Hoodlums," *Journal of Criminal Law, Criminology and Police Science* 48: 12–17 (May–June 1957). A similar concept was presented in a later article by Scott Briar and Irving Piliavin, "Delinquency, Situational Inducements, and Commitment to Conformity," *Social Problems*, Summer 1965, pp. 35–45.

5. Ibid., p. 14.

the single most important source of social control for adolescents.[6] He argued that most delinquent behavior was the result of insufficient social control, and that delinquent behavior "caused" by positive factors was relatively rare.[7] *Social control* was used as a broad term that included direct controls imposed by means of restrictions and punishments, internal control exercised through conscience, indirect control related to affectional identification with parents and other noncriminal persons, and the availability of legitimate means to satisfy needs.[8] With respect to the final type of social control, Nye argued that "if all the needs of the individual could be met adequately and without delay, without violating laws, there would be no point in such violation, and a minimum of internal, indirect, and direct control would suffice to secure conformity."

Nye surveyed 780 boys and girls in grades 9 through 12 in three towns in the state of Washington in order to test the theory. Included in the survey were a wide variety of questions on family life, as well as seven items intended to measure delinquency. Those seven items were: skipped school without a legitimate excuse; defied parents' authority to their face; took things worth less than $2; bought or drank beer, wine, or liquor (including at home); purposedly damaged or destroyed public or private property; and had sexual relations with a person of the opposite sex.[9] On the basis of how often they said they had committed these acts since the beginning of grade school, about one-fourth of the youths were placed in a "most delinquent" group, and the remainder in a "least delinquent" group.[10]

Nye found that youths in the "most delinquent" group were significantly more likely to be given either complete freedom or no freedom at all, to have larger sums of money available, to be rejecting of their parents and to disapprove of their parents' appearance, to have parents who were seldom cheerful and often moody, nervous, irritable, difficult to please, dishonest, and who "took things

6. F. Ivan Nye, *Family Relationships and Delinquent Behavior,* John Wiley, New York, 1958.

7. Ibid., p. 4.

8. Ibid., p. 5–8.

9. Ibid., pp. 13–14.

10. Youths who said that they had never committed the act since the beginning of grade school were given 0 points, those who said they committed it once or twice were given 1 point, and those who said they committed it three or more times were given 2 points. Boys 15 and younger who accumulated five or more points for the seven offenses were placed in the "most delinquent" group, along with boys 16 and over who accumulated 7 or more points. Nye argued that such a division adequately differentiated between institutionalized and noninstitutionalized adolescents. See ibid., pp. 15–19, and Nye and James F. Short, Jr., "Scaling Delinquent Behavior," *American Sociological Review* 22: 26–31 (June 1957).

out" on the youth when things went wrong. Youths whose mothers worked outside the home and who were rejected by their parents were slightly more likely to fall in the "most delinquent" group. In contrast, youths in the "least delinquent" group were significantly more likely to come from families that attended church regularly, did not move often, and were from rural areas. They were likely to be the oldest or only child, from a small family, to have a favorable attitude toward their parents' disciplinary techniques and toward recreation with their parents, to agree with their parents on the importance of a variety of values, to be satisfied with the allocation of money by their parents, and to get information and advice concerning dating and religion from their parents. In all, Nye tested 313 relationships between youths and their parents. He found that 139 of those were consistent with his control theory, 167 were not significant, and only 7 were inconsistent with it.[11]

Nye's contribution to the development of control theory was quite significant because of the theory he proposed and because he undertook a broad empirical test of the theory. His findings in support of the theory are impressive, but one can question the extent to which they apply to groups that are normally referred to as delinquents. Nye's sample did not include any youths from large cities, and included only negligible numbers of nonwhite youths or youth with foreign-born parents. Toby pointed out that "the group which Professor Nye calls 'most delinquent' would be considered nondelinquents by many criminologists."[12] Also, because the questionnaire was administered in high schools, the sample would not include any youths age 15 or younger who were more than one year behind in school (they would still be in grade school), or any youths age 16 or over who had legally dropped out of school. Only two behaviors on the questionnaire constituted criminal offenses: taking things worth less than $2 and purposely damaging or destroying public or private property. Thus the results of Nye's study might be interpreted as describing the effect of family relationships on minor delinquent activities among basically nondelinquent youths.

Toby also pointed out that Nye's research apparently assumes that the same causal processes would be involved with more serious delinquents, but that other researchers might very well disagree with the assumption. Finally, Toby noted that a response bias among the youths answering the questionnaire could account for many of Nye's

11. Nye, *Family Relationships*, p. 155.

12. Jackson Toby, "Review of *Family Relationships and Delinquent Behavior* by F. Ivan Nye," *American Sociological Review* 24:282–83. (Feb. 1959).

findings. Youths who were more willing to report their delinquent activities may also have been more willing to describe the less desirable aspects of their family life. Other youths may have both underreported their delinquent activities and described their family life in more positive terms. Thus the study would show that better family relationships are associated with fewer delinquent activities. Toby concluded that Nye's results should be interpreted with great caution.

In 1961 Walter C. Reckless proposed a containment theory, in which he attempted to organize many of the concepts and variables found in earlier theories into a general theory of crime and delinquency.[13] He argued that all individuals are affected by a variety of forces driving them toward, and a variety of other forces restraining them from, crime and delinquency. The driving forces include what Reckless called *social pressures* that bear down on the individual, including adverse living conditions, family conflicts, minority group status, and lack of opportunities. The driving forces also include what Reckless called *social pulls* that draw the person away from accepted norms of living, such as bad companions, delinquent or criminal subculture, deviant groups, mass media, and so on. There are also biological or psychological *pushes* from within each individual that drive him or her toward crime and delinquency. Those include restlessness, discontent, inner tensions, hostility, aggressiveness, need for immediate gratification, rebellion against authority, and so on.

Aligned against these forces are the forces of internal and external containment restraining the individual from moving in the direction of criminality. *External containment* consists in effective family living and support groups, and includes such items as consistent moral front, institutional reinforcement, reasonable norms and expectations, cohesiveness, effective supervision and discipline, fostering a sense of belongingness and identity, and so on. *Inner containment* is the product of internalization and consists in self-control, ego strength, superego, frustration tolerance, sense of responsibility, resistance to diversions, goal orientation, ability to find substitute satisfactions, and so on. Reckless maintained that containment theory was a general theory that could better explain crime and delin-

13. Walter C. Reckless, "A New Theory of Delinquency and Crime," *Federal Probation* 25: 42–46 (Dec. 1961); also *The Crime Problem*, 3rd ed., Appleton-Century-Crofts, New York, 1961, pp. 335–59. Earlier theories that took a similar form include Arthur L. Beeley, "A Socio-Psychological Theory of Crime and Delinquency: A Contribution to Etiology," *Journal of Criminal Law, Criminology and Police Science* 45: 394–96 (Dec. 1945), excerpted in Reckless, *The Crime Problem*, 5th ed. Goodyear, Pacific Palisades, Calif. 1973; and Lowell Julliard Carr, *Delinquency Control*, rev. ed., Harper and Row, New York, 1950.

quency than could other theories that only described specific pressures, pulls, pushes, or containments.

Reckless and various collaborators had done a good deal of research on the self-concept of nondelinquent boys who lived in high-delinquency areas, arguing that good self-concept was an "insulator" against delinquency.[14] The idea of inner containment and of containment theory generally grew out of these studies. More recent research, however, has found only moderate relationships between self-concept and delinquency, and Reckless's studies have been criticized as involving faulty methodology.[15] Containment theory has also been subjected to criticism. Schrag points out that its key terms are vague, and that *pressures, pulls,* and so on are defined only by asserting their functions and providing a list of illustrations.[16] That makes it unclear which variables belong in which categories. Some variables seem to be assigned to one category when they provide forces in favor of conformity, and to another when they provide forces in favor of delinquency. For example, "bad companions" are listed as pulls, but "supportive relationships" (which would seem to entail good companions) are listed as outer containment. A similar problem is encountered in attempting to separate inner containment and pushes. Problems of this type make the theory difficult to test.

Reckless's theory can be regarded as an overall framework within which the many theories of crime and delinquency can be viewed. But it does not seem to add anything to those theories, and it has

14. Walter C. Reckless, Simon Dinitz, and Ellen Murray, "Self-Concept as an Insulator Against Delinquency," *American Sociological Review* 21: 744–56 (Dec. 1956); Reckless, Dinitz, and Murray, "The 'Good Boy' in a High Delinquency Area," *Journal of Criminal Law, Criminology and Police Science* 48: 18–25 (May–June 1957); Reckless, Dinitz, and Barbara Kay, "The Self-Component in Potential Delinquency and Potential Nondelinquency," *American Sociological Review* 22: 566–70 (Oct. 1957); Dinitz, Kay, and Reckless, "Group Gradients in Delinquency Potential and Achievement Scores of Sixth Graders," *American Journal of Orthopsychiatry* 28: 598–605 (July 1958); Jon Simpson, Dinitz, Kay, and Reckless, "Delinquency Potential of Pre-Adolescents in a High Delinquency Area," *British Journal of Delinquency* 10: 211–15 (Jan. 1960); Frank R. Scarpitti, Murray, Dinitz, and Reckless, "The 'Good Boy' in a High Delinquency Area: Four Years Later," *American Sociological Review* 25: 555–58 (Aug. 1960); Dinitz, Scarpitti, and Reckless, "Delinquency Vulnerability: A Cross Group and Longitudinal Analysis," *American Sociological Review* 27: 515–17 (Aug. 1962); Reckless and Dinitz, "Pioneering with Self-Concept as a Vulnerability Factor in Delinquency," *Journal of Criminal Law, Criminology and Police Science* 58: 515–23 (Dec. 1967).

15. Michael Schwartz and Sandra S. Tangri, "A Note on Self-Concept as an Insulator against Delinquency," *American Sociological Review* 30: 922–26 (Dec. 1965); Tangri and Schwartz, "Delinquency Research and the Self-Concept Variable," *Journal of Criminal Law, Criminology and Police Science* 58: 182–90 (June 1967); James D. Orcutt, "Self-Concept and Insulation against Delinquency: Some Critical Notes," *Sociological Quarterly* 2: 381–90 (Summer 1970).

16. Clarence Schrag, *Crime and Justice: American Style,* U.S. Government Printing Office, Washington, D.C., 1971, pp. 82–89.

problems because the divisions it proposes are not very precise.[17] Its contribution to control theory was the attention it focused on the concepts of internal and external containment. However, the criticisms leveled against it have been severe, and even in the latest edition of Reckless's text it is no longer provided an important place.[18]

## 2. MATZA'S *DELINQUENCY AND DRIFT*

While the early control theories presented above have been soundly criticized, they provided the basic concepts and framework for the modern control theories of David Matza and Travis Hirschi. Those control theories present a strong challenge to the more common view that juvenile delinquency is caused by special biological, psychological, or social factors.

In *Delinquency and Drift* Matza stated that traditional theories of delinquency emphasize constraint and differentiation: Delinquents are said to be different from nondelinquents in some fundamental way, and that difference constrains them to commit their delinquencies.[19] In some theories the differences are said to be biological or psychological, and the constraint takes the form of compulsion. In other theories the differences are said to be social and the constraint takes the form of commitment to delinquent values. Matza maintained that these theories predicted and explained too much delinquency. Most of the time delinquents are engaged in routine, law-abiding behaviors just like everyone else, but if you believe the picture painted in these theories, delinquents should be committing delinquencies all the time. In addition, these theories cannot account for the fact that most delinquents "age out" of delinquency and settle down to law-abiding lives when they reach late adolescence or early adulthood. The factors that supposedly explained the delinquency are still present (for example, lack of legitimate opportunities), but the delinquency itself disappears.[20]

Matza proposed an alternate image for delinquents that emphasizes freedom and similarity rather than constraint and differentia-

17. Ibid., p. 88–89.

18. Reckless, *The Crime Problem*, op. cit., 5th ed. pp. 55–57.

19. David Matza, *Delinquency and Drift*, John Wiley, New York, 1964, pp. 1–27.

20. For an alternative explanation, see Charles A. Murray and Louis A. Cox, *Beyond Probation*, Sage, Beverly Hills, Cal., 1979, pp. 67–77. Murray and Cox maintain that delinquents do not "age out." Rather, the decrease in involvement in delinquency occurs after intervention by the state, independent of the age at which that intervention takes place. If there is no intervention, delinquency continues to increase with age.

tion. That image was *drift.*[21] Drift is said to occur in areas of the social structure in which control has been loosened, freeing the delinquent to respond to whatever conventional or criminal forces happen to come along. The positive causes of delinquency, then, "may be accidental or unpredictable from the point of view of any theoretical frame of reference, and deflection from the delinquent path may be similarly accidental or unpredictable."[22] Within the context of such an image a theory of delinquency would not attempt to describe its positive causes, but rather would describe "the conditions that make delinquent drift possible and probable," that is, the conditions under which social control is loosened. Matza did not deny that there were "committed" and "compulsive" delinquents, as described by the traditional theories. However, he argued that the vast majority of delinquents were "drifters" who were neither.

Matza's criticism of traditional theories of delinquency focused on the sociological argument that their behaviors are generated by commitment to delinquent values. Matza argued that delinquents portray themselves this way because they are unwilling to appear "chicken."[23] But private interviews reveal that delinquents do not value delinquent behavior itself. Rather, they describe the behavior as morally wrong but argue that there are extenuating circumstances, so that their own delinquent actions are "guiltless."[24] The delinquent's portrayal of these circumstances is similar to, but much broader than, the extenuating circumstances defined in the law relating to intent, accident, self-defense, and insanity. Thus the delinquent does not reject conventional moral values, but "neutralizes" them in a wide variety of circumstances so that he is able to commit delinquent actions and still consider himself guiltless. This *sense of irresponsibility* is reinforced by the ideology of the juvenile court, which declares that juveniles are not responsible for their actions.

The sense of irresponsibility is the immediate condition that makes delinquent drift possible, but the delinquent is prepared to accept the sense of irresponsibility by a pervasive *sense of injustice.*[25] Just as the sense of irresponsibility is derived from a broad interpretation of conventional legal standards for extenuating circumstances, so the sense of injustice is derived from a broad interpretation of conven-

21. Matza, op. cit., pp. 27–30.

22. Ibid., p. 29.

23. Ibid., pp. 33–59.

24. Ibid., pp. 59–98.

25. Ibid., pp. 101–177. See also Marvin Krohn and John Stratton, "A Sense of Injustice?" *Criminology* 17 (4): 495–504 (Feb. 1980).

tional legal standards for justice. For example, by conventional legal standards of justice it is necessary to prove beyond a reasonable doubt that a given individual has committed a given criminal act. The delinquent uses excessively legalistic standards to argue that "they didn't prove it." Thus he may passionately argue that he was unjustly treated even though he admits that he committed the act.

Once the moral bind of the law has been loosened by the sense of irresponsibility and the sense of injustice the juvenile is in a state of drift and is then free to choose among a variety of actions, some delinquent, some lawful. At this point Matza suggests that there are some "positive" causes of delinquency in the sense that there are reasons why the juvenile chooses delinquent, as opposed to lawful, behaviors.[26] The juvenile feels that he exercises no control over the circumstances of his life and the destiny awaiting him. In such a mood he moves to make something happen, to experience himself as a cause of events. This mood of desperation provides the motivation to commit new acts of delinquency. Once those actions have been committed, he is motivated to continue committing them because he has learned the moral rationalizations necessary to consider himself guiltless, and because he has learned the technical means to carry out the offenses.

### 3. HIRSCHI'S *CAUSES OF DELINQUENCY*

The theorist who is most closely identified with control theory is Travis Hirschi. Hirschi argued that it is not necessary to explain the motivation for delinquency, since "we are all animals and thus all naturally capable of committing criminal acts."[27] He then proposed a comprehensive control theory that individuals who were tightly *bonded* to social groups such as the family, the school, and peers would be less likely to commit delinquent acts.[28] The most important element of the social bond is *attachment*, affection for and sensitivity to others. Attachment is said to be the basic element necessary for the internalization of values and norms, and thus is related to Reiss's conception of personal controls and Nye's conceptions of internal and indirect controls. A second element is *commitment*, the rational investment one has in conventional society and the risk one takes when engaging in deviant behavior. Commitment is similar to

---

26. Matza, op. cit., pp. 181–91. Compare with Hirschi, *Causes of Delinquency*, pp. 33–34.

27. Hirschi, op. cit., p. 31.

28. Ibid., pp. 16–34.

what Toby described as a "stake in conformity." The third element is *involvement* in conventional activities. This variable is based on the commonsense observation that "idle hands are the devil's workshop," and that being busy restricts opportunities for delinquent activities. The final element of the social bond is *belief*. Matza had argued that delinquents had conventional moral beliefs, but neutralized them with excuses so that they could commit delinquent acts without feeling guilty. Hirschi, in contrast, argued that "there is variation in the extent to which people believe they should obey the rules of society, and, furthermore, that the less a person believes he should obey the rules, the more likely he is to violate them."[29] Thus Matza's theory had emphasized that delinquents are tied to the conventional moral order and must free themselves from it in order to commit delinquent acts, while Hirschi's theory assumes that they are free from the conventional order to begin with.

Like Nye, Hirschi tested his theory with a self-report survey. The sample consisted of about 4,000 junior and senior high school youths from a county in the San Francisco Bay area. The questionnaire contained a variety of items related to family, school, and peer relations, as well as six items that served as an index of delinquency.[30] Three of those six items referred to stealing (things worth less than $2, things worth between $2 and $50, and things worth more than $50), while the other three asked whether the youth had ever "taken a car for a ride without the owner's permission," "banged up something that did not belong to you on purpose," and "beaten up on anyone or hurt anyone on purpose" (not counting fights with a brother or sister). Youths were given one point for each of the six offenses they reported committing in the last year, regardless of how often they reported committing it.[31] Hirschi also used school records and official police records as data for the study.

Hirschi was particularly concerned to test the adequacy of his control theory against theories that argued the motivation for delinquency was to be found in social strain (such as Merton's, Cohen's, or Cloward and Ohlin's) and theories that explained delinquency in terms of cultural or group influence (such as Sutherland's or Miller's).[32] Each of these three types of theories can explain many of the

29. Ibid., p. 26.

30. Ibid., p. 54.

31. Ibid., p. 62. This was defined as the "recency" index, and was used throughout the study.

32. Strain theories are reviewed in Chapter 11 of this book, while what Hirschi called "cultural deviance" theories are reviewed in Chapter 12. One of the arguments made in Chapter 12 is that the description of Sutherland's theory as a cultural deviance theory is inaccurate.

well-known facts about delinquency, such as that delinquents do poorly in school, but each proposes a different chain of causation. Much of Hirschi's book is devoted to attempts to test the different chains of causation found in the three types of theories.

Hirschi reported that, in general, there was no relationship between reported delinquent acts and social class, except that children from the poorest families were slightly more likely to be delinquent.[33] In addition, he found only minimal racial differences in self-reported delinquency, although their official arrest rates were substantially different.[34] Hirschi concluded that these findings were most difficult to reconcile with strain theories, since those were explicitly class-based theories.[35]

Hirschi then analyzed the effects of attachment to parents, schools, and peers on reported delinquent acts. He found that, regardless of race or class, and regardless of the delinquency of their friends, boys who were more closely attached to their parents were less likely to report committing delinquent acts than those who were less closely attached.[36] That finding is consistent with control theory but inconsistent with cultural theories, where attachment to deviant friends or deviant parents would theoretically be associated with increased reporting of delinquency. Hirschi also found that youths who reported more delinquent acts were more likely to have poor verbal scores on the Differential Aptitude Test, to get poor grades in school, to care little about teachers' opinions, to dislike school, and to reject school authority. He argued that these findings are consistent with control theory, since such boys would be free from the controlling forces of schools. However, he argued that they were inconsistent with strain theories such as Cohen's, since the most "strained" youths would be those who did poorly but who continued to care about success in the school. Youths who did poorly and did not care about school success would not be "strained."[37] He also found that boys who reported more delinquent acts were less attached to their peers than boys who reported fewer delinquent acts. Again Hirschi argued that this finding is consistent with control theory, since attachment

---

33. Hirschi, op. cit., pp. 66–75.

34. Ibid., pp. 75–81.

35. Ibid., pp. 226–27.

36. Ibid., pp. 97, 99.

37. Hirschi admits that his formulation may not adequately test strain because of Cohen's idea of reaction formation: Boys may care about school success, but if they are unable to succeed, they may then deny that they care at all. However, Hirschi argues that such an argument is virtually impossible to falsify; ibid., pp. 124–126.

to peers would be conducive to delinquency only if those peers valued delinquent behavior. However, it is inconsistent with cultural theories, where the assumption is made that the motivation for delinquency is passed through intimate, personal relationships. Hirschi found that association with delinquent companions could increase delinquent behavior, but only when social controls had been weakened. Youths with large stakes in conformity are unlikely to have delinquent friends, and when they do have such friends, they are unlikely to commit delinquent acts themselves. For youths with low stakes in conformity, however, the greater the exposure to "criminal influences," the more delinquent activities the youth reported.[38]

Having examined the effect of attachment on reported delinquent acts, Hirschi examined the effects of the other three elements of his theory. He found that the educational and occupational aspirations of delinquents are lower than nondelinquents, as are the educational and occupational expectations. This finding is consistent with control theory, since a youth with low aspirations and low expectations has little commitment to conformity—that is, he risks little by committing delinquent acts. In contrast, the findings are inconsistent with strain theories, since those theories locate the source of strain in the gap between aspirations and expectations. According to strain theories, youths with high aspirations but low expectations (because of blocked opportunities) should be the most delinquent. Hirschi found that "the higher the aspiration, the lower the rate of delinquency, regardless of the student's expectations."[39] Hirschi also found that youths who worked, dated, spent time watching TV, reading books, or playing games were more likely to report delinquencies.[40] That finding was the opposite of what was expected from his theory, since these behaviors represent involvement in conventional activities. Hirschi did find, however, that boys who spent less time on homework, reported being bored, spent more time talking to friends and riding around in cars were more likely to report delinquent acts. These can be considered measures of the lack of involvement in conventional activities. Finally, Hirschi found a strong correlation between reported delinquent activities and agreement with the statement "It is alright to get around the law if you can get away with it."[41] He took this to be a measure of the extent to which boys believe they

38. Ibid., pp. 159–161.
39. Ibid., p. 183.
40. Ibid., p. 190.
41. Ibid., pp. 202–203.

should obey the law. He also found support for the neutralizing beliefs that Matza had described as freeing the delinquent from the moral bind of the law, although he argued that "the assumption that delinquent acts come before the justifying beliefs is the more plausible causal ordering with respect to many of the techniques of neutralization."[42] Finally, Hirschi found no support for a separate lower-class culture as described by Miller. Hirschi found instead that these beliefs are held by academically incompetent youths, whether lower or middle class, and that academically competent youths, whether lower or middle class, held what are often called "middle-class values." Thus he concluded that lower-class values are not cultural in that they are not transmitted as a valued heritage. Rather, they "are available to all members of American society more or less equally; they are accepted or rejected to the extent they are consistent or inconsistent with one's realistic position in that society."[43] Thus Hirschi believes that "the class of the father may be unimportant, but the class of the child most decidedly is not.[44]

### 4. ASSESSING CONTROL THEORIES

Control theories have generated a fairly large number of empirical studies, many of which have produced supportive results.[45] Most of those studies, however, focused on relatively trivial offenses committed by essentially nondelinquent youths. Both Hirschi's study and Nye's study, as reported above, are of this type. Hirschi admits that some theorists may hold that "delinquents are so obviously underrepresented among those completing the questionnaires that the results need not be taken seriously."[46] However, he argues that in-

---

42. Ibid., p. 208.

43. Ibid., p. 230.

44. Ibid., p. 82.

45. See, for example, Michael J. Hindelang, "Causes of Delinquency: A Partial Replication and Extension," *Social Problems* 20: 471–87 (1973); John R. Hepburn, "Testing Alternative Models of Delinquency Causation," *Journal of Criminal Law and Criminology* 67: 450–60 (1977); Eric D. Poole and Robert M. Regoli, "Parental Support, Delinquent Friends and Delinquency," *Journal of Criminal Law and Criminology* 70 (2): 188–93 (1979); and Michael D. Wiatrowski, David B. Griswold, and Mary K. Roberts, "Social Control Theory and Delinquency," *American Sociological Review* 46: 525–41 (Oct. 1981). For a review of other empirical data supporting Hirschi's control theory, see LaMar T. Empey, *American Delinquency*, rev. ed., Dorsey Press, Homewood, Ill., 1982, pp. 269–75. A more general review of empirical evidence supporting the control perspective can be found in Gwynn Nettler, *Explaining Crime*, 3rd ed., McGraw-Hill, New York, 1984, pp. 288–314.

46. Hirschi, op. cit., p. 41. See Thomas J. Bernard, "Control Criticisms of Strain Theories," *Journal of Research in Crime and Delinquency* 21 (4): 353–72 (Nov. 1984), for an argument that there were few serious delinquents in Hirschi's sample to begin with, and that he lost most of his data on them due to nonresponse.

cluding serious delinquents would have made the final relationships even stronger. Such an argument is valid only if the same causal processes are at work for seriously delinquent youths as for basically nondelinquent but "wild" youths. If different processes are at work, then the inclusion of serious delinquents would weaken Hirschi's results. This is the same criticism that Toby raised about Nye's earlier study, and it is consistent with Matza's argument that serious delinquents may not be "drifters," but instead may be committed or compulsive.

A remark in Hirschi's book illustrates the problem. Hirschi found that increased involvement in conventional activities was related to more delinquency, which is the opposite of what his theory predicted:[47]

Something is wrong with our theory. The difficulty, it seems, is that the definition of delinquency used here is not the definition that makes the involvement hypothesis virtually tautological. When Cohen, for example, says the delinquent gang "makes enormous demands upon the boy's time," he is of course not saying that delinquency as here defined takes an enormous amount of the boy's time. In fact, as defined, delinquency requires very little time: *the most delinquent boys in the sample may not have devoted more than a few hours in the course of a year to the acts that define them as delinquent.*

Control theory may adequately explain delinquency in boys who spend only a few hours per year engaged in it, but whether it explains delinquency among the boys that Cohen was talking about is another question entirely.

This problem is related to the control theory assumption that criminal and delinquent behaviors are "naturally motivated," and that there are no outside pressures generating them. It is relatively easy and appealing to think of the trivial offenses in Hirschi's and Nye's studies as being naturally motivated, requiring no other explanation than that they are "fun." But that image is less appealing when one considers the aggressive and violent nature of much serious gang delinquency and adult criminality.

Control theories ultimately attribute such serious criminality to our

---

47. Hirschi, op. cit., p. 190 (emphasis added). Hirschi (ibid., p. 46) defines delinquency as follows: "Delinquency is defined by acts, the detection of which is thought to result in punishment of the person committing them by agents of the larger society." Under that definition, virtually all youths may be classified as delinquents. Toby ("Review," op. cit.) raised a similar problem with Nye's definition of delinquency.

innately aggressive and violent animal heritage. But the question of whether humans are inherently peaceful or inherently aggressive has been the subject of debate for over 2,000 years by philosophers, theologians, psychologists, sociologists, anthropologists, and now criminologists.[48] The debate is by no means resolved at the present time, and to that extent it is not possible to evaluate fully the control theory explanation of crime.

Despite this ongoing debate, there appears to be a growing agreement on a narrower issue that concerns the type of violence and aggression that is defined as serious crime. Some who hold the view that aggression is an innate human characteristic now also argue that serious criminal behavior represents a degeneration of the aggressive instincts caused by biological or social pathologies.[49] That would be consistent with the finding, as discussed in Chapter 11, that empirical research on serious delinquency has provided considerable support for the basic contentions of strain theories. If this view ultimately prevails, then the control theory explanation could only be applied to less serious forms of delinquency and crime.

## 5. IMPLICATIONS AND CONCLUSIONS

After a number of years of being dominated by strain theories, criminological theory and research has come increasingly under the influence of control theories, particularly as formulated by Hirschi. Control theories appeal to criminologists for several reasons. First, they provide criminologists with very testable theories. Many other criminological theories, in contrast, are much more difficult to test in that their concepts and variables (like "an excess of definitions favorable to law violation") are very difficult to operationalize. Second, control theories have been linked from the outset with a new research technique, the self-report survey. That research technique has consistently produced results that support the basic contentions of control theories. The combination of a testable theory with a research technique that produces supportive results is very attractive, to say the least.

A number of criminologists have concluded that control theory in general, and Hirschi's control theory in particular, is supported by

48. See Thomas J. Bernard, *The Consensus-Conflict Debate: Form and Content in Social Theories*, Columbia University Press, New York, 1983.

49. Luigi Valzelli, *Psychobiology of Aggression and Violence*, Raven Press, New York, 1981, chapter 4.

empirical research, while other types of theories are not.[50] That conclusion, however, does not seem warranted either by general research on human behavior or by specifically criminological research focusing on the explanation of criminal and delinquent behavior. A more restricted but better-supported assessment is that control theories are generally supported by one type of data—self-report surveys—and that they provide a good explanation of one type of crime, the less serious forms of juvenile delinquency. However, they are not as yet supported by studies that focus directly on more serious delinquency or on adult criminality.

RECOMMENDED READINGS

Travis Hirschi, *Causes of Delinquency*, University of California Press, Berkeley, 1969. The most important control theory.

Ruth Rosner Kornhauser, *Social Sources of Delinquency*, University of Chicago Press, Chicago, 1978. A comprehensive defense of control theories.

Gwynn Nettler, *Explaining Crime*, 3rd ed., McGraw-Hill, New York, 1984. A general review of theory and research in criminology, generally interpreting it as supporting control theory.

William R. Arnold and Terrance M. Brungardt, *Juvenile Misconduct and Delinquency*, Houghton Mifflin, Boston, 1983. A general delinquency text that presents a new control theory and organizes the presentation of materials around that theory.

Thomas J. Bernard, "Control Criticisms of Strain Theories: An Assessment of Theoretical and Empirical Adequacy," *Journal of Research in Crime and Delinquency* 21 (4): 353–72 (Nov. 1984). Empirical research supporting control theories should be interpreted as explaining the variation between underconformity and overconformity ("wild" youth and "square" youth) in a basically nondelinquent population.

Freda Adler, *Nations Not Obsessed with Crime*, Rothman, Littleton, Col., 1983. Successful crime control is associated with the existence of effective systems of popularly accepted and culturally harmonious social controls, capable of maintaining, generating, and transmitting shared values.

M. Phillip Feldman, *Criminal Behavior: A Psychological Analysis*, John Wiley, London, 1977. Places "learning not to offend" in a much broader context that includes biological and personality differences, "learning to offend" through differential reinforcements, social modeling and situational inducements, and the effects of social labeling.

Nancy Eisenberg, ed., *The Development of Prosocial Behavior*, Academic Press, New York, 1982. Developmental psychologists examine theory and research on the process of developing "prosocial" behavior in children.

50. Nettler, op. cit., pp. 313–14; William R. Arnold and Terrance M. Brungardt, *Juvenile Misconduct and Delinquency*, Houghton Mifflin, Boston, 1983; Ruth Rosner Kornhauser, *Social Sources of Delinquency*, University of Chicago Press, Chicago, 1978.

# CHAPTER FOURTEEN

# Deviance and Social Reaction

Thomas Szasz has written that a person who studied slaves might find that "such persons are generally brutish, poor, and uneducated, and might conclude that slavery is their 'natural' or appropriate social status."[1] His point was that in order to genuinely understand slaves, it is necessary to study the whole institution of slavery, including the masters and the entire social and economic system of which slavery was a part. Similarly, social reaction theorists maintain that it is not possible to understand crime merely by studying criminals, but that crime must be viewed in its entire social context. In particular, they argue, criminal behavior can only be understood in the context of the reactions to it by other people, including the official reactions in which specific people and events are legally defined as criminal.

This is a relatively recent area of theory and research in criminology and it can be quite confusing. Theorists who present these views often deny that they are stating a "theory," and say instead that they are taking a new "perspective" on crime.[2] Exactly what that means is not entirely clear, except that it seems to entail a broad look at many topics, all tied together by the common framework of symbolic

1. Thomas S. Szasz, "Involuntary Mental Hospitalization: A Crime Against Humanity," in Thomas S. Szasz, ed., *Ideology and Insanity*, Doubleday Anchor, Garden City, N.Y., 1970, pp. 123–24.

2. See, for example, Howard S. Becker, "Labelling Theory Reconsidered," in Sheldon Messinger et al., eds., *The Aldine Crime and Justice Annual—1973*, Aldine, Chicago, 1973, p. 6; Edwin M. Schur, *Labelling Deviant Behavior*, Harper, New York, 1971, p. 27; John I. Kitsuse, "The 'New Conception of Deviance' and its Critics," in Walter R. Gove, ed., *The Labelling of Deviance: Evaluating a Perspective*, 2nd ed., Sage, Beverly Hills, Cal., 1980, p. 383.

interactionism. Symbolic interactionism was briefly discussed in Chapter 12 of this book, since it also forms the basis of Sutherland's differential association theory.[3] Its key argument is that human actions are best understood in terms of the *meaning* that those actions have for the actors, rather than in terms of preexisting biological, psychological, or social conditions. These meanings are to some extent created by the individual, but primarily they are derived from intimate personal interactions with other people.

Using this general frame of reference, social reaction theorists make theoretical arguments in four general areas related to criminology: (1) the definition of crime; (2) the origins of criminal behaviors and the effect that defining an individual as a criminal has on that individual's behavior; (3) the processes by which agents of the criminal justice system arrive at official definitions of specific people and events as criminal; and (4) the processes by which general categories of behavior are defined as crimes in the criminal law. This chapter reviews arguments made by social reaction theorists on each of these topics.

## 1. REACTIVE DEFINITIONS OF CRIME

Most, but not all, social reaction theorists present a general argument that criminal behavior is defined solely by the reaction that other people have to it.[4] These theorists use the terms *deviance* and *social reaction* to express the relationship between criminal behavior and the social processes of defining specific people and events as criminal. Criminal behavior is said to be a part of deviance, where that term implies only that the activity is different from activities considered normal or usual in the society.[5] The distinguishing characteristic of deviance is said to be that there exists some form of negative *social reaction*—that is, other people view the behavior as "wrong" or "bad." In symbolic interactionist terms, other people attribute a certain meaning to the deviant behavior and then act on the basis of that meaning.

3. This theory was more extensively summarized in the second edition of the present book. See George B. Vold, *Theoretical Criminology*, 2nd ed. prepared by Thomas J. Bernard, Oxford University Press, New York, 1979, pp. 255–58.

4. A social reaction theorist who does not present a reactive definition of deviance is Edwin M. Lemert, *Human Deviance, Social Problems and Social Control*, Prentice-Hall, Englewood Cliffs, N.J., 1967, pp. 40–64. See also his *Social Pathology*, McGraw-Hill, New York, 1951, pp. 75–76. Within Lemert's theory, primary deviation is normatively defined.

5. Jess Stein, editor-in-chief, *The Random House Dictionary of the English Language, the Unabridged Edition*, Random House, New York, 1971, p. 395.

The behaviors that are considered deviant differ from time to time and from place to place. A Nazi in the United States today is considered deviant but was not considered deviant in Germany in the 1930s. A person who shoots another person may or may not be considered deviant, depending on the legal and cultural conditions of the society. Sometimes those conditions are not clearly specified, so that some people regard the person as a criminal while others regard the person as a hero.[6] Many behaviors considered deviant by one group of people are viewed as perfectly normal by another group of people. To that extent deviance, like beauty, is in the eye of the beholder.[7] Thus deviance and social reaction are reciprocal terms that can only be understood in conjunction with each other. Social reaction theorists make a similar point about criminal behaviors and the social processes of defining these behaviors as criminal.

This can be called a *reactive* definition of crime, since it argues that crime is defined solely by the reactions of other people to it. Reactive definitions can be contrasted with *normative* definitions, in which crime is said to be defined by the fact that it violates rules for behavior (norms) with which most people in a society agree.[8] Normative definitions are older and more intuitive, but reactive definitions have arisen as a result of problems with normative definitions. Gibbs states that normative definitions have failed to grapple with the problem of consensus (is there a norm against marijuana smoking in our society?), the problem of differences between actions and behaviors (what people say they ought to do versus what they actually do), and the problem of differences in power (do the norms of more powerful people count more than the norms of less powerful people, since they have more input into the content of law?).[9]

Despite these problems with normative definitions, Gibbs continues to advocate them, since he argues that reactive definitions are faced with similar problems. Reactive definitions have failed to precisely identify the social reactions that define particular actions and people as criminal. Is it the reaction of any individual, or is it the

---

6. See, for example, the case of Bernhard Goetz who, on December 23, 1984, shot four youths in a New York City subway after they harassed him and asked him for $5. The case received almost daily coverage in the *New York Times* following the incident. See in particular the column by Sydney Schanberg in the Dec. 29, 1984, issue; the letters to the editor responding to that column in the Jan. 11, 1985, issue; and "The Editorial Notebook" by David C. Anderson and the column by Kenneth B. Clark in the Jan. 14, 1985, issue.

7. J. L. Simmons, *Deviants*, Glendessary Press, Berkeley, 1969, pp. 3–11.

8. Jack P. Gibbs, *Norms, Deviance, and Social Control*, Elsevier, New York, 1981, pp. 22–35.

9. Ibid., pp. 9–18.

reaction of social groups? If groups, how large must the group be? Do the reactions of powerful groups count more than the reactions of powerless groups? Or is it only reactions by official agents of social control? Different social reaction theorists provide different answers. Gibbs asks: "If the meaning of an act is so problematical that a sociologist cannot justifiably classify the act as deviant by reference to norms, why is the meaning of a reaction to the act not equally problematical?"[10] Thus it is not clear on a general level whether reactive definitions of crime have any advantages over normative definitions.

## 2. SOCIAL REACTION THEORIES OF CRIMINAL BEHAVIOR

One of the most important "meanings" within symbolic interaction theory is the meaning that people give to themselves, their self-image. People may define themselves as handsome, cowardly, kindly, faithful, smart, worthless, or all of the above. They then act toward themselves according to the meanings they have for themselves. Each person's self-image is constructed primarily through interactions with other people. That is what Mead called "the self as a social construct"[11] and what Cooley called "the looking glass self."[12] Cohen describes this point of view well:[13]

The self is built up in the process of interacting with others. In doing business with them, we discover what we are—i.e., the categories to which we have been assigned—and to some extent we determine what we shall be. We may lay claims to being a certain sort of person, but this claim must make sense in terms of the culture of those we are dealing with, and we must make these claims stick. To lay a claim is to say, in effect: "I am such-and-such a sort of person; I invite you to deal with me on this basis; you may expect certain things of me." To make the claim stick, we must validate it by meeting the cultural criteria of the role. We know we have done this when others, by their responses, indicate acceptance of us as valid specimens of the role. In so doing, we also confirm our conception of ourselves. We cannot really tell whether we are "leaders," "glamour girls," "pool sharks," or "brains" without venturing into the icy waters of social interac-

---

10. Ibid., p. 27.

11. For discussion of Mead's view, see Bernard N. Meltzer, "Mead Social Psychology," in Jerome G. Manis and Bernard N. Meltzer, eds., *Symbolic Interaction*, Allyn and Bacon, Boston, 1967, pp. 9–13.

12. Charles H. Cooley, *Human Nature and the Social Order*, Charles Scribner's Sons, New York, 1902, pp. 183–85, 196–99, reprinted in Manis and Meltzer, op. cit., pp. 217–19.

13. Albert K. Cohen, *Deviance and Control*, Prentice-Hall, Englewood Cliffs, N.J., 1966, p. 98. Reprinted by permission of the publisher.

tion, trying our hand at the role, and seeing how others respond. Everyone is continually engaged in a lifelong process of building, maintaining, or refashioning a self.

One might expect that people who commit criminal behaviors would think of themselves as criminals—that is, have a criminal self-image. In fact, many of them do not. Yochelson and Samenow found that even the most hardened, consistent offenders were unwilling to admit that they were criminals, although they could easily recognize criminality in others.[14] Cameron pointed out that nonprofessional shoplifters often deny that their actions constitute theft, and tend to rationalize their behavior as "merely naughty or bad" or as "reprehensible but not really criminal."[15] Cressey's analysis of embezzlement is quite similar.[16] Embezzlers are people who hold positions of trust and normally conceive of themselves as upstanding citizens. Therefore they must define their actions as "only borrowing the money" before they can proceed. Matza and Sykes argue that most juvenile delinquents do not have an overt commitment to delinquent values and do not conceive of themselves as criminals.[17] Their own delinquent behavior contradicts their self-image, and therefore they often justify the behavior by arguing that it is "not really criminal." Five "techniques of neutralization" may be used in this way: denial of responsibility ("It wasn't my fault"); denial of injury ("They can afford it"); denial of victims ("They had it coming"); condemn the condemners ("Everyone is crooked anyway"); and appeal to higher loyalties ("I did it for the gang"). Police who use illegal violence justify it in terms of the need to accomplish their jobs.[18] Illegal activities by government agencies may be justified in terms of "national security." Antiwar activists who committed illegal acts stated that the "real criminals" were the ones who were running the war. And, in general, Chambliss and Seidman state: "It is a truism that every person arrested for crime perceives himself as innocent, for there are

14. Samuel Yochelson and Stanton E. Samenow, *The Criminal Personality*, vol. I, Jason Aronson, New York, 1976, p. 19.

15. Mary Cameron Owen, *The Booster and the Snitch*, The Free Press, New York, 1964, pp. 159, 161, 168.

16. Donald R. Cressey, *Other People's Money: A Study of the Social Psychology of Embezzlement*, The Free Press, Glencoe, Ill., 1953.

17. Gresham M. Sykes and David Matza, "Techniques of Neutralization: A Theory of Delinquency," *American Sociological Review* 22: 667–70 (Dec. 1957).

18. William A. Westley, "Violence and the Police," *American Journal of Sociology* 59: 34–41 (July 1953).

always circumstances which to him seem to place his action outside the appropriate definition of the crime."[19]

These examples illustrate the fact that criminal behaviors are frequently committed by persons who do not conceive of themselves as criminals. In order to maintain a noncriminal self-image, these persons "define the situation" so that they can maintain that their actions are not really crimes. They are then free to continue committing criminal behaviors without changing their self-image.

The maintenance of a noncriminal self-image is very important to most people. Pressure to accept a criminal self-image depends in part on the number of others who define the person as a criminal, and the process of informing others is frequently used as a technique of social control. For example, consider the case of a person who has a noncriminal self-image, but who is caught shoplifting and is brought to the store office. Store officials communicate to the person that "you *are* a shoplifter." This is threatening to the person precisely because the self is constructed in the process of interacting with others, including the store officials. The officials can increase the power of the threat by increasing the number of persons who know about the new identity. The ultimate threat to the identity, however, involves the process of arrest and conviction in which the person is officially declared to be a criminal in the view of the society at large. From this point of view a criminal trial can be interpreted as a "status degradation ceremony" in which the public identity of the person is lowered on the social scale. Garfinkel maintains that literally every society has such ceremonies as a method of social control, and that the structure of these ceremonies is essentially similar although the societies differ dramatically.[20]

Criminal behavior that occurs in the context of a noncriminal self-image may originate in any number of biological, psychological, or social factors in the person's life. Lemert calls such a person a "primary deviant."[21] But criminal behavior generates a negative social reaction in other people, which attacks the persons noncriminal self-image. If the person is unwilling or unable to stop the criminal behavior, then at some point it may be necessary to reorganize the self-image to incorporate the criminal behavior—that is, to take on a

19. William J. Chambliss and Robert B. Seidman, *Law, Order and Power*, Addison-Wesley, Reading, Mass., 1971, p. 71.

20. Harold Garfinkel, "Conditions of Successful Degradation Ceremonies," *American Journal of Sociology* 61 (5): 420–24 (Mar. 1965).

21. Edwin M. Lemert, *Human Deviance, Social Problems, and Social Control*, Prentice-Hall, Englewood Cliffs, N.J., 1967, pp. 17, 40.

criminal self-image. This may be done as a defense against the attacks of the social reaction, since those who already think of themselves as criminals or as juvenile delinquents are less threatened when other people define them that way. Lemert calls such a person a "secondary deviant."[22] The redefinition of self opens the door to full participation in the criminal life and allows the person to make a commitment to a criminal career. At this point, Lemert argues, criminal behavior is no longer generated by the various biological, psychological, and social factors in the person's life, but is generated directly by the person's criminal self-image.

Criminal justice agencies, as the institutionalized means of social reaction, may play a role in the process by which a person comes to accept a criminal self-image. These agencies "label" people as criminals in formal status degradation ceremonies, as well as in informal interactions. Once applied, Becker has argued, the criminal label overrides other labels, so that other people think of the person primarily as a criminal.[23] Such a person may then be forced into criminal roles because of public stereotypes about criminals.[24] For example, on release from prison a person may be unable to obtain legitimate employment due to the criminal conviction and may then return to crime in order to survive. Finally, those who have been labeled criminal may associate primarily with other people who have been similarly labeled, either because they are all institutionalized together or because other people refuse to associate with them.[25] Membership in an exclusively criminal group can increase the likelihood that individuals will resort to a criminal self-image rather than attempt to retain a noncriminal self-image.

This discussion represents one of the basic arguments of the so-called labeling approach to crime: that the formal and informal processes of social control can have the effect of increasing criminal behavior because the labeling process increases the likelihood that the person will develop a criminal self-image. Several criticisms of the labeling approach should be mentioned. First, labeling theorists

---

22. Lemert, op. cit., pp. 40–64; also Lemert, *Social Pathology*, McGraw-Hill, New York, 1951, pp. 75–76.

23. Howard S. Becker, *Outsiders—Studies in the Sociology of Deviance*, Free Press of Glencoe, New York, 1963, pp. 32–33. See also Kai T. Erikson, "Notes on the Sociology of Deviance," *Social Problems* 9: 311 (Spring 1962). An example would be Ray's argument that a cured heroin addict relapses in part because other people continue to treat him as an addict. See Marsh B. Ray, "The Cycle of Abstinence and Relapse among Heroin Addicts," *Social Problems* 9: 132–40 (Fall 1961).

24. Becker, op. cit., pp. 34–35.

25. Ibid., pp. 37–39.

sometimes have overemphasized the importance the official labeling process can have. As Akers has remarked:[26]

One sometimes gets the impression from reading this literature that people go about minding their own business, and then—"wham"—bad society comes along and slaps them with a stigmatized label. Forced into the role of deviant the individual has little choice but to be deviant.

Second, labeling theory generally portrays the deviant as resisting the deviant label, and accepting it only when it can no longer be avoided. Although this may be true in some cases, in others it would appear that the deviant identity is actively sought and that the person may form a deviant identity without ever having been officially or unofficially labeled. For example, youths who join a delinquent gang may form a deviant identity centered on their gang activities. Although official labeling may make it harder to change that identity in the future, it would not have pushed the youth into the identity in the first place, and there is no particular reason to believe that failure to label the youth would lead him to seek a law-abiding identity instead.

Third, it is generally recognized that for the typical, law-abiding member of society who has a noncriminal self-image, the the labeling or stigmatizing function of the criminal court is the primary technique of social control and is much more important than the actual imposition of punishments.[27] The average citizen is deterred from committing most crimes because he or she fears the conviction itself rather than the punishment associated with it. This is why courts are frequently able to suspend sentence or impose such minor punishments as small fines or unsupervised probation with no loss of effectiveness. Only in cases in which conviction does not hold a stigma—for example, traffic offense cases—do the courts rely heavily on the actual imposition of punishments in the social control of the average citizen. Reducing the stigmatizing or labeling effects of the criminal court could possibly lead to an increase in the incidence of criminal behaviors and to an increase in the imposition of other, harsher punishments for those behaviors. Thus the basic question is not whether the labeling function creates crime, but whether it creates more crime than it eliminates. Although this is a very complicated question to

26. Ronald L. Akers, "Problems in the Sociology of Deviance: Social Definitions and Behavior," *Social Forces* 46: 455–65 (1967).

27. Franklin E. Zimring and Gordon J. Hawkins, *Deterrence*, University of Chicago Press, Chicago, 1973, pp. 190–94.

analyze, it seems probable that labeling does not create more crime than it eliminates.[28] This means that the policy implications of labeling theory are not at all clear.

## 3. SOCIAL REACTION VIEWS OF ENFORCING CRIMINAL LAWS

Gibbs points out one clear advantage for reactive definitions of crime: Criminologists most often use reactive data such as official police, court, and corrections statistics.[29] These data are at best a rough approximation of behavior that violates social norms, but they are a very precise and accurate account of the social reactions of official criminal justice agents. Particular events are officially crimes only if they are "defined" as such by agents of the criminal justice system. In symbolic interaction terms, those agents must attribute a certain meaning to a situation, and then must act on that meaning.

A number of researchers have examined the processes by which criminal justice agents define an event as criminal. They find that, in addition to legal factors, there are certain nonlegal factors that regularly affect whether an event is defined as a crime. These nonlegal factors include the interaction with the offender; the interaction with the complainant, the organizational structure, and policy of the agency; and the demands of the particular job. These studies do not attempt to explain the causes or origins of criminal behaviors; rather, they attempt to explain the distribution of official crime rates by looking at factors that enter into the enforcement of criminal laws. As such, they can be described as part of a theory of the behavior of criminal law, as discussed in the first chapter of this book.

The *interaction with the offender* can strongly influence whether the police officer officially defines the situation as a crime. For example, Piliavin and Briar studied one metropolitan police department in which officers could choose from five possible responses to delinquent behavior, ranging from outright release to arrest and confinement in juvenile hall.[30] The authors found that in all cases involving minor offenses, and in some cases involving serious offenses, the decision on how to handle the case was made on the ba-

---

28. Charles R. Tittle, "Labelling and Crime: An Empirical Evaluation," in Walter R. Gove, ed., *The Labelling of Deviance—Evaluating a Perspective*, John Wiley, New York, 1975, pp. 181–203.

29. Gibbs, *Norms, Deviance, and Social Control*, pp. 31–32.

30. Irving Piliavin and Scott Briar, "Police Encounters with Juveniles," *American Journal of Sociology* 69: 206–14 (Sept. 1964).

sis of the officer's assessment of the personal character of the youth
rather than on the basis of the offense itself. The officer, for example, might define the youth as a "serious delinquent" or as a "mis-
guided youth" or as a "good boy who happened to be in the wrong
place at the wrong time." This definition was based less on factual
data (which were usually not available at the time) than it was on a
variety of "cues" that arose in the interaction between the officer and
the youth and from which the officer inferred the youth's character.
These cues included the youth's group affiliation, age, race, groom-
ing, dress, and demeanor.

The most important of these cues was clearly the demeanor of the
youth, which the officers themselves estimated was a major factor in
50 to 60 percent of their decisions.[31]

Juveniles who were contrite about their infractions, respectful to officers,
and fearful of the sanctions that might be employed against them tended to
be viewed by patrolmen as basically law-abiding or at least "salvageable."
For these youths, it was usually assumed that informal or formal reprimand
would suffice to guarantee their future conformity. In contrast, youthful offenders who were fractious, obdurate or who appeared nonchalant in their
encounters with patrolmen were likely to be viewed as "would-be tough
guys" or "punks" who fully deserved the most severe sanction: arrest.

For the juvenile, however, the hostile attitude may not represent a
commitment to delinquent values, but may be a response to having
been repeatedly interrogated by police precisely because of his
physical appearance:[32]

Negro gang members are constantly singled out for interrogation by the police, and the boys develop their own techniques of retaliation. They taunt
the police with jibes and threaten their authority with gestures of inso-
lence, as if daring the police to become bigots and bullies in order to defend their honor. Moreover, these techniques of retaliation often do succeed in provoking this response. When suspect after suspect becomes hostile
and surly, the police begin to see themselves as representing the law among
a people that lack proper respect for it. They, too, begin to feel maligned
and they soon become defensively cynical and aggressively moralistic.

31. Ibid., pp. 210–211. For additional information on the role of demeanor in police encounters with juveniles, see Donald J. Black and Albert J. Reiss, Jr., "Police Control of Juveniles,"
*American Sociological Review* 35: 63–77 (Feb. 1970).

32. Carl Werthman and Irving Piliavin, "Gang Members and the Police," in David J. Bordua,
ed., *The Police*, John Wiley, New York, 1967, p. 46. See also Westley, "Violence and the
Police," in which police were asked to name situations in which the use of violence would be
justified. The most frequent response was when the offender showed "disrespect for police."

The police officer's definition of the situation can also emerge when he *interacts with a complaining citizen* on the scene of an alleged crime. The definition he constructs determines whether he writes an official report. That, in turn, determines whether the event is recorded as a crime in the official statistics and whether further action is taken to arrest and prosecute the offender. Black studied this process by having trained observers accompany police officers in three major cities.[33] He found that police wrote reports in only 72 percent of the felony situations and 53 percent of the misdemeanor situations, with the following factors appearing to influence their decisions.

1. Complainant's preference: there were no cases in which an official report was written when the complainant expressed a preference for unofficial action. In cases where the complainant preferred official action, the officer complied with the preference in 84% of the felony situations and 64% of the misdemeanor situations.

2. Relation to the offender: police wrote reports in 84% of the cases where the offender was presumed to be a stranger (including 91% of the felony situations). However, they wrote reports in only 51% of the cases involving friends, neighbors, or acquaintances, and in only 41% of the cases involving family. The police were more likely to report misdemeanors involving strangers (74%) than they were to report felonies involving friends, neighbors, or acquaintances (62%).

3. Complainant's attitude: official reports were written in 91% of the situations in which the complainant was very deferential and respectful to the police (including 100% of the felony situations). Seventy-three percent of the cases were reported where the complainants were "civil," but only 30% where they were "antagonistic."

4. Complainant's race and class: there was little evidence of discrimination on the basis of the complainant's race, since reports were written in 72% of the cases where the complainants were black, and in 76% of the cases where they were white. However, police reported 100% of the felonies involving white-collar complainants (both black and white), but only 77% of the felonies involving blue-collar complainants.

Black concludes by stating that "the life chances of the criminal violator may depend on who his victim is and how his victim presents his claim to the police."

Differences in *organizational structure* of the criminal justice agency can produce substantial differences in the set of people defined as

33. Donald J. Black, "The Production of Crime Rates," *American Sociological Review* 35: 733–48 (Aug. 1970).

criminal. For example, Cicourel analyzed the differences in rates of delinquency in two cities of similar size. He found that they did not reflect differences in juvenile behavior, but were generated by differences in the organizational structures of the juvenile control agencies.[34] City A had higher general rates of delinquency, as well as higher rates of recidivism. This was attributed to the fact that the juvenile division in this city was larger, better organized, more professional, and maintained better records. Because of these factors, juveniles who were heavily engaged in delinquent activities were more likely to be identified and aggressively pursued. On the other hand, City B had higher rates of Mexican-American and black delinquency, and this was attributed to the fact that the police department in that city was heavily oriented toward viewing minorities as "troublemakers." Thus the police more aggressively monitored those groups.

Changes in *departmental policy* can also affect the way police define situations, and this sometimes results in dramatic changes in the crime rates.[35]

In Chicago, the number of known robberies increased from 1,263 to 14,544 in a three-year period, and burglaries increased from 879 to 18,689 in the same period. This change was due almost completely to a change in the recording practices of the police following an investigation by the Chicago Crime Commission. Similarly, in the 1952 annual report of the New York City Police Department, a revised system of recording crimes was a major factor in the 254 percent rise in the city's crime rate between 1950 and 1951. A community apparently cut its delinquency rate in half by establishing a youth bureau attached to the police department, but investigation indicated that the rate actually increased and that the reported drop was the result of a change in the reporting system.

Political pressures can generate unofficial departmental policies that have the same effects. For example, in 1969 the Nixon administration instituted an extensive crime control program in Washington, D.C., and a great deal of pressure was brought on the police department to reduce crime.[36] The reduction was achieved, but after

34. Aaron V. Cicourel, *The Social Organization of Juvenile Justice,* John Wiley, New York, 1968, pp. 58–110.

35. Edwin H. Sutherland and Donald R. Cressey, *Criminology,* 8th ed., Lippincott, Philadelphia, 1970, p. 28.

36. David Seidman and Michael Couzens, "Getting the Crime Rate Down: Political Pressure and Crime Reporting," *Law and Society Review* 8 (3): 457–94 (Spring 1974). See also Kurt Weis and Michael E. Milakovich, "Political Misuses of Crime Rates," *Society* 11 (5): 27–33

analyzing the statistics Seidman and Couzens concluded that at least part of it was due to downgrading offenses. For example, larcenies of $50 or more were recorded as larcenies of under $50, and burglaries were recorded as larcenies if the entry was not forced.

Sometimes it is the way the officer *defines his job* that determines the way he defines a particular situation. Bittner describes patrol work on Skid Row as primarily "playing it by ear," in which the objective of the patrol is "reducing the aggregate total of troubles in the area" rather than "evaluating individual cases according to merit."[37] Different officers develop very different styles of operation on Skid Row, and these styles originate in the officer's definition of the Skid Row situation and the people in it. These different styles result in very different sets of people being defined as criminals. Again, if the department itself advocated a different policy, a still different set of people would end up defined as criminals.

Individuals may deliberately attempt to define their situations in such a way that their jobs are more easily accomplished. Sudnow studied the functioning of an adult criminal court.[38] He found that both the district attorney and the public defender had developed conceptions of "normal crimes," which they regarded as "the typical manner in which offenses of given classes are committed, the social characteristics of the persons who regularly commit them, the features of the settings in which they occur, the types of victims often involved, and the like." Whereas private defense attorneys usually attempt to discover as many differences between their client's situation and the "normal crime" in the attempt to construct an adequate defense, the public defender in this court typically attempted to find as many similarities as possible in the interest of processing the case as routinely as possible. For example, the defendant would be asked only a very few questions about the crime itself, and these questions would be designed to confirm in short order that the crime could be defined as a "normal crime." The routine handling of a

(July–Aug. 1974). This pressure is evidenced by Police Chief Jerry Wilson's later statement at a press conference that "I never had any doubt that my function in this city was to reduce crime and that if crime was not reduced I would probably be replaced as chief of police." (Quoted in Seidman and Couzens, op. cit., p. 488.) The *Washington Star* had reported that Wilson told his commanders that if they were unable to reduce crime in their jurisdictions, they would be replaced by men who could (ibid., p. 469).

37. Egon Bittner, "The Police on Skid Row: A Study in Peace Keeping," *American Sociological Review* 32 (5): 699–715 (Oct. 1967).

38. David Sudnow, "Normal Crimes: Sociological Features of the Penal Code in a Public Defender Office," *Social Problems* 12 (3): 255–76 (Winter 1965). See also Abraham S. Blumberg, "The Practice of Law as a Confidence Game: Organizational Cooptation of a Profession," *Law and Society Review* 1: 15–39 (June 1967).

"normal crime" consisted of a predetermined plea bargain in which
the new charge was chosen because it produced a reasonable reduction in the sentence; at times it had no relationship to the original
charge or even to the event that actually occurred. Even if the defendant insisted he was innocent the public defender presumed his
guilt, although he did not reveal this presumption. He argued instead that the defendant would probably be convicted anyway and
would receive a much more severe sentence. If the defendant insisted on pleading innocent, the public defender typically prepared
the case in such a way that he could not be faulted in his defense of
the client, but the defense would not seriously interfere with the
routine court conviction process.

Job demands also affect the way juvenile court workers define situations and people with whom they deal. The role of the juvenile
court is not to determine innocence or guilt, but to diagnose the
conditions that caused the delinquent behavior and to act in the best
interest of the child to alleviate those conditions. Cicourel demonstrated that the agents of the juvenile court routinely act to define
situations so that they are readily understandable within the philosophy of the juvenile court, and so that the courses of action that are
indicated as necessary by the situation are among those actually
available to the court.[39] The result of this process is that the factors
generally thought to be causes of delinquency (bad home environment, poverty, poor school performance, disorganized neighborhood, racial minority, etc.) become the criteria used by court workers to select juveniles for official action.

All of these examples demonstrate that the official definition of individuals as criminals, as well as the official portrayal of criminal actions, is strongly affected by the organizational structures and policies of the criminal justice agencies, as well as by the characteristics
of the criminal justice personnel. To the extent that criminologists
use official crime data, the goal of criminological theory should be to
explain the official crime rates themselves rather than to explain the
criminal behavior.[40] The explanation of official crime rates should take
into account the "true" rate of criminal behavior, as well as the disposition of officials to officially record and process it.

39. Cicourel, op. cit., Chs. 4–7. See also Robert M. Emerson, *Judging Delinquents*, Aldine,
Chicago, 1969.
40. Gibbs, op. cit., pp. 40–43.

## 4. SOCIAL REACTION VIEWS OF ENACTING CRIMINAL LAWS

One of the most important factors in determining the distribution of official crime rates is the "true" rate of criminal behavior. But that "true" rate of criminal behavior is determined by the legal definitions of crime contained in the criminal law. Legally speaking, society "creates" crime by passing laws.[41] For example, if a criminal law is passed concerning political contributions or truth in advertising or pollution control, then a whole new class of crimes exists where none existed before. If marijuana smoking or homosexuality or public drunkenness is decriminalized, then a whole class of crimes simply disappears. In every society there are people who would kill their spouses if they found them having an affair. Some societies will declare this to be murder, others will find it regrettable but understandable, and still others will consider it honorable behavior. As with the views of law enforcement, social reaction views of the enactment of criminal laws are part of the theory that attempts to explain the distribution of official crime rates rather than the behavior of individual criminals. As such, these views are part of a theory of the behavior of criminal law rather than of criminal behavior.

Social reaction theorists view the process of defining actions as crimes as part of the more general process in society of defining and suppressing deviance. Societies define deviance by declaring (either formally or informally) certain human behaviors to be "bad," and then by attempting to minimize or eliminate these behaviors. Because the specific behaviors chosen for this process vary widely from time to time and from place to place, social reaction theorists maintain that the process of defining and suppressing deviance is itself important to social solidarity, independent of the particular behaviors involved.[42] The process works by simplifying the problems of good and evil for the average member of society.[43] Defining the deviants as evil and inferior implies that the remaining members of society are good and superior, thus strengthening their commitment to each other. Combating the evil of deviance consolidates individuals into

---

41. See Clayton A. Hartjen, *Crime and Criminalization*, Praeger, New York, 1974, pp. 1–39, for a discussion of this view.

42. This point was originally made by Durkheim in his discussion of "crime as normal." See Ch. 9, this volume. Kai T. Erikson made a similar point when he described deviance as forming the "boundaries" of society. See Erikson, op. cit.; also Erikson, "On the Sociology of Deviance," in *Wayward Puritans*, John Wiley, New York, 1966, pp. 3–19.

43. This description is taken from the description of the benefits of anti-Semitism in J.-P. Sartre, *Anti-Semite and Jew*, Schocken, New York, 1965, as described by Thomas S. Szasz, *The Manufacture of Madness*, Harper & Row, New York, 1970, p. 270–72.

a tightly knit group and makes it possible for them to use the most ignoble methods to control deviance without questioning these methods. Thus the average member of society is not faced with difficult moral choices, which might undermine a commitment to the path society has taken.

The behavior of the individual is the normal criterion used to select those who will be defined as deviants in a society, but the process works in exactly the same way when other criteria are used. "Heretical" beliefs have been used as a criterion for selecting deviants in a number of societies, including the early Puritan colonies on Massachusetts Bay.[44] Hitler defined deviance on the basis of race and attempted a "final solution" by exterminating the Jews. Sometimes deviant behaviors are imagined and attributed to particular individuals. For example, in Renaissance Europe approximately one-half million persons were executed as witches,[45] and in the great purge under Stalin, millions of loyal Soviet citizens were declared traitors or saboteurs and were executed or shipped to Siberia.[46] Szasz argues that these all represent various manifestations of a deep-seated need for people to ritually expel evil from their communities, and that in primitive communities this took the form of the ritual destruction of a scapegoat.[47]

Campaigns to define and suppress deviance are always launched in the name of benefiting the whole society, but they are often promoted and supported primarily by those who benefit directly. For example, Chambliss's analysis of the law of vagrancy indicates that it was originally created in England shortly after the Black Death had wiped out approximately 50 percent of the population.[48] The result was a serious labor shortage and a great increase in wages. The vagrancy statute made it a crime to give alms to any person who was unemployed while being of sound mind and body, and required that any such person serve any landowner who needed him at the wage level paid before the Black Death. Up to this time beggars had been common and tolerated in England, and there is little doubt that they were defined as criminals to provide a source of cheap labor for landowners.

44. Erikson, *Wayward Puritans*, op. cit.

45. Elliott P. Currie, "Crimes Without Criminals: Witchcraft and Its Control in Renaissance Europe," *Law and Society Review* 3 (1): 7–32 (Aug. 1968).

46. Walter D Connor, "The Manufacture of Deviance: The Case of the Soviet Purge, 1936–1938," *American Sociological Review*, 37: 403–13 (Aug. 1972).

47. Szasz, *The Manufacture of Madness*, op. cit., pp. 260–75.

48. William J. Chambliss, "A Sociological Analysis of the Law of Vagrancy," *Social Problems*, 12 (1): 66–77 (Fall 1964).

Sometimes the benefits of a campaign against deviance are primarily the acquisition of political or bureaucratic power. An example can be found in the campaign to define narcotics users as criminals.[49] In the nineteenth century narcotics were widely available in the form of patent medicines, and addiction was viewed more or less as alcoholism is today—addicts were tolerated and pitied, but not considered criminals. In an attempt to control narcotics distribution, Congress passed the Harrison Narcotics Act in 1914, which required that official records be kept on all sale and distribution of narcotics, and that a nominal tax of one cent per ounce be paid. There is no indication in the law of any legislative intent to restrict or deny addicts access to legal drugs, and the law was passed with little publicity. A narcotics bureau was set up in the Internal Revenue Division of the Treasury Department to enforce the registration procedures and collect the tax. From this tiny beginning the narcotics control bureaucracy promoted its own growth and expansion by launching an extensive public relations campaign against narcotics use and by sponsoring a series of court cases that resulted in the reinterpretation of the Harrison Act so that all narcotics use was declared illegal. As a result of these efforts "(t)he Narcotics Division succeeded in creating a very large criminal class for itself to police . . . instead of the very small one Congress has intended."[50]

Sometimes the benefits of a campaign against deviance are not so much economic as symbolic. Gusfield has analyzed the temperance movement and the resulting enactment of Prohibition as a "symbolic crusade" to reassert the traditional values of rural, middle-class Protestants over the increasing influence of urban, lower-class Catholics in national life.[51] This law created a huge class of criminals by forbidding the manufacture, sale, or transportation of alcoholic beverages, and resulted in the establishment of organized crime syndicates to meet the demand for illegal alcohol. The volume of crime created by this act was so great that it ultimately had to be repealed. Campaigns for and against homosexual rights also can be viewed as symbolic crusades.[52] Opponents of gay rights are asserting traditional moral and religious values regarding sexual behavior. They want homosexuals to be officially recognized as deviants, and want the right

49. Donald T. Dickson, "Bureaucracy and Mortality: An Organizational Perspective on a Moral Crusade," *Social Problems*, 16 (2): 143–56 (Fall 1968). For other examples, see Isadore Silver, ed., *The Crime Control Establishment*, Prentice-Hall, Englewood Cliffs, N.J., 1974.

50. Rufus King, "The Narcotics Bureau and the Harrison Act: Jailing the Healers and the Sick," *Yale Law Journal* 62: 736–49 (1953), p. 738, quoted in Dickson, op. cit., p. 151.

51. Joseph Gusfield, *Symbolic Crusade*, University of Illinois Press, Urbana, 1963.

52. See "Battle Over Gay Rights," *Newsweek Magazine*, June 6, 1977.

to discriminate against them in specific situations, such as when hiring teachers for high schools. Proponents of gay rights are asserting such values as tolerance, liberality, and respect for the rights of minority groups, and are fighting to have discrimination against homosexuals declared illegal. Thus they want official recognition that those who practice such discrimination are deviants, and that homosexuals are not. For homosexuals, the success of their campaign would also lead to practical economic benefits in such areas as housing and employment.

Since campaigns against deviance usually result in the redistribution of benefits from some groups (the deviants) to others (the promoters and supporters of the campaigns), it seems likely that the social solidarity produced depends at least partially on the solidification of power relationships between groups in the society.[53] This is most apparent when two competing groups are attempting to define each other as deviants, as is the case with the "battle for gay rights." One group will succeed in defining the other as deviant only if it is able to generate sufficient power to overcome the support the other group has. This group then obtains the support of the official social control agencies, which normally has the effect of solidifying their power base and institutionalizing their dominance over the other group. In most campaigns against deviance, the role of power is not as apparent because deviants are normally isolated, disorganized, and almost powerless. For example, merchants have traditionally been a powerful group in society, and laws have reflected the maxim "Let the buyer beware." If consumers had been a powerful group instead (and they are now becoming one), the saying might have been "Let the seller beware." Neither approach is inherently more just than the other. The effect of laws has traditionally been to define those who steal from the merchant as dishonest, and to define those from whom the merchant steals as stupid. There is a negative social reaction to both behaviors, but whether this reaction becomes translated into law depends on the relative power of the opposing groups.

## 5. IMPLICATIONS AND CONCLUSIONS

The concept of social reaction appears to combine and confuse two separate phenomena: the official reaction of the social control agen-

---

53. This would be similar to the establishment of pecking order among chickens, where each chicken pecks those below him in the pecking order, but is pecked by those above him. See R. H. Masure and W. C. Allee, "The Social Order in Flocks in the Common Chicken and Pigeon," *Auk* 51: 306–27 (1934).

cies and the personal reaction of particular individuals and groups in society. Individuals and groups construct behavioral norms based on their own moral values and personal self-interest, and react to specific behaviors as deviant when those behaviors violate their norms. They then compete among themselves in an attempt to have their norms enforced by the official social control agencies. Their success in this competition depends directly on the degree of power they possess and are willing to use. Official policies are the result of the conflict and compromise process among these groups. To the extent that the group is successful in having its norms enforced by the social control agencies, it arrogates to itself the right to speak in the name of the entire society. But the mere fact that one group has sufficient power to define another group as deviant does not imply that there is any broad consensus on the matter (there may or may not be) and does not preclude the possibility that the other group may be able to reverse the power distribution in the future.

Liazos points out that deviance theorists frequently state that those who define others as deviants must be more powerful than the deviants themselves.[54]

But this insight is not developed. In none of the 16 [textbooks in the field of deviance] is there an extensive discussion of how power operates in the designation of deviance. Instead of a study of power, of its concrete uses in modern, corporate America, we are offered rather fascinating explorations into the identities and subcultures of "deviants," and misplaced emphasis on the middle-level agents of social control.

The role of power in the definition of crime is the central focus of conflict criminology, which will be the subject of the next chapter.

## RECOMMENDED READINGS

Edwin M. Lemert, "Deviance," in Sanford H. Kadish, ed., *Encyclopedia of Crime and Justice*, vol. 2, Macmillan and the Free Press, New York, 1983, pp. 601–11. A broad overview of the development of deviance theories from their origins in social

---

54. Alexander Liazos, "The Poverty of the Sociology of Deviance: Nuts, Sluts and 'Preverts,' " *Social Problems* 20 (1): 103–20 (Summer 1972), especially p. 115. Since Liazos made this comment, several books have been published in the area of deviance that focus on power relations. See Pat Lauderdale, ed., *A Political Analysis of Deviance*, University of Minnesota Press, Minneapolis, 1980; and Edwin M. Schur, *The Politics of Deviance: Stigma Contests and the Uses of Power*, Prentice-Hall, Englewood Cliffs, N.J., 1980. See also Ruth-Ellen Grimes and Austin Turk, "Labeling in Context: Conflict, Power and Self-Definition," in Marvin D. Krohn and Ronald L. Akers, eds., *Crime, Law, and Sanctions*, Sage, Beverly Hills, Cal., 1978, pp. 39–58; and the readings in H. Laurence Ross, ed., *Law and Deviance*, Sage, Beverly Hills, Cal., 1981.

pathology, social disorganization, and anomie theories. Presents a general discussion of labeling theory, and concludes with a discussion of the politicization of deviance and the relationship to conflict theories.

Lonnie Athens, *Violent Acts and Actors: A Symbolic Interactionist Study*, Routledge and Kegan Paul, London, 1980. A general theory of violent crime, based on symbolic interactionism.

Michael Fabricant, *Deinstitutionalizing Delinquent Youth: The Illusion of Reform?*, Schenckman, Cambridge, Mass., 1980. An analysis of the closing of juvenile correctional institutions in Massachusetts. Symbolic interactionist principles are used to analyze police, courts, and corrections interactions with youths.

Stuart Hall et al., *Policing the Crisis: Mugging, The State, and Law and Order*, Macmillan, London, 1978. The term *mugging* was introduced in Britain in the early 1970s to refer to certain violent crimes, and was used to create a "panic" in the media that played on racial fears.

Jack P. Gibbs, *Norms, Deviance, and Social Control: Conceptual Matters*, Elsevier, New York, 1981. Many of the thornier theoretical issues are addressed.

Michael Phillipson, *Understanding Crime and Delinquency*, Aldine, Chicago, 1974. A general text on crime and delinquency, presented from the interactionist perspective.

Jason Ditton, *Contrology: Beyond the New Criminology*, Humanities Press, Atlantic Highlands, 1979. Crime is explained as a function of "control waves" by agents of the criminal justice system, and the labeling effect those control waves have on the behavior of individuals.

Francis T. Cullen and John B. Cullen, *Toward a Paradigm of Labeling Theory*, University of Nebraska Press, Lincoln, 1978. An ambitious attempt at reformulating labeling theory.

Ronald A. Farrell and Victoria L. Swigert, *Deviance and Social Control*, Scott,Foresman, Glenview, Ill., 1982. This general deviance text examines the research from six theoretical perspectives, including labeling theory and conflict theory. A general structural theory integrating the six perspectives is proposed.

Donald Black, *The Manners and Customs of the Police*, Academic, New York, 1980. The quantity and style of social control exerted by the police depends on the locations of the offender and victim in "social space," which has vertical, horizontal, cultural, corporate, and normative dimensions.

# CHAPTER FIFTEEN

# Conflict Criminology

Throughout the long history of thinking about human societies, social theorists have repeatedly presented two contrasting views that have very different implications for criminology.[1] In the *consensus* view, society is said to be based on a consensus of values among its members, and the state is said to be organized to protect the general public interest. To the extent that societies are composed of groups with conflicting values and interests, the organized state is said to mediate between these conflicting groups and to represent the values and interests of society at large. The contrasting *conflict* view has a history as long as that of the consensus view and is also based on the argument that societies are composed of groups with conflicting values and interests. However, the organized state is not said to represent the values and interests of the society at large. Rather, it is said to represent the values and interests of groups that have sufficient power to control the operation of the state.

The most famous conflict theorist was Marx, who argued that the organized state in capitalist societies represents the economic interests of the people who own the means of production, and that the state would have to assume ownership of the means of production before it could represent the common interests of all the people. Criminology theories based on Marxism will be presented in Chapter 16. The present chapter looks at conflict criminology theories, which are also based on a conflict view of society but which do not

1. A history of the consensus-conflict debate, going back to Plato and Aristotle, can be found in Thomas J. Bernard, *The Consensus-Conflict Debate: Form and Content in Social Theories*, Columbia University Press, New York, 1983.

imply that changes in the capitalist economic system will result in a
society based on consensus.

## 1. SELLIN'S CULTURE CONFLICT THEORY

An early conflict theory appeared in 1938, when Thorsten Sellin
presented a theory of crime based on the conflicts between different
cultural groups in society.[2] He argued that different cultures have
different "conduct norms," that is, rules that require certain types of
people to act in specific ways in certain circumstances. Within a simple, homogeneous society, many of these conduct norms are enacted
into law and actually represent a consensus in the society. But as the
society becomes more complex, it becomes increasingly likely that
there will be overlap and contradiction between the conduct norms
of different groups. Sellin defined "primary cultural conflicts" as those
occurring between two different cultures.[3] These conflicts could occur at border areas between two divergent cultures; or, in the case
of colonization, when the laws of one culture are extended into the
territory of another; or, in the case of migration, when members of
one cultural group move into the territory of another. "Secondary
cultural conflicts" are said to occur when a single culture evolves into
several different subcultures, each having its own conduct norms.[4]
In each of these cases law would not represent a consensus of the
various members of the society, but would reflect the conduct norms
of the dominant culture.

## 2. VOLD'S GROUP CONFLICT THEORY

Sellin's culture conflict theory was based on the conflict of norms and
for that reason was quite similar to Sutherland's differential association theory. In the original edition of *Theoretical Criminology*, published in 1958, George B. Vold presented a group conflict theory that
was based instead on the conflict of interests. Vold's theory relied
on the sociology of conflict presented by Simmel.[5] Vold's work has

2. Thorsten Sellin, *Culture Conflict and Crime*, Social Science Research Council, New York,
1938, pp. 32–33.

3. Ibid., pp. 63, 104.

4. Ibid., p. 105.

5. Cf. *The Sociology of Georg Simmel*, translated by and with an Introduction by Kurt H.
Wolff, The Free Press, Glencoe Ill., 1950; also Simmel's *Conflict* (trans. by Kurt H. Wolff)
and *The Web of Group Affiliations* (trans. by Reinhard Bendix), The Free Press, Glencoe Ill.,
1955. Simmel's work is analyzed in Lewis A. Coser, *The Functions of Social Conflict*, The

been highly influential in the later development of conflict theory in criminology, where it now holds an important place. The following is a summary of his argument, presented to a considerable extent in his own words.

Group conflict theory is based on a view of human nature that holds that people are fundamentally group-involved beings whose lives are both a part of and a product of their group associations.[6] Groups are formed out of situations in which members have common interests and common needs that can best be furthered through collective action.[7] Thus the behavior of individuals is best understood in its group context as part of the general theories and conceptions of "collective behavior."[8]

New groups are continuously being formed as new interests arise, and existing groups weaken and disappear when they no longer have a purpose to serve.[9] Groups become effective action units through the direction and coordination of the activities of their members. For the members, the experience of participating in group activities and sharing troubles and satisfactions operate to make the individual a group-conscious person. Out of this experiential background group identification and group loyalty become psychological realities. Group loyalty and identification tend to be emotionally toned attachments not closely related to any rational understanding the individual may

---

Free Press, Glencoe, Ill., 1956. See also the series of articles under "Groups" in *International Encyclopedia of the Social Sciences*, vol. 6, Macmillan and the Free Press, New York, 1968, pp. 259–93. A review of Simmel's theory, along with a comparison to Durkheim's consensus theory, can be found in Bernard, op. cit., pp. 111–42. A review of the more recent conflict theory of Ralf Dahrendorf, together with a comparison with the consensus theory of Talcott Parsons, can be found on pp. 145–90 of the same work.

6. Cf. Simmel, *The Web of Group Affiliations;* also Kenneth E. Boulding, *Conflict and Defense: A General Theory*, Harper & Row, New York, 1962, pp. 105–22.

7. Cf. Simmel, *The Web of Group Affiliations*, pp. 128–30. See also Morton Deutsch, *The Resolution of Conflict*, Yale University Press, New Haven, 1973, "Group Formation," pp. 48–66; and Muzafer Sherif and Carolyn W. Sherif, "Group Formation," *International Encyclopedia of the Social Sciences*, vol. 6, pp. 276–83.

8. Cf. Robert E. Park and Ernest W. Burgess, *Introduction to Science of Sociology*, University of Chicago Press, Chicago, 1924, "Competition," pp. 504–10; "Conflict," pp. 475–79; "Collective Behavior," pp. 865–74. See Anthony Oberschall, *Social Conflict and Social Movements*, Prentice-Hall, Englewood Cliffs, N.J., 1973, pp. 1–29, for the history and development of theories of collective behavior as they relate to conflict theory; and James F. Short, Jr., "Collective Behavior, Crime, and Delinquency," in Daniel Glaser, *Handbook of Criminology*, Rand McNally, Chicago, 1974, pp. 403–49, for current uses of this concept in the explanation of crime.

9. Cf. Charles H. Cooley, *Social Organization*, Scribner, New York, 1924, "Primary Aspects of Organization," pp. 3–57. See also Coser, *The Functions of Social Conflict*, op. cit. pp. 104–10, for a discussion of the search for new group purposes to avoid dissolution of the group; and Boulding, op. cit., pp. 123–44, for a model of changes in group membership.

have of the place or significance of the group in the general scheme of things.[10]

Groups come into conflict with one another as the interests and purposes they serve tend to overlap, encroach on one another, and become competitive. Conflict between groups tends to develop and intensify the loyalty of group members to their respective groups.[11] This is clearly one of the most important elements in developing "group-mindedness" attitudes on the part of individual members. The individual is most loyal to the group for which he has had to fight the hardest and to which he has had to give the greatest measure of self for the common end of group achievement.[12]

Implicit in this social-psychological view of human nature is a *social process* view of society as a collection of groups held together in a dynamic equilibrium of opposing group interests and efforts.[13] The continuity of group interactions, the endless series of moves and countermoves, of checks and cross-checks, provides opportunity for a continuous possibility of shifting positions, of gaining or losing status, with the consequent need to maintain an alert defense of one's position.[14] The result is a more or less continuous struggle to maintain, or to improve, the place of one's own group in the interaction of groups. Conflict is therefore one of the principal and essential social processes in the continuous and ongoing functioning of society.[15]

These social interaction processes grind their way through varying kinds of uneasy adjustment to a more or less stable equilibrium of

10. Muzafer Sherif, *An Outline of Social Psychology*, Harper, New York, 1948, Ch. 13, "Adolescent Attitudes and Identification," pp. 314–38. See also John H. Schaar, "Loyalty," *International Encyclopedia*, vol. 9, pp. 484–87.

11. Simmel, *Conflict*, op. cit., pp. 87–107; Coser, *The Functions of Social Conflict*, pp. 87–110. See also Anatol Rapoport, *Conflict in Man-Made Environment*, Penguin, Baltimore, 1974, pp. 200–201; and Charles H. Cooley, op. cit., "Hostile Feelings between Classes," pp. 301–9.

12. Muzafer Sherif, *An Outline*, Ch. 7, "The Formation of Group Standards or Norms," pp. 156–82. See also L. Festinger, "The Psychological Effects of Insufficient Reward," *American Psychologist* 16: 1–11 (1961), in which it is argued that "rats and people come to love the things for which they have suffered."

13. Cf. Bertram M. Gross, "Political Process," *International Encyclopedia*, vol. 12, pp. 265–73.

14. R. E. Park and E. W. Burgess, op. cit., p. 865; also Muzafer Sherif, *An Outline*, Ch. 5, "Properties of Group Situations," pp. 98–121. See Kurt Lang and Gladys Engel Lang, "Collective Behavior," *International Encyclopedia*, vol. 2, pp. 556–65, for a discussion of the current uses of this term.

15. For a discussion of the relation between the principal social processes and the resulting social order, see Park and Burgess, op. cit., pp. 506–10. The importance of conflict in the maintenance of the social order is discussed in Simmel, *Conflict*, pp. 16–20, and in Coser, op. cit., pp. 33–85. See also Lewis Coser, "Social Conflict and the Theory of Social Change," *British Journal of Sociology* 8: 197–207 (Sept. 1957), reprinted in Coser, *Continuities in the Study of Social Conflict*, The Free Press, New York, 1967, pp. 37–51.

balanced forces. The resulting condition of relative stability is what is usually called social order or social organization. The adjustment, one to another, of the many groups of varying strengths and of different interests is the essence of society as a functioning reality. The normal principle of social organization, then, is the relatively stable balance of opposing group forces in which each group attempts to obtain and maintain the best possible position with respect to its own interests and purposes.

The conflict between groups seeking their own interests is especially visible in legislative politics, which is largely a matter of finding practical compromises between antagonistic groups in the community.[16] Conflicts between opposing group interests exist in the community before there is any legislative action. As one group lines up against another, both may seek the assistance of the organized state to help them defend their rights and protect their interests. This general situation of group conflict gives rise to the familiar cry "There ought to be a law!" which is essentially the demand by one of the conflicting groups that the power of the organized state be used to support them in their conflict with the other group. Naturally, the other group, against whom the proposed law is directed, opposes its passage. Whichever group interest can marshal the greatest number of votes will determine whether or not there will be a new law to hamper and curb the interests of the opposing group.[17]

Once the new law has been passed, those who opposed the law in the legislature are understandably not in sympathy with its provisions and do not take kindly to efforts at law enforcement. They are more likely to violate the law, since it defends interests and purposes that are in conflict with their own. Those who promoted the law, in contrast, are more likely to obey it and more likely to demand that the police enforce it against violators, since the law defends interests and purposes they hold dear. In other words, those who produce legislative majorities win control of the police power of the state and decide the policies that determine who is likely to be

16. Harold D. Lasswell, *Politics: Who Gets What, When, How*, McGraw-Hill, New York, 1936; Harold D. Lasswell and Abraham Kaplan, *Power and Society*, Yale University Press, New Haven, 1950; V. O. Key, Jr., *Politics, Parties, and Pressure Groups*, Crowell, New York, 1959; Earl Latham, *The Group Basis of Politics*, Cornell University Press, Ithaca, N.Y., 1952; David B. Truman, *The Governmental Process*, Knopf, New York, 1953; David Easton, *The Political System*, Knopf, New York, 1971.

17. Richard Quinney, *The Social Reality of Crime*, Little, Brown, Boston, 1970, pp. 29–97; William J. Chambliss and Robert B. Seidman, *Law, Order, and Power*, Addison-Wesley, Reading, Mass., 1971, pp. 56–74; Clayton A. Hartjen, *Crime and Criminalization*, Praeger, New York, 1974, pp. 16–39.

involved in the violation of laws.[18] Thus the whole process of law-making, lawbreaking, and law enforcement directly reflects deep-seated and fundamental conflicts between group interests and the more general struggles among groups for control of the police power of the state. To that extent, criminal behavior is the behavior of *minority power groups*, in that these groups do not have sufficient power to promote and defend their interests and purposes in the legislative process.

A great deal of criminal behavior is carried out by groups rather than by individuals acting alone. From the point of view of group conflict theory, this may be interpreted as the banding together for protection and strength of those who are in some way at odds with organized society and with the police forces maintained by that society. For example, a delinquent boys' gang is almost always a "minority power group" in the sense that they are out of sympathy with and in more or less direct opposition to the rules and regulations of the dominant majority, that is, the established world of adult values and power.[19] Police ordinarily represent the power and values of the adult world, whereas the gang seeks to get benefits and advantages not permitted under the adult code. The gang cannot achieve its objectives through regular channels, making use of, and relying for protection on, the police powers of the state. It therefore resorts to direct action with the typical social-psychological reaction of a conflict group, for example, loyalty to group and leaders, subordination of individual wishes to group ends, adherence to an approved code of values and behavior.[20]

Criminals of all kinds who have significant group identifications react in very much the same manner. Those who reject the majority view and refuse to follow required behavior patterns are generally de-

18. E. H. Sutherland, "Crime and the Conflict Process," *Journal of Juvenile Research* 13: 38–48 (1929); Quinney, op. cit., pp. 101–204; Chambliss and Seidman, op. cit., pp. 261–472; Hartjen, op. cit., pp. 74–157. See also Sutherland's "sociological definition of crime" in Edwin H. Sutherland and Donald R. Cressey, *Criminology*, 10th ed., Lippincott, Philadelphia, 1978, p. 12: "crime can be seen to involve four elements: (1) a value which is appreciated by a group or a part of a group which is politically powerful; (2) isolation of or normative conflict in another part of this group so that its members do not appreciate the value or appreciate it less highly and consequently tend to endanger it; (3) political declaration that behavior endangering the value is henceforth to be a crime; and (4) pugnacious resort to coercion decently applied by those who appreciate the value to those who disregard the value. When a crime is committed, all these relationships are involved. Crime *is* the set of relationships when viewed from the points of view of a social system rather than of the individual."

19. See Short, op. cit., pp. 413–27.

20. Cf. William F. Whyte, *Street Corner Society*, University of Chicago Press, Chicago, 1943; also Solomon Kobrin, "The Conflict of Values in Delinquency Areas," *American Sociological Review*, 16: 653–62 (Oct. 1951); and Frederick Thrasher, *The Gang*, 2nd ed. rev., University of Chicago Press, Chicago, 1936.

fined and treated as criminals. Members of such minority power groups do not accept the definition of themselves, or of their behavior, as criminal. Looking to their own group of like-thinking associates, they readily persuade themselves that their course of action is acceptable and, from their point of view, entirely honorable. The basic problem, therefore, is the conflict of group interests and the struggle for the control of power that is always present in the political organization of any society.

A great deal of criminal behavior results from the conflict among groups struggling over control of power in the political organization of the state. For example, numerous crimes result from the direct political reform type of protest movement, such as the civil rights and antiwar movements of the 1960s and 1970s.[21] The ultimate form of political struggle is rebellion and revolution. A successful revolution makes criminals out of the government officials previously in power, and an unsuccessful revolution makes its leaders into traitors subject to immediate execution. In both cases the criminals are a minority power group in that they lost the struggle for power.

Such political conflicts often involve a great deal of what would otherwise be called ordinary criminal behavior. Revolutions are almost always accompanied by murder, sabotage, seizure of private property, and many other offenses against the criminal code.[22] Many an election in many a democratic country has been accompanied by a similar collision of opposing groups, with resulting personal violence, bribery, perjury, and even burglary and theft, all for the sake of gaining or keeping control of political power.[23] On the surface these offenses seem to be ordinary crimes, but on closer examination they are revealed as the acts of good soldiers fighting for a cause and against the threat of enemy encroachment.[24] The age-old psychological principle of group conflict comes to the fore—the end (i.e., the defense of group position) justifies the means.

21. Jerome Skolnick, *The Politics of Protest*, U. S. Government Printing Office, Washington, D.C., 1969, especially Chapter 7; James F. Short and Marvin E. Wolfgang, eds., *Collective Violence*, Aldine-Atherton, Chicago, 1972.

22. Cf. Carl Leiden and Karl M. Schmitt, eds., *The Politics of Violence*, Prentice-Hall, Englewood Cliffs, N.J., 1968; Robert Moss, *The War for the Cities*, Coward, McCann and Geoghegan, New York, 1972; or Richard Clutterbuck, *Protest and the Urban Guerrilla*, Abelard-Schuman, New York, 1974.

23. Cf. Lincoln Steffens, *The Shame of the Cities*, McClure, Phillips, New York, 1904; Ovid Demaris, *Captive City*, Lyle Stuart, New York, 1969; or any of the many books dealing with the criminal events associated with the U.S. presidential election of 1972, such as Theodore H. White, *Breach of Faith*, Atheneum, New York, 1975, or Anthony Lukas, *Nightmare*, Viking, New York, 1976.

24. Cf. G. Gordon Liddy, *Will*, Dell, New York, 1981.

Similar criminal behaviors are associated with many situations of group conflict, where one group seeks political or economic changes and the other group resists such changes. There are violent confrontations between labor and management in strikes and lockouts, and between labor unions with jurisdictional disputes;[25] between white and black community members over school busing and neighborhood integration;[26] and between the police and minority members of the community.[27] In these confrontations both sides may resort to force, resulting in the killing or injuring of individuals and the destruction of private and public property. The participants on either side of the dispute condone whatever criminal behavior is deemed necessary for the maintenance of their side of the struggle. The end is said to justify the means, and the participants in the struggle do their duty as good soldiers, even if what has to be done is contrary to law and something that they would not do otherwise. These individuals may regret doing cruel and brutal things and may hope for an early peace settlement that favors their side in the conflict, but they have the support of the group and therefore feel no guilt over their criminal actions.

Group conflict theory points to one of the fundamental conditions of life in organized political society, and suggests that a considerable amount of crime is intimately related to group conflict situations. For these situations the criminal behavior of the individual is best viewed in the context of the course of action required for the group to maintain its position in the struggle with other groups. A sociology of conflict therefore is the basis for understanding and explaining this kind of criminal behavior. On the other hand, group conflict theory is strictly limited to those kinds of situations in which the individual criminal acts flow from the collision of groups whose members are loyally upholding the in-group position. Such a theory does not explain many kinds of impulsive and irrational criminal acts that are

---

25. Philip Taft and Philip Ross, "American Labor Violence: Its Causes, Character, and Outcome," in Hugh Davis Graham and Ted Robert Gurr, *The History of Violence in America,* Praeger, New York, 1969, pp. 281–395.

26. See, for example, the illustrated accounts of the Boston school busing riots in the October 21, 1974, issues of *Time, Newsweek,* and *U.S. News and World Report.*

27. Otto Kerner, *Report of the National Advisory Commission on Civil Disorders,* Bantam, New York, 1968. The use of police violence against community members is explained using group conflict theory in William A. Westley, *Violence and the Police,* MIT Press, Cambridge, Mass., 1970. An analysis of recent British riots comparable to that of the Kerner Commission is found in Philip Jenkins and Fred Hutchings, "New Patterns of Urban Riots," in Israel L. Barak-Glantz and Elmer H. Johnson, eds., *Comparative Criminology,* Sage, Beverly Hills, Cal., 1983, pp. 69–85.

quite unrelated to any battle between different interest groups in organized society.

## 3. QUINNEY'S THEORY OF THE SOCIAL REALITY OF CRIME

Many contemporary conflict criminologists have acknowledged their indebtedness to Vold's formulation. Among these is Richard Quinney, whose theory of "the social reality of crime" is expressed in the following six propositions[28]:

Proposition 1 (Definition of Crime): Crime is a definition of human conduct that is created by authorized agents in a politically organized society.

Proposition 2 (Formulation of Criminal Definitions): Criminal definitions describe behaviors that conflict with the interests of the segments of society that have the power to shape public policy.

Proposition 3 (Application of Criminal Definitions): Criminal definitions are applied by the segments of society that have the power to shape the enforcement and administration of criminal law.

Proposition 4 (Development of Behavior Patterns in Relation to Criminal Definitions): Behavior patterns are structured in segmentally organized society in relation to criminal definitions, and within this context persons engage in actions that have relative probabilities of being defined as criminal.

Proposition 5 (Construction of Criminal Conceptions): Conceptions of crime are constructed and diffused in the segments of society by various means of communication.

Proposition 6 (The Social Reality of Crime): The social reality of crime is constructed by the formulation and application of criminal definitions, the development of behavior patterns related to criminal definitions, and the construction of criminal conceptions.

Each of Quinney's propositions is derived from earlier work in criminology or sociology. The first proposition is based on the interactionist view that deviance is defined by the social reaction to it. Quinney argues that crime is a "definition" of behavior that is "created" by the authorities. Thus crime is not a matter of individual pathology, "but is a judgment made by some about the actions and characteristics of others."[29]

The second and third propositions are drawn from Vold's earlier

---

28. Richard Quinney, *The Social Reality of Crime*, Little, Brown, Boston, 1970, pp. 15–23.
29. Quinney, op. cit., p. 16.

conflict theory.[30] For example, the second proposition is quite comparable to Vold's statement that "whichever group interest can marshall the greatest number of votes will determine whether or not there is to be a new law to hamper and curb the interests of some opposition group,"[31] and the third proposition is comparable to the statement "Those who produce legislative majorities win control over the police power and dominate the policies that decide who is likely to be involved in violation of the law."[32] There is, however, a major difference between the two theories. Vold discussed conflict between organized interest groups, whereas Quinney discussed conflict between "segments" of society. Segments are said to share the same values, norms, and ideological orientations, but they may or may not be organized in defense of those commonalities.[33] Some segments, such as business and labor, have been organized into interest groups for many years, but other segments, such as women, poor people, and homosexuals, have organized themselves only recently. There are also segments of society that have only minimal organization, such as young and old people, and segments that have no organization at all, such as prisoners and the mentally ill.

Because of this difference, Quinney used conflict theory to explain all crime instead of merely some of it. Vold had specifically excluded "impulsive, irrational acts of a criminal nature that are quite unrelated to any battle between different interest groups in organized society."[34] He also implied that at least some "ordinary common-law offenses involving persons and property" are not related to any political struggle, and must be explained by other theories.[35] Quinney, on the other hand, would hold that even irrational and impulsive people represent a segment of society who have common values, norms, and ideological orientations, although this segment is not organized into any interest group.[36] Their behavior is defined as crim-

---

30. Quinney (ibid., p. 17, n. 42, and p. 18, n. 44) cites Vold for these two propositions, stating in the footnote: "I am obviously indebted to the conflict formulation of George B. Vold, *Theoretical Criminology.* . . ."

31. George B. Vold, *Theoretical Criminology*, Oxford University Press, New York, 1958, p. 208; this volume, p. 273.

32. Ibid., p. 209; this volume, pp. 273–74.

33. Quinney, op. cit., p. 38.

34. Vold, op. cit., p. 219; this volume, pp. 276–77.

35. Ibid., p. 214; this volume, p. 275.

36. For example, see Quinney's discussion of violent crime in *The Social Reality*, pp. 249–52. Austin Turk made a similar point about Vold's theory by stating that "this residual category [of impulsive, irrational acts] seems to be unnecessary if one avoids equating social conflict with quasi-military encounters between organized groups deliberately engaged in a strug-

inal by those who have more power and who are protecting their own interests. The absence of overt political struggle does not mean that there is no conflict between the segments. It indicates rather that the one segment has complete superiority of power over the other, to the point where the struggle takes the form of individual acts of resistance by the disorganized segment.

Quinney's fourth proposition relies on Sutherland's differential association theory. Different segments of society are said to have different behavior patterns and normative systems, each of which is learned in its own social and cultural setting. The probability that any individual will violate the criminal law depends, to a large extent, on how much power and influence his segment has in enacting and enforcing laws. Those with little or no power will find many of their normal behavior patterns criminalized, whereas those with great power will find few of their normal behavior patterns criminalized.

Quinney's two final propositions rely on contemporary sociology of knowledge, which holds that the world in which humans live is primarily subjective and socially constructed.[37] He argued that the term *crime* can be taken to refer to concrete happenings that individuals personally experience, or it can refer to conceptions of reality that are created and communicated to individuals through various forms of social interaction, including the media. Different conceptions of crime can be created and communicated as part of the political process of promoting a particular set of values and interests. For example, during the Viet Nam War, antiwar groups argued that the real criminals were those running the war. Consumer and ecology groups have argued that the real criminals are in big business. Community organizers in inner-city neighborhoods argue that the real criminals are the absentee landlords and the greedy store owners. But these conceptions of crime are generally disregarded by most people because their proponents do not have very much power. Conceptions of crime that are created and communicated by people in powerful segments of society, however, are widely accepted by other people in the society as their own view. This legitimizes the authority of power segments and allows them to carry out policies in the name of the common good that really promote their own interests. For example, Richard Nixon promoted a certain conception of

gle to assert their respective interests." Austin T. Turk, "Conflict and Criminality," *American Sociological Review*, 31: 342, n. 21 (June 1966).

37. See particularly Peter L. Berger and Thomas Luckmann, *The Social Construction of Reality*, Doubleday, Garden City, N.Y., 1966.

crime in his campaign for the presidency in 1968. When Nixon said that "we're going to have a new Attorney General of the United States of America" in order to restore law and order,[38] it was clear that he was talking about lower-class urban street crime, not the upper-class corporate and political crime that would drive him from office and send his new attorney general (John Mitchell) to prison.

Quinney concludes:[39]

Conceptions of crime . . . are constructed with intentions, not merely to satisfy the imagination. We end up with some realities rather than others for good reason—because someone has something to protect. That protection can be achieved by the perpetuation of a certain view of reality. Realities are, then, the most subtle and insidious of our forms of social control. . . . The reality of crime that is constructed for all of us by those in a position of power is the reality we tend to accept as our own. By doing so, we grant those in power the authority to carry out the actions that best promote their interests. This is the *politics of reality*. The social reality of crime in politically organized society is constructed as a political act.

### 4. TURK'S THEORY OF CRIMINALIZATION

Austin Turk also proposed a conflict analysis of how power groups achieve authority and legitimacy in society.[40] Although consensus theorists maintained that social order arose from the internalization of the norms embodied in the law, Turk argued that social order is based in a consensus-coercion balance maintained by the authorities. Authorities must prevent this balance from shifting to either "an excessively coercive, power relationship or an excessively consensual, egalitarian relationship."[41] To the extent that they are able to prevent this, people in the society will become conditioned to live with the social roles of authorities and subjects in such a way that no one will question these roles. It is this conditioning that underlies the social order in all societies[42]:

The stability of an authority relationship appears to depend far less upon subjects' conscious or unconscious belief in the rightness or legitimacy of the rank order than upon their having been conditioned to accept as a fact of life that authorities must be reckoned with as such. As long as people

---

38. Quoted in Quinney, op. cit., p. 312.
39. Ibid., p. 304.
40. Austin T. Turk, *Criminality and Legal Order*, Rand McNally, Chicago, 1969.
41. Ibid., p. 42.
42. Ibid., p. 44.

accept the inevitability of their social order, and operate within it with little or no questioning of why it should be at all, authority is secure.

Within this view of society, Turk presented a "theory of criminalization" that specified "the conditions under which cultural and social differences between authorities and subjects will probably result in conflict, the conditions under which criminalization will probably occur in the course of conflict, and the conditions under which the degree of deprivation associated with becoming a criminal will probably be greater or lesser."[43] Turk first distinguished between cultural norms and social norms. Cultural norms are associated with verbal formulations of values, and social norms with actual behavior patterns.[44] From the point of view of the authorities, cultural norms are associated with the law as it is written, and social norms with the law as it is enforced. Conflict will be most likely when there is "close agreement between the cultural norm announced by authorities and their actual behavior patterns, and similarly high congruence between the way in which subjects who possess the attribute or commit the act evaluate it and their social norms."[45] In this case, "neither side is likely to give in without a contest, as in each case they not only 'talk that way' but come close to acting in accord with the way they talk."[46] In this formulation there is the presupposition that no norm will be announced or enforced unless there is a cultural or social difference between authorities and subjects to begin with. The probability of conflict will be greatest when the subjects have a full-blown language and philosophy with which to defend their behaviors.[47]

The likelihood of conflict is also affected by the degree of organization and the level of sophistication of both authorities and subjects.[48] Authorities are presumed to be organized, since organization is a prerequisite for achieving and retaining power. Subjects may or may not be organized. Conflict will be more likely when subjects are organized, since "an individual who has group support for his behavior is going to be more stubborn in the face of efforts to make him change than is someone who has only himself as an ally." The term *sophistication* is used by Turk to mean "knowledge of patterns in the

43. Ibid., p. 53.
44. Ibid., pp. 36–38.
45. Ibid., p. 55.
46. Ibid., pp. 55–56.
47. Ibid., p. 57.
48. Ibid., pp. 58–61.

behavior of others which is used in attempts to manipulate them."
Conflict is more likely when either subjects or authorities are less
sophisticated, since the more sophisticated subjects will be able to
achieve their goals without precipitating a conflict with the superior
powers of the state, and the less sophisticated authorities will have
to rely more strongly on overt coercion to achieve their goals rather
than more subtle, alternative tactics.

Given these conditions that affect the likelihood of conflict between authorities and subjects, Turk goes on to discuss the conditions under which it will be more likely that this conflict will result
in the criminalization of the subjects. The primary factor, Turk argues, will be the meaning the prohibited act or attribute has for the
first-line enforcers (i.e., the police), and the extent to which the
higher-level enforcers (i.e., the prosecutors and judges) agree with
the evaluation of the police.[49] If all levels of enforcers find the prohibited act or attribute very offensive, then it is likely that there will
be high arrest rates, high conviction rates, and severe sentences. If,
due to class and status differences between police and the higher-
level enforcers, police find the behavior offensive but the higher-level
enforcers do not, there will likely be more severe deprivation associated with arrests, but low conviction rates and less severe sentences. If police find the behavior inoffensive but higher-level enforcers find it offensive, then there will be low arrest rates but high
conviction rates and severe sentences.

The second factor affecting criminalization will be the relative power
of the enforcers and resisters.[50] In general, criminalization will be
greatest when the enforcers have great power and the resisters are
virtually powerless. In situations in which the power of the resisters
and the power of the enforcers is approximately equal, the criminalization process is tempered by the potential costs involved. Here
the enforcers become cautious, which is likely to keep the criminality rate low. If the resisters achieve greater power than the enforcers, then the law will usually be changed.

The third factor affecting criminalization rates is what Turk calls
the "realism of the conflict moves"; here the "degree of realism" is
defined as[51]

its consequences for increasing or decreasing one's chances of success. In
the case of the enforcers this means the maintenance of an authority rela-

49. Ibid., pp. 65–67.
50. Ibid., pp. 67–70.
51. Ibid., p. 70.

tionship necessitating relatively little investment of resources in enforcement, and in the case of resisters means forcing norm enforcers either to retract the announced norm, to stop trying to enforce it, or at least to compromise in some fashion (e.g., by making only token gestures at enforcement).

He states that unrealistic conflict moves by either party will tend to increase criminalization, which is a measure of the overt conflict between the two groups.

## 5. CHAMBLISS AND SEIDMAN'S ANALYSIS
## OF THE CRIMINAL JUSTICE SYSTEM

In recent years a number of criminologists have analyzed the functioning of the criminal justice system from the perspective of conflict theory.[52] Perhaps the most thorough analysis is Chambliss and Seidman's *Law, Order, and Power*.[53] These authors note that the consensus perspective and the conflict perspective provide radically different versions of how the criminal justice system actually functions. Therefore they examined the day-to-day functioning of that system in order to determine which (if either) of the two models could be considered correct. Specifically, they sought to discover whether the power of the state (as embodied in the criminal justice system) is "a value-neutral framework within which conflict can be peacefully resolved," as described by consensus theory, or whether, as conflict theory would have it, "the power of the State is itself the principal prize in the perpetual conflict that is society."[54]

The criminal justice process begins with the legislative activity of lawmaking. Consensus theory would describe this process as "a deliberative assembly of one nation, with one interest, that of the whole, where, not local purposes, nor local prejudices, ought to guide, but the general good, resulting from the general reason of the whole."[55]

52. See, for example, Stuart A. Scheingold, *The Politics of Law and Order: Street Crime and Public Policy*, Longman, New York, 1984; Stuart L. Hills, *Crime, Power, and Morality: The Criminal Law Process in the United States*, Chandler, New York, 1971; Richard Quinney, *Critique of Legal Order*, Little, Brown, Boston, 1973; Erik Olin Wright, *The Politics of Punishment*, Harper & Row, New York, 1973; Clayton A. Hartjen, *Crime and Criminalization*, Praeger, New York, 1974; Barry Krisberg, *Crime and Privilege*, Prentice-Hall, Englewood Cliffs, N.J., 1975; and Harold E. Pepinsky, *Crime and Conflict*, Academic Press, New York, 1976.

53. William J. Chambliss and Robert B. Seidman, *Law, Order, and Power*, Addison-Wesley, Reading,, Mass., 1971.

54. Ibid., p. 4.

55. Edmund Burke, *Works*, H. J. Bohn, London, 1893, p. 447; quoted in Chambliss and Seidman, op. cit., p. 63.

The authors argue, however, that "every detailed study of the emergence of legal norms has consistently shown the immense importance of interest-group activity, *not 'the public interest,'* as the critical variable in determining the content of legislation."[56] In addition, when the law expresses moral values rather than economic interests, they will be the values of some groups rather than others. Chambliss and Seidman maintain that "the higher a group's political and economic position, the greater is the probability that its views will be reflected in the laws."[57]

Rule making in the criminal justice system also occurs in the appellate courts, where decisions establishing precedents have the effect of creating law. These decisions concern "trouble cases" where no law clearly applies to the case or where more than one law can be seen to apply. Appellate courts are examined closely because it is said that they "are the institution *par excellence* for which society most carefully cherishes the idea of value-neutrality."[58]

These rule-making decisions have always been justified in written opinions by referring to factors beyond the personal values of the judge. Originally judges referred to "natural law" to support their decisions, but it later became apparent that the natural law described by the judges really embodied their personal values.[59] Later justifications have usually been phrased in terms of preexisting laws and the principles embodied in those laws.[60] Dissenting opinions, however, can just as well be justified on legalistic grounds as can majority opinions, indicating that the decision is actually being based on other factors. There is now a move to justify these decisions on the basis of what is best for society,[61] but judgments about what is "best" depend on a set of values. Roscoe Pound, the originator of this school of thought, attempted to state the common values that would underlie these judicial decisions, but his formulation did not meet with widespread acceptance and has been criticized as reflecting primarily his own personal values.[62] Therefore the authors conclude that, in the last analysis, judges must rely on their personal values when they create rules in deciding "trouble cases."[63]

56. Chambliss and Seidman, op. cit., p. 73.
57. Ibid., pp. 473–74.
58. Ibid., p. 75.
59. Ibid., pp. 125–28.
60. Ibid., pp. 128–31.
61. Ibid., pp. 131–45.
62. Ibid., pp. 141–42.
63. Ibid., p. 151.

Chambliss and Seidman give a number of reasons why the values of appellate judges will be primarily oriented to the wealthy rather than the poor.[64] Appellate judges are largely from the more privileged segments of society. They are usually lawyers who have been trained in law schools by the "casebook" method. This method confines the issues studied to those raised in earlier litigation, which are predominantly issues related to the wealthy. As lawyers, future judges tend to focus on cases involving the wealthy, since these are the clients who are able to pay high legal fees. The successful lawyer who becomes a trial judge will have achieved a socially prominent position and can be expected to socialize with the more privileged classes; he thus becomes more attuned to their needs. Promotion of a trial judge to the appellate level is inevitably tied in one way or another to the political process, so that those trial judges who do not deal appropriately with the politically powerful will often not be promoted.

Thus there are many subtle pressures encouraging judges to consider, carefully and thoroughly, issues related to persons of power and wealth. But there are also organizational pressures to restrict the total amount of litigation before the court to prevent overloading the docket. These pressures, together with the fact that appeals to higher court depend in part of the ability of the defendant to pay for the cost of the litigation, have the result that the majority of case law concerns issues relating only to the wealthy and powerful.

The examination of the functioning of law enforcement agencies focuses on the bureaucratic nature of those organizations and their connections to the political structure. The authors summarize their theory in the following points:[65]

1. The agencies of law-enforcement are bureaucratic organizations.

2. An organization and its members tend to substitute for the official goals and norms of the organization ongoing policies and activities which will maximize rewards and minimize the strains on the organization.

3. This goal-substitution is made possible by:

a) the absence of motivation on the part of the role-occupants to resist pressures towards goal-substitution;

b) the pervasiveness of discretionary choice permitted by the substantive criminal law, and the norms defining the roles of the members of the enforcement agencies; and

64. Ibid., pp. 95–115.
65. Ibid., p. 269.

c) the absence of effective sanctions for the norms defining the roles in those agencies.

4. Law enforcement agencies depend for resource allocation on political organizations.

5. It will maximize rewards and minimize strains for the organization to process those who are politically weak and powerless, and to refrain from processing those who are politically powerful.

6. Therefore it may be expected that the law-enforcement agencies will process a disproportionately high number of the politically weak and powerless, while ignoring the violations of those with power.

Chambliss and Seidman conclude that both in structure and in function the law operates in the interests of existing power groups. The public interest is represented only to the extent that it coincides with the interests of those power groups.[66]

## 6. A UNIFIED CONFLICT THEORY OF CRIME

The following conflict theory is derived principally from the theories of Vold, Quinney, and Chambliss and Seidman presented in this chapter.[67] It also uses the language of social learning theory, as developed by Akers and presented in Chapter 12.[68]

I. Schedules of Reinforcement in Complex Societies

1. The conditions of one's life determine the schedules of reinforcement one experiences. These schedules of reinforcement include both evaluative definitions of behaviors (values) and the past and present rewards and punishments attached to behaviors, either directly or vicariously experienced (interests).

2. Complex societies are composed of groups with widely different life conditions.

3. Therefore complex societies are composed of groups with widely different schedules of reinforcement, including disparate and conflicting sets of values and interests.

II. Behavior Patterns of Individuals

4. Behavior is acquired and persists to the extent that it is differentially reinforced over alternative behavior and is evaluated as desirable or jus-

66. Ibid., p. 503.

67. An earlier version can be found in Thomas J. Bernard, "The Distinction Between Conflict and Radical Criminology," *Journal of Criminal Law and Criminology* 72 (1): 362–79 (Spring 1981).

68. Ronald L. Akers, *Deviant Behavior: A Social Learning Approach*, 2nd ed., Wadsworth, Belmont, Cal., 1977.

tified. Thus individuals generally behave in ways that are consistent with their values and interests.

5. Because the conditions of one's life, and therefore one's values and interests, tend to remain relatively stable over time, groups tend to develop relatively stable behavior patterns that differ in varying degrees from the behavior patterns of other groups.

III. The Enactment of Criminal Laws

6. The enactment of criminal laws is part of the general legislative process of conflict and compromise in which different groups attempt to promote and defend their own values and interests.

7. Individual laws usually represent a combination of the values and interests of many groups, rather than the specific values and interests of any one particular group. Nevertheless, the greater a group's political and economic power, the more the criminal law in general tends to represent the values and interests of that group.

8. Therefore, in general, the greater a group's political and economic power, the less likely it is that the behavior patterns characteristic of that group (behaviors consistent with their values and interests) will violate the criminal law, and vice versa.

IV. The Enforcement of Criminal Laws

9. In general, the greater the political and economic power of individuals, the more difficult it is for official law enforcement agencies to process them when their behavior violates the criminal law. There are many reasons for this. For example, the types of violations may be more subtle and complex, or the individuals may have greater resources to conceal the violation, legally defend themselves against official action, or exert influence extralegally on the law enforcement processes.

10. As bureaucracies, law enforcement agencies tend to process the easier, rather than the more difficult, cases.

11. Therefore, in general, law enforcement agencies tend to process individuals with less, rather than more, political and economic power.

V. The Distribution of Official Crime Rates

12. Because of the processes of criminal law enactment and enforcement described above, the official crime rates of groups tend to be inversely proportional to their political and economic power, independent of any other factors that might also influence the distribution of official crime rates (e.g., social, psychological, or biological factors affecting the behavior of offenders or the behavior of criminal justice agents).

This is a theory of the behavior of criminal law, as described in the first chapter of this book, since it explains the differences in official crime rates in terms of differences in the enactment and the enforcement of criminal laws. It includes and is based on a theory of criminal behavior, a social learning theory that argues that criminal behavior is normally learned behavior responding to different reinforcement schedules operating in different social structural locations. Thus the theory presents a theoretical chain that begins with general social structural characteristics, moves through the processes by which individuals in similar social structural locations learn similar patterns of behavior, and concludes by relating those patterns of behavior to the processes of enacting and enforcing criminal laws in order to explain the distribution of official crime rates.[69] Because it combines and interrelates a theory of criminal behavior with a theory of the behavior of criminal law, the above theory is described as a "unified theory of crime."

There are several differences between this theory and Vold's original group conflict theory, each reflecting developments that have occurred in the field of criminology since he wrote. The first of those differences concerns the nature of the normal learning process. Vold based his conflict theory on the view that criminal behavior was "normal learned behavior," which he identified with Sutherland's theory of differential association.[70] As discussed in Chapter 12, Sutherland's theory has been updated by several criminologists to include modern learning principles. These more recent theories maintain Sutherland's basic view that criminal behavior is normally learned behavior but they provide a more complex view of what normal learning entails. Since Vold's use of Sutherland's theory did not depend on the specific description of the normal learning process, the more recent theories of normal learning can be incorporated into Vold's conflict theory without changing its basic argument. The above theory incorporates into the context of Vold's argument the principles of operant conditioning and social learning, as developed by Ronald Akers.[71]

A second difference concerns the definition of the term *group*. Vold considered only conflict between organized interest groups and excluded "many kinds of impulsive, irrational acts of a criminal nature" from his theory because he believed that those behaviors required explanations other than normal learning. Akers, however, explains

69. Akers, ibid., pp. 61–68, makes a similar argument about structural sources of behavior and social processes of learning those behaviors. The present argument extends the theoretical chain to the distribution of official crime rates.

70. Cf. Vold, *Theoretical Criminology*, 1st ed., pp. 201–2.

71. Akers, op. cit., pp. 39–60.

the same behaviors with social learning theory.[72] Thus, these behaviors can be encompassed within Vold's theory along with the more modern learning theory. That requires a broader definition of the term *group* that Vold used. Such a broader definition is used by Quinney, who based his conflict theory on the conflict between segments of society.[73] *Segments* were defined as "broad statistical aggregates containing persons of similar age, sex, class, status, occupation, race, ethnicity, religion, or the like." Quinney's description is comparable to what are called "quasi-groups" in Dahrendorf's theory of class conflict[74] and to what is translated as "groups" in Simmel's conflict theory.[75] This broader definition includes, in addition to organized interest groups, unorganized aggregates of individuals in structurally similar situations.

This broader definition of the term *group* is adopted here both because it is more consistent with the sociological conflict tradition than is Vold's narrower definition and because most high-crime-rate "groups" are unorganized aggregates of individuals in structurally similar situations—for example, young urban poor black males. These groups are characterized by similar values and interests generated by their common social structural location, although they are not organized to promote and defend those values and interests in the larger society.

Vold's use of the narrower definition of *group* was consistent with Sutherland's theory, where the origin of behaviors is said to lie in commonly held or shared ideas, loosely described as "culture." The actions of an isolated individual cannot be incorporated within Sutherland's theory since culture is necessarily a group phenomenon. Akers, however, views culture primarily as a product of the similar reinforcements generated in common social structural locations. The focus on structure as the ultimate source of behaviors is consistent with Vold's emphasis on conflicts of interests as the source of conflicting behaviors. Vold himself did not link conflicting interests to their origins in social structure, but such a link is consistent with his

---

72. Ibid., pp. 259–65. Some "impulsive, irrational" actions can also be incorporated in Vold's original group conflict theory, despite his statement. See Short, op. cit., p. 412, who, in discussing juvenile gang behavior, states: "What appears to be 'impulsive' behavior—or pathological—may in fact be collectively cultivated, part of a group's complex adjustment to a hostile and demanding environment."

73. Quinney, op. cit., p. 38.

74. Ralf Dahrendorf, *Class and Conflict in Industrial Society*, Stanford University Press, Stanford, Cal., 1959, pp. 167–68.

75. See Translator's Note by Rinehard Bendix in Simmel, *Conflict and the Web of Group Affiliations*, p. 127, n. 1.

basic argument and is incorporated into the above theory. It is this link that makes the broader definition of the term *group* possible, since an unorganized aggregate of isolated individuals in structurally similar situations will tend to act alike even if they do not share intimate personal interactions. These similar actions are referred to as "behavior patterns," a term that is taken from Quinney.[76]

The third difference between the above theory and Vold's original group conflict theory lies in the role the criminal law enforcement process is said to play. Vold described the enforcement of laws merely as an extension of their enactment; he did not describe law enforcement as a separate process that could itself influence the distribution of official crime rates. In effect, Vold's theory skipped section IV of the above theory entirely, moving directly from differences in the enactment of criminal laws to differences in official crime rates. Vold's focus on the criminal law enactment process is consistent with his narrow definition of *group*, since only organized interest groups enter into the criminal law enactment process. The above description of the criminal law enforcement processes, and especially the emphasis on its bureaucratic nature, is derived from the work of Chambliss and Seidman.[77]

A final difference is terminological rather than substantive. Vold argued that conflict groups were formed on the basis of "common interests," although he also wrote of "common purposes" and "common needs." Vold's terminology is taken from Simmel, who wrote about "interests in a common purpose."[78] Neither Simmel's nor Vold's use of the term *interests* should be construed narrowly to mean only economic interests, and both are broad enough to incorporate what are normally considered values. Thus, the addition of the term *values* clarifies rather than extends Vold's original argument.

7. CONFLICT EXPLANATIONS OF THE BEHAVIOR
OF CRIMINAL LAW

The unified conflict theory presented above is primarily a theory of the behavior of criminal law; it explains the distribution of official crime rates in terms of differences in the enactment and enforcement of criminal laws. Specifically, it asserts that the behaviors typical of relatively powerless people are more likely to be officially de-

76. Quinney, op. cit., pp. 207–74.
77. Chambliss and Seidman, op. cit., p. 269.
78. Simmel, *Conflict and the Web of Group Affiliations*.

fined as crimes by the criminal law (section III) and that relatively powerless people are more likely to be officially processed as criminals by the criminal justice system (section IV). These two assertions can be described as the "differential enactment" and "differential enforcement" of criminal laws.

The evidence for the differential enforcement of criminal laws is contradictory. Some studies have concluded that the primary factor considered in the decision to process people in the criminal justice system is the seriousness of the criminal behavior.[79] Other studies argue that there are small differences in processing at each stage of the system, and that those differences accumulate so that their overall effect is quite large.[80] Even those who reject the view that the system handles the poor and powerless differently admit that there is some truth to it. Nettler, for example, extensively reviews studies to show that the law enforcement system does not discriminate against poor and powerless people, but he also admits that wealthy and powerful people are necessarily handled more leniently by that system.[81]

The differential enforcement argument, as presented above, relies on a general argument about the problems of bureaucracies. These bureaucratic problems are difficult to overcome, even when law enforcement officials have the best of intentions. For example, James Q. Wilson documents the extensive difficulties that the FBI and the Drug Enforcement Administration had in attempting to redirect their enforcement efforts from essentially powerless low-level operatives to the much more powerful individuals who ran things.[82] Criminal justice agencies are not immune from the bureaucratic problems that affect virtually every other organization. Thus there is little doubt that differences in power have some effect on processing by the criminal justice system. The real question is how extensive that effect is, and how much it contributes to the distribution of official crime rates.

As mentioned above, the major alternative argument is that law enforcement processing is determined primarily by the "serious-

---

79. An extensive review of these studies is presented in Gwynn Nettler, *Responding to Crime,* Anderson, Cincinnati, 1982, Chapter 2.

80. R. L. McNeely and Carl E. Pope, "Race, Crime and Criminal Justice: An Overview," in McNeely and Pope, eds., *Race, Crime and Criminal Justice,* Sage, Beverly Hills, Cal., 1981, p. 20; Allen E. Liska and Mark Tausig, "Theoretical Interpretations of Social Class and Racial Differentials in Legal Decision-Making for Juveniles," *Sociological Quarterly* 20: 199 (Spring 1979).

81. Nettler, *Responding to Crime,* pp. 57–59.

82. James Q. Wilson, *The Investigators,* Basic, New York, 1978.

ness" of criminal behavior. But "seriousness" is defined by the content of criminal law, which raises the argument about differential enactment: whether the definition of "serious" crimes found in the criminal law is itself somehow related to the distribution of power in society. A number of studies have shown that there is a fairly widespread consensus, both within societies and between them, on what constitutes "serious" crime.[83] These studies have been interpreted as contradicting the differential enactment argument. But even within such widespread agreements, the differential enactment of criminal laws can affect official crime rates in three ways.

At the simplest level there seem to be at least some value conflicts within complex societies, even if those who hold the conflicting values are a relatively small portion of the population. If members of the conflicting groups achieved a sufficient degree of power, they could be expected to demand that the criminal law be changed so that their valued behaviors would be legal. Recent changes in the laws on homosexuality and marijuana use reflect just such a process. The sale and possession of heroin is generally described as an extremely serious offense in the consensus studies mentioned above, but if heroin dealers and users achieved considerable power in a society, they might very well legalize it in much the same manner that alcohol is legal today. The present law of homicide recognizes certain "excuses" such as self-defense and insanity. If the members of a "subculture of violence" achieved a significant degree of political power, they could be expected to demand that the laws of homicide be rewritten so that a broader range of "excuses" was legally accepted. Such changes in the content of criminal law would have the effect of redistributing official crime rates away from the newly powerful groups.

A second way that the content of criminal law affects the distribution of official crime rates occurs where there is agreement on what is valued, but the criminal law protects and defends a certain distribution of that valued commodity. These are conflicts of interest, not conflicts of values. For example, in a society in which property is valued, the criminal law protects and defends those who have property against those who do not. Those who do not have property may steal it, but they would not want laws against stealing changed, since they themselves would not want to be victims of theft. If those who have little or no property achieve a substantial degree of power in a

---

83. Thorsten Sellin and Marvin E. Wolfgang, *The Measurement of Delinquency*, John Wiley, New York, 1964; Graeme Newman, *Comparative Deviance*, Elsevier, New York, 1976.

society, they could be expected to accomplish through the law what they have been attempting to accomplish through crime, redistribute property from others to themselves. Once that redistribution had been carried out, then the set of people likely to steal would change, since the set of people without property would have changed. Thus the criminal law may protect the interests of the more powerful groups even if there are no conflicts of values between the powerful and powerless. Changes in the relative power of conflicting groups would then result in changes in the sets of people likely to break the law, but would not result in changes in the content of the criminal law itself.

A third way that differential enactment of laws affects the distribution of official crime rates is through the failure of the laws to define as criminal the socially harmful and victimizing behaviors of more powerful groups. From this point of view the criminal behaviors of less powerful people are indeed "socially harmful," and the public has a right to expect protection from those behaviors by agents of the criminal justice system. The problem is that by any objective measure the socially harmful and victimizing behavior of more powerful people vastly exceeds the socially harmful and victimizing behavior of less powerful people.[84] These actions are generally taken purely for the pursuit of personal gain and result in many more deaths and serious injuries and greater destruction of property than the acts that are defined as crimes in the criminal law.

From the point of view of conflict theory, these socially harmful behaviors are not defined as crimes because of the relative power of the groups committing them. A number of recent developments in criminal law reflect the increased ability of the general public to protect themselves against these types of predatory activities.[85] However, these changes can only occur very slowly, since they reflect deep-seated changes in the relative power of conflicting interest groups in society.

As with the differential enforcement argument, there is little doubt that the differential enactment of criminal laws has at least some effect on the distribution of official crime rates. It is inevitable that more powerful groups will be able to influence, at least to some extent, the definitions found in criminal laws so as to deflect attention away from their own behaviors to the behaviors of the less powerful.

84. See Jeffrey H. Reiman, *The Rich Get Richer and the Poor Get Prison,* 2nd ed., John Wiley, New York, 1983.

85. Daniel Glaser, *Crime in Our Changing Society,* Holt, Rinehart and Winston, New York, 1978, Chapter 1.

The real question is whether the processes of differential enactment and enforcement have a substantial impact on the distribution of official crime rates or whether they have a relatively small impact. That question is left open in the final point of the above unified conflict theory, which acknowledges that other social, psychological, and biological factors may also influence the distribution of official crime rates.

## 8. CONFLICT EXPLANATIONS OF CRIMINAL BEHAVIOR

The above conflict theory is primarily a theory of the behavior of criminal law, but it includes and is based on a theory of criminal behavior. Theories of criminal behavior and theories of the behavior of criminal law are two sides of the same coin and must be consistent with each other if they are to comprise a "unified" theory of crime.[86] In the present case, the conflict theory of the behavior of criminal law argues that behaviors typical of relatively powerless people are more likely to be officially defined and processed as criminal. If one turns that statement around, it suggests a theory of criminal behavior: relative powerlessness should explain the development of patterns of behaviors that are likely to be officially defined and processed as criminal. That is, relative powerlessness can be viewed as a cause of criminal behaviors.

That suggestion is consistent with a considerable amount of the theory and research associated with explanations of criminal behavior, as discussed in other chapters of this book. For example, crime does not appear to be systematically related to poverty but may be related to economic inequality. There is probably no better measure of relative powerlessness than the lack of material wealth in a society where other people have it. Shaw and McKay pointed to social disorganization in rapidly changing inner-city areas as the cause of crime. But both Shaw and McKay apparently later came to the conclusion that the ultimate cause of that disorganization was the powerlessness of the residents to protect their neighborhoods from invasion by business and industry. The inner-city neighborhoods with more powerful residents were not similarly invaded and did not suffer similar disorganization. The strain theories of Merton and of Clo-

---

86. See Donald Black, *The Behavior of Law*, Academic Press, New York, 1976, pp. 9–10, and Donald R. Cressey, "Fifty Years of Criminology," *Pacific Sociological Review* 22 (4): 457–80 (Oct. 1979). Cressey concludes his article with a comment about "a need for a theory which explains why criminals behave as they behave and, *at the same time*, explains why criminal law officials label the way they label and otherwise behave as they behave" (p. 467, emphasis in original).

ward and Ohlin suggest that crime and delinquency are associated with lack of legitimate opportunities, which is an obvious effect of relative powerlessness. Programs designed to alleviate this problem failed because more powerful groups turned the programs to serve their own interests rather than the interests of the less powerful groups. "Cultural" theories suggest that there are at least some normative differences among groups about rules for expected behavior in specific situations. But groups with criminal norms are necessarily low-power groups, or they would protect and defend their norms in the processes of the enactment and enforcement of criminal law.

Hirschi's control theory contains the variable of commitment, which "assumes that the organization of society is such that the interests of most persons would be endangered if they were to engage in criminal acts." But different societies are organized in defense of different sets of interests (e.g., the United States and the Soviet Union), so that different sets of people in those societies "lack commitment." In any particular society, those who "lack commitment" must also lack political and economic power, or they would use that power to influence the organization of society so that it would be in their interests to obey the law.

Social reaction theories have increasingly focused on the argument that those who define others as deviant are necessarily more powerful than the deviants themselves. That implies that relative powerlessness is a key variable in the explanation of deviance. Finally, Marxist theories argue that the criminal law enactment and law enforcement agencies ultimately serve the long-term economic interests of those who own the means of production. One consequence is that these agencies tend to officially criminalize the socially harmful behavior of powerless groups and to ignore socially harmful behavior of more powerful groups.

Each of these areas of theory and research can be interpreted as pointing to relative powerlessness as the ultimate structural condition underlying the development of patterns of behavior that are likely to be officially defined and processed as criminal. Thus, conflict criminology is consistent with a broad range of theory and research on the causes of criminal behaviors.

## 9. POLICY IMPLICATIONS

Conflict criminology implies that greater equality in the distribution of power among groups in society should result in greater equality in the distribution of official crime rates. Crime rates should be redistributed for two reasons. First, there should be a general reduction in the crime rates of groups that presently have high crime rates, as those groups use their newly acquired power to legally pursue and defend their values and interests. Second, there should also be a general increase in the crime rates of groups that presently have low crime rates, as those groups find their ability to pursue and defend their values and interests increasingly hindered by other groups.

Within the context of conflict theory, the specific process by which a redistribution of power can be effected is through the establishment of organized groups by which the presently unorganized aggregates of individuals would be able to pursue and defend their values and interests.[87] This implication bears a resemblence to the policy implication of control theory, since it entails bonding the previously isolated individual to a group that will interact with other groups according to mutually agreed upon rules. The difference is that control theory generally implies that the individual be bonded to "conventional" groups, whereas conflict criminology implies that the individual should be bonded to other individuals who have similar values and interests and who occupy similar social structural locations. To the extent that a particular individual is considered deviant rather than conventional, the group that best represents his or her values and interests will also be considered deviant rather than conventional. The view that the best solution to social conflict lies in the representation of diverse aggregates of individuals by an equally diverse number of organized groups under conditions of relative equality is the reason why conflict theory in general is most comfortable with pluralist democracy as a form of government.[88]

The organization of interest groups out of previously unorganized aggregates of individuals is a difficult process that is frequently subject to severe abuses. Especially at their beginnings, these groups are often taken over by the most aggressive members, who make unrealistic and ultimately unproductive demands on behalf of their members, while reaping many personal benefits for themselves. This pattern can be found, for example, in the history of a number of American labor unions, and it is for reasons such as these that many wardens oppose the formation of prisoner unions.[89] These types of

---

87. Dahrendorf, op. cit., pp. 225–27.

88. Bernard, "The Distinction Between Conflict and Radical Criminology"; Bernard, *The Consensus-Conflict Debate;* Dahrendorf, op. cit.; Coser, *The Functions of Social Conflict.*

89. J. E. Baker, "Inmate Self-Government," *Journal of Criminal Law, Criminology and Police Science* 55: 39–47 (1964). Sometimes wardens oppose inmate self-government because it genuinely represents the interests of the inmates and therefore challenges the interests of the prison administration. See G. T. Tyrner-Stastny and C. Stastny, "The Changing Political Culture of a Total Institution," *Prison Journal* 57: 43–55 (1977).

problems are especially severe when the groups of people being organized have been defined as deviant by their society. Sagarin argues that such groups generally either promote overconformity to conventional norms as a means of soliciting approval from society, or seek to change societal attitudes and instill pride in the deviant by "thumbing their noses" at society.[90] Nevertheless, Irwin argues that such groups should be allowed to form in prisons in order to reduce the level of violence associated with conflicts there,[91] and Murton argues that where such groups have been successfully organized the violence associated with prison conflicts has decreased markedly.[92] More equality has also been shown to reduce violence in youth institutions,[93] and "mediating structures" have been shown to reduce violence associated with youth crime in the community.[94]

## 10. CONCLUSION

Conflict criminology presents a theory of the behavior of criminal law. That theory argues that behaviors typical of relatively powerless people are more likely to be officially defined as criminal, and relatively powerless people themselves are more likely to be processed by criminal justice agencies. Conflict criminology also suggests a theory of criminal behavior, which argues that relative powerlessness is a key structural characteristic associated with the development of patterns of behavior that are likely to be officially defined and processed as criminal. These theories of criminal behavior and the behavior of criminal law are two sides of the same coin and together constitute a unified theory of crime.

Conflict criminology asserts that there is a general tendency for power and official crime rates to be related in a certain way. Specifically, the more power a group has the lower its official crime rates tend to be, while the less power a group has the higher its official crime rates tend to be. In the context of that assertion, it is interesting to consider Lord Acton's famous observation that power corrupts, and absolute power corrupts absolutely. Power may corrupt, but it does not lead to crime unless there is some greater power that,

90. Edward Sagarin, *Odd Man In*, Quadrangle, Chicago, 1969.

91. John Irwin, *Prisons in Turmoil*, Little, Brown, Boston, 1980.

92. Thomas O. Murton, *The Dilemma of Prison Reform*, Holt, Rinehart and Winston, New York, 1976.

93. Craig A. McEwan, *Designing Correctional Organizations for Youths*, Ballinger, Cambridge, Mass., 1978.

94. Robert L. Woodson, *A Summons to Life: Mediating Structures and the Prevention of Youth Crime*, Ballinger, Cambridge, Mass., 1981.

for whatever reason, defines that corruption as criminal. Otherwise, no matter how corrupt the action is, it either will not be defined as a crime in the criminal law, or the person will not be processed as a criminal through the criminal justice system. Absolute power may corrupt absolutely, but people with absolute power are never officially defined as criminals.[95]

### RECOMMENDED READINGS

Victoria Lynn Swigert and Ronald A. Farrell, *Murder, Inequality and The Law*, Heath, Lexington, Mass., 1976. A study of differential legal treatment of approximately 1,000 persons charged with homicide. A theory similar to Quinney's social reality theory is developed.

Stuart A. Scheingold, *The Politics of Law and Order: Street Crime and Public Policy*, Longman, New York, 1984. An analysis of criminal justice policies from a conflict perspective.

Austin Turk, *Political Criminality: The Defiance and Defense of Authority*, Sage, Beverly Hills, Cal., 1982. An extension of Turk's theory of criminalization, focusing on the political uses of police power.

Thorsten Sellin, *Culture Conflict and Crime*, Social Science Research Council, New York, 1938. Crime as the conflict of conduct norms of different cultures and subcultures.

Stuart Nagel, Erika Fairchild, and Anthony Champagne, *The Political Science of Criminal Justice*, Thomas, Springfield, Ill., 1983. A book of readings analyzing criminal justice policies in terms of "who gets what, how, and why."

Donald Black, *The Behavior of Law*, Academic Press, New York, 1976. A theory explaining the amount and style of governmental social control in terms of five general social variables.

Daniel Glaser, *Crime in Our Changing Society*, Holt, Rinehart and Winston, New York, 1978. A general criminology text that links a conflict theory of law with a theory of criminal behavior as normal learned behavior.

Thomas J. Bernard, *The Consensus-Conflict Debate: Form and Content in Social Theories*, Columbia University Press, New York, 1983. A history and analysis of the consensus-conflict debate, comparing seven pairs of theorists. The differences between the two types of theories are derived from assumptions about human nature and value judgments about existing societies.

---

95. See Thomas Hobbes, *Leviathan*, E. P. Dutton, New York, 1950, Chapter 18, p. 148.

# CHAPTER SIXTEEN

# Marxist Criminology

Some Marxists have argued that there can be no "Marxist" criminology, since Marxism is an economic theory of history and crime plays no role in the economic forces that Marx described as the basic causes of fundamental social change.[1] On the other hand, it is possible to view criminal behavior, crime policy, and criminology itself within the context of the historical processes that Marx described. Such a view is Marxist in that it is influenced by and dependent on the Marxist theory of history, whether or not it is considered a part of the theory itself. This chapter reviews a number of such views that have been presented by criminologists who have a basic allegiance to the broader Marxist view of history and social change.

In some ways Marxist criminology can be described as a more specific form of the general conflict argument presented in the last chapter.[2] Like conflict criminology, Marxist criminology contains both theories of criminal behavior and theories of the behavior of criminal law. But where conflict criminology describes power as the key

1. See Paul Q. Hirst, "Marx and Engels on Law, Crime, and Morality," in Ian Taylor, Paul Walton, and Jock Young, eds., *Critical Criminology*, Routledge & Kegan Paul, London, 1975, pp. 203–32. For a general discussion of whether it is legitimate to speak of a Marxist criminology, see Steven Spitzer, "Leftwing Criminology: An Infantile Disorder?" in James A. Inciardi, ed., *Radical Criminology*, Sage, Beverly Hills, Cal., 1980, pp. 169–90.

2. The relationship between conflict and radical criminology theories is a matter of some discussion and dispute. See Thomas J. Bernard, "The Distinction Between Conflict and Radical Criminology," *Journal of Criminal Law and Criminology* 72 (1): 362–79 (Spring 1981); Robert F. Bohm, Radical Criminology: An Explication," *Criminology* 19 (4): 565–89 (Feb. 1982); and David O. Friedrichs, "Radical Criminology in the United States," C. Ronald Huff, "Conflict Theory in Criminology," and Austin T. Turk, "Analyzing Official Deviance," all in Inciardi, ed., *Radical Criminology*, op. cit.

structural variable in the explanation of crime, Marxist criminology looks behind power, to political and economic systems, for the ultimate explanation. Crime is explained by the specific characteristics of the political and economic systems that exist during particular historical periods.

Marxist criminology theories are difficult to summarize for several reasons. First, they are based on an extremely complex theory of society and of social change. That complexity leads to many profound disagreements among different Marxist theorists. In addition, these theories are evolving rapidly at the present time, so individual theorists frequently change their own positions as their thinking develops. Consequently one can only summarize some of the major themes, but many other arguments must be left out. The chapter begins with a discussion of Marx's writings, and then presents the applications of Marxist theory to the topics of crime, crime policy, and criminology.

## 1. GENERAL OVERVIEW OF MARXIST THEORY

Karl Marx (1818–83) wrote in the immediate aftermath of the massive social changes brought about by the Industrial Revolution. In one lifespan (approximately 1760–1840), the world as it had been for a thousand years suddenly changed.[3] Marx attempted to explain why those profound changes had occurred when they did, and to give some sense of what was coming next.[4] Marx's theory linked economic development to social, political, and historical change, and was not in itself a theory of individual or group behavior.

The principal conflict that Marx presented in his theory, and on which the theory is based, was the conflict between the material forces of production and the social relations of production.[5] The term *material forces of production* generally refers to a society's capacity to produce material goods. This includes technological equipment and the knowledge, skill, and organization to use that equipment. The term *social relations of production* refers to relationships between people. These include property relationships, which determine how

3. Michel Foucault, *Discipline and Punish*, Pantheon, New York, 1977.

4. This account of Marx's theory is taken from Thomas J. Bernard, *The Consensus-Conflict Debate: Form and Content in Social Theories*, Columbia, New York, 1983, pp. 95–98. Other summaries of Marx's work can be found in David Greenberg, *Crime and Capitalism*, Mayfield, Palo Alto, Cal., 1980, pp. 13–17; and Richard Quinney, *Class, State and Crime*, 2nd ed., Longman, New York, 1980, pp. 41–51.

5. A summary of this argument is found in Karl Marx, *Critique of Political Economy* (1859), English translation, International Library, New York, 1904, pp. 11–13.

the goods produced by the material forces of production are distributed—that is, who gets what.

The development of the material forces of production is relatively continuous throughout history, since it consists in the development of technology, skills, etc. The social relations of production, however, tend to freeze into particular patterns for long periods of time. When first established, the social relations enhance the development of the material forces of production, but as time goes by they become increasingly inconsistent with them and begin to impede their further development. At some point the social relations change abruptly and violently, and new social relations are established that once again enhance the development of the material forces of production.

Marx used this general model to explain the profound changes that had just occurred in European societies. When the social relations of feudalism were first established, they were "progressive" in the sense that they were necessary for the further development of the material forces of production. After a thousand years, however, the material forces of production had developed extensively, but the social relations had hardly changed at all. At that point the social relations of feudalism were hindering the further development of the material forces of production. The massive changes of the Industrial Revolution reflected a sudden and violent restructuring of the social relations of production. The new social relations—bourgeois capitalism—were "progressive" in the sense that they were necessary for the further development of the material forces of production.

Having analyzed the causes of the violent and abrupt social changes that had just been completed, Marx went on to use his theory to predict what would happen next. The material forces of production would continue to develop under capitalism, but the social relations would remain fixed, just as they had under feudalism. As the development of the material forces proceeded, the social relations of capitalism would increasingly become a hindrance rather than a help to the further development of the material forces. Ultimately, Marx predicted, there would be a sudden and violent restructuring of those social relations in which capitalism would be replaced by socialism.

Marx was fairly specific on why he thought that would happen. The logic of capitalism is "survival of the fittest," so that the "fittest" gobble up the "less fit." As part of this process, property is increasingly concentrated into fewer and fewer hands, and more and more people become wage laborers instead of working for themselves. At the same time, increasing mechanization in business and industry means that fewer workers are needed, so that there is an increasing pool of underemployed and unemployed workers. Because so many workers are available who want jobs, those who have jobs can be paid low wages because they can be replaced by others who will work for less.

In the long run, this means that capitalist societies will tend to polarize into two conflicting groups. One of these groups consists of the people who, as they gobble up their competitors, own an increasing portion of the property in the society. As Marx said: "One capitalist always kills many."[6] Thus the number of people in this group will grow smaller over time as some of them get gobbled up by others. As this group becomes smaller, it grows richer and richer. The other group, consisting of employed and unemployed wage laborers, keeps getting larger over time. But as unemployment increases with increasing mechanization, real wages tend to decrease because the supply of labor exceeds the demand for it. Thus, while this group becomes larger and larger over time, it also grows poorer and poorer.

Thus, Marx argued, capitalist societies would inevitably tend to polarize into two groups, one growing smaller and smaller while getting richer and richer, and the other growing larger and larger while getting poorer and poorer. This tendency toward polarization is what Marx called the "contradiction" in capitalism, and as it became more extreme, it would act as a greater hindrance to the further development of the material forces of production. A revolutionary restructuring of the social relations of production would be inevitable at some point. That restructuring, according to Marx, would consist of establishing collective ownership of the means of production and instituting centralized planning to end the cycles of overproduction and depression that plague capitalism.[7]

## 2. EARLY MARXIST VIEWS OF CRIME

Marx himself did not discuss the problem of crime or its relation to the economic system at length, although he did address the subject in several passages.[8] Hirst argues that Marx's idea of crime centered

6. Karl Marx, *Capital*, vol. 1, International, New York, 1967, p. 763.

7. See, in general, Karl Marx, *Critique of the Gotha Programme*, International, New York, 1970. See also D. Ross Gandy, *Marx and History: From Primitive Society to the Communist Future*, University of Texas Press, Austin, 1979, pp. 72–95.

8. For discussions of Marx's views of crime, see Ian Taylor, Paul Walton, and Jock Young, *The New Criminology*, Harper and Row, New York, 1973, pp. 209–36. Original passages from

on the concept of demoralization.[9] Marx believed that it was essential to human nature that people be productive in life and in work. But in industrialized capitalist societies there are large numbers of unemployed and underemployed people. Because these people are unproductive, they become demoralized and are subject to all forms of crime and vice. Marx called these people the *lumpenproletariat*.

In another passage Marx argued against the classical philosophy that was dominant in his day.[10] That philosophy held that all people freely and equally joined in a social contract for the common good, and that the law represented a consensus of the general will. Marx maintained that this view ignored the fact that unequal distribution of wealth in a society produced an unequal distribution of power. Those with no wealth have no power in the formation of the social contract, whereas those with great wealth can control it to represent their own interests. Thus Marx did not see crime as the willful violation of the common good, but as "the struggle of the isolated individual against the prevailing conditions."[11]

An early Marxist criminologist, Willem Bonger, provided an extensive theory of crime in his book *Criminality and Economic Conditions*, published in 1916.[12] Bonger argued that the capitalist economic system encouraged all people to be greedy and selfish and to pursue their own benefits without regard for the welfare of their fellows. Crime is concentrated in the lower classes because the justice system criminalizes the greed of the poor while it allows legal opportunities for the rich to pursue their selfish desires. He argued that a socialist society would ultimately eliminate crime because it would promote a concern for the welfare of the whole society and would remove the legal bias that favors the rich.

After the mid-1920s Marxist criminology virtually disappeared from the scene, at least in the English-speaking world.[13] Two new versions appeared around 1970, one in the United States, which developed from conflict theory and was exemplified in the works of Rich-

---

Marx and Engels can be found in Maureen Cain and Alan Hunt, eds., *Marx and Engels on Law*, Academic Press, New York, 1979, or Paul Phillips, *Marx and Engels on Law and Laws*, Barnes and Noble, Totowa, N.J., 1980.

9. Hirst, op. cit., pp. 215–21.

10. Karl Marx and Friedrich Engles, *The German Ideology*, Lawrence and Wishart, London, 1965, pp. 365–67.

11. Ibid., p. 367.

12. Willem Bonger, *Criminality and Economic Conditions*, Little, Brown, Boston, 1916; reprinted by Agathon, New York, 1967. See also the excellent Introduction by Austin Turk in the abridged edition, Indiana University Press, Bloomington, 1969. See also the brief discussion of Bonger and other early Marxist criminologists in Greenberg, op. cit., pp. 11–12.

13. Greenberg, op. cit., p. 1.

ard Quinney,[14] and the other in Great Britain, which developed from
the social reaction perspective and was exemplified in the works of
Taylor, Walton, and Young.[15] The British version originated with the
notion that deviant behavior should be considered fully authentic
human action rather than the product of some form of individual or
social pathology; that is, deviance was seen as a manifestation of human diversity. The criminalization of deviance was considered to be
a societal need unrelated to the quality of the behavior. Taylor, Walton, and Young maintained that this need to criminalize deviance is
a function of the social, economic, and political structures of existing
societies and that, therefore, "it is possible to envisage societies free
of any material necessity to criminalize deviance."[16] It was to envisage those new societies that the authors turned to Marxism.

The conflict theory path to Marxism was somewhat different. In
general, non-Marxist conflict theory exposes the inequalities of the
power relationships underlying the criminalization of some behaviors rather than others and can lead very naturally to a desire to change
those relationships. That is, it can lead from an "objective" analysis
of the criminalization process to a "political" effort to aid powerless
groups in their struggle against the powerful. The development of
Marxism also seems to be related to Quinney's earlier conception of
social reality. The creation of a particular social reality of crime is
seen as a political act reinforcing the status quo and the existing power
relationships. Quinney concluded that "objective" criminology is invariably used by the system to reinforce the existing social reality or,
if it cannot be so used, it is ignored.[17] This conclusion led him to
take a radically oppositional, negativistic stance toward the existing
system and to concentrate on the construction of new social realities
based on more equitable power relationships.[18] It was for these new
social realities that Quinney turned to Marxism.

These early versions of Marxist criminology were criticized by other
Marxists as misinterpreting Marx's thought.[19] Block and Chambliss,

14. See Richard Quinney, *Critique of Legal Order*, Little, Brown, Boston, 1973; Quinney
with John Wildeman, *The Problem of Crime*, 2nd ed., Harper & Row, New York, 1977.

15. See Taylor, Walton, and Young, *The New Criminology*, and *Critical Criminology*.

16. Taylor, Walton, and Young, "Critical Criminology in Britain: Review and Prospects," in
*Critical Criminology*, p. 20. See also the concluding statement of *The New Criminology*, p.
282: "The task is to create a society in which the facts of human diversity, whether personal,
organic or social, are not subject to the power to criminalize."

17. Quinney, *Critique*, pp. 26–32.

18. Quinney, "From Repression to Liberation," in Robert A. Scott and Jack D. Douglas, *Theoretical Perspectives on Deviance*, Basic Books, New York, 1972, pp. 317–41.

19. Hirst, op. cit.; also R. Serge Denisoff and Donald McQuarie, "Crime Control in Capitalist
Society: A Reply to Quinney," *Issues in Criminology* 10 (1): 109–19 (Spring 1975).

for example, criticized the early theories for their simplistic portrayal of the "ruling class" as a unified and monolithic elite; for the argument that the enactment and enforcement of laws reflects only the interests of this ruling class; and for the argument that criminal acts are a political response to conditions of oppression and exploitation.[20] Greenberg raised some of the same criticisms and also pointed out that these theories ignored studies that showed a widespread consensus on legal definitions of crime; that underprivileged people are most frequently victims of crime by other underprivileged people, so that they have an interest in the enforcement of criminal laws; and that it is unrealistic to expect that crime will be eliminated in socialist societies.[21] Greenberg later described these early theories as primarily political statements associated with New Left politics of the 1960s and the early 1970s rather than genuine academic arguments about the nature of crime.[22] With the collapse of the New Left in the early 1970s, "leftists who retained their political commitments dug in for the long haul." Some turned to community organizing while others turned to Marxist theory to deepen their understanding of the broader social processes. Greenberg concludes: "By the mid 1970s, a specifically Marxian criminology began to take shape."[23] This new and more rigorous Marxist criminology attempts to use the broad social theories of Marxism to provide a view of criminal behavior, crime policies, and criminology itself. In particular, it relates these topics to the political economy of the particular societies in which they occur, and relies primarily on historical and cross-cultural studies for support, since only in such studies can societies with different political economies be compared.

## 3. MARXIST VIEWS OF CRIMINAL BEHAVIOR

Marxist criminologists initially described criminal behavior in terms of "primitive rebellion" against conditions of exploitation and oppression.[24] That view has now been widely rejected by Marxists,

20. Alan A. Block and William J. Chambliss, *Organizing Crime*, Elsevier, New York, 1981, pp. 4–7. For a much harsher but less substantive criticism of these early theories, see Tony Platt, "Crime and Punishment in the United States: Immediate and Long-Term Reforms From a Marxist Perspective," *Crime and Social Justice*, Winter 1982, pp. 38–45.

21. David F. Greenberg, "On One-Dimensional Criminology," *Theory and Society* 3: 610–21 (1976).

22. Greenberg, *Crime and Capitalism*, pp. 6–10.

23. Ibid., p. 10.

24. See the discussion on "the image of criminality" in Ronald Hinch, "Marxist Criminology in the 1970s: Clarifying the Clutter," *Crime and Social Justice*, Summer 1983, pp. 69–71.

who look for more complex explanations of crime within the context of the Marxist theory of history and of social change.[25] A number of such explanations have been proposed. These explanations have considerable similarity to explanations found in more traditional criminological theories, except that they link their basic concepts to a broader view of political-economic systems and the historical processes in which those systems change.

For example, Greenberg presented a class-based theory of delinquency that has some similarities to so-called strain theories of delinquency.[26] Strain theories describe *class* in terms of the economic or occupational status of the parents, but Greenberg used the traditional Marxist view that class should be defined in terms of the relationship to the means of production. Juveniles occupy a unique position with respect to the means of production in that they are excluded from economically productive activity but are required to engage in extensive training for their future productive role. Thus they can be described as comprising a class of their own. Membership in this class is associated with a number of special strains. Exclusion from the labor market means that they cannot finance the leisure activities that are valued in the peer culture, which leads to stealing to generate desired funds. At the same time, many youths have negative and degrading experiences in schools, which provoke hostile and aggressive responses. Finally, some youths have deep-seated anxieties about achieving the status expected of adult males in our culture, which leads to the establishment of alternate status structures in which status is achieved through criminal acts. Greenberg concluded that programs to reduce delinquency would have little effect unless they were accompanied by broader changes in the capitalist economic system. Later, however, he commented that his conclusion may have been too pessimistic, and pointed to the system of apprenticeships in Switzerland, where delinquency is low, and suggested that such a system may have some beneficial effects.[27]

25. See, for example, Platt, op. cit., p. 40. He states: In general, the New Left either glossed over "street" crime as an invention of the FBI to divert attention away from corporate crimes or romanticized it as a form of primitive political rebellion. But as we well know from both experience and knowledge, "street" crime is not a fiction, but rather a very real and serious problem, especially in the superexploited sectors of the working class and its reserve army of labor. . . . This [view] was irresponsible and dangerous, a reflection of the profound alienation of the New Left from the daily conditions of life in working class communities.

26. David F. Greenberg, "Delinquency and the Age Structure of Society," in Greenberg, *Crime and Capitalism*, pp. 118–139. See also M. Colvin and J. Pauly, "A Critique of Criminology: Toward an Integrated Structural-Marxist Theory of Delinquency Production," *American Journal of Sociology* 89 (3): 513–51 (1983).

27. Greenberg, *Crime and Capitalism*, p. 66.

Other Marxist criminologists have suggested that high-crime groups are under special strains in the context of a capitalist economic system. Quinney, for example, described street crimes as crimes of "accommodation" to capitalist social relations in the sense that they are the actions of people who have been brutalized by the conditions of capitalism.[28] These criminals reproduce the exploitative relations of capitalism in their own criminal activities—that is, they treat their victims the way they themselves have been treated. Quinney's description relies on Marx's arguments about the lumpenproletariat, as described above.

While Greenberg's and Quinney's theories described special strains generating crime and delinquency, other theories have described crime in capitalist societies in terms of the breakdown of social controls. Friedrichs,[29] for example, argued that the effectiveness of a legal order depends largely on the extent to which it is perceived to be "legitimate." He then pointed out that American society is widely described as being in a crisis of legitimacy, indicated by a significant erosion of faith in leaders and in governmental institutions, disillusionment with the basic values on which those institutions are based, and the perception that those institutions are ineffective. In such a situation there is a general rise in various types of illegal behavior, including crime, riots, and revolutionary activity. The state has no choice but to respond to these activities with increasingly coercive and repressive measures, but the long-term effect of these responses is to worsen the crisis. Thus the crisis of legitimacy is a "contradiction" in the sense that it cannot be resolved without changing the basic structural arrangements of capitalism.

While these Marxist views use causal descriptions similar to those found in strain and control theories, the most common Marxist view is similar to those found in the traditional criminology theories that describe criminal behavior as normal learned behavior. These Marxist theories describe criminal behaviors as the rational responses of rational individuals confronted with a situation structured by the social relations of capitalism. This view is consistent with the general view found in Marxist theory that, in general and in the long run,

28. Richard Quinney, *Class, State and Crime*, pp. 59–62.

29. David O. Friedrichs, "The Law and the Legitimacy Crisis," in R. G. Iacovetta and Dae H. Chang, eds., *Critical Issues in Criminal Justice*, Carolina Press, Durham, N.C., 1979, pp. 290–311. See also Friedrichs, "The Legitimacy Crisis: A Conceptual Analysis," *Social Problems* 27 (5): 540–55, 1980. Other radical articles that have a control orientation include John R. Hepburn, "Social Control and the Legal Order," *Contemporary Crises* 1: 77–90 (1977); and Raymond J. Michalowski and Edward W. Bohlander, "Repression and Criminal Justice in Capitalist America," *Sociological Inquiry* 46 (2): 99–104 (1976).

individuals act and think in ways that are consistent with their economic interests.

One such description of criminal behavior was by Gordon, who focused on the economic precariousness of capitalist societies.[30] Gordon argued that crime is simply a way to make money for poor people, who are faced with situations of chronic unemployment and underemployment in low-paying and demeaning jobs. The violent nature of these crimes are a result of the fact that, unlike more powerful groups, poor people do not have the option to steal in more sophisticated ways, that is, with a pen rather than with a gun.

Gordon argued that organized crime was similarly a rational response to economic conditions in which there was a demand for illegal goods and services. This type of business is available to poorer people as a method of making money, whereas other legitimate forms of business are largely unavailable. Chambliss used a similar view in his extensive analysis of organized crime in Seattle.[31] Chambliss argued that at one time most of these goods and services were legal and that they were declared illegal for various historical reasons, but the demand for them did not disappear. He also pointed out that in our political system politicians have a strong need to generate funds in order to run for political office, and that, at the same time, they control the conditions under which laws against these illegal goods and services are enforced. This creates a very strong pressure for a coalition between politicans and organized crime figures, and Chambliss claimed that he found such a coalition at the heart of organized crime in Seattle. Chambliss was fairly pessimistic about the possibilities for reform to eliminate such crime, except to argue that decriminalization would be helpful. However, he said that most reforms replaced the people in key positions but did nothing about the basic political-economic forces (demand for illegal goods and services, need for money by politicians) that gave rise to organized crime in the first place. As the new, "reform" people responded to those same forces, they tended to do the same kinds of things done by the corrupt politicians they had replaced.

In a later book with Block, Chambliss generalized some of his arguments, relating various types of crime to the political-economic

30. David M. Gordon, "Class and the Economics of Crime," *Review of Radical Political Economics* 3: 51–75 (Summer 1971). See also Gordon, "Capitalism, Class, and Crime in America," *Crime and Delinquency* 19: 163–86 (April 1973).

31. William J. Chambliss, *On The Take: From Petty Crooks to Presidents*, Indiana University Press, Bloomington, Ind., 1978.

systems of societies in which they occur.[32] They argued that every political-economic system contains contradictions that cannot be resolved without changing the fundamental structure of the society. Crime in a society is essentially a rational response to those contradictions. The problem with crime control policies in general is that they attempt to deal with the symptoms without changing the basic political-economic forces that generate those symptoms to begin with.

Chambliss's analysis suggests a moving away from the early utopian position that crime would disappear when the social relations of capitalism were replaced by socialism. He retains the basic argument that crime is caused by capitalism in the sense that its ultimate social structural sources are found in the political and economic system of the society. Greenberg takes a similar position:[33]

There is no question that the historical development of capitalism transformed criminal law, patterns of crime, and methods of crime control. . . . At least in this sense, the basis for asserting that capitalism causes crime and criminal justice is empirically well-grounded. If, however, one interprets the word "cause" more narrowly to mean that only in capitalist societies does one find crime or formal methods of crime control, then the assertion is clearly false. Crime was unquestionably present in precapitalist societies. There is equally no doubt that crime and criminal justice institutions are found in societies that are considered socialist. . . .

Greenberg states that the persistence of crime in socialist societies should not be considered a refutation of Marxist theories of crime, but rather should be the occasion of Marxist theories linking the nature of crime in those societies to their political and economic arrangements. Three types of theories have been advanced to account for such crime: the view that crime is a "relic" of capitalism in the sense that elements of capitalist and bourgeois consciousness persist among the people despite the establishment of socialism; the view that crime is rooted in the social inequalities and relative deprivation of present socialist societies, which retain elements of exploitation and domination as they are being transformed into a genuinely communist society; and the view that crime springs from the social relations of socialism itself, with an entrenched bureaucracy interested in preserving its own privileges and centralized planning resulting in the powerlessness and alienation of workers. Greenberg

32. Block and Chambliss, op. cit.
33. Greenberg, *Crime and Capitalism*, pp. 23–25.

regards the persistence of crime in socialist societies as one of the major areas for future theorizing within the Marxist perspective.

## 4. MARXIST VIEWS OF THE BEHAVIOR OF CRIMINAL LAW

Like the initial Marxist theory of criminal behavior, there was an initial Marxist theory of the behavior of criminal law that is now widely rejected by Marxists. That theory is the so-called instrumentalist view that the enactment and enforcement of criminal laws are solely the "instruments" of a unified and monolithic ruling class that conspires to seek its own advantage at the expense of other groups. That view was actually inconsistent with Marx's description of the ruling class, and has been significantly modified as Marxist criminologists have moved away from overtly political statements to more sound academic arguments based on Marxist theory.[34]

Marx had argued that, although there were many conflicts in societies, the most important conflict in capitalist society is the conflict of economic interests generated by private ownership of the means of production. The owners of the means of production could be described as a class (the ruling class) because their similar positions in the social structure would result in similarities in their beliefs and actions. The term *ruling class* did not necessarily imply that they had organized themselves into a cohesive group. Marx made a similar argument about the working class, that they could be described as a class because they shared interests whether or not they were organized to defend those interests. The conflict between these two groups was a long-range, structurally determined conflict between sets of people who were defined by their relation to the means of production, rather than necessarily an overt conflict that occurred between two organized groups at a particular historical point.

Marx's argument that the state is a tool of the ruling class was based on the argument that the economic well-being of a society depends on the development of the material forces of production. If the social relations of production include private ownership of the means by which goods are produced, then the economic well-being of the society depends on the economic well-being of a set of private citizens. The state, then, has no choice but to arrange things so that the economic interests of those people are served, regardless of what

---

34. See the discussion on class in Hinch, op. cit., pp. 65–69.

consequences that has for the economic interests of other groups.[35] It is for that reason, Marx argued, the state should assume ownership of the means of production.

This more complex view of the ruling class is incorporated into so-called structuralist views of the state in capitalist societies, as developed by Althusser and others.[36] In this view the primary function of the state is not to directly serve the short-term interests of capitalists, but rather to ensure that the social relations of capitalism will persist in the long run. This requires that many different interests be served at different times, in order to prevent the rise of conditions that will lead to the collapse of capitalism. Thus, on any particular issue, including the enactment and enforcement of criminal laws, the actions of the state may serve other interests besides those of the owners of the means of production. Nevertheless, the owners of the means of production can still be described as a ruling class in that the organized state serves their economic interests in the long run, and they have an excessive amount of political power in comparison to other groups, with a disproportionate ability to get the state to serve their interests in the short run.

In the context of this view, Marxist criminologists have presented a number of analyses of the historical origins of the criminal law and of criminal justice agencies, as well as of their present operations. Marx himself presented the first such analysis, and it was very instrumental in shaping his later views.[37] As a young man Marx was a follower of the philosopher Hegel. At that time he wrote a number of articles on the crime of the theft of wood in Germany around 1840. Traditionally, rights to the forest were divided between the rights of the nobility to hunt and chase and the rights of the peasants to the use of forest products such as wood. In the early 1800s, however, the value of wood increased dramatically with the burgeoning markets for fuel, shipbuilding, railroad building, mining timbers, and so

35. It is most interesting that this argument is also central to the economic policies of President Ronald Reagan, who, through his taxing and spending programs, has directed economic resources to the owners of the means of production. Reagan, like Marx, argues that this policy is necessary for the economic health of the entire society. The difference between the two does not lie in the analysis of the situation but in the response to it.

36. A useful summary of the instrumentalist vs. structuralist views of the state and the legal order is found in William Chambliss and Robert Seidman, *Law, Order, and Power*, 2nd ed., Addison-Wesley, Reading, Mass., 1982, pp. 306–9. Chambliss and Seidman then propose their own "dialectical, institutionalist" model on pp. 309–16.

37. See Peter Linebaugh, "Karl Marx, the Theft of Wood, and Working Class Composition," in Greenberg, *Crime and Capitalism*, pp. 76–97. See also Greenberg's comments on pp. 60–63 and 484.

on. This resulted in the passage of a number of acts that took away the traditional rights of the peasants and defined the taking of wood from the forest as a crime. The enforcement of these laws then became a major function of criminal justice agencies, which processed enormous numbers of peasants who persisted in taking wood. Marx was outraged at the unfairness of these laws. On the basis of his Hegelian philosophy, Marx argued that the "true" state would uphold the rights of all citizens, whereas these laws defended only the interests of the forest owners. Marx later rejected the more overtly idealistic strains of Hegelianism, stating: "The philosphers have only *interpreted* the world in various ways; the point, however, is to change it."[38]

Marx later argued in *Capital* that the economic basis of capitalism rested on a similar theft of the traditional rights of the peasants.[39] Prior to capitalism most peasants were independent producers with hereditary rights to the use of state-owned, church-owned, or commonly held lands. Through a variety of legal means the peasants' rights to these lands were terminated, their traditional ways of earning a living declared illegal, and the lands they had used turned over to private capitalists. Having been deprived of their traditional means of support, many of these peasants then became beggars and vagabonds or formed roving bands of robbers. All of these methods of earning a living were also defined as criminal, so that peasants were virtually forced by the criminal law to become wage laborers working for the capitalists themselves. Marx documented that, whenever given a choice, peasants attempted to remain independent producers rather than become wage laborers. Thus, he argued, the economic basis of capitalism had been laid by a theft of the grandest scale imaginable, a theft that had been accomplished through the coercive power of the criminal law.

Marxist criminologists have done a number of more recent studies of the criminal law, arguing that it responds to the needs of the capitalist class.[40] In these descriptions of the enactment and enforce-

38. Karl Marx, "Theses on Feuerbach," in Lewis S. Feuer, ed., *Marx and Engles' Basic Writings on Politics and Philosophy,* Anchor, New York, 1959, p. 245; quoted in Greenberg, *Crime and Capitalism,* p. 484.

39. Karl Marx, *Capital,* quoted in Greenberg, ed., *Crime and Capitalism,* pp. 45–48. See also Greenberg's comments on pp. 38–39.

40. See in general the readings in the following edited volumes: Greenberg, ed., *Crime and Capitalism;* Piers Beirne and Richard Quinney, eds., *Marxism and Law,* John Wiley, New York, 1982; and David Kairys, ed., *The Politics of Law: A Progressive Critique,* Pantheon, New York, 1982. See also two "review essays" by David F. Greenberg and Nancy Anderson, *Contemporary Crises* 5 (3): 293–322, July, 1981, and David O. Friedrichs, *ALSA Forum* 8 (2): 329–47 (1984).

ment of criminal laws, Marxists generally take the same view of human behavior that they take in their descriptions of criminal behavior. Individuals, including those who write and enforce the criminal laws, in the long run and in general tend to think and to act in ways that are consistent with their economic interests. Their actions are essentially the rational responses of rational individuals in situations that are structured by the social relations of capitalism. This results in a certain general consistency in the outcome of their actions in that they tend to support the interests of the owners of the means of production, although that outcome is not necessarily the result of a conspiracy by a ruling class elite.

### 5. MARXIST VIEWS OF CRIMINOLOGY·

The general view that people tend to think and act in ways that are consistent with their economic interests can be applied to criminologists as well as to criminals and criminal justice agents. Marxists have therefore argued that criminology itself can be described as a "cultural product" that, through various subtle or obvious ways, will tend to support the interests of the ruling class, regardless of whether criminologists see themselves in that way.[41]

At least to some extent, the interests of criminologists are shaped by the needs of the political-economic order of capitalism. At the most general level, most criminologists have done reasonably well under that system and therefore are not radicals and do not favor the overthrow of capitalism. They tend to accept the capitalist economic system as a given and attempt to analyze the causes of and possible responses to criminal behaviors within the context of that system. Such a view generally excludes theory and research that focuses on the capitalist system itself as a cause of criminal behavior. To that extent, traditional criminology is built on the assumption that capitalist social relations will continue, and it limits the examination of the causes of criminal behavior to factors that do not require changes in that system. Marxists therefore argue that it can be interpreted as part of the general effort to shore up capitalism, regardless of whether that is the conscious intention of criminologists.

A more specific point is that the major sources of funding for criminological research are the federal government and private foundations that are or have been associated with large corporate enterprises. These funding sources tend to focus criminological research

41. Quinney, *Critique*, pp. 26–32.

onto individuals and their immediate social environments, and away from research into the broader political-economic contexts of crime. It would be unrealistic to expect any group to fund studies that would tend to undermine their most important interests. To the extent that these funding sources focus criminological research on some topics rather than others, they determine the content of criminology itself. Again, no conspiracy theory is required here, only the argument that people in general, including those that fund criminological research, will tend to act and think in ways that are consistent with their own economic interests. To the extent that such funding is determined ultimately by the people who own the means of production, it will tend to focus on ways to deal with crime within the context of capitalist social relations rather than through a change in those relations.

In order to escape these tendencies, Marxists maintain that criminologists must become "reflexive" and "critical," aware of themselves as self-interested persons and aware of the ultimate ethical implications of their own work.[42] In addition, Quinney argues that criminologists must become self-conscious advocates for working-class interests in their conflict with the ruling class.[43] Other Marxists, however, reject Quinney's position as theoretically inadequate and ultimately harmful to the development of a truly Marxist social science.[44] An alternate position has been taken by Greenberg, who maintains that there are a number of things that Marxist criminologists can do.[45] They can discredit the many false public beliefs about crime and criminals that are elements of bourgeois ideology and part of the way the capitalist economic system is sustained; they can support many types of reform movements, attempting to make the criminal justice system in our present society more fair and just; but most important, Greenberg argues, Marxists can develop and disseminate superior ways of understanding crime.

## 6. CONCLUSION

Marxist criminology is a very recent development, having its beginnings in the early 1970s in its more rigorous form. Most assessments

---

42. Robert M. Bohm, "Reflexivity and Critical Criminology," in Gary F. Jensen, ed., *Sociology of Delinquency*, Sage, Beverly Hills, Cal., 1981, pp. 29–47.

43. Richard Quinney, "The Production of a Marxist Criminology," *Contemporary Crises* 2 (3): 277–92 (1978).

44. Milton Mankoff, "On the Responsibility of Marxist Criminologists: A Reply to Quinney," *Contemporary Crises* 2 (3): 293–301 (1978). See also Greenberg, *Crime and Capitalism*, pp. 486–87.

45. Greenberg, *Crime and Capitalism*, pp. 488–93.

of Marxist criminology by traditional criminologists consider only the initial versions, which were clearly inadequate and unscientific.[46] But Marxist criminologists themselves have offered the most brutal criticisms of those early versions. An assessment of the more recent Marxist criminology is more difficult and ultimately rests on an assessment of general Marxist theory. Such an assessment is beyond the scope of the present examination. It is clear, however, that these more recent theories must be viewed only as initial attempts. Marxists today speak primarily of the challenges of the future, not the accomplishments of the past. Platt, for example, states:[47]

It is time to go beyond a "radical" criminology that simply exposes the horrors of capitalism and the injustices of criminal justice. . . . At the same time, we need to do a great deal of difficult theoretical work, to escape from the intellectual straightjacket of "criminology" and use the complex science of Marxism to get beyond muckraking radicalism. And given that Marxism is, after all, a guide to action, our policy proposals and theoretical enterprises must be informed by and tested in practice. The tasks before us, then, pose a considerable challenge which will require stamina and serious determination.

## RECOMMENDED READINGS

David F. Greenberg, ed., *Crime and Capitalism*, Mayfield, Palo Alto, Cal., 1981. The most readable account of Marxist criminology to date. See especially the excellent introductions to the various readings.

William Chambliss and Robert Seidman, *Law, Order, and Power*, 2nd ed., Addison-Wesley, Reading, Mass., 1982. A difficult and complex work that constitutes a powerful analysis of the criminal justice system from a Marxist perspective. Adapted from the earlier, conflict-oriented first edition.

Julia R. Schwendinger and Herman Schwendinger, *Rape and Inequality*, Sage, Beverly Hills, Cal., 1983. Exploitative relations in capitalism produce inequalities that result in violence. The prevalence of rape is linked to political, ideological, and economic contexts.

Richard Quinney, *Class, State and Crime*, 2nd ed., Longman, New York, 1980. A general theory of crime and criminal justice in advanced capitalist societies.

Richard Quinney, *Social Existence: Metaphysics, Marxism, and the Social Sciences*, Sage, Beverly Hills, Cal., 1982. An extended look at the possible future society which could emerge under Christian Marxism.

---

46. See, for example, Don C. Gibbons, *Society, Crime, and Criminal Behavior*, 4th ed., Prentice-Hall, Englewood Cliffs, N.J., 1984, pp. 143–48; and Gwynn Nettler, *Explaining Crime*, 3rd ed., McGraw-Hill, New York, 1984, pp. 192–203.

47. Platt, op. cit., p. 44.

Alan A. Block and William J. Chambliss, *Organizing Crime*, Elsevier, New York, 1981. The nature of organized crime is derived from the political and economic arrangements of the society in which it occurs.

James A. Inciardi, ed., *Radical Criminology*, Sage, Beverly Hills, Cal., 1980. A book of readings convering a variety of topics related to radical criminology. See especially the accounts of the development of radical criminology in Great Britain (by Mungham) and in the United States (by Friedrichs).

Jeffrey H. Reiman, *The Rich Get Richer and the Poor Get Prison*, 2nd ed., John Wiley, New York, 1983. Crime could be controlled, but the failure of criminal justice policies serves important interests among the wealthy.

Larry Tifft and Dennis Sullivan, *The Struggle to Be Human: Crime, Criminology and Anarchism*, Cienfuegos Press, Sanday, U.K., 1980. The search for a different world, without crime or criminology, without the hierarchical institutions of the state or capitalism.

Eileen B. Leonard, *Women, Crime and Society: A Critique of Theoretical Criminology*, Longman, New York, 1982. A feminist and radical perspective is required to resolve the past inadequacies of criminology theories and to provide an understanding of women and crime.

David O. Friedrichs, "The Problem of Reconciling Divergent Perspectives on Urban Crime: Personal Experience, Social Ideology and Scholarly Research," *Qualitative Sociology* 4 (3): 217–28 (Fall 1981). A personal statement about how one criminologist came to take an overtly partisan, leftist stance on crime, although with a pragmatic and humanistic bias.

# CHAPTER SEVENTEEN

# Criminology Theory
# and Specific Types of Crime

This chapter looks at three specific types of crime: victimless crime, organized crime, and white-collar crime. Despite the fact that most people have a reasonably clear idea of what these crimes involve, they are the subject of many disputes among criminologists—for example, whether victimless crime is really victimless, whether white-collar crime is really crime, and how much organization is really found in organized crime. In this chapter, as in the book generally, the focus of the discussion is not on the various facts known about these types of crime but rather on their implications for criminology theory.

## 1. VICTIMLESS CRIMES

A number of behaviors are widely prohibited by law that do not have a victim in the traditional sense of the term. Bedau names four characteristics of so-called victimless crimes, although they do not apply in every case.[1] First, there is consensual participation of all the persons involved in the crime, although in the case of abortion this is true only if the fetus is not considered a person. Second, no participant in the crime complains to the police, although a nonparticipant may do so. The absence of a complainant-participant makes these laws

---

1. Hugo Adam Bedau, "Are There Really 'Crimes Without Victims,'" in Edwin M. Schur and Hugo Adam Bedau, *Victimless Crimes: Two Sides of A Controversy*, Prentice-Hall, Englewood Cliffs, N.J. 1974, pp. 66–76. Bedau questions the validity of the concept. A N.J., review of the main facts and issues involved in connection with these major social problems as crimes may be found in Gilbert Geis, *Not the Law's Business?* Schocken, New York, 1979.

difficult to enforce. Third, the participants generally believe that they are not harmed by the crime, although other people believe that they are. Fourth, the crimes generally involve the willing exchange, among adults, of strongly desired but legally proscribed goods or services, although crimes like public drunkenness or narcotics use do not have this characteristic.

Victimless crimes include the following: (1) drunkenness and related offenses; (2) vagrancy and begging; (3) gambling; (4) prostitution and other adult consensual sexual offenses; (5) drug and narcotics law violations; and (6) juvenile status offenses (curfew, truancy, runaway). These offenses are of special significance to police and law enforcement officials everywhere because of the large numbers of people involved in them. Police figures in these matters cannot be taken to mean much as to the frequency of occurrence of the behavior in the community, but they give a rough idea of the relative importance of these categories in the total workload of handling complaints and prosecuting cases in the United States. Table 17–1[2] presents the total arrest statistics for each type of nontraffic offense in the year 1982. Thus, from a police standpoint, drunkenness and related behaviors accounted for about 36 percent of all nontraffic arrests, while vagrancy, gambling, sex offenses, drug law violations, and status offenses accounted for another 10 percent. That means that "victimless" crimes, as a group, accounted for about 46 percent of all nontraffic arrests in 1982.[3] How many more individuals are involved in similar behaviors, but are not arrested for them, is not known. It is reasonable to assume that the majority of people who engage in these behaviors escape police attention, so that these figures represent only a small fraction of the total number of times these offenses are actually committed.

. Most criminological theories focus on the question of the causes of the criminal behavior. That question can be asked about these offenses also, and the answer would focus on the biological, psychological, or social characteristics of the individuals involved. For example, there may be underlying biological differences that make some people susceptible to addiction to alcohol or other drugs, while other people may be able to use these substances with some frequency

2. Federal Bureau of Investigation, *Uniform Crime Reports for the United States, 1982,* U. S. Government Printing Office, Washington, D.C., 1983, Table 31.

3. That percentage has been decreasing rapidly in recent years. In 1956 these categories accounted for over 70 percent of all persons held for prosecution, according to the first edition of this book (pp. 142–43). 1972 was the first year in statistical recording history that American police arrested fewer drunks than serious crime offenders (*Criminal Justice Newsletter,* December 10, 1973).

TABLE 17–1   Total Arrests for Nontraffic Offenses, 1982

| Offense Category | Number | Percent |
| --- | --- | --- |
| Drunkenness | 1,034,527 | 10.3 |
| Driving while intoxicated | 1,404,646 | 14.0 |
| Disorderly conduct | 764,324 | 7.6 |
| Violation of liquor laws | 404,797 | 4.0 |
| Subtotal | 3,608,294 | 35.9 |
| Vagrancy | 32,158 | .3 |
| Gambling | 36,569 | .4 |
| Prostitution | 111,029 | 1.1 |
| Sex offenses (except forcible rape and prostitution) | 66,320 | .7 |
| Narcotic drug laws | 565,182 | 5.6 |
| Juvenile status offenses | 194,020 | 1.9 |
| Total | 4,613,572 | 45.9 |
| All other nontraffic arrests | 5,448,771 | 54.1 |
| Total | 10,062,343 | 100.0 |

without becoming addicted.[4] There may be various psychological factors involved, such as conflicts generated by repressed tendencies buried deep within the personality.[5] Or the person may be trapped in inescapable social circumstances that block every attempt to make a meaningful life.[6]

On the other hand, these offenses may also be explained by cultural differences about what constitute appropriate behaviors in given circumstances.[7] Many of these offenses involve commercial transactions for gain and provide opportunities for profitable employment. Prostitution, for example, may simply be a "job" for those involved in its practice, and gambling and the sale of narcotics involve large profits to at least some of the people who engage in these activities. Even vagrancy and begging have certain advantages as a way of making a living. There are many pleasures involved in alcohol and drug use,

4. See, for example, D. W. Goodwin, *Is Alcoholism Hereditary?* Oxford University Press, New York, 1976; J. H. Mendelson and N. K. Mello, "Biological Concomitants of Alcoholism," *New England Journal of Medicine* 301 (17): 912 (1979) and D. D. Rutstein and R. L. Veech, "Genetics and Addiction to Alcohol," *New England Journal of Medicine* 298 (20): 1140 (1978).

5. See, for example, G. Lolli, "Alcoholism as a Disorder of the Love Disposition," *Quarterly Journal of Studies on Alcohol* 17: 96 (1956); S. Rado, "Narcotic Bondage," *American Journal of Psychiatry* 114: 165 (1975).

6. See, for example, Elliot Liebow, *Tally's Corner*, Little, Brown, Boston, 1967.

7. This argument was made in greater detail in earlier editions of this book. See George B. Vold, *Theoretical Criminology*, Oxford University Press, New York, 1958, pp. 151–54; also 2nd ed., prepared by Thomas J. Bernard, 1979, pp. 334–37.

and some people, at least, may simply not see anything wrong with getting drunk or high, even though the law forbids it.

There are also many fine distinctions between these victimless crimes and perfectly legal behaviors, and these distinctions vary in different cultures. Gambling is illegal, but investing in the stock market, where one bets on whether the price of the stock will go up or down, is an honored and encouraged practice in our economy. On the other hand, such economic speculation is illegal in socialist economies. "Playing the numbers" has always been a widespread illegal way of gambling in poor urban neighborhoods, but it provides gainful employment for those who operate the games as well as for the "runners," who deal with the players. Recently many states have instituted lotteries that are identical to the illegal numbers game. The only difference is that the criminals who run numbers games pay out a larger percentage of the money to winners than do the state lotteries.[8] Marijuana use is an accepted part of the culture in rural Jamaica, as is the use of cocaine in the Peruvian highlands.[9] Nicotine (in cigarettes) is approximately as addictive as heroin, and being addicted to cigarettes is much more physically harmful since it can cause cancer and heart disease.[10] But cigarettes are widely and legally available, and the federal government even subsidizes the tobacco industry, while heroin use and sale are regarded as serious crimes. With respect to these victimless crimes, the differences between the illegal and legal behaviors are generally peculiar to a specific culture and involve specific rationalizations of many kinds that are acceptable within that culture.

The question of why people engage in these behaviors, then, may be less interesting for criminology than the question of why these particular behaviors, and not others, are defined as crimes. It appears that, for various reasons, these behaviors offend the moral sensibilities or the economic interests of groups with significant degrees of political power, with the result that they were defined as crimes by legislatures.[11] In other countries, with other configurations of

8. Numbers games normally pay off at 600–1 (see Lowell L. Kuehn, "Syndicated Crime in America," in Edward Sagarin and Fred Montanino, eds., *Deviants: Voluntary Actors in a Hostile World*, General Learning Press, Morristown, N.J., 1977, p. 169). State lotteries pay off at 500–1, so that they keep 10 percent more of the money as profits than do the numbers games.

9. Louis S. Goodman and Alfred Gilman, eds., *The Pharmacological Basis of Therapeutics*, 3rd ed., Macmillan, New York, 1965, p. 299; Melanie C. Dreher, *Working Men and Ganja: Marihuana Use in Rural Jamaica*, Institute for the Study of Human Issues, Philadelphia, 1982.

10. Edwin M. Brecher, *Licit and Illicit Drugs*, Consumers Union, Mount Vernon, N.Y., 1972, pp. 209–44.

11. See, for example, Donald T. Dickson, "Bureaucracy and Morality: An Organizational Perspective on a Moral Crusade," *Social Problems* 16 (2): 143–56 (Fall 1968); William J. Cham-

powerful groups, different sets of behaviors became defined as crimes. Other behaviors that are as socially or personally harmful as these victimless crimes have not been defined as violations of the criminal law because the people who engaged in those behaviors had sufficient power to protect themselves within the context of the criminal law process. These behaviors might be compared to blasphemy and heresy, which in past times were commonly prosecuted as criminal offenses. Both have disappeared as categories of crimes calling for police control in Western nations, although they remain crimes in some other countries. These behaviors persist in the community, and may even be regarded by some people as serious problems, but it is no longer considered appropriate to respond to them with criminal prosecution.

In a similar way it would be possible to eliminate current victimless crimes simply by changing the law so that the behaviors were no longer defined as criminal. The behaviors themselves would remain, of course, and to the extent that they constitute problems for the individual and for society generally, they would have to be dealt with in some other way. On the other hand, we have been punishing these behaviors as crimes for many years, and they still are with us. In addition, there is widespread recognition of the fact that these behaviors are much more prevalent than would appear from arrest statistics. Penalizing these behaviors as crimes, then, seems not to have been particularly successful in controlling or eliminating them.

Changing the legal definitions of these behaviors would imply a prior change in the ideas and opinions held by powerful groups in society, but such a change in fact seems to be well under way at the present time. Various individuals and organizations are now urging that victimless crimes be decriminalized, and there appears to be some substantial movement in that direction. For example, at least 25 states have now decriminalized public drunkenness, 8 states have stopped arresting people for possession of small amounts of marijuana, and a number of states have legalized various forms of gambling.[12] Prostitution is legal in parts of one state (Nevada) as well as in a number of European countries, and a number of states have also decrimi-

---

bliss, "A Sociological Analysis of the Law of Vagrancy," *Social Problems* 12 (1): 66–77 (Fall 1964); Joseph Gusfield, *Symbolic Crusade*, University of Illinois Press, Urbana, Ill., 1963; A. R. Lindesmith, "A Sociological Theory of Drug Addiction," *American Journal of Sociology* 43: 593–613 (Jan. 1983); and E. H. Sutherland and Harvey J. Locke, *Twenty Thousand Homeless Men*, Lippincott, Philadelphia, 1936.

12. "An Update on Victimless Crimes," National Council on Crime and Delinquency, Hackensack, N.J., 1977.

nalized other types of adult consensual sexual activity.[13] England now has heroin maintenance programs in which physicians can legally prescribe heroin for addicts, and similar programs have been urged as a partial solution to the heroin problem in the United States.[14] The decriminalization movement is not necessarily based on the argument that there is nothing "wrong" with these behaviors—many of them may still be considered harmful to the participants as well as to society at large—but those who advocate decriminalization argue that defining and punishing these behaviors as crimes has not been an effective way of dealing with these problems, and may in fact have made the problems worse.[15]

With respect to these victimless crimes, theories of the causes of criminal behavior (why people act this way) seem to be less interesting for criminology than are theories of the behavior of criminal law (why these behaviors are defined as crimes). There seems to be a growing perception that classical theories (punishing these behaviors as crimes in order to reduce their incidence) have failed and, in at least some instances, caused more problems than they have solved. While many of these offenses are not considered "serious" crimes (with the exception of the possession and sale of heroin), criminology theories can hardly ignore them, since they account for nearly half of all nontraffic arrests in the United States.

2. ORGANIZED CRIME

In law-abiding society nearly everyone works with someone else to earn a living. Everywhere people are interested in getting a maximum return for a minimum expenditure of effort and energy, and working with other people in a division of labor is simply the most efficient way to get things done. This is the basic reason for the organization of business and the coordination of specialized efforts to achieve a higher level of industrial production. The incentive of a more efficient and effective way to achieve one's ends as well as a more profitable return for the effort, is also the key to understanding

13. Daniel Glaser, *Crime in Our Changing Society*, Holt, Rinehart and Winston, New York, 1978, pp. 345–410.

14. Arnold S. Trebach, *The Heroin Solution*, Yale University Press, New Haven, Conn., 1982.

15. Norval Morris and Gordon Hawkins, *The Honest Politician's Guide to Crime Control*, University of Chicago Press, Chicago, 1970; Sanford H. Kadish, "The Crisis of Overcriminalization," *The Annals* 374: 157–70 (Nov. 1967); National Council on Crime and Delinquency, "Crimes Without Victims: A Policy Statement," *Crime and Delinquency* 17 (2): 129 (Apr. 1971).

organization in the field of crime.[16] Like most other people, criminals are interested in obtaining more money with less effort and fewer risks. Thus the motivation for organization in criminal activities is largely the same as that of legitimate business.

The lowest level of organization in criminal activities is a temporary *partnership* in which two or three people work together to pull a particular "job." Partnerships can develop into somewhat larger, permanent associations that can be described as *gangs*. These are characterized by a stable division of labor in which different members, under a recognized leadership, use different specialized skills in a coordinated effort to pull more difficult and profitable types of "jobs." Criminal gangs tend to develop the social-psychological orientations of a conflict group, with loyalty and emotionally toned attachments to other group members, much like the loyalties that develop among a group of soldiers engaged in combat.

The highest level of criminal organization is found in the *syndicate*, which is a large, permanent association of criminals that operates like a large business organization. The term *organized crime* is frequently used to refer only to the activities of these highly organized, large-scale associations of criminals, and not to the less-organized, smaller criminal organizations described above. For example, the President's Commission of Law Enforcement and Administration of Justice stated that organized crime "involves thousands of criminals, working within structures as complex as those of any large corporation, subject to laws more rigidly enforced than those of legitimate governments."[17] They distinguish three principal aspects of organized crime activity.[18]

---

16. The President's Commission on Law Enforcement and Administration of Justice, *Task Force Report: Organized Crime*, U.S. Government Printing Office, Washington, D.C., 1967, pp. 1–5; also Daniel Bell, "Crime as an American Way of Life," *Antioch Review* 13: 131–54 (June 1953). Extensive bibliographies dealing with the subject of "organized" crime may be found in Lowell L. Kuehn, "Syndicated Crime in America," in Edward Sagarin and Fred Montanino, eds., *Deviants: Voluntary Actors in a Hostile World*, General Learning Press, Morristown, N.J., 1977, pp. 214–19; and James A. Inciardi, "Vocational Crime," in Daniel Glaser, ed., *Handbook of Criminology*, Rand McNally, Chicago, 1974, pp. 381–401.

17. *Task Force Report—Organized Crime*, p. 1. See Donald R. Cressey, "The Functions and Structure of Criminal Syndicates," in *Task Force Report*, Appendix A, pp. 25–60, for a detailed presentation of this structure. See also the discussions of formal organizations in Donald R. Cressey, *Criminal Organization*, Harper & Row, New York, 1972, pp. 1–17. Francis A. J. Ianni rejects this model of organization, maintaining instead that criminal syndicates are organized along "family" or "kinship" lines, or are similar to small businesses rather than to huge corporations. See Ianni's *A Family Business: Kinship and Social Control in Organized Crime*, Russell Sage, New York, 1972, and *Black Mafia: Ethnic Succession in Organized Crime*, Simon and Schuster, New York, 1974. This debate is discussed in Kuehn, op. cit., pp. 184–97.

18. *Task Force Report*, p. 1.

The core of organized crime activity is the supplying of illegal goods and services—gambling, loan sharking, narcotics, and other forms of vice—to countless numbers of citizen customers. But organized crime is also extensively and deeply involved in legitimate business and in labor unions. Here it employs illegitimate methods—monopolization, extortion, tax evasion—to drive out or control lawful ownership and leadership and to exact illegal profits from the public. And to carry on its many activities secure from governmental interference, organized crime corrupts public officials.

Although these activities are interrelated, a somewhat artificial distinction will be made, for the purposes of discussion, between the criminal syndicate, organized for the provision of illegal goods and services, and the rackets, involved in the invasion of legitimate organizations. Both forms of organized crime will be discussed, along with the political graft and corruption associated with them.

In contrast to the criminal gang, which is an active, mobile group directly involved in crime activity, the *criminal syndicate* is a relatively stable type of business organization. Its business is to integrate and coordinate existing crime opportunities, practices, and personnel into a smoothly functioning, large-scale enterprise devoted to the assurance of a high level of profits for the organization. The word *syndicate* is taken directly from the language of legitimate business. The significance of the term in the present context lies in the fact that it represents an important, large-scale combination of capital and skilled personnel devoted to criminal activity. This may make it a very powerful influence in the local community, or in the state, and sometimes even in the nation. Like the truly "big business" corporation on which it is patterned, it can afford to buy the best talent available in services and in technical skill that it may need but not to be able to furnish directly from within the organization.

The syndicate is in the business of providing forbidden and illegal services or commodities desired by customers who are able and willing to pay for what they want.[19] Illicit sex, drugs, alcohol, loans, and gambling are the main staples sold to willing customers at prices high enough to give a substantial profit to management after meeting all the costs of carrying on the business.

The crime syndicate flourishes only because people with money in their pockets are willing to pay the price asked for the service provided or the commodity sold. No one is forced to patronize a crime syndicate and there is no compulsion on the public to contribute to

19. See Cressey, *Theft of the Nation*, Harper & Row, N.Y., 1969, pp. 72–108, "Demand, Supply, and Profit."

its profits. In this sense it is a business organization, functioning on merit and profitable only when it can give the customer what he wants at a price he is willing to pay. He may be asked to pay an outrageous price for what he wants, but that is equally true of many legitimate commodities. The syndicate must also keep the customers coming without the support of the advertising ballyhoo of the mass media.

The *racket* in crime is the systematic practice of extortion under threat of some kind, usually of personal injury or of property damage. Typically, the racketeer insists on being "cut in" for a percentage of the returns from some existing, profitable enterprise under threat of some penalty for refusal. If the business is illegal, or only marginally within the law, the opportunities for the racketeer are normally greatly increased, since no appeal for redress can then be made to the police or other public authorities.

Racket operations are almost infinitely varied and extensive as to the kind of business enterprise that may be vulnerable.[20] An illustration of one of its simplest forms is the so-called protective association that forces retail business establishments to pay high dues and regular "fees" for the privilege of operating without molestation. The "hazards" against which the merchant is "protected" are interference by "enemy" gangsters but in actuality originate with and are under the control of the racketeers themselves. Should the merchant refuse to go along with the demands made on him, he may find his windows broken, his shop bombed, or his goods damaged. In case of continuing obstinacy, beatings, eye-gouging, and so on may be used as more effective arguments of persuasion. The "sales talk" of the racketeer may include the suggestion that the added costs of "protection" be passed on to the customers, thus making it a more profitable business both for the merchant and for the protective association.

*Political graft and corruption* are always intimately related to the effective organization of crime.[21] The politician or bureaucrat, es-

---

20. For detailed accounts of specific racket and syndicate operations and for interpretations of "who worked what racket," see especially accounts like those of Frederic Sondern, Jr., *Brotherhood of Evil*, Farrar, Straus, and Cudahy, New York, 1966; Peter Maas, *The Valachi Papers*, Putnam, New York, 1968; Donald R. Cressey, *Theft of the Nation;* Ralph Salerno and John S. Tompkins, *The Crime Confederation,*, Doubleday, Garden City, N.Y., 1969; Ed Reid, *The Grim Reapers*, Regnery, Chicago, 1969; and Fred J. Cook, *The Secret Rulers*, Duell, Sloan and Pearce, New York, 1966.

21. *Task Force Report*, p. 6. For a detailed discussion of such corruption, see William J. Chambliss, *On The Take: From Petty Crooks to Presidents*, Indiana University Press, Bloomington, Ind., 1978. See also Alan A. Block and William J. Chambliss, *Organizing Crime*, Elsevier, New York, 1981; Cressey, *Theft of the Nation*, pp. 248–89; Stuart L. Hills, *Crime, Power, and Morality*, Chandler, New York, 1971, pp. 119–29; and Clark Mollenhoff, *Strike Force: Organized Crime and the Government*, Prentice-Hall, Englewood Cliffs, N.J., 1972.

pecially in the anonymity of city life, can easily become corrupt and a ready and willing partner with various organized criminal elements. The primary tool for this corruption is money, either offered as a direct bribe, kickback, or payoff, or in the more subtle form of a "campaign contribution."[22] In return for this money, the criminal expects to receive various forms of "protection" from the criminal justice system. Police may simply look the other way, prosecutors may dismiss cases, and judges may suppress evidence, issue favorable instructions to the jury or find the defendant innocent, or impose minimal sentences. More subtle forms of protection may also be provided. Police may deliberately use illegal or unconstitutional methods in making arrests in order to ensure that the charges will be thrown out in court. Or they may selectively enforce the laws against all but a certain group, thereby granting those groups a virtual monopoly in crime. Criminals may be tipped off when search warrants are issued or raids are planned, police investigating units and prosecution units in the district attorney's office may be deliberately underfunded and overworked, and anticrime legislation may be defeated or watered down. Finally, government officials can make decisions that result in massive profits for legitimate businesses controlled by organized crime. Zoning regulations can be altered, resulting in windfall profits in real estate deals; construction contracts may be awarded to companies who did not submit the lowest or best bid; liquor licenses may be granted to some people, but not to others. The list seems to be endless.

This, in brief, is the general nature of the unholy alliance between the corrupt political machine and organized crime that all too often has characterized local, city, and county government in the United States.[23] The problem must not be confused with that of the occasional personal dishonesty among individual politicians in their dealings with other individuals, ostensibly businessmen, who are connected with criminal gangs and syndicates. The problem lies in the widespread corruption and favoritism of a group of politicians who are accustomed to working and maintaining contacts with organized

22. See Alexander Heard, *The Costs of Democracy,* University of North Carolina Press, Chapel Hill, N.C., 1960, pp. 154–68.

23. Chambliss, *On the Take;* George Amish, *The American Way of Graft,* The Center for Analysis of Public Issues, Princeton, N.J., 1976; Larry L. Berg, Harlan Hahn, and John R. Schmidhauser, *Corruption in the American Political System,* General Learning Press, Morristown, N.J., 1976; David Caputo, *Organized Crime and American Politics,* General Learning Press, Morristown, N.J., 1974; John Gardiner, *The Politics of Corruption,* Russell Sage, New York, 1970. See also Gardiner's "Wincanton: The Politics of Corruption," in *Task Force Report,* Appendix B, pp. 61–79.

crime syndicates that can well afford to pay for special services or special immunities. The cooperation of numerous individuals is usually involved in obtaining approvals and signatures necessary for government action of any kind, and therefore corruption and graft involving public officials is seldom a matter of a few individuals. It is not so much a question of individual or personal dishonesty as the chicanery, double-dealing, and general dishonesty on the part of a whole clique or group of government officials—thus the phrase *corrupt government*—joining the criminal syndicate to exploit a relatively inarticulate and essentially helpless general public. Any sense of personal wrongdoing on the part of individual public officials in these situations seems to have been blunted by the psychological support of the group situation, whereby they have the acceptance and assurance of support of fellow officials. "What so many others do without self-incrimination cannot be really so very bad" is the usual justification of individuals in such situations.

One basic fact stands out from this discussion, namely, that organized crime must be thought of as a natural growth of or as a developmental adjunct to our general system of private profit economy.[24] Business, industry, and finance are all competitive enterprises within the area of legal operations. But there is also an area of genuine economic demand for commodities and services not permitted under our legal and social codes. Organized crime functions in this area. It, too, is competitive, and hence must be organized to protect itself and to compete.

Three questions can be asked about organized crime in the context of criminology theories. The first of these questions is associated with theories of criminal behavior: Why do people act this way? At least with respect to the criminal associations that provide illegal goods and services, the explanation for the criminal behavior appears to be basically the same as the explanation of the behavior of any legitimate businessman: These criminals are making a profit by providing goods and services that are strongly desired by customers who are willing to pay for them. The second question is associated with theories of the behavior of criminal law, and asks why these particular goods and services are illegal. The answer to that question requires an examination of the historical distribution of power among groups in society, and the moral sensibilities and economic interests of those groups. As with victimless crimes, the question of why these goods and services are defined as criminal appears to be more interesting

24. Chambliss, *On the Take.*

for criminology than the question of why some people desire to obtain, and other people attempt to provide, these goods and services.

The third question is associated with classical theories and concerns whether defining and punishing the behaviors as criminal has led to a decrease in their incidence. It appears that it has not. Defining these behaviors as criminal may actually contribute to many of the more harmful aspects associated with organized crime. The political graft and corruption necessary for organized crime to flourish would be unnecessary if it were possible legally to provide these goods and services. Many of the more violent practices associated with organized crime appear to be extreme examples of the cutthroat competitive practices engaged in by legitimate businesses, where the excessive nature of these practices is derived from the fact that criminal businesses operate totally outside the rule of law.[25] Legitimate businessmen, in contrast, may occasionally send someone to firebomb their competitor's factory, but it is generally easier to control the excesses of such cutthroat competition because these businesses are exposed to regulations of legitimate society. Legitimate businessmen can also appeal to the police and courts for redress of grievances when their competitors engage in unfair practices against them, whereas organized crime figures have to rely on their own organizations to right whatever wrongs they might believe have been done to them. In general, the violence associated with organized crime would be considerably reduced if the goods and services they deliver were legal instead of illegal.

Finally, defining these goods and services as illegal actually contributes to the profits available from them. Most drugs, for example, are relatively inexpensive to produce, and the enormous profits they generate are possible only because drug use is illegal. Otherwise, legitimate competition would drive the price down and the profit margin would become much smaller. This means that organized criminals may not favor decriminalization of their operations, since they might then lose their base of operations. That, after all, is what happened when Prohibition was repealed. The criminal organizations that had been providing illegal alcohol were replaced by legitimate organizations that provided a better-quality product at a more reasonable price. Criminal organizations largely went out of the alcohol business and had to move into new markets, much as any other business would, in order to remain viable. In the meantime most of

25. This point is discussed more extensively in the second edition of the present book. See George B. Vold, *Theoretical Criminology*, 2nd ed. prepared by Thomas J. Bernard, Oxford University Press, New York, 1979, pp. 351–53.

the violence that had been associated with alcohol production and sales simply disappeared.

Under the present arrangement it can be argued that organized criminals have a very attractive setup. They are marketing goods and services for which there are substantial demands. There are enormous profits available, since these goods and services are defined as illegal. Political graft and corruption prevent the effective enforcement of the laws, which in effect means that organized criminals are free to market their products as long as they share some of their profits with law enforcement officials and politicians. And, finally, organized criminals are free to use the most violent methods to eliminate any competition that might arise from others who attempt to sell the same goods and services at a better price. As with victimless crimes, classical criminology appears to be the least relevant to understanding organized crime, since punishing these behaviors as crimes has not seemed to decrease their incidence. These operations seem to be much more significantly affected by the economic facts of supply and demand, and the fads and foibles in consumer habits, than by legislation and attempts at formal control.[26]

## 3. WHITE-COLLAR CRIME

The term *white-collar crime* has been in frequent use since the 1939 presidential address of the late Edwin H. Sutherland to the American Sociological Society.[27] Since then, the term has gained widespread popularity among the public, but it is still remains ambiguous and controversial in criminology. It nevertheless relates to some special aspects of criminal behavior that have important implications for criminological theory.

Sutherland addressed himself to the problem of crime in modern business practices. He argued that the usual reports, which picture the criminal populations as made up largely of lower-class, economically underprivileged persons, give a misleading and essentially false impression of noncriminality on the part of the upper classes, including respected and highly placed business and political personages.[28] More explicitly, white-collar criminality was said to take place

26. Cf. Kuehn, op. cit., pp. 206–11.

27. Edwin H. Sutherland, "White Collar Criminality," *American Sociological Review* 5: 1–12 (Feb. 1940). See also Sutherland, "Is 'White Collar Crime' Crime?" *American Sociological Review* 10: 132–39 (Apr. 1945); *White Collar Crime*, Dryden Press, New York, 1949; and "Crime of Corporations," in Albert Cohen, Alfred Lindesmith, and Karl Schuessler, eds., *The Sutherland Papers*, Indiana University Press, Bloomington, Ind., 1956.

28. E.H. Sutherland, "White Collar Criminality," p. 2.

most frequently in misrepresentation of the financial statements of corporations, in manipulation of the stock exchange, in the bribery of public officials to secure desirable contracts or immunities, in bribery in commercial transactions, in misrepresentation in advertising and salesmanship, in embezzlement and misuse of trust funds, in dishonest bankruptcies, and so on. The Chicago gangster Al Capone was quoted as calling such practices "the legitimate rackets"[29] in which respectable people could participate, in contrast to the more familiar and violent types of rackets characteristic of the underworld.

Sutherland defined white-collar crime as "a violation of criminal law by the person of the upper socio-economic class in the course of his occupational activities."[30] The crucial question, however, concerned the criterion used to determine whether a violation of the criminal law had occurred. The criterion normally used was conviction in criminal court. But Sutherland argued that[31]

white-collar criminals are relatively immune (from criminal conviction) because of the class bias of the courts and the power of their class to influence the implementation and administration of the law. This class bias affects not merely present-day courts, but also, to a much greater degree, affected the earlier courts which established the precedents and rules of procedure of the present-day courts.

As a result of this class bias, the crimes of the upper class are generally handled differently than the crimes of the lower class. Thus:[32]

The crimes of the lower class are handled by policemen, prosecutors, and judges with penal sanctions in the form of fines, imprisonment, and death. The crimes of the upper class either result in no official action at all, or result in suits for damages in civil courts, or are handled by inspectors and by administrative boards or commissions with penal sanctions in the form of warnings, orders to cease and desist, occasionally the loss of a license, and only in extreme cases by fines or prison sentences. Thus, the white-collar criminals are segregated administratively from other criminals and, largely as a consequence of this, are not regarded as real criminals by themselves, the general public, or the criminologists.

In order to compensate for this class bias, Sutherland argued that official conviction statistics must be supplemented by evidence of

29. Ibid., p. 3.

30. E. H. Sutherland, "Crime and Business," *The Annals of the American Academy of Political and Social Science* 217: 112–18 (Sept. 1941).

31. E. H. Sutherland, "White Collar Criminality," p. 7.

32. Ibid., pp. 7–8.

criminal violations from other sources. Specifically, Sutherland included hearings before regulatory commissions, civil suits for damages, and various other procedures outside of criminal court prosecution and conviction. All such actions resulting in decisions against a person or corporation, Sutherland insisted, should be taken as instances of conviction of white-collar crime, since such decisions are sufficient proof of violation of law and of the carrying on of a practice legally defined as injurious to the public. Similarly, in his view, civil suit judgments in which the injured party has been more interested in restitution or damages than in punishment would be considered as evidence of white-collar crime, as would settlements made by surety companies of embezzlement cases in which prosecutions of crime usually do not occur because such prosecution interferes with the recovery of funds taken. He would also include as white-collar crime procedural findings of "unfair labor practices," "infringement on patents," and "discrimination between buyers."

White-collar crimes should not be confused with ordinary crimes committed by upper-class people. If upper-class people commit murder, robbery, rape, ordinary theft, or other crimes under the ordinary criminal law, they are simply ordinary criminals and are prosecuted as such; in no sense are they white-collar criminals merely because they happen to be upper-class persons. White-collar crimes, in contrast, involve evasions of regulations and violations of law carried on as part of an occupation or business in order to secure greater profit and without concern for the injury inflicted on the public. Sutherland maintained that the reason this kind of behavior was not handled through the criminal courts was that "because of their social status [white-collar criminals] have a loud voice in determining what goes into statutes and how the criminal law as it affects themselves is implemented and administered."[33] Thus he called these actions crimes even though no criminal conviction had been obtained and even though in some cases no criminal law was violated, but only civil law or administrative regulations.

In the years since Sutherland wrote there have been numerous examples of white-collar crime, and the public is generally more aware of and concerned about these behaviors than they were at the time he introduced the term.[34] Nevertheless, the term remains contro-

---

33. Ibid., p. 8.

34. For examples of more recent incidences of "white-collar" crime, see Lester A. Sobel, ed., *Corruption in Business*, Facts on File, New York, 1977. See also such books as Gilbert Geis and Robert F. Meier, *White Collar Crime*, rev. ed., The Free Press, New York, 1977; Jack D. Douglass and John M. Johnson, eds., *Official Deviance*, Lippincott, Philadelphia, 1977;

versial in criminology because of its use in describing behaviors that do not result in criminal convictions and in some cases do not even involve violations of the criminal law. The controversy has centered on the objection that the term ignores legal distinctions between civil and criminal violations, and is so ambiguous and uncertain that it is useless for research purposes.

One of the most outspoken critics of the term was Paul Tappan.[35] He pointed to the impropriety of introducing what he said tends to become purely personal definitions of what is socially injurious. It is necessary, obviously, to do more than condemn such offenses in the abstract; it is equally necessary to specify what particular type of deviation, and in what degree for each type, shall be considered criminal. This, Tappan insisted, the criminal code does better and more explicitly than any nonlegal system, such as the "system of private values" in the area of economic ethics that are the principal component of the popular extension of the term *white-collar crime.* He therefore argued that a basic requirement for meaningful research is definitive terminology, so that the categories of enumeration and analysis do not overlap. This he found impossible with the many interpretations available as to what should be considered white-collar crime and what should be taken to be something else.[36]

In statistical studies of white-collar crime, any official action, civil or criminal (mostly the actions of administrative commissions or boards), that has been undertaken by government administrators to bring about compliance with regulations is usually considered evidence of criminality. Thus a desist order, a purely civil action, is usually counted as an instance of criminality and interpreted as the equivalent of "conviction of crime." This tendency to count all violations of all kinds of laws and regulations as crime, provided there is a penalty attached, brought forth a critical protest from E. W. Burgess, who insisted that a distinction must be made "between crimes recognized by law for generations and disapproved of by the mores . . . [and] new offenses as the result of recent legislation or regulations by government agencies carrying with them a penalty for

M. David Ermann and Richard J. Lundman, eds., *Corporate and Governmental Deviance,* Oxford University Press, New York, 1978; John M. Johnson and Jack D. Douglas, eds., *Crime at the Top,* Lippincott, Philadelphia, 1978; David R. Simon and D. Stanley Eitzen, *Elite Deviance,* Allyn and Bacon, Boston, 1982; and Frank Pearce, *Crimes of the Powerful,* Pluto Press, London, 1976.

35. Paul W. Tappan, "Who Is the Criminal?" *American Sociological Review* 12: 96–102 (Feb. 1947).

36. Ibid., pp. 99–100.

violation."[37] He added the offhand sociological definition: "A criminal is a person who regards himself as a criminal and is so regarded by society," and declared that the white-collar criminal did not fit the definition.[38] In response to Burgess's comment, Conklin has argued:[39]

To suggest that white collar crime should be defined by the attitudes of the perpetrators would logically imply that murders and rapists should also be questioned about their attitudes toward the criminality of their acts. It is the law rather than the opinion of the offender which defines behavior as criminal or noncriminal.

The comments by Burgess and Tappan concerning the ambiguity of the white-collar crime concept and the failure to distinguish between civil and criminal law miss the fundamental point Sutherland had raised. Sutherland insisted that his analysis of white-collar crime was "an attempt to reform the theory of criminal behavior" rather than an attempt to reform society.[40] If a theory of criminal behavior is to be scientifically adequate, then it must explain all behaviors that have the same essential characteristics, whether or not the behavior has been defined as a crime by the criminal justice agencies. After reviewing upper-class white-collar crimes and the common crimes of the lower class, Sutherland concluded that "the crimes of the two classes differ in incidentals rather than essentials. They differ principally in the implementation of the criminal laws which apply to them."[41] Because criminologists did not consider the activities of upper-class persons as crimes, their theories of criminal behavior have been focused almost exclusively on poverty and the personal pathologies associated with poverty. But these theories could not explain white-collar crime, which differed only in incidentals and not in essentials from the common crimes of the lower class. Therefore, Sutherland argued that conventional theories of crime were invalid, and that "a theory of criminal behavior which will explain both white-collar criminality and lower-class criminality is needed."[42]

37. E. W. Burgess, "Comment," *American Sociological Review* 56: 32–33 (July 1950).

38. Ibid., p. 34.

39. John E. Conklin, *"Illegal but Not Criminal,"* Prentice-Hall, Englewood Cliffs, N.J., 1977, p. 10.

40. Sutherland, *White Collar Crime*, p. v.

41. Sutherland, "White Collar Criminality," p. 7.

42. Sutherland, *White Collar Crime*, p. v.

Sutherland then suggested just such a theory. He argued that, from the point of view of the individual, white-collar crime as well as lower-class crime could be explained by the theory of differential association and, from the point of view of society, both could be explained by anomie and culture conflict theories.[43] He offered case histories to demonstrate that white-collar criminality was learned in a process of association with employers and coworkers who defined such behavior favorably. He also demonstrated that illegal practices devised by an individual or a firm soon diffuse throughout the industry as the competition adopts the practices in what is clearly a learning situation. Finally, he argued that white-collar criminals act in isolation from significant unfavorable definitions of their behaviors. Media representatives and governmental officials who define other behaviors as crimes (that is, those of the lower class) do not so define these white-collar behaviors, both because they are often engaged in the same behaviors themselves and because they are often intimately connected in a profitable web of alliances with the "criminals."

Although differential association theory was used to explain how the individual became involved in white-collar criminality, Sutherland used anomie and culture conflict theories to explain the presence of that criminality in society. Anomie theory described a lack of standards for regulating business practices that had been caused by the rapid economic changes associated with the decline of the free competition system and the rise of governmental regulation. A period of uncertainty resulted in which neither the business community nor the general public was certain of the forms they wished that regulation to take, and the resulting "normlessness" was the source of much criminality.

Culture conflict resulted because the set of standards and norms for acceptable business practices that had evolved in the business community was quite different from that held in the political community. In a formulation directly comparable to his differential association theory, Sutherland argued that crime resulted when the organization that favored violation of law was more powerful than the organization against it. The business community was strongly united in favor of white-collar criminality, but the political community was weak and uncommitted in their organization against it. This explained the prevalence of white-collar crime in society. The obvious implication was that illegal business practices would continue until the political community was effectively organized against it.

43. Sutherland, "White Collar Criminality," p. 7.

A number of other theories explaining white-collar criminal behavior have been proposed by other theorists.[44] While these theories of criminal behavior are interesting, it might be more interesting to look at the question of white-collar crime from the point of view of a theory of the behavior of criminal law. Such a view focuses on explaining the enactment and enforcement of laws against these behaviors, rather than explaining why some people commit them.

From that point of view the whole white-collar crime controversy can be seen as not merely an academic argument among criminologists, but as part of the struggle among groups in society over the processes of enacting and enforcing criminal laws. Many of those who favor the white-collar crime concept are not merely making a theoretical argument, but are also urging that the coercive power of the criminal justice system be used to repress these behaviors. Many others who have objected to the concept do so because they think that it is inappropriate to respond to those behaviors within the context of the criminal justice system. Whichever side prevails in this struggle will determine whether white-collar groups have low or high official crime rates in the future.

Extensive nonconformity of the type found in white-collar crimes is a reflection of basic differences in how people think about the role of government in the private affairs of individuals. The traditional American view, from the earliest days of the Republic, has been firmly set against government interference in business transactions. The "American way" has been dedicated to a glorification of the free market, where the primary goal of business is to maximize profit.[45] Whether or not this is good economic philosophy is not the question. The real questions are whether it is possible to enact laws that are opposed by a significant and powerful segment of the population and, once they are enacted, whether it is possible to enforce them. The American experiments with prohibition of alcohol from 1917

---

44. See, for example, Marshall B. Clinard, "Criminological Theories of Violations of Wartime Regulations," *American Sociological Review* 11: 258–70 (June 1946); Vilhelm Aubert, "White Collar Crime and Social Structure," *American Journal of Sociology* 58: 263–71 (Nov. 1952), reprinted in Geis and Meier, op. cit., pp. 168–79; Donald R. Cressey, *Other People's Money*, The Free Press, Glencoe, Ill., 1953; Richard Quinney, "Occupational Structure and Criminal Behavior: Prescription Violations by Retail Pharmacists," *Social Problems* 11: 179–85 (Fall 1963), reprinted in Geis and Meier, op. cit., pp. 189–96; William N. Leonard and Marvin Glenn Weber, "Automakers and Dealers: A Study of Criminogenic Market Forces," *Law and Society Review* 4 (3): 407–24 (Feb. 1970), reprinted in Geis and Meier, op. cit., pp. 133–48.

45. One bank vice-president stated: "The goal of a business corporation is to make a profit . . . *more fully*, the only goal of a business corporation is to make the *maximum possible profit*. . . . *Completely*, the only goal of a business corporation is to make the maximum possible profit *over a long period*." Cited in Fred J. Cook, *The Corrupted Land*, Macmillan, New York, 1966, p. 93.

to 1933 and with price control legislation during World War II illustrate the difficulty of enforcing laws that are opposed by large or powerful segments of the population.[46] In both cases there were widespread and systematic violations of the law. There were also earnest efforts expended by government agents to bring about compliance, including an extensive battery of legal coercion brought to bear on offenders, running all the way from civil and administrative findings and penalties to prosecutions in criminal courts. But there was a similar cumulative failure in the sense that the whole phenomenon of lawlessness and noncompliance increased with each passing month. In both cases the crime problem was finally solved by abandoning the law, and the practices that had been illegal were again made legal and respectable.

A more recent attempt at price controls produced equally discouraging results.[47] In response to the oil crisis in the 1970s, price controls were imposed on oil in order to promote the discovery of new oil wells in the United States. Accordingly, a higher price was allowed for "new" domestic oil than for "old" domestic oil or for imported oil. The response of the oil industry was to engage in what Rep. Albert Gore (D.—Tenn.) called "the largest fraud, in monetary terms, that has ever been committed on the American public." By relabeling "old" domestic oil and imported oil as "new" domestic oil, approximately $3 billion in illegal profits were made. Although the controls had been imposed because of the judgment that independence from foreign oil was vital to the national security, the response of the government to their widespread violation was to cease all enforcement activities and ultimately to remove the controls.

The simple fact of the matter is that the business community does not view the violation of laws regulating business transactions as being as serious as the violation of laws governing the criminal activity typically committed by poor people. Because this segment of the population has substantial influence on the legislative enactment of laws, the majority of such violations are viewed as civil wrongs, as violations somehow less serious than those of the criminal law covering theft, burglary, and so on. The basic difference in the enforcement of the law bearing on business transactions reflects the power this group has in influencing the policies of the criminal justice system. In countries in which the business community has less influence, one finds a different situation. For example, in the Soviet Union and the

---

46. Report of the National Commission on Law Observance and Law Enforcement, Washington, D.C., June 26, 1931; Marshall B. Clinard, *The Black Market*, Rinehart, New York, 1952.

47. ABC News, "Close-up: The Oil Game," broadcast on June 20, 1982.

People's Republic of China, white-collar offenders are executed for offenses which in America would ordinarily be a civil offense or a criminal offense punished normally by probation and restitution.[48]

The efforts at prohibition and price control discussed above can be explained by Sutherland's arguments about culture conflict. Efforts at enforcement failed because those who organized in favor of law violation were so strong that they crushed those who organized against it. Whether enforcement efforts against today's white-collar crime will prevail is yet to be determined. Because of recent increases in public support, it seems highly unlikely that there will be any dismantling of enforcement efforts in the near future, as happened with prohibition and price control. On the other hand, it also seems unlikely that enforcement efforts will become so powerful that they will be able to overwhelm those who favor law violation. Rather, like enforcement efforts against lower-class crimes, there will probably be a protracted struggle between relatively balanced forces, with neither side routing the other.

Considering white-collar crimes from the three general perspectives in criminology, it would seem that classical theories have considerable potential, since they treat individual criminals as rational actors weighing costs and benefits before deciding whether to commit a crime. No one is more rational and calculating than a white-collar executive deciding, within the context of a large business organization, how to pursue a profit more efficiently. Thus if there is any type of crime in which the classical system of justice should work, it is white-collar crime. The law simply needs to establish punishments that outweigh the benefits of the crime and white-collar offenders, as rational actors, will certainly decide to obey the law.

But, in fact, the classical system of justice has failed miserably in its efforts to control white-collar crime.[49] The problem is that, because of the power of white-collar groups, the criminal law imposes maximum penalties for white-collar crimes that are dramatically lower than the anticipated level of profits from them. Attempts to increase the level of penalties have failed, so that it is in the interests of white-collar groups to continue committing these offenses. This points to the main problem with classical theories generally: They fail to con-

48. See George Feifer, "Russia Shoots Its Business Crooks," *New York Times Magazine*, May 2, 1965, pp. 32–33ff., reprinted in Gilbert Geis, ed., *White Collar Crime*, 1st ed., Atherton, New York, 1968, pp. 320–26; Charles A. Schwartz, "Economic Crime in the U.S.S.R.," *International and Comparative Law Quarterly*, 30 (2): 281–96 (1981); Hungdah Chiu, "Capital Punishment in Mainland China," *Journal of Criminal Law and Criminology* 68 (3): 374–98 (1977).

49. Cf. Christopher D. Stone, *Where the Law Ends*, Harper, New York, 1975.

sider the power of different groups in society and their ability to influence the enactment and enforcement of laws. Classical theories are simply inadequate to deal with the problem of white-collar crime as it exists in the real world because they ignore a major fact in that world, that some groups have more power than others.

As with victimless and organized crimes, theories of criminal behavior do not seem terribly interesting when applied to white-collar crimes. The question of why white-collar offenders behave the way they do can be answered in a relatively straightforward way: they want to make a profit. The more interesting questions for criminology seem to be associated with theories of the behavior of criminal law. How do the processes of enacting and enforcing the criminal laws operate with respect to these behaviors, and with what result for the distribution of official crime rates?

### 4. CONCLUSION

This chapter illustrates that, for victimless, organized, and white-collar crimes at least, theories that examine the processes of the enactment and enforcement of criminal laws are the most interesting and relevant ways to gain an understanding of crime as a social phenomenon. In contrast, classical theories appear to be misleading because the process of defining and punishing these behaviors as crimes has not generally resulted in decreases in their incidence, and theories that examine the causes of criminal behaviors seemed somewhat uninteresting and irrelevant since there are fairly obvious reasons why people engage in them.

Sutherland argued that his theories on white-collar crime were an attempt to reform criminology, not an attempt to reform society. That statement can be interpreted as an attempt to get criminologists to examine the behavior of criminal law in addition to examining the behavior of criminals and the effectiveness of enforcement and punishment systems. While much has been done since Sutherland wrote, the fact remains that criminologists have not yet responded fully to his challenge.

### RECOMMENDED READINGS

Edwin H. Sutherland, *White Collar Crime*, Holt, Rinehart and Winston, New York, 1961. A landmark work in criminology, ahead of its time, and still not fully appreciated.

Edward Sagarin and Fred Montanino, eds., *Deviants: Voluntary Actors in a Hostile World*, General Learning Press, Morristown, N.J., 1977. Contains excellent chapters on syndicated crime (by Lowell L. Kuehn) and white-collar crime (by Carl B. Klockars).

Gilbert Geis, *Not the Law's Business?* Schocken, New York, 1979. An examination of homosexuality, abortion, prostitution, narcotics use, and gambling, focusing on whether victimless crimes can be considered socially harmful.

Edwin M. Schur and Hugo Adam Bedau, *Victimless Crimes: Two Sides of a Debate*, Prentice-Hall, Englewood Cliffs, N.J., 1974. A philosopher and a sociologist present two perspectives on the rationale for decriminalizing victimless crimes.

Sanford H. Kadish, "The Crisis of Overcriminalization," *The Annals* 374: 157–70 (Nov. 1967). An examination of the questionable functions of the criminal law concerning victimless crimes and the costs of using law enforcement to control the behaviors.

Edward M. Brecher, *Licit and Illicit Drugs*, Consumers Union, Mount Vernon, N.Y., 1972. A review of historical, medical, pharmacological, sociological, psychiatric, and psychological literature on legal and illegal drugs, and a critical examination of drug laws, policies, and attitudes.

Alan A. Block and William J. Chambliss, *Organizing Crime*, Elsevier, New York, 1981. The many interrelationships between organization in criminal activities and the political-economic systems of the societies in which they occur.

Francis A. J. Ianni, with Elizabeth Reuss-Ianni, *A Family Business: Kinship and Social Control in Organized Crime*, Russell Sage, New York, 1972. A detailed and intimate portrayal of one Italian-American criminal "family."

Francis A. J. Ianni, *Black Mafia: Ethnic Succession in Organized Crime*, Simon and Schuster, New York, 1974. A study of the black, Puerto Rican, and Cuban crime syndicates that are replacing the Italian-American "families" in New York and New Jersey.

James A. Inciardi, "Vocational Crime," in Daniel Glaser, ed., *Handbook of Criminology*, Rand McNally, Chicago, 1974, pp. 299–401. A detailed history of professional crime from fifteenth-century Europe through the gangs of the early American West to contemporary organized crime; extensive bibliography.

# CHAPTER EIGHTEEN

# Theory, Research, and Policy

In the traditional view of scientific methodology, facts necessarily precede theories.[1] Facts are established through empirical research, so that, with respect to criminology, empirical research establishing the facts about crime must precede any theories used to explain those facts. At the same time, crime policies cannot be directly derived from the facts established by empirical research. Rather, policies can only come from interpretations that are part of the theories used to explain facts. Therefore crime policies can only flow from theories, which, in turn, can only come from facts established by research. Thus it would seem that criminology should consist in an orderly progression from (1) empirical research establishing the facts, to (2) theories explaining these facts, to (3) policies derived from the theories.

While this is consistent with the traditional view of scientific methodology, it is clear that things do not work that way in criminology.[2] Some of the most basic facts crucial to criminology theories are still disputed, despite numerous efforts at empirical research to

1. Bryan Magee (*Karl Popper*, Viking Press, New York, 1973, p. 50) defines the traditional scientific methodology as "the following stages in the following order, each giving rise to the next: (1) observation and experiment; (2) inductive generalization; (3) hypothesis; (4) attempted verification of hypothesis; (5) proof or disproof; (6) knowledge.

2. Things apparently do not work that way in the physical sciences either. Magee (ibid., p. 50) gives Popper's view of the scientific methodology as follows: "(1) problem (usually rebuff to existing theory or expectation); (2) proposed solution—in other words, a new theory; (3) deduction of testable propositions from the new theory; (4) tests, i.e., attempted refutations by, among other things (but only among other things), observation and experiment; (5) preference established between competing theories."

resolve the questions.[3] Other facts are not disputed, but there are as many interpretations of those facts as there are theories in criminology. There are attempts to test the different theories against each other, with the result that one is supported and another is disconfirmed, or that some combination of theories seems best suited to explain the particular data used in the particular study.[4] Research is also used to test the effectiveness of policies derived from the different theories, sometimes finding that they reduce crime while other times finding that there is no effect or even that they increase crime. But such findings are taken with a grain (or a pound) of salt by criminologists, who generally do not see them as sufficient reason to change their positions.

Why is the field of criminology in such a state? How can so many different theories be held by so many different criminologists? Why can't the field straighten itself out, establish the facts about crime through research, determine the appropriate theoretical interpretation of those facts, and infer the proper policy recommendations from that theory? The present chapter examines some of the interrelationships between theory, research, and policy in criminology.

## 1. THEORY AS THE BASIS FOR RESEARCH

The term *research*, when used as a verb, quite literally means "to search again."[5] But it is impossible to search with any degree of effectiveness unless one has some idea of what one is looking for. It is the underlying theory of criminality that guides criminologists in their search for the facts that ultimately will have to be explained by theories of crime. So while there is a sense in which facts must always precede theories, there is another sense in which theories almost always precede facts, since theories guide the search for facts.

3. For example, do lower-class people commit more criminal actions than other people? For conflicting answers to this question, with extensive citations of research, see Ruth Rosner Kornhauser, *Social Sources of Delinquency*, University of Chicago Press, Chicago, 1978, pp. 88–100; Charles R. Tittle, Wayne J. Villemez, and Douglas A. Smith, "The Myth of Social Class and Criminality," *American Sociological Review* 43 (5): 643–56 (Oct. 1978); Donald Clelland and Timothy J. Carter, "The New Myth of Class and Crime," *Criminology* 18: 319–36 (1980); and Delbert Elliott and Suzanne Ageton, "Reconciling Race and Class Differences in Self-Reported and Official Estimates of Delinquency," *American Sociological Review* 45: 95–110 (1981). In general, see Michael Hindelang, "Class and Crime," in Sanford Kadish, *Encyclopedia of Crime and Justice*, Macmillan and the Free Press, New York, 1983.

4. See, for example, Robert E. Johnson, *Juvenile Delinquency and Its Origins*, Cambridge University Press, Cambridge, U.K., 1979; Delbert S. Elliott, Suzanne S. Ageton, and Rachelle J. Canter, "An Integrated Theoretical Perspective on Delinquent Behavior, *Journal of Research in Crime and Delinquency* 16 (1): 3–27 (Jan. 1979).

5. Cf. *Webster's Collegiate Dictionary*, 5th ed., G. & C. Merriam Co., 1947, p. 847.

An example will make that point clear. Some criminologists do empirical research on the relationship between biological factors and criminality. That research is designed to discover the facts that must precede any theory linking biology to crime. At the same time, a criminologist who did not have some confidence in the theory would probably not be interested in doing the research to begin with. Thus, while it is true that facts must precede theories, it is also true that adherence to theories determines where one looks as one is searching for facts. A similar point can be made about criminologists who seek to establish linkages between crime and any number of other factors, such as legitimate and illegitimate opportunities, political-economic systems, attachments to families or peers, cultural beliefs, poverty, income inequality, intelligence, neighborhood characteristics, psychopathology, or powerlessness. In each case adherence to a theory determines where one looks for facts, and in that sense determines the facts one is likely to discover.

What, then, determines a criminologist's initial adherence to a theory, before the start of the search for facts? In general, a theory is a way of understanding or "making sense" of a phenomenon. Criminology theories can make sense for many reasons. Three such reasons are: (1) because the theory is consistent with the person's general and unscientific ideas about crime and criminals; (2) because the theory has certain policy implications about how to respond to crime which make sense to the person; and (3) because the theory is consistent with a body of theoretical knowledge and empirical research techniques that the person acquired before beginning the study of crime and criminals.

Preexisting ideas of crime and criminals may be derived from a variety of sources. Some people form ideas about crime and criminals primarily by reading newspapers and watching television. Others have worked with criminals either within the criminal justice system or within some type of community program, or they have grown up in an environment in which they had many personal experiences with criminals. Whatever the source, most people, including criminologists, form general and relatively unscientific ideas about crime and criminals that make sense to them. These unscientific views influence the general characteristics of the more scientific theories that makes sense to the person. Theories that are consistent with those general views are explored in more detail, and empirical research is undertaken to test them out. Theories that are totally inconsistent with those general views may be dismissed out of hand. After all, "experience is the best teacher." Criminologists, like most other people, put little credence in theories that contradict what they have seen with their own eyes.

Closely related to the general and unscientific views of crime and criminals are the general and unscientific views a person forms about appropriate ways to respond to crime. Some people, on the basis of their experience, believe that punishment is the appropriate response to crime, while other people are favorably oriented toward treatment in correctional institutions or in the community. Some people are favorably oriented toward decriminalization of specific offenses, while others oppose it. Some people believe that solving the crime problem will require major social and political reorganizations, while others believe that such views are not only wrongheaded but dangerous.

There is an obvious and logical interconnection between what one wants done about crime and the explanation of crime in which one believes. Every theory of crime implies policies about how to best handle the crime problem. Conversely, every crime policy makes certain theoretical assumptions about crime that a person must believe in order to believe that the policy will work. In principle, policy ought to be derived from theory, but in reality practical measures often do not wait for theoretical explanations. Rather, policies that seem necessary at the time are implemented, and theoretical explanations come along afterwards to rationalize and justify what has occurred. In this situation people tend to believe in one or another theory of crime because its policy implications are consistent with what they believe should be done about crime; that is, they have a strong belief in particular crime policies and adopt a theory of crime that supports those policies.

Finally, many people come into the field of criminology from other disciplines and bring with them an entire body of knowledge and research techniques. A recent example would be the entrance of economists into the field of criminology. Economics is based on a particular theory of human nature and has developed extensive techniques for statistical analysis. Beginning in the late 1960s, economists began branching out to other fields, believing that their general theories and research techniques would be useful in explaining other phenomena besides the economic system. A number of these economists began to use econometric theories and research techniques to explain the behavior of criminals and the policies of the criminal justice system.[6] Most of these economists had little or no

6. These studies are briefly described in Chapter 2.

experience with criminals and the criminal justice system; their commitment and beliefs were formed by their adherence to economic theory.

Many other groups have come to criminology bearing extensive loads of theory and research techniques. Some sociologists bring Durkheim, Parsons, and Kingsley Davis; others bring Simmel, Weber, and Ralf Dahrendorf; still others bring Marx, Althusser, Habermas, and Thompson; and still others bring symbolic interactionism ethnomethodology, and phenomenology. Some psychologists bring operant and classical conditioning and arguments about differential reinforcement; others bring personality inventories or intelligence tests; still others bring Freudian psychoanalysis. Some biologists bring the anatomy and chemistry of the brain and central nervous system, others bring theory and research on the autonomic nervous system, and still others bring biochemical views on hormones and diet. The list goes on and on.

This presents a major problem for the systematic accumulation of knowledge within the field of criminology. Rock has argued that most of the truly innovative work in criminology has been done by individuals who only passed through the field on their way to other goals.[7] These "criminological innovators" were not criminologists and did not continue to work in the field after making their innovations. The innovations themselves were based on extensive bodies of theory and research that were also new to the field. Criminologists are then faced with a very large problem: They must attempt to absorb large and essentially foreign bodies of knowledge and to integrate them into the preexisting body of theory and research on crime. Just about the time that criminologists have finally absorbed one innovation, another one from another field comes along and the whole process starts over. As a consequence, Rock describes the field of criminology as "a number of fitful leaps from one partially examined thesis to another," and as "a sequence of relatively disconnected and underdeveloped analytical episodes."[8]

One could still expect that the systematic process of gathering and analyzing facts through empirical research would lead to a progressive discarding of theories as they are disconfirmed, and a progressive focusing on one theory as more consistent with the data than any of the others. Such a view would be consistent with Popper's argument that preferences are established between competing the-

---

7. Paul Rock, "Has Deviance a Future?" in Herbert M. Blalock, ed., *Sociological Theory and Research*, The Free Press, New York, 1980, pp. 290–303.

8. Ibid., pp. 293, 295.

ories through "falsification" rather than "verification."[9] That is, the competition among theories is resolved when all the theories except one have been systematically eliminated because they are shown through empirical research to be inconsistent with the facts. The remaining theory is not verified, since no one has proved it is correct. The best that one can say is that "it is supported by every observation so far, and yields more, and more precise, predictions than any known alternative. It is still replaceable by a better theory."[10]

A number of criminologists would argue that such a process has indeed taken place in criminology, and that one theory has shown itself to be more consistent with the data than any other theory. Unfortunately, these criminologists do not agree among themselves on which theory that is. Some criminologists have said that the data about crime are best interpreted within the context of differential association theory;[11] others say social learning theory;[12] still others say control theory;[13] still others, Marxist theory;[14] and so on. The authors of the present book adhere to the view that the data about crime can best be interpreted within the framework of conflict criminology. Again, we can ask why such a situation arises within criminology. Why doesn't the scientific process operate to resolve these controversies systematically?

Over time, it probably will. It must be remembered that, in comparison to sciences such as physics and chemistry, criminology and the other social sciences are very young. The systematic study of physical matter goes back at least to the ancient Greeks, and is more than 2,000 years old. These sciences have had a great deal of time to falsify competing theories, and consequently have reached a considerable degree of agreement on the basic assumptions of their field. In contrast, there was little systematic inquiry into the phenomenon of crime prior to the classical school, beginning about 200 years ago, and the scientific study of the causes of criminal behavior began just over 100 years ago with Lombroso. The history of criminology since then has primarily been one in which new views have been added to the field but old ones have not been eliminated. We no longer believe Lombroso's theory that criminals are atavistic, but some the-

9. Magee, op. cit.

10. Ibid., p. 22.

11. Edwin H. Sutherland and Donald R. Cressey, *Criminology*, 10th ed., Lippincott, Philadelphia, 1978.

12. Ronald L. Akers, *Deviant Behavior*, 2nd ed., Wadsworth, Belmont, Cal., 1977.

13. Gwynn Nettler, *Explaining Crime*, 3rd ed., McGraw-Hill, New York, 1984.

14. Richard Quinney, *Criminology*, 2nd ed., Little, Brown, Boston, 1979.

ories still link crime to physical appearance, others link crime to biological defects such as XYY chromosomes, and still others link crime to biological "inferiority" such as lower autonomic nervous system arousal. There has been very little falsification in criminology so far, and that is why every chapter in this book begins with early theory and research within a certain framework and concludes with a description of similar theory and research going on at the present time.

Criminology's problems in this regard are no different than those of social science generally. The specific problem is that social science theory attempts to describe a very complex reality, but research techniques require that variables be defined in a relatively simple manner so that they can be carefully measured.[15] In general, then, there is a gap between the needs of theory for complexity and the needs of research for simplicity. There are basically two ways to address this problem: One treats the needs of theory as primary and attempts an accurate description of the very complex reality, and the other treats the needs of research as primary and focuses on the analysis of relatively simple but measurable variables. Obviously neither approach solves the problem itself, and both have advantages and disadvantages.

The first approach attempts to describe the total interrelationships of individuals, events, and changing perspectives involved in the phenomenon of crime. These studies may be based on a real-life experience with the subject, and may utilize and organize a great deal of measurable data, but the basic concepts and arguments they propose are not precisely measurable. Many of the theories presented in this book take this approach. Their advantage is that they present views that are more likely to make sense as descriptions of the phenomenon of crime. Their basic problem is that they involve broad generalizations that cannot be specifically tested. There is always the danger that the observer will select out of the totality of impressions and information those items and events that fit the preexisting conception of what to look for. That is, the observer may be able to see only what the theory of criminology has prepared him or her to see.

The other approach deals primarily with measurable variables in the hopes that they will accurately represent the broader and more complex reality. Blalock has written extensively on problems associated with this approach, having turned to it after engaging in frustrating attempts to make sense of the theoretical and empirical lit-

---

15. Hubert M. Blalock, Jr., *Basic Dilemmas in the Social Sciences*, Sage, Beverly Hills, Cal., 1984.

erature in the areas of ethnic and racial relations.[16] He describes the
basic situation of the social scientist (and criminologist) as one in which
there are a large number of independent variables (e.g., race, class,
intelligence, neighborhood of residence, extent of criminal and delinquent associates, and so on), all of which are moderately correlated with the dependent variable (crime) and all of which are moderately correlated with each other. Competing theories generally
include all of the different variables, but place different degrees of
importance on them, or argue for different causal relationships. In
this situation relatively simple decisions about how to define and
measure the variables can produce dramatic differences in the empirical results. The situation is made even more complicated because many of the variables of greatest interest are extremely difficult to measure. Some of them are defined in such a way that it is
not immediately clear how to measure them (e.g., "differential associations" or "commitment to conformity"), while others are more
readily measurable but may require expensive data-collection efforts
when the funds are simply not available. In this situation the social
scientist may simply "select whatever remotely connected indicators
he or she can locate and then merely announce that these will serve
as measures of some highly abstract theoretical construct."[17] As a result of these and other related problems a great deal of social science
research takes the following form:[18]

The investigator points to inadequacies in previous research, which has found
only weak to moderate relationships between a dependent variable and explanatory factors that the investigator wishes to dismiss. An "alternative"
explanation is advanced, the relevant variables imperfectly measured, controls for one's opponent's variables introduced (with these variables also being
imperfectly measured), and then some conclusions reached that usually favor the investigator's preferred explanation. Often, however, the differences in explanatory power are slight and easily accounted for on the basis
of a combination of sampling and measurement errors. The latter, however, are usually ignored and tests are made only for the former. The reader
is then left with an uncomfortable feeling that neither theory is very satisfactory.

16. Hubert M. Blalock, Jr., "Measurement and Conceptualization Problems: The Major Obstacle to Integrating Theory and Research," *American Sociological Review* 44: 881–94 (Dec.
1979). An abridged version is presented in Blalock, ed., *Sociological Theory and Research*,
pp. 31–47.

17. Hubert M. Blalock, Jr., *Conceptualization and Measurement in the Social Sciences*, Sage,
Beverly Hills, Cal., 1982, p. 19.

18. Ibid., p. 16.

Blalock states that the failure to face up to such fundamental issues of conceptualization and measurement is one of the major reasons for the lack of consensus in the social sciences, and for the frus-
tratingly slow pace at which genuine knowledge is accumulated in
these fields. He summarizes his basic message as follows: [19]

Unless very careful attention is paid to one's *theoretical* assumptions and
conceptual apparatus, no array of statistical techniques will suffice. Nor can
a series of ad hoc empirical studies produce truly cumulative knowledge,
except in the sense of producing dated and situation-specific findings of immediate and practical significance. The basic message is that theoretical and
methodological concerns must go hand in hand. Progress in the one area
without similar progress advanced in the other cannot be more than minimal.

Blalock states that this message is especially discouraging for the highly
pragmatic, research-oriented social scientist.[20] Such a person, "constrained by serious data limitations, usually finds it convenient to
sidestep these issues. The theorist, trying to make sense of diverse
empirical studies, is then confronted with an almost hopeless task
and may be tempted to use the empirical information either selectively or anecdotally—or even to ignore it."[21]

Problems associated with the gap between the needs of theories
for complexity and the needs of research for simplicity explain the
general tendency in the field of criminology to expand with the addition of new views but to fail to eliminate older views through falsification. Criminologists adhere to theoretical views of crime that
make sense to them for some reason. Each theoretical perspective
tends to be supported by some empirical studies, but tends to be
disconfirmed by other empirical studies. None of these studies has
sufficient credibility among criminologists to result in a general
agreement that certain viewpoints have been falsified. So research
in all areas continues simultaneously, and there is little appearance
of progress in the field.

Hirschi commented that there has been "too much theory and too
little testing of theory" in criminology research.[22] Blalock's com-

19. Ibid., p. 9.

20. Ibid., p. 9.

21. Blalock, "Measurement and Conceptualization Problems," p. 883.

22. Travis Hirschi, *Causes of Delinquency*, University of California Press, Berkeley, Cal., 1969,
p. 243.

ments can be construed as arguing that there has been too much testing of theory but too little *thinking about* the testing of theory. It is the nature of science to be progressive, in the sense that scientists systematically attack and ultimately solve the problems that hinder progress in their field.[23] Thus one can expect that these problems will be straightened out in the long run. In the meantime they present the major challenge for criminology theory and research in the foreseeable future.

## 2. CRIMINOLOGY THEORY AND CRIME POLICY

Crime policies are the different ways in which the organized state responds to the serious social problems described by the term *crime*. There are many types of crime policies. Some deal with individual offenders, including imprisonment policies that attempt to restrain them by locking them up, to deter them through punishment, or to treat the causes of their behaviors. Other policies attempt to change the social conditions in the communities that offenders come from, or to change the physical environments in the communities where offenders commit their offenses. Still other crime policies address social and political conditions in the society at large, or decriminalize specific offenses in order to take those problem behaviors out of the criminal justice system. The major way in which organized states have always responded to the problems of crime has been via policies that deal with individual offenders. The most common term used to describe these policies at present is *corrections*. That term will be used here, although it is not entirely appropriate for policies that focus on punishing, restraining, or deterring offenders.

There have been some rather clear trends in corrections policies over the long run of history. The major trend has been from overtly brutal and violent policies to policies that are more lenient and mild. Associated with this major trend has been a general shift from capital and corporal punishments to imprisonment as the most frequent response to criminal behavior. There has also been a general change in thinking about the purpose of the state's response, from that of punishment itself to that of some "treatment" intended to change the criminal behavior. Finally, there also may have been a tendency for the state to respond to greater numbers of people and behaviors as

23. Cf. Thomas S. Kuhn, *The Structure of Scientific Revolutions*, University of Chicago Press, Chicago, 1970, pp. 160–73.

criminal as those responses become milder and more focused on imprisonment.[24] That general tendency may be continuing at present with the move to community corrections.[25]

Crime policies that respond to the individual offender, when viewed from the point of view of criminology theory, can basically be interpreted in the context of the ideas and attitudes represented by the terms *punishment* and *treatment*. Punishment involves the intentional infliction of pain and suffering (not necessarily physical) upon the offender by official authority because it is believed that some good will be produced by the pain itself. In general, the infliction of pain as an object in itself can produce benefits only if offenders (or potential offenders) reevaluate their actions as a result of this suffering and choose not to continue committing crimes. This is the process described in classical criminology, so that the concept of punishment is generally associated with the classical school.

Use of the term *treatment* has come into corrections through the analogy with medicine. A sick patient is treated to the end that he may recover from his illness and be restored to normal functioning. He is not punished for having become sick, nor to teach him a lesson so that he will not again become sick. The treatment varies with each case, depending on the diagnosis of what is wrong, which in turn is based on the accumulated knowledge about the disease or condition and on experience with the appropriate action to be taken for different kinds of illness. By the same logic, in corrections the term implies a knowledge of crime causation together with procedures whereby the criminal may be studied and treated appropriately in order to control and change his behavior and restore him to normal functioning in society. Use of the term follows from the general point of view that understands crime as naturally caused, the product of antecedent conditions, circumstances, and events and therefore to be dealt with in terms of the conditions that produce it. That point of view, of course, is associated with theories of the causes of criminal behavior.

Present-day correctional practices can be understood in terms of the basic contradictions between punishment and treatment. Imprisonment *as punishment* is justified by the same logic, and by the same assumptions about human nature, as any other form of punishment, the principal difference being that it would usually be con-

24. Michel Foucault, *Discipline and Punish*, Pantheon, New York, 1977.
25. See, for example, James Austin and Barry Krisberg, "Wider, Stronger, and Different Nets: The Dialectics of Criminal Justice Reform," *Journal of Research in Crime and Delinquency*, January 1981, p. 171.

sidered to be milder and more humane than the punishments it has replaced. As punishment, therefore, imprisonment is to be understood as the present form or stage of the long historic process of mitigating the severity and barbarity of earlier practices. *As treatment,* imprisonment similarly is justified by the same logic and assumptions used in connection with care of the physically ill, the mentally ill, or the congenitally defective. The objective is to return the individual to the community a better citizen than when he or she entered the institution.

Treatment programs in the modern prison generally have been of two kinds, psychological or psychiatric counseling and educational or vocational training programs.[26] Counseling is assumed to be useful in uncovering the deeper frustrations and anxieties thought to underlie individual misconduct. When the individual obtains more insight into his or her own unconscious motivations, it should follow that he or she will be ready to seek a more intelligent life orientation than criminality. Such service provided by the institution should therefore be a positive contribution to rehabilitation. Together with this specialized service goes a general program of education and training in the trade or industrial skills needed for successful life-adjustment outside. Such training programs seek to correct the ignorance, poor habits, and lack of skill that are assumed to have been important factors in the inmate's past criminality.

All of these policies make theoretical assumptions about crime and criminal behaviors, whether the people who adhere to these policies are conscious of those assumptions or not. Punishment policies assume that people are free to change their behaviors in response to punishment; otherwise it is the mindless infliction of pain and discomfort on people with no useful purpose whatsoever. Individual counseling programs assume that criminal behavior is at some level a response to personality problems and that dealing with such problems will have some influence on later criminal behavior. Unless one makes such an assumption, then inmates who participate in such programs would only be expected to gain insight about themselves, so that they lead richer and more fulfilling lives while they are pursuing their careers in crime. Similarly, educational and vocational programs assume that criminal activity is at some level a response to

---

26. For a detailed discussion of programs emphasizing psychiatric or psychological treatment, see the readings in Robert G. Leger and John R. Stratton, eds., *The Sociology of Corrections,* John Wiley, New York, 1977, pp. 301–87. For educational and vocational training programs, see Ronald L. Goldfarb and Linda R. Singer, *After Conviction,* Simon and Schuster, New York, 1973, pp. 610–74.

the lack of opportunities to make a living in legitimate ways and that providing inmates with some legitimate skills and abilities will resolve that problem. But crime may not be a response to the absence of legitimate opportunity, or it may be that the absence of legitimate opportunities has nothing to do with the skills and abilities of the offender but rather is a function of much broader economic trends and political policies. In either case, providing the individual offender with vocational skills and educational abilities will not solve the problem.

It is obvious that the treatment policies used in prisons are based on very few of the criminology theories that have been discussed in this book. It is equally obvious why correctional policies are based on some criminology theories and not others. The criminology theories that are used as the basis for correctional treatment are those that can be implemented entirely within a prison setting and do not require any adjustments or modifications in the broader functioning of society. That is, correctional policies are based on theories that are oriented entirely to the adjustment of the prisoner to the larger society, and not on theories that imply that some adjustments must be made in the larger society itself.

For example, many kinds of criminality are the product of the conflicts among competing groups with different values and interests. The victimless, organized, and white-collar crimes discussed in Chapter 17 might be considered as examples of this type of crime. Correctional workers, both in theory and in practice, usually ignore this social conflict aspect of criminality and seek to change the orientation and the behavior of the individuals concerned. These workers cannot change the society of which they are a part, they cannot modify the forces in conflict outside the institution, but they do hope to do something with the individuals inside the institution. Hence they ignore what they cannot manipulate, and construct a correctional theory to rationalize what they hope to do. This may well be the principal reason for the popularity of environmental theories of crime causation among correctional workers and for the frequent emphasis on the significance of traumatic experience in accounting for the psychological idiosyncracies of criminals.

An obvious question must be asked: How effective have these programs been? Numerous studies have been done on individual treatment programs with a great variety of results. In order to evaluate the effectiveness of rehabilitation programs in general, Walter C. Bailey in 1966 analyzed 100 of these reports published between

1940 and 1960.[27] He concluded that "evidence supporting the efficacy of correctional treatment is slight, inconsistent, and of questionable reliability." A much broader study was carried out by Lipton, Martinson, and Wilks in the late 1960s.[28] They undertook a six-month search of the literature for all available reports on the effects of rehabilitation programs published in English between 1945 and 1967. A large number of these studies were eliminated because of methodological problems that made evaluation impossible. The remaining 231 studies were then evaluated in terms of the effect of the various programs on recidivism, as well as on other measures of offender improvement such as adjustment to prison life, vocational success, educational achievement, personality and attitude change, and general adjustment to the outside community. Although rehabilitation programs were found to benefit offenders in a variety of ways, in general these programs did not appear to affect recidivism. Martinson summarized this point as follows: "With few and isolated exceptions, the rehabilitative efforts that have been reported so far have had no appreciable effect on recidivism."[29]

This finding indicates that participation in rehabilitation programs apparently has little effect on whether a criminal does or does not return to crime. It does not necessarily mean, however, that most criminals do return to crime. In fact, it would appear that recidivism rates, with or without rehabilitation programs, are much lower than previously thought. Martinson and Wilks have carried out a survey of recidivism studies similar to the survey of rehabilitation studies.[30] Preliminary findings indicate that the mean recidivism rate in the 1970s is about 23 percent, having dropped from around 33 percent in the 1960s. These figures are substantially below most estimates that recidivism rates are somewhere around 60 to 70 percent, but are consistent with Glaser's earlier analysis of recidivism studies.[31] He had argued that the higher recidivism statistics were generally

---

27. Walter C. Bailey, "Correctional Outcome: An Evaluation of 100 Reports," *Journal of Criminal Law, Criminology and Police Science* 57 (2): 153–60 (June 1966).

28. Douglas Lipton, Robert Martinson, and Judith Wilks, *The Effectiveness of Correctional Treatment*, Praeger, New York, 1975. A shorter version of this study is found in Robert Martinson, "What Works? Questions and Answers About Prison Reform," *The Public Interest* 35: 22–54 (Spring 1974).

29. Martinson, "What Works?" op. cit., p. 25.

30. Robert Martinson and Judith Wilks, *Knowledge in Criminal Justice Planning—A Preliminary Report*, Center for Knowledge in Criminal Justice Planning, New York, 1976.

31. Daniel Glaser, *The Effectiveness of a Prison and Parole System*, Bobbs-Merrill, Indianapolis, 1964, pp. 13–35.

based on surveys of prison populations, which usually found that about
two-thirds of the inmates in a particular prison had previously been
incarcerated. That type of survey ignores the fact that repeat offenders usually receive longer sentences than first offenders, so that
they tend to "pool" in the prison system, whereas the first offenders
turn over more rapidly. In addition, many of these estimates were
taken from maximum security institutions, where there are likely to
be more repeat offenders and fewer first offenders. Glaser estimated
that only about one-third of all men released from a prison system
would be returned to prison within five years.

What sense can criminology theories make of this situation in correctional policies? First, the general finding that recidivism rates are
reasonably low, and that they are not affected by participation in rehabilitation programs, suggests that the effectiveness of prisons as a
response to crime is probably derived primarily from their punishment, rather than their rehabilitative, aspect. This general observation would support the general point of view of classical criminology,
and would suggest that the present policies that attempt to treat the
causes of criminal behaviors are unsuccessful.

Second, the high crime rates in the United States, as compared
to other countries, suggests that criminal behaviors are generated by
the particular social arrangements found in this country. The lower
crime rates found in many other countries suggests that changes in
the social arrangements of this country could have a impact on crime
rates here. It is obvious that the present correctional policies to punish or treat criminal behavior do not attempt to change these larger
social arrangements. Rather, it may be that on the one side there is
a gigantic social assembly line that mass-produces criminals, and on
the other side there is a criminal justice system, with its punishment
and treatment programs, that attempts to grab many of the criminals
as they come off the line and remake them into upstanding citizens.

In earlier periods criminology theory focused directly on the individual criminal, and the policies derived from these theories were
easily implemented without changing any broader social arrangements. As criminology has developed more recently, it has focused
more and more on the broader social arrangements thought to generate higher crime rates. Policies derived from these theories generally have not been implemented. Two attempts to implement such
policies were discussed in earlier chapters of this book. Chapter 10
discussed the attempt of Shaw and McKay to deal with social disorganization in rapidly changing urban areas, and Chapter 11 discussed the attempts of the War on Poverty to redistribute legitimate

opportunities to groups without them. In each case, these attempts were derailed when they conflicted with the moral values and economic interests of more powerful groups. The lesson of this is clear: Crime policies can only be implemented if they do not disturb the economic interests and moral values of larger, more powerful groups.

Here, then, is the heart of the problem between criminology theory and crime policy. Criminology theory attempts to explain the basic problem of crime. In so doing it looks at any number of different variables, from those associated with the individual offender to those associated with the political and economic systems of the society itself. Crime policies can be derived from all aspects of criminology theory, but only policies that do not disturb the larger group interests can be implemented. Thus only those policies derived from criminology theories that focus on offenders and their immediate environments can be implemented, and only to the extent that the larger social arrangements are not disturbed.

In a sense, the problem between criminology theory and crime policy is comparable to that between criminology theory and empirical research. Just as empirical research must reduce complex theoretical arguments to simple concepts that can be precisely measured, so crime policies must reduce complex theoretical arguments to simple programs that can be implemented administratively without stepping on any large toes. Criminology theory has no such limitation, and has focused more and more on those large toes as involved in the basic problems of crime. The end result is an impasse in which the policy implications of most criminology theories are never implemented and criminology itself is viewed as having little or nothing practical to say about crime policy.[32]

## 3. CONCLUSION

Policy choices are value choices, and scientific experts should not be in the business of making value decisions, although as private citizens they are entitled to their value commitments as are other persons. As scientific experts, however, they should use their expertise to determine accurately what the effects of various public policies are likely to be. In theory, at least, public officials will then be able to make informed and intelligent value choices about important public concerns such as crime.[33]

32. See James Q. Wilson, *Thinking About Crime*, rev. ed., Basic Books, New York, 1984, ch. 3.

33. This is the position taken by John Monahan, *Predicting Violent Behavior*, Sage, Beverly Hills, Cal., 1981.

Criminologists will not be able to function in this role until they achieve some agreement among themselves on the facts about crime and the basic theoretical interpretation of those facts. That requires solving the problems of conceptualization and measurement described earlier in this chapter. Until then, policymakers are able to select as experts those criminologists who support policies similar to the policymaker's own ideas. Those policies tend to be ones that are consistent with the policymaker's interests and the interests of powerful groups to whom the policy maker must respond. Other criminologists are then reduced to the role of saying that the policies preferred by the policymaker will not work but of not being able to offer any other alternatives that, from the policymaker's viewpoint, are acceptable.

The traditional view is that policies are derived from theories, while theories are based on empirical research to discover facts. It appears that, more often than not, this sequence is reversed in criminology. People adhere to theories of crime because those theories are consistent with preferred crime policies. Adherence to the theory then determines the nature of empirical research, which is designed to discover facts to support the preferred theory and discredit competing theories. Criminology will not achieve the status of a science until it conforms to the traditional relationship, so that criminology theories will indeed be based on the discovery of facts through empirical research, and policy recommendations will flow from the implications of theory.

## RECOMMENDED READINGS

Hubert M. Blalock, Jr., *Basic Dilemmas in the Social Sciences*, Sage, Beverly Hills, Cal., 1984. A nontechnical review of problems arising from the study of a complex reality in the light of practical problems of data collection.

Denis Szabo, *Criminology and Crime Policy*, Heath, Lexington, Mass., 1978. A complex analysis of the relationship between theory in criminology and crime policies.

Ysabel Rennie, *The Search for Criminal Man: A Conceptual History of the Dangerous Offender*, Heath, Lexington, Mass., 1978. The history of theoretical criminology viewed from the perspective of policy implications, showing their cyclical tendencies.

Daniel Glaser, "The Interplay of Theory, Issues, Policy, and Data," and James F. Short, Jr., "Evaluation as Knowledge-Building—and Vice Versa," in Malcolm W. Klein and Katherine S. Teilmann, eds., *Handbook of Criminal Justice Evaluation*, Sage, Beverly Hills, Cal., 1980, pp. 123–42 and 303–26, respectively. Unless theoretical frameworks guide and are the product of program evaluations, those evaluations may contribute little to our knowledge base.

J. David Hawkins, Paul A. Pastor, Jr., Michelle Bell, and Sheila Morrison, *A Typology of Cause-Focused Strategies of Delinquency Prevention*, U.S. Government Printing Office, Washington, D.C., 1980. The various types of criminology theories are examined for their policy implications about preventing delinquency.

# CHAPTER NINETEEN

# Assessing Criminology Theories

Theories must be based on facts. Thus, assessments of criminology theories are essentially statements about whether and to what extent those theories are consistent with and supported by the facts. But, as pointed out in Chapter 18, the state of empirical research in criminology is such that there are many disagreements about the basic facts related to the phenomenon of crime. Even when there are agreements about the facts, there are disagreements about their proper theoretical interpretation. Nevertheless, at the end of each chapter of this book, some assessment is made about the theories presented in that chapter. Those assessments are necessarily somewhat subjective, but they represent the best judgment of the authors.

It also seems appropriate to offer some general assessment of criminology theories, now that we have come to the end of the book. This is an attempt to draw together the various assessments made at the end of each chapter and to that extent can serve as a summary and overview of the field. The assessment also attempts, in a somewhat speculative way, to draw together the different types of theories into one coherent view. To that extent it is even more subjective than the assessments offered at the end of the different chapters. This, of course, is only one view, and other authors who review the state of theory and research in criminology come to very different conclusions.[1]

---

1. See, for example, Gwynn Nettler, *Explaining Crime*, 3rd ed., McGraw-Hill, New York, 1984, pp. 315–16.

## 1. THEORIES OF CRIMINAL BEHAVIOR

Two types of theories of criminal behavior are discussed in this book. The first, referred to as *classical criminology*, describes criminal behavior as freely chosen. In this frame of reference criminals are described as rational individuals who calculate the costs and benefits of committing crime and choose to commit crime when its benefits are greater than its costs. The second type of theory, referred to as *positive criminology*, describes criminal behavior as caused by factors beyond the individual's control. The causes of criminal behavior were originally thought to be biological factors, but later the focus shifted to psychological factors and then to social factors.

In recent years most criminology theories have focused on social factors as causes of criminal behaviors. Given the present state of empirical research, it seems reasonable to conclude that this present focus is appropriate. A substantial majority of criminals are apparently biologically and psychologically normal individuals whose criminal behaviors arise because they are placed in particular kinds of social situations. The major role for biological and psychological theories in criminology, therefore, is to describe the normal processes by which normal individuals learn normal human behaviors, both criminal and noncriminal. Theories focusing on abnormal biological and psychological characteristics may be useful for understanding some criminal behaviors but are less useful for explaining the broad range of criminality.

If biological and psychological abnormalities are not present in most criminals, then the distinction between positive and classical views of criminal behavior largely disappears. Specifically, the modern theories of normal learning are similar to, although more complex than, the classical view. Instead of describing individuals as freely deciding their actions on the basis of a calculation of costs and benefits, these theories describe human behaviors as shaped by reinforcements and punishments. When applied to criminal behavior, it is relatively apparent that one type of reinforcement is the inherent benefit of committing the criminal act, and one type of punishment is that imposed by criminal justice agencies. These are the costs and benefits described by classical theory. But modern learning theory, as applied to the learning of criminal behaviors, goes beyond these costs and benefits to describe a wide variety of other reinforcements and punishments that shape the person's behavior. In classical terms, these are additional costs and benefits that enter into the person's decision-making process.[2]

Many criminology theories presented in this book can be interpreted as describing social factors that direct specific reinforcements and punishments to groups of people who face particular kinds of social situations. The result is that individuals in some groups are more likely to engage in criminal behaviors, while individuals in other groups are more likely to avoid them.[3] In classical terms, one would say that rational individuals who calculate their costs and benefits in different kinds of social situations will come to different conclusions about whether to engage in criminal behaviors. Social factors therefore determine the overall distribution of criminal behaviors among groups in society.

At the most general level, the reinforcements and punishments experienced by a person are influenced by his or her position within the structural organization of the broader society. This includes the degree of modernization; the nature of the political-economic system; the distribution of opportunities, power, and wealth within that system; and the presence or absence of rapid social change. Reinforcements and punishments are also influenced by the values, norms, and expectations for behavior that are embedded within the person's cultural and social context. Finally, reinforcements and punishments are also influenced by personal relationships, such as attachments to conventional others and the effects of being labeled a criminal. With respect to any individual, the explanation of criminal behavior may involve any combination of these elements. To that extent, all criminology theories may be considered useful in that they can sensitize the observer to the many kinds of factors that may be involved in the person's life.

On the other hand, some types of factors are more likely to be involved in some types of situations and therefore with some types of people. The results of empirical research on this subject are quite tentative, but the following suggestions appear to make sense at the present time:

1. The gradual long-term decline in criminal behavior over the centuries is probably best explained by the gradual expansion of cultural and structural controls as part of the modernization process.

2. The classical view can be considered a cognitive learning theory, whereas most modern learning theories are behavioral. See Chapter 12 of this book. This distinction does not affect the present argument.

3. This is similar to the position taken by Ronald L. Akers, *Deviant Behavior: A Social Learning Approach*, 2nd ed., Wadsworth, Belmont, Cal., 1977.

2. Short-term increases in that long-term decline may be associated with a variety of factors, including the breakdown of cultural and structural controls, such as during periods of rapid social change; changes in cultural attitudes toward criminal behavior, such as the legitimization of violence during times of war; and changes in the structural organization of the society, such as the distribution of legitimate opportunities, material goods, or political power.

3. Juvenile delinquency, most cases of which consist of less serious offenses, is probably best explained by the relative absence of structural and cultural controls during adolescence. These behaviors generally cease as the person enters adulthood.

4. The presence of higher rates of serious criminal behavior in some societies rather than others, and in some groups within a particular society, is probably best attributed to strains associated with the social structural organization of the society. This includes serious forms of delinquency that persist into adulthood.

5. The persistence of those higher rates of serious criminal behavior for one or two generations after the disappearance of the underlying structural conditions can be attributed to cultural ideas that first develop in response to the structural conditions and then achieve an independent causal effect on behaviors.

6. The persistence of serious criminal behavior for a longer period of time is probably best attributed to structural conditions rather than cultural ideas, unless there are cultural differences in attitudes about whether the behavior is really criminal. Few such differences exist about the behaviors traditionally described as serious crimes.

7. When a criminal ceases committing serious criminal behaviors with no change in the structural and cultural conditions and no change in the overall crime rate of the society, it is probably due to the effects of the classical system of punishment.

## 2. THEORIES OF THE BEHAVIOR OF CRIMINAL LAW

In order to present a complete explanation of the phenomenon of crime, it is necessary to explain not only why people behave the way they do but also why their behaviors are officially defined and processed as crimes. That is, criminology must include both theories of criminal behavior and theories of the behavior of criminal law. These two types of theories must be consistent with each other since they both ultimately explain the same phenomenon. A theory of criminal behavior that is joined to and consistent with a theory of the behavior of criminal law constitutes a unified theory of crime.

Theories of the behavior of criminal law have always been associated with theories of criminal behavior. For example, Beccaria presented many ideas about how the criminal law behaved. Most of those ideas were quite radical, and Beccaria was unable to solve the conceptual problems they caused in the context of his classical theory. Those problems were solved by the later neoclassical theorists, who simply discarded Beccaria's ideas and replaced them with the argument that the criminal law protects the common interests. Beccaria himself had described the behavior of criminal law in very different terms.

The early positive criminologists explained the behavior of criminal law in their "natural" definitions of crime: the behavior of criminal law was said to be determined by the inherent characteristics of criminal behaviors. More recent theories of the causes of criminal behavior are implicitly based on similar theories of the behavior of criminal law. Kornhauser, for example, states that most criminology theories are based on the assumption that "within any entity sufficiently knit to be called a society, there are some minimum rules required for its mere existence. . . . These pan-human 'rules of the game'—rules about the safety of the person and his possessions, rules without which sustained social interaction cannot occur—are everywhere and always embodied in law."[4] This is a theory of the behavior of criminal law, although, as Kornhauser points out, it is not made explicit in any of the criminology theories.

These implicit theories of the behavior of criminal law are often relatively simplistic. They may involve only the most general assertions, applied to a fairly restricted range of the criminal law, with the admission that there are numerous (although unspecified) exceptions. Theorists may defend those assertions with the argument that the behavior of criminal law is relatively obvious and needs no explicit or detailed explanation. Nevertheless, the failure to develop explicit and detailed theories may result from the fact that a close examination of the actual behavior of criminal law leads to innumerable conceptual problems that the theorists are unable to solve within their own frames of reference.

Explicit theories of the behavior of criminal law have been presented within only three of the frames of reference discussed in this book. *Social reaction* theorists view the enactment and enforcement of criminal laws in terms of the social psychological processes of attributing meanings to certain situations and then acting on these

---

4. Ruth Rosner Kornhauser, *Social Sources of Delinquency*, University of Chicago Press, Chicago, 1978, p. 40.

meanings. *Conflict* theorists argue that the enactment and enforcement of criminal laws reflects in a general way the distribution of power among groups in societies. *Marxist* theorists argue that the criminal law is one of the many means by which the state serves the long-term economic interests of the owners of the means of production, particularly with respect to maintaining capitalist social relations. These theorists also present theories of criminal behavior in association with their theories of the behavior of criminal law, so that their theories can be described as unified theories of crime. However, all of these theories would require substantial additional development before they could be said to offer satisfactory explanations of the phenomenon of crime, and none at present is supported by a fairly broad range of empirical research specifically designed to test it against competing theories.

## 3. CONCLUSION

The challenge for criminologists is to construct such unified theories of crime. This will require a more precise description of the biological, psychological, and social factors associated with the emergence of criminal behaviors among particular individuals and groups in society. It will also require the development of explicit theories focusing on the behavior of criminal law. Like theories of criminal behavior, these theories must be empirically supported, that is, they must reflect the reality of how the criminal law actually behaves rather than the ideal of how it is supposed to behave. These two types of theories must be joined to each other in a consistent and unified theory in order to explain fully the phenomenon of crime.

Meeting this challenge requires the generation of new knowledge about crime through rigorous empirical research. But more important, it requires the organization and coordination of existing knowledge in a coherent theoretical framework. Much is already known about the phenomenon of crime. Future developments in theoretical criminology will result primarily from making sense out of what we already know.

# Index

Abuse, child, 101
Academic competence. *See* Intelligence; Schools and delinquency
Adler, Alfred, 111
Adler, Mortimer J., 6, 209
Adoptees, 90–92
Aichhorn, August, 114–15, 116, 232
Akers, Ronald L.
  on labeling theory, 256
  social learning theory, 223–24, 228, 229, 286, 288–89
Alihan, M. A., 174–75, 176
Althusser, L., 311, 344
Anomie
  as a control perspective, 143–44, 158, 232
  Durkheim's theory, 143, 146, 150–52, 185, 186, 188–89
  Lander's study, 177
  Merton's theory, 143, 185–89
  Sutherland's theory, 334
Anthropology, criminal, 36–38, 43–44, 50–57
Antisocial personality. *See* Psychopathy
Anxiety reaction to punishment, 103–4
Appearance, physical. *See* Physical characteristics
Aristotle, 9, 48, 206, 208
Aspirations, 199, 244
Association, Aristotle's laws of, 206, 208
Association, differential. *See* Differential association theory
Atavistic criminal, Lombroso's theory of, 37–40, 50–53, 345–46

Autonomic nervous system, 103–6, 232–33, 344, 346

Bailey, Walter C., 352–53
Bandura, Albert, 207–8
Bartol, Curt R., 106, 127–28
Beccaria, Marchese de, 18–30
  behavior of criminal law and, 362
  Durkheim and, 155
  Lombroso and, 36
  physiognomy and, 48
Becker, Gary S., 31
Becker, Howard S., 254
Bedau, Hugo Adam, 317
Behavior of criminal law
  conflict theories, 286–94
  as a frame of reference, 13–15, 16, 361–63
  Marxist theories, 299–300, 310–13
  organized crime and, 327–28
  social reaction theories, 257, 263
  victimless crimes and, 322
  white-collar crime and, 335, 338
Behavioral learning theories, 206–7
Beliefs. *See* Ideas
Berk, Richard A., 134
Berman, Louis, 96–97
Binet, Alfred, 70–72
Biochemical imbalance, 96–99
Biological behaviorism, 224–25
Biological factors, 81–107, 359, 363. *See also* Genetics, Intelligence; Physical characteristics

Biological factors (*continued*)
  control theories and, 232–33, 237, 239, 247
  econometric theories and, 31
  as a frame of reference, 11, 16, 33
  social factors and, 64, 78, 84–85, 106–7
  social reaction theories and, 254–55
  unified conflict theory of crime, 287, 294
  victimless crimes and, 318–19
Biosocial theories, 64, 84–85. *See also* Biological factors; Social factors
Bittner, Egon, 261
Black, Donald J., 259
Blacks and crime. *See* Racial and ethnic groups
Blalock, Hubert M., Jr., 347–48, 349
Block, Alan A., 304–5, 308–9
Blumstein, Alfred, 153–54
Body type theories, 57–65
Bohn, Martin J., Jr., 119
Bonesana, Cesare. *See* Beccaria, Marchese de
Bonger, William, 303
Bordua, David J., 199
"Born" criminal
  Lombroso, 38–40, 50–53
  Ferri, 41
Bowlby, John, 115
Brain allergies, 98–99
Brain damage, 100–101
Brain dysfunction, 100–103
Brenner, Harvey, 134
Briar, Scott, 257
Broca, Paul, 70
Brodsky, Stanley L., 125–26
Bronner, Augusta, 115
Burgess, Ernest W., 162–64, 332–33
Burgess, Robert L., 223–24
Bursik, Robert J., Jr., 175–76

Calvin, Allen D., 134
Cameron, Mary Owen, 253
Capital punishment. *See* Death penalty
Capitalist economic system, 269–70, 299–316
Capone, Al, 223, 330
Carrara, Francesco, 41
Causes of criminal behavior. *See also* Biological factors; Positivist theories; Psychological factors; Social factors

  as a frame of reference, 10–12, 16, 33, 45–46, 359
  multiple factor causation, 11, 37–38, 45, 106–7, 359–61, 363
Central nervous system, 99–103, 344
Cerebral allergies, 98–99
Chambliss, William J.
  conflict theory, 154, 283–86, 290
  Marxist theory, 304–5, 308–9
  self-image of criminals, 253–54
  vagrancy, 264
Chicago area projects, 180–82
Chicago School of Human Ecology, The, 160–84, 212
  and Durkheim, 143
Cho, Y. H., 135
Christiansen, Karl O., 89
Christie, Nils, 153
Chromosomes, XYY, 92–95, 346
Cicourel, Aaron V., 260–62
Class and crime. *See also* Poverty; White-collar crime
  classical criminology, 27–28
  cultural and subcultural theories, 214–19
  Hirschi's theory, 243, 245
  intelligence and, 77–82
  Marxist theories, 303, 306–13
  social reaction theories, 259–62, 264, 265
  strain theories, 187–89, 193–97, 200–203
  Sutherland's theory, 226, 329–34
  XYY chromosomes and, 95
Classical conditioning, 207
  autonomic nervous system, 103–6
Classical theories, 18–35
  correctional policies and, 354
  Durkheim's theory and, 143
  as a frame of reference, 10, 13, 15–17, 359
  Marx's theory and, 303
  organized crime and, 328
  victimless crimes and, 322
  white-collar crime and, 337–38
Cleckley, Hervey, 116, 122–23
Cloward, Richard A.
  gang delinquency, 195–97, 199–200, 201, 216, 242, 294
  illegitimate opportunities, 193–94, 205
Cognitive learning theories, 206–7. *See also* Culture; Ideas
  Glaser's theory as, 223
  Sutherland's theory as, 211–12, 222, 228–29

Tarde's theory as, 208
Cohen, Albert K.
  gang delinquency, 194–95, 196, 199, 200, 216, 242, 243, 246
  self-image, construction of, 252
Collective conscience, 146–50
Colson, Charles, 8
Community control theory, 179–80
Community organization, 180–82
Comte, Auguste, 144, 145
Conditioning, classical, 207
  autonomic nervous system, 103–6
Conditioning, operant, 207
  criminal behavior as normally learned, 222–25
  unified conflict theory of crime, 288
Conflict theories, 269–98, 363
  and ecological research, 178
  and Marxist theories, 269–70, 299–300
  and social reaction theories, 225–26
Conklin, John E., 333
Consensus vs. conflict, 269, 280, 283–84
Constitutional school. *See* Physical characteristics
Containment theory, 237–39
Control perspective, 232–33
  and autonomic nervous system, 103–6
  in conflict theories, 295, 296
  in Durkheim's theory, 143–44, 158–59
  in Glaser's theory, 223
  in the Gluecks' research, 61, 220–22
  and IQ, 76–78
  in Marxist theories, 307
  and phrenology, 49
  in psychoanalytic theory, 114–16
  in Shaw and McKay's theory, 160, 165, 171, 173, 179–80
  social control theories, 232–48, 360–61
Cooley, Charles H., 252
Corrections, 349–55
Cortés, Juan B., 62–65
Couzens, Michael, 260–61
Cressey, Donald R.
  definition of crime, 12
  differential association theory, 213, 219, 228
  embezzlement, 219, 253
  personality inventories, 118
Crime policies, 349–55
  conflict theories, 295–97
  cultural and subcultural theories, 216, 218

ecology theories, 180–82
  strain theories, 201–2
Crime rates, official
  in conflict theories, 287–88, 290–94, 295–98
  historical trends in, 136–37, 157–58, 360
  in social reaction theories, 257, 262, 263
  white-collar crime, 226, 330–31, 335
Criminal anthropology, 36–38, 43–44, 50–57
Criminalization, Turk's theory of, 280–83
Crowe, Raymond R., 90
Cultural and subcultural theories, 213, 214–19, 242–44, 295
Culture deviance theory, 227
Cultural transmission theory, 179–80
Cultural values. *See* Values
Culture. *See also* Values; Expectations; Ideas; Norms
  Akers' theory, 228, 289
  cultural and subcultural theories, 214–19, 245, 295
  IQ test bias, 74, 79–80
  Marxist theory, 313
  strain theories, 186–89, 193, 194, 197, 198, 200–201
  Sutherland's theory, 212–13, 289
  Turk's theory, 281
  victimless crimes, 319–20
Culture conflict
  Sellin, 270
  Shaw, 172–73
  Sutherland, 212, 227, 334
Curtis, Lynn A., 217–18, 229

Dahrendorf, Ralf, 289, 344
Dalgaard, Steffen Odd, 89–90
Dangerous offender laws, 125–27
Danser, Kenneth R., 133
Darwin, Charles, 36–37, 40, 44, 68
Davis, Kingsley, 344
Death penalty,
  Beccaria, 24, 29
  Behavior of criminal law, 14–15, 337
  Garofalo, 44
Decriminalization, 321–22, 328
Definitions of crime and criminals, 9
  labeling, 15, 250–52
  legal, 10, 12
  natural, 12, 43
De Fleur, Melvin L., 220–21

Degeneracy
  mental, 67–69
  physical, 47, 50–57
Deterrence, 30–32
Deviance and social reaction, 248–68, 362
  conflict theories and, 295
  Durkheim's theory and, 144, 154
  Marxist theories and, 304
Devil. *See* Spiritual explanations
Dickman, Toby, 39
Diet and crime, 84, 98–99
Dietrick, David C., 198–99
Differential anticipation theory, 222–23
Differential association theory, 209–14.
  *See also* Sutherland, Edwin H.
  assessments of, 225–30
  Cloward and Ohlin's theory and, 193, 197
  Quinney's social reality theory and, 279
  Sellin's culture conflict theory and, 270
  Shaw and McKay's theory and, 179
  symbolic interactionism and, 211–12, 250
  tests and reformulations of, 216, 219–25, 242–43
  Vold's group conflict theory and, 225–27, 288, 289
  white-collar crime and, 334
Differential social organization, 213
Dinitz, Simon, 120
Disorganization, social, 170–72, 180–82, 212–13, 294, 354
Drift, 239–41, 246
Dugdale, Richard, 68–69
Durkheim, Emile, 143–59,
  control theories and, 143–44, 156, 158–59, 232
  ecology theories and, 143, 156, 179
  strain theories and, 143, 156, 185, 186, 188–89

Ebbinghaus, H., 69, 206
Ecology, 160–84
Ecological fallacy, 176
Econometrics, 30–32, 343–44
Economic conditions and crime, 130–41
  in Kornhauser's theory, 179–80
  in Lander's work, 177
  in Shaw and McKay, 169
Economic inequality, 130–31, 138–41, 294
Ehrlich, Isaac, 135
Electroencephalograph (EEG), 99–100

Ellis, Lee, 86–87
Enacting criminal laws. *See* Behavior of criminal law; Official crime rates
Enforcing criminal laws. *See* Behavior of criminal law; Official crime rates
Environmental vs. genetic models of human behavior, 6, 8, 85–92, 157
Environmental factors in crime causation. *See* Social factors
Environmental studies, 178–79
Epilepsy, 100
  in Lombroso's theory, 38
Erikson, Kai, 153, 154
Expectations. *See also* Culture; Ideas
  in Cloward and Ohlin's theory, 199
  in Glaser's theory, 223
  in Hirschi's theory, 244
  in subculture of violence theories, 216, 228
  in Sutherland's theory, 227–28
Eysenck, H. J.,
  as control perspective, 232–33
  autonomic nervous system, 104–06

Facts and theories, relationship between, 3–6, 340–49, 358
Falsification of theories, 5–6, 344–46
Family, crime runs in, 86–87
Family and delinquency, 86, 114–16, 234–37, 243–44, 262
Fascism and positivism, 42, 45
Felony murder laws, 14–15
Ferracuti, Franco, 215–17, 218, 228
Ferri, Enrico, 37, 40–42
Frame of reference, theory as a function of, 9–10, 15–17
Free will, crime as a product of, 10, 359.
  *See also* Classical theories
  Ferri's rejection of, 40
  and phrenology, 49–50
French code, 25, 26
French revolution, 21, 25, 144
Freud, Sigmund, 110, 111–13, 233
Friedrichs, David O., 307

Gall, Franz Joseph, 39, 48–50
Galton, Francis, 85
Gangs, juvenile
  Cloward and Ohlin's theory, 195–97
  Cohen's theory, 194–95
  Miller's theory, 214–15
  as sociopaths, 123
  in Vold's theory, 274

Garfinkle, Harold, 254
Garofalo, Raffaelo, 37, 42–45
Genetics
  and biological defectiveness, 84–95
  and environmental theories of human
    behavior, 6, 8, 157
  and mental defectiveness, 74–82
  and parental neglect and battering, 101
  and theories of normal learning, 205
Geographic studies, 178–79
Gibbons, Don C., 63
Gibbs, Jack P., 251–52, 257
Gillin, John, 25, 43
Gland dysfunction, 96–99
Glaser, Daniel, 133, 222–23, 353
Glueck, Eleanor T., 61–62, 63, 118–19,
  220
Glueck, Sheldon, 61–62, 63, 118–19,
  220, 221–22
Goring, Charles
  refutation of Lombroso, 52–55
  theory of hereditary defectiveness, 78,
    85–87
Goddard, H. H., 71–73, 78
Gordon, David M., 308
Gordon, Robert, 75–77, 78–79
Gore, Albert, 336
Gould, Stephen Jay, 6
Greenberg, David F., 305, 306, 307,
  309–10, 314
Group conflict theory, 270–77, 288–90
Guerry, A. M., 39, 131–32
Gurr, Ted Robert, 136–37, 155, 158
Gusfield, Joseph, 265
Guze, Samuel, 123–25

Habermas, Jurgen, 344
Habitual criminal laws, 125–27
Halley, Edmund, 131
Hawkins, Gordon, 125
Hayner, Norman S., 175
Head injuries, 100–101
Healy, William, 115
Henderson, C. R., 69, 72
Heredity, 84, 85–92. *See also* Biological
  factors; Genetics
Hill, R. H., 135, 140
Hindelang, Michael J., 77–78, 79, 80
Hirschi, Travis
  on Cohen's theory, 198
  control theory, 239, 241–45, 246, 247
  on criminology theories, 348
  Durkheim and, 143–44
  on intelligence, 77–78, 79, 80

Hirst, Paul Q., 302–3
Hobbes, Thomas, 9, 18, 19, 28, 206
Hooton, E. A., 55–57, 61
Hormones, 97–98, 344
Human nature
  in conflict theories, 271–72
  in control theories, 232, 241, 246–47
  in Durkheim's theory, 151, 188
  in strain theories, 197–98
Hunter, H., 95
Hutchings, Barry, 90–92
Hypoglycemia, 98–99

Ideas. *See also* Cognitive learning theo-
    ries; Culture; Expectations; Norms;
    Values
  in Sutherland's theory, 211, 225, 228–
    29
  in cultural theories, 214–19, 361
  in social reaction theories, 250–57
Illegitimate opportunities, 193–94, 197,
  205
Inequality
  in Beccaria's theory, 28–29
  in conflict theory, 273–98
  in Durkheim's theory, 143
  economic, 130–31, 132, 138–41, 294
  in Marxist theory, 299–300, 303–13
Injuries and crime, 84, 100–01
Insanity, 109–11
  in Lombroso's theory, 38
  Acquittal by reason of, 123
Intelligence, 67–83
  blacks and delinquency, 74–78
  poverty, crime, and, 75, 130
  sex chromosomes and, 93, 95
  in Shaw's work, 171
Interests
  and crime policies, 320–21, 327, 337,
    355, 356
  in classical theories, 10, 28–29, 30–32
  in conflict theories, 269–80, 283–87,
    288, 292–93, 296–98
  in Marxist theories, 310–14
Interstitial areas, 172
IQ. *See* Intelligence
Irwin, John, 297

Jacobs, D., 135
Jacobs, Patricia, 93–94
Jeffery, C. Ray, 224–25
Jensen, Arthur R., 75, 77
Johnson, Lyndon B., 185, 201

Jonassen, Christen T., 175
Jukes family, 68–69
Jung, Carl, 104, 111

Kallikak family, 72–73
Kennedy, Robert F., 201
Kessler, S., 95
Kitsuse, John I., 198, 199
Klinefelter's syndrome, 93
Kornhauser, Ruth Rosner
    on behavior of criminal law, 362
    community control theory, 179–80
    on cultural deviance theories, 227–28
    on strain theories, 199–200
Kozol, Harry L., 126–27
Krestschmer, Ernst, 57–58
Kringlen, Einar, 89–90

Labeling
    definition of crime, 15
    and English ecological studies, 178
    and learning disabilities, 102
    and psychiatry, 124
    in Shaw's work, 172
    theory, 252–57, 360
Lander, Bernard, 176–77
Lange, Johannes, 88
Laub, John H., 133
Lavater, Johan Caspar, 48
Learning, criminal behavior as a prod-
    uct of, 205–31, 288–89, 307–8, 359–
    60
Learning disabilities, 101–3
Learning, general theories of, 205–8, 225
Legal definitions of crime, 10, 12
Legitimate opportunities, 189, 196–203,
    235, 239, 244, 294–95, 351-52, 360
Lemert, Edwin, 198, 254–55
Levin, Yale, 39
Lewis, Dorothy Otnow, 101
Liazos, Alexander, 267
Liebow, Elliot, 200, 201
Lindesmith, Alfred A., 39
Lipton, Douglas, 353
Locke, John, 18, 28, 206
Lodhi, A. Q., 156
Loftin, Colin, 135, 140
Lombroso, Cesare, 36–40, 50–52, 68,
    345
    classical criminology and, 33
    Durkheim and, 143
    Goring's challenge to, 52–55
    Tarde and, 208–9

Lower-class crime. *See* Class and Crime;
    Culture; Poverty

Mannheim, Hermann, 12
Martinson, Robert, 353
Marx, Karl, 269, 299, 300–303, 311–12,
    344
Marxist theories of crime, 299–316
    conflict theories and, 269, 295, 299–
    300
    ecological research and, 178
    as theories of behavior of criminal law,
    310–13, 363
    as theories of criminal behavior, 11,
    305–10
Matza, David, 239–41, 242, 245, 253
McCord, William, 124
McDonald, Lynn, 156
McKay, Henry D., 81, 164–71, 173–83,
    193, 294, 354
Mead, George Herbert, 209, 211–12, 252
Mednick, Sarnoff A., 90–92, 99–100,
    105–6
Megargee, Edwin I., 121
Mendel, Gregor, 73
Menstrual tension, 97–98
Mental deficiency. *See* Intelligence
Mental disease, 109–11. *See also* Psy-
    chological factors
    and prediction of dangerousness, 125–
    27
    psychoanalysis, 111–17
    psychopathy, 122–25
Mercer, Jane, 79
Merton, Robert K., 185–94, 195, 196,
    197, 198, 200, 205,
    conflict theory and, 294
    control theory and, 242
    Durkheim's theory and, 143, 185–86,
    188–89
Mesomorphy, 59–65
Messner, Steven F., 140–41
Michael, Jerome, 6, 209
Miller, J. E., 94
Miller, Walter B.
    delinquency control project, 181
    lower-class culture, 214–15, 216, 242,
    245
Minimal brain dysfunction, 101–3
Minnesota Multiphasic Personality In-
    ventory (MMPI), 119–22
Modeling, 207–08
Modernization, 143–59, 360
Monahan, John, 126–27

Moos, R. H., 95
Morris, Norval, 125, 126
Morris, Terence, 181–82
Multiple factor causation, 11, 37–38, 45, 106–7, 359–61, 363
Murton, Thomas O., 297
Mussolini, Benito, 42, 45

Nagel, William G., 134
Nationality. *See* Racial and ethnic groups
Natural definitions of crime, 12, 43, 362
Natural explanations of crime, 8–10, 16, 68
Neglect, child, 101
Nervous system, 99–106, 346
Neoclassical school of criminology, 18, 26–27, 30, 32
Nettler, Gwynn, 198, 202, 291
Neutralization, techniques of, 240, 253
Nisbet, Robert A., 144
Nixon, Richard M., 8, 201, 260, 279–80
Normal crimes, Sudnow's study of, 261–62
Normal in society, Durkheim's theory of crime as, 144, 146–50
Normal learned behavior, criminal behavior as, 205–31, 288–89, 307–8, 359–60
Norms. *See also* Culture; Expectations; Ideas, Values
  cultural and subcultural theories, 215–16, 227–28
  definition of crime and, 251–52
  deviant groups and, 297
  ecological theory, 179
  Sellin's theory, 270
  social reaction theories, 251–52, 257, 267
  Sutherland's theory, 213, 227–28
  Turk's theory, 281
Nutrition, 98–99, 130
Nye, F. Ivan, 234–37, 241, 242, 246

Official crime rates. *See* Crime rates, official.
Ohlin, Lloyd E., 195–97, 199–200, 201, 216, 242, 294
Operant conditioning, 207
  criminal behavior as normally learned, 222–25, 288
Opportunities, illegitimate, 171, 193–94, 197, 205

Opportunities, legitimate, 171, 189, 196–203, 235, 239, 244, 294–95, 351–52, 360
Opportunity theories. *See* Strain theories.
Organized crime, 82, 308–9, 317, 322–29
Orsagh, Thomas, 134

Park, Robert E., 161–64
Passingham, R. E., 106
Pavlov, Ivan, 104–5, 207
Pearson, Karl, 52, 85, 87
Personality of offender, 108–29. *See also* Psychological factors
  autonomic nervous system, 104–5
  gland dysfunction, 96–99
  temperament and physique, 57–65
Personality tests, 117–22
Phrenology, 48–50
Physical characteristics, 47–66, 346
Physiognomy, 48
Piliavin, Irvin, 257
Platt, Tony, 315
Ploscowe, Morris, 136
Policy crime, 349–55
  conflict theories, 295–97
  cultural theories, 216, 218
  ecology theories, 180–82
  strain theories, 201–2
Political-economic system, 299–300, 306, 360
Popper, Karl, 344–45
Positivist theories. *See also* Biological factors; Psychological factors; Social factors
  and classical theories, 33, 359–60
  as a frame of reference, 10–12, 13, 16, 33, 45–46, 359
  multiple factor causation, 11, 37–38, 45, 106–7, 359–61, 363
  the positive school, 36–46
Pound, Roscoe, 284
Poverty, 130–42. *See also* Economic inequality; Class and crime
  behavior of criminal law and, 14–15
  Bonger's theory, 303
  conflict theory, 294
  Goring's research, 86
  intelligence and, 75
  Shaw and McKay's theory, 163–64, 169
  strain theories, 200–203
  Sutherland's theory, 333

Power
  conflict theories, 269–98, 360
  ecology theories, 182
  Marxist theories, 299–300, 303, 304
  McClelland's test, 62, 63
  organized crime, 327
  in Puritan Massachusetts, 154
  social reaction theories, 251–52, 265, 266–67
  victimless crimes, 320–21
  white-collar crime, 337–38
Prediction of dangerousness, 125–27
Premenstrual tension, 97–98
Prince, Morton, 110
Psychiatry, 108–17, 233–34. *See also* Biological factors; Personality of offender
Psychoanalysis, 111–17
Psychological factors, 108–29, 359, 363. *See also* Personality of offender
  control theories and, 232–33, 237, 239
  econometric theories and, 31
  as a frame of reference, 11, 16, 33
  intelligence, theories related to, 67–83
  normal learning, crime as a product of, 205–31
  social reaction theories and, 254–55
  unified conflict theory of crime and, 287, 294
Psychopathy, 120–25
  and adoption studies, 90
  in Eysenck's theory, 105
  on the MMPI, 120–22
  similarities in Lombroso's theory, 38
Punishment
  in Beccaria's theory, 20, 21, 23–24
  in classical theory, 10, 19, 33
  in Durkheim's theory, 147–48, 153–54
  in econometric theory, 30–32
  Ferri's substitutes for, 41
  Garofalo's theory of, 44
  history of, 349–51
  response of autonomic nervous system to, 103–6

Quetelet, Adolphe, 39, 131–32
Quinney, Richard
  differential association theory, 220
  Marxist theory, 304, 307, 314
  social reality of crime, 277–80, 286, 289, 304

Racial and ethnic groups
  Hirschi's theory, 243
  and intelligence, 74–82
  Kornhauser's theory, 179–80
  Shaw and McKay's theory, 170–71, 175–76
  social reaction theories, 258–59, 260, 262
  subculture of violence theory, 215–19
Radzinowicz, Leon, 39
Reactive definitions of crime, 250–52, 257
Recidivism, 353–54
Reckless, Walter C., 237–39
Redl, Fritz, 115–16
Rehabilitation programs, 351–53
Reiss, Albert J., Jr., 220, 233–34, 241
Relative deprivation, 138–39. *See also* Economic inequality
Research, 340–49
Residential succession, 169–71, 175–76
Rhodes, A. Lewis, 220
Rice, Kent, 133
Robinson, W. S., 176
Robison, Sophia M., 173–74, 176
Rock, Paul, 344
Role theory, 222–23
Rose, Stephen M., 201–2

Sagarin, Edward, 297
Samenow, Stanton E., 253
Sarbin, Theodore R., 94, 126
Savitz, Leonard, 39, 40
Schlapp, Max G., 96
Schools and delinquency, 79, 101–3, 194–95, 234, 243, 245, 262, 306
Schuessler, Karl F., 118
Schrag, Clarence, 238
Schulsinger, Fini, 90
Science and crime, 4–6, 340–49, 356
Seidman, David, 260–61
Seidman, Robert B., 253–54, 283–86, 290
Self-report surveys, 77, 174, 235–37, 242–45, 247–48
Sellin, Thorsten, 12, 40, 42, 270
Sex hormones, 97–98
Sexual psychopath laws, 125–27
Shah, Saleem A., 126
Shaw, Clifford R., 81, 164–83, 193, 294, 354
Sheldon, William H., 58–60
Shelley, Louise I., 158
Shockley, William, 74–75

Short, James F., Jr., 219–20
Siddle, David A. T., 105
Simmel, Georg, 270, 289, 290, 344
Simon, Theodore, 70
Simons, Ronald L., 80
Skin conductance response, 105–6
Skinner, B. F., 207
Smith, Adam, 20, 131
Smith, Edward H., 96
Snodgrass, Jon, 182
Social area analysis, 177
Social change, rapid, 360, 361
  in Durkheim's theory, 151–52
  in Quetelet's theory, 132
  in Sutherland's theory, 334
Social contract theory, 18–20, 21, 27–28
Social control theories, 232–48, 295, 296,
    345. *See also* Control perspective
Social disorganization, 172–73, 180–82,
    212–13, 294, 354
Social factors, 130–315, 359–61, 363. *See
    also* Causes of criminal behavior
  biological factors and, 78, 84–85, 106–
    7
  classical theories and, 29–30, 31
  as a frame of reference, 11–12, 16, 33
  in the Gluecks' research, 62
  intelligence and genetics, 74–82
  learning disabilities and, 102–3
  positivist theories and, 37–38, 41
  psychological factors and, 108, 127–28
Social learning theory, 207–8, 223–24,
    286–88
Social reaction theories, 248–68, 362
  conflict theory and, 295
  Durkheim's theory and, 144
  Marxist theory and, 304
Social reality of crime, 277–80
Social structure. *See* Structure, social
Sociopathy. *See* Psychopathy
Socrates, 9, 47–48, 149
Spiritual explanations, 6–8, 16, 32–33,
    67–68, 109
Spitzer, Steven, 154–55
Spurzheim, John Gasper, 48–49
Stekel, Wilhelm, 111
Stern, W., 71
Strain theories, 185–204, 361
  control theories and, 242–44, 247
  Durkheim's theory and, 143
  Glaser's theory and, 223
  Marxist theories and, 306–7
  relative deprivation and, 139
Structure, social
  conflict theories, 288–90, 295, 297

cultural theories, 216–19, 228–29
  Marxist theory, 310–11
  social learning theory, 228
  strain theories, 187–89, 198, 200–203
  Sutherland's theory, 212–13
Subcultural theories
  Cloward and Ohlin's gang theory, 195–
    97, 199–200, 201, 216, 242, 294
  Cohen's gang theory, 194–95, 196,
    199, 200, 216, 242, 243, 246
  cultural and subcultural theories, 213,
    214–19, 242–44, 295
Subculture of violence, 139–40, 215–18,
    292
Sudnow, David, 261
Sullivan, Richard F., 31, 32
Sutherland, Edwin H. *See also* Differ-
    ential association theory
  definition of crime, 12
  differential association theory, 179,
    193, 197, 209–14, 216, 219, 222–30,
    242, 250, 270, 279, 288, 289
  on IQ, 78
  on Sheldon, 60
  white-collar crime, 225–27, 230, 329–
    34, 337–38
Sykes, Gresham M., 253
Symbolic interactionism, 209, 211–12,
    249–50, 252, 344
Szasz, Thomas S., 249

Tappan, Paul, 332
Tarde, Gabriel, 208–9
Taylor, Ian, 304
Techniques of neutralization, 240, 253
Temperament and physique, 57–65
Terman, Lewis, 71, 72
Testosterone, 98
Theories in criminology. *See also* Be-
    havior of criminal law; Classical
    theories; Positivist theories; Uni-
    fied theories of crime
  assessments of, 358–63
  overview of, 3–17
  research and crime policy, 340–56
Thompson, E. P., 344
Thorndike, E. L., 206
Tilly, Charles, 156
Toby, Jackson, 234–35, 236–37, 242
Treatment of criminals, 349–55
Turk, Austin T., 280–83
Turner, Stanley H., 39
Twins, 5–6, 80, 87–90

Unemployment, 132–34, 255, 302–3, 308
Unified theories of crime, 286–90, 297, 361–63

Values. *See also* Culture; Expectations, Ideas, Norms
 and criminology, 6
 and crime policies, 320–21, 354–55
 conflict theories, 269, 284–85, 286–87, 290, 292, 296
 control theories, 240, 242, 245, 253
 cultural and subcultural theories, 214–17, 361
 ecology theories, 172, 179
 social reaction theories, 258
 strain theories, 186–88, 194–95, 196–97, 198, 200
 Sutherland's theory, 211, 227–28
Victimless crimes, 317–22
Violence, subculture of, 215–19
Vitamin deficiencies, 98–99
Vold, George B., 225–26, 270–77, 278, 286

Waldo, Gordon P., 120
Walton, Paul, 304

War on poverty, 185, 201–3, 354–55
Webb, Jim, 175–76
Weber, Max, 344
White-collar crime, 14–15, 82, 226–27, 230, 329–38
Wilks, Judith, 353
Wilson, James Q., 291
Wineman, David, 115–16
Witkin, Herman A., 95
Wirth, Lewis, 177
Wohler, Frederich, 96
Wolfgang, Marvin E., 154, 215–17, 218, 228

XYY chromosomal complement, 92–95, 346

Yablonsky, Lewis, 123
Yochelson, Samuel, 253
Young, Jock, 304

Zehr, Howard, 156–57